Claude A. Swanson

Claude A. Swanson of Virginia

A Political Biography

HENRY C. FERRELL, Jr.

THE UNIVERSITY PRESS OF KENTUCKY

Publication of this book has been assisted
by a grant from East Carolina University

Scholarly publisher for the Commonwealth,
serving Bellarmine College, Berea College, Centre
College of Kentucky, Eastern Kentucky University,
The Filson Club, Georgetown College, Kentucky
Historical Society, Kentucky State University,
Morehead State University, Murray State University,
Northern Kentucky University, Transylvania University,
University of Kentucky, University of Louisville,
and Western Kentucky University.

Editorial and Sales Offices: Lexington, Kentucky 40506-0024

Library of Congress Cataloging in Publication Data

Ferrell, Henry C., 1934-
  Claude A. Swanson of Virginia.

  Bibliography: p.
  Includes index.
  1. Swanson, Claude Augustus, 1862-1939.   2. Legislators
—United States—Biography.   3. United States.   Congress—
Biography.   4. Virginia—Governors—Biography.   I. Title.
E748.S92F47   1985   975.5′042′0924 [B]   84-27031
ISBN 0-8131-1536-1

To Martha

Contents

Illustrations and Photo Credits

Frontispiece: Claude A. Swanson as governor of Virginia (1906-1910). Portrait by Harry Franklin Waltman. Virginia State Library.

Text Illustrations

"As the Game Is Being Played in Virginia" (p. 59). *Washington Post*

"The Latest Successful 'Come Back'" (p. 94). *Washington Post*

"The American Delegation Crosses Lake Geneva" (p. 188). From Alois Derso and Imre Kelen, *Pages Glorieuses—Days of Hope and Glory* ([Paris?] *ca.* 1933)

Following Page 150

Claude A. Swanson as freshman senator. Library of Congress

Swanson as Fifth District congressman. William R. Perkins Library, Duke University

Governor Swanson at the Jamestown Tercentennial. Virginia State Library

Thomas Staples Martin. Library of Congress

John W. Daniel. "1901 Virginia Constitutional Convention Album" (#7373), Manuscripts Department, University of Virginia Library

Rorer A. James. *Danville Register*

Westmoreland Davis. Virginia State Library

Andrew J. Montague. Virginia State Library

Carter Glass. "1901 Virginia Constitutional Convention Album" (#7373), Manuscripts Department, University of Virginia Library

Henry D. Flood. "1901 Virginia Constitutional Convention Album" (#7373), Manuscripts Department, University of Virginia Library

Walter A. Watson. "1901 Virginia Constitutional Convention Album," (#7373), Manuscripts Department, University of Virginia Library

Richard E. Byrd. Virginia State Library

Harry F. Byrd, Sr. Manuscripts Department, University of Virginia Library

Swanson and Ray Stannard Baker. Library of Congress

Franklin D. Roosevelt and his first Cabinet. Wide World Photos, Inc., courtesy of the Franklin D. Roosevelt Library

Swanson, Roosevelt, and Josephus Daniels. Copyright 1934, New York News, Inc. Reprinted by permission. Courtesy of the Franklin D. Roosevelt Library

Swanson at Pearl Harbor. National Archives

Swanson as Secretary of the Navy. Photo by D.W. Miller, courtesy of the U.S. Naval Historical Center

Preface

Covering most of the years of the one-party South, Claude Augustus Swanson's public career as congressman, governor, senator, and secretary of the navy spanned from Grover Cleveland's administration to that of Franklin D. Roosevelt. In Virginia, he perfected political skills and acquired a world view that led him to become a dominant figure in the state's leadership. His accomplishments, when carefully assessed, raise serious questions concerning previous interpretations of Virginia politics between 1892 and 1932 that feature a powerful Democratic "organization" dispersing would-be reformers in its eagerness to placate corporate oligarchs.

Swanson had a penchant for finding the sources of power. Enmeshed in the challenges of the day, he was too involved in resolving divisive class and partisan conflicts to compose many introspective statements. An evaluation of his actions and decisions presents, however, an extraordinary political personality. At the state level, his effectiveness and achievements were equaled by few Virginia chief executives. Nationally, he was an insider, treating with the sinew and structure of the Democratic party, sectional competition, economic interests, presidential authority, and untoward events that give a political era shape and substance. From the 1890s through the inauguration of Franklin Roosevelt, an investigation of Swanson's political career furnishes insight into regional and national politics. Delineation of his service as secretary of the navy reveals additional contours of the New Deal.

During the years of research and preparation of this study, I have been assisted by many persons. A complete list would consume many columns of print. Three professional historians must be cited: William B. Hamilton, for introducing me to the complexities of history; Richard L. Watson, Jr., for perceptively guiding me into advanced research; and, most important, Edward E. Younger, for his dedication to Virginia history which inspired me and a generation of graduate students at the University of Virginia. The professional staffs of a host of libraries have been true to their craft in aiding my efforts. I especially appreciate the contributions of Edmund Berkeley, Jr. and his past and present colleagues in the Manuscripts Department of the University of Virginia Library and those of Mary Frances Morris and her fellow reference librarians of Joyner Library at East Carolina University. The University's Research Committee furnished several stipends to help defray research expenses and the work would not have been completed without funds from the East Carolina University Foundation.

Beyond these and other contributions, to my wife Martha Smith Ferrell, who hunted with me in the faded papers of many collections and who understood the need to keep at it, I give my lasting gratitude.

1

Rising Young Politician
1862-1892

A few weeks before the Second World War ignited Europe, *Time* reviewed the life of a "lank, long-nosed Southern politician," Claude Augustus Swanson, late secretary of the navy in Franklin D. Roosevelt's cabinet. Noting that the former congressman, governor, senator, and cabinet minister was "no mediocrity, but a shrewd, hard-working careerist," the article surmised that Swanson, who held "his job for reasons of political expediency was one of the best secretaries of the Navy the U. S. ever had." Lacking wide perspective, the summary illumined but one aspect of a multifaceted, seventy-seven-year career politician whose forebears lived among the southern Virginia hills and waterways.[1]

Under the patronage of John Dennis, indentured Englishman Robert Swanson settled in 1643 near the Wicomico River and established the Virginia Swansons. His descendants tied their future to land acquisition, moved south of the Appomattox trading posts, and eventually reached present day Franklin, Henry, and Pittsylvania counties. Cathedral forests, interspersed with savannahs and riding slopes between high ground, awed early English visitors. Great Bermuda rain systems watered these natural farm sites and spawned dozens of creeks and runs. The primary river, the Dan, received its name from William Byrd and his wrangling crew of surveyors, sighting a boundary between Virginia and North Carolina in October 1728. Blinded partially by the descending sun, they imagined they saw gold dust littering the river bottom but discovered instead "small flakes of isinglass." Silica deposits would combine, however, with gray, sterile soil to grow pungent stands of tobacco, generating wealth that transformed the river basin.[2]

The economy and culture of the great rural colony encouraged restless seventeen-year-old William Swanson I to settle in Goochland in 1747 and to speculate in land. He bought and sold two thousand acres in ten years and, by 1762, secured title to six hundred more in Bedford near the Blue Ridge Mountains. He turned southward and, in 1768, held five hundred acres in modern Franklin County. In September 1777, he and his sons swore allegiance to the new commonwealth of Virginia and sold supplies and horses to Continental troops. A decade later, his eyes on the main chance, he shifted his family to a three-hundred-acre plot in Wilkes County, Georgia. Thirty-five-year-old William Swanson II remained behind to cultivate the family land in Pittsylvania

County where he established his home. Before his death in 1827, representing the county and its growing mercantile heart, Danville, William Swanson II won four terms in the House of Delegates. His son, William Graves Swanson, left his farm by the Pigg River to serve as a captain in the 101st Virginia Regiment during the War of 1812. First elected delegate in 1818, he held six consecutive terms as a Whig during the tumultuous 1830s and struggled for a greater government role in developing Pittsylvania.[3]

State action had earlier sponsored navigable access to the sea. The Dan River had enticed exporters of agricultural produce, livestock, and timber, but it ran the long way, first to the northeast, then into its master river the Roanoke, which spread into North Carolina and emptied into Albermarle Sound. After 1800, Virginia and North Carolina cooperated to form the Roanoke Navigation Company. By 1825, bateaux of over ten thousand pounds' capacity slipped over water from Danville to Norfolk via the Dismal Swamp Canal. These advances stimulated commerce and manufacturing in Danville, which featured grist and saw mills, tobacco factories, warehouses, and a cotton mill.[4]

In 1816, Virginia created a fund for internal improvements awarded by a board of public works. Immediately, political intrigue entangled local rivalries in the state legislature. William Graves Swanson, in 1837, led Pittsylvania County's Whig delegation to seek funding for a railroad from Danville to Richmond. Contests between localities, railroads, and canal companies delayed a through rail system to the west. Not until 1846 did the Danville railroad receive a charter, with the state furnishing three-fifths of construction funds. Quickly, Pittsylvanians purchased $150,000 additional shares. The rails were completed in 1856, but by then William Graves Swanson had moved to Georgia. A land-conscious society, competitive and suspicious localities, speculative dreams, pride in the Richmond and Danville Railroad, and a dependency upon government in a mixed economy were legacies of the era.[5]

Born in 1799, John Swanson, son of William Graves Swanson, married Julia Cook and built their home at Swansonville, seventeen miles northwest of Danville near the Franklin Pike. He directed slaves to build and to staff a spacious, two-story building of homemade red bricks to process tobacco for local and regional markets. His son, John Muse Swanson, born in 1829, participated at a young age in family business activities that included the Swansonville General Store, managed by his brother James. By 1840, Pittsylvania County ranked first in Virginia with its tobacco crop of 6,439,000 pounds. In 1859, over seventy tobacco factories in the county supported foundries, tin and machine shops, and lumberyards. The Swansons bought annually from the crop and stored it for eventual resale or processing. They loaned $14,000 in 1860 to neighborhood growers and purchased 100,000 pounds of their tobacco.[6]

Tobacco prosperity enabled John Muse Swanson to marry Catherine Pritchett of Brunswick County and to raise their family in Swansonville. He sold "Swanson's Twist" on his travels throughout the southeastern states and observed Danville entrepreneurs taking advantage of the Richmond and Danville Railroad. Enhancing their control of tobacco purchases, Dr. J.B. Stovall of Halifax and Danville tobacconists Thomas D. Neal and William P. Graves chartered in 1860 Neal's Warehouse which began to supplant the noisy and unsystematic street auctions. But the harsh smell of exploding gunpowder replaced momentarily the aroma of cured leaf. In April 1861, the Civil War engulfed Virginia.[7]

Upon assembly of thousands of troops, war conditions increased demands for Southside foodstuffs and tobacco. Encouraged by Confederate railroad practices and commodity gamblers, Pittsylvania County growers and their factors abandoned staid agricultural practices for wild speculation. By late 1864, only two-sevenths of the freight traveling the Richmond and Danville Railroad was government stores; individual speculators held the remainder. Representative of this group, William T. Sutherlin, tobacconist, scientific farmer, banker, and former Whig, served at Danville's army post as chief quartermaster. He emerged from the conflict as the town's primary entrepreneur and political broker. Although John Muse Swanson joined the Confederate army during its last seven months, the Swansons benefited from the war's economic opportunities.[8]

In Swansonville on March 31, 1862, amid discussions over prospects for profit and victory, John and Catherine Swanson welcomed their third son, Claude Augustus, into a large family circle of brothers and sisters.[9] Their home was well furnished with life's necessities yet simple in its routine. Family attendance at the Methodist Episcopal Church, South, marked the apex of the week. Sowing and harvesting measured the meter of the months. As surely as Turkey Cock Mountain rimmed the northwest horizon, an established order and sense of permanence pervaded the child's universe. He acquired a cultural empathy with blacks and with the small, independent white farmers. He absorbed and understood their need to hold and to use the land.

Preceding generations bequeathed Claude a sinewy, angular body. The dominating quality of his eyes continued throughout his life; even in old age "his eyes still sparkled." An 1893 sketch described his figure as "slender and beautifully proportioned," featuring a head with a prominent nose, "abundant wavy, dark hair, a handsome mustache and brave black eyes." One journalist recalled that "even in repose his eyes seemed to smile." Another observer perceived him as one who "undoubtedly attract[ed] attentions from the ladies gallery." He presented an initial impression of viewing life not only "knowingly" but "whimsically." Frequently, Swanson was given to a fanciful and comical capriciousness. Amid his large family, he developed an inclination to search the world for comedic themes rather than for order. Traveler and storyteller, his father may have strengthened this tendency, or his mother, surrounded by children, may have encouraged maternal approval through laughter. Certainly, the rural culture strengthened ribald exchanges that skirted vulgarity to stitch over tragedies of crop failures, war, disease, and death. Whatever the source, his humorous and open personality, paired with a tall, lean physique, influenced his future public success.[10]

Political adversaries occasionally overlooked a third element of Swanson's nature: a wide-ranging, flexible intellect. He had a quick-witted, hard-working, and analytical mind, a tool that accumulated knowledge to forge compromise from political adversity, to persuade men, and to shape events. One politician commented: "No idle bread did he eat; no time did he lose in frivolity or the shades of ease." Given such a work ethic, in part from his Methodist heritage, in 1869 he enrolled in a private school organized by wealthier landowners and taught by Swansonville native Celestia Susannah Parrish. Swanson remembered the twenty-two-year-old Parrish as "one of the most brilliant women and . . . best teachers" graduated from Virginia State Normal School at Farmville.[11]

A surviving letter written to his mother emulates the formal phrases of Claude's copybook. Ailing, she visited fashionable Botetourt Springs in August 1873, leaving Claude bereft of his usual fishing partner in Swansonville. In his letter he described the new Methodist "preacher," but more important among childhood priorities, he wrote of ripening peaches and watermelons ready for eating. Failing to regain her health, his mother died one month later and was buried in the family plot at the Swansonville Methodist Church.[12]

Profits from Swanson's Twist in the lower South continued into the 1870s. Operating the tobacco factory at full tilt through early spring into summer, John Muse Swanson departed for the cotton country during the August harvest days and remained throughout the market season. Shipments of Twist were sent along his selling routes before his arrival. Other neighbors, such as R.J. Reynolds in nearby Patrick County, followed similar commercial patterns. Avoiding federal tax collectors when possible, Claude's father escaped the Panic of 1873 and, encouraged by poor crop years, continued successfully to speculate. His father's success allowed Claude to be enrolled during his twelfth year at Whitmell Academy, six miles down the Danville Pike. Taught by thirty-eight-year-old North Carolinian Joseph Venable, a first honors bachelor of arts graduate from the University of North Carolina, Swanson described him as a "thorough teacher and disciplinarian." Discipline was "usually harsh and severe" in these academies. Their curricula varied but most were intended to prepare students of the upper class for college through instruction in Latin, Greek, mathematics, and rhetoric. Parental concerns demanded that "practical" courses be taught; thus, chemistry and physics were often requirements.[13]

A prevailing theme of practicality in postwar Virginia boosted entrepreneurial activities. Their confidence in the planter oligarchy sundered by the Civil War, young Confederates studied to replicate the patterns of northern capitalism whose products had beaten them on the battlefields. Proposing that reunion be as painless and as profitable as possible, former Whigs and aspiring businessmen attracted them. As one of the committee of nine who gained approval of the Reconstruction Underwood constitution, Sutherlin in 1869 participated in leading Virginia into both the Union and the newly established Conservative party that pledged universal suffrage and amnesty, "political peace, prosperity and persistent whiggery." Urban-oriented Conservatives ruled Virginia for a decade and public conjecture in Pittsylvania County frequently centered upon the state's role in business affairs. As a residue of these years, identifiable class lines were etched between the interests of Danville residents and those of "country people."[14]

Virginia governmental actions affected Pittsylvania County. Free public schools were required by the new Underwood constitution. Federal land grant monies helped charter Virginia Agricultural and Mechanical College at Blacksburg and underwrote Hampton Normal and Agricultural Institute. Both institutions were expected to contribute to the "material resources of the Country." The Assembly increased interest rates to attract capital. To recruit labor to replace black field hands departing to the cities, a new Board of Immigration was created. State tobacco inspection ceased and the local warehouses now received fees for that service. Commended as sound laissez-faire business practice, the legislature sold the state's interest in nearly all of its railroads. Revenue and accelerated rail construction resulted, but railroad companies' participation in politics grew as well. The Funding Act of 1871 refinanced the state debt at face value through the issuance of 6 percent bonds, whose coupons could be used to pay state taxes. This latter feature eventually forced the state treasury into deficits, but additional paper was provided for credit-shy Virginia in the 1870s. Moderate to well-to-do farmers gained more from these developments than planters or day laborers. Debate over the public debt factionalized the Conservatives into "Funders" and "Readjusters."[15]

Southside speculators and entrepreneurs projected a vast expansion of tobacco markets exported by a refurbished Richmond and Danville Railroad. Sutherlin and North Carolina-born railroad president Algernon S. Buford schemed accordingly with Richmond interests to build an alliance with Tom Scott's Pennsylvania Railroad. This alliance would counter the threat to Danville by William Mahone, whose railroad combine reached from Petersburg along a Norfolk axis. In Swansonville and elsewhere, with an exuberance equal "to an old prospector in finding a long sought lode," farmers exploited the popular bright leaf. Yearly crops suffered from unstable market conditions, adverse weather, and flea beetles that altered quality and quantity. Given these fluctuations, one dealer admitted it was "natural that under such circumstances a speculative feeling should spring up." Between 1870 and 1876, Danville market prices were encouraging, but in 1878 a tidal wave of 27 million pounds, 11 million more than the previous year, struck the warehouses. A massive market shakedown rocked tobacco country.[16]

That year's average of eight cents per pound consumed operating capital at the Swansonville red brick manufacturing building. Seriously shaken, forty-eight-year-old John Muse Swanson returned to farming to provide funds for the debilitated family store. His oldest son William Graves remained with him while John Pritchett Swanson moved to Danville to lay the foundations of Swanson Brothers Company, wholesale grocers. Later commentaries cite these events as producing in young Claude a major catharsis. He recalled reading a life of Warren Hastings which encouraged him to restore his family's fallen fortunes. In the glittering coals of the Swanson hearth, perhaps he saw future political office, but, recounted in the afterglow of a successful gubernatorial campaign, the story has a mythic quality. More important, indicative of family political influence, Claude was hired in 1877 for thirty dollars a month to teach public school.[17]

Swanson remembered the experience. "Every person . . . who had a child too bad to keep at home and who was too stingy to hire a nurse for it, sent it to me to nurse during my school hours." In a flimsy, "wretched" building, "scorched by summer suns and shivered by winter winds," he questioned which created more noise: the wind whistling through log walls or "whirl of the switch" as he "belabored the bad boys." Compensated "not half enough . . . for nursing those infants and teaching that school," he polished his insights by reading about historical and contemporary events. Despite the exertions of rural spokesmen to maintain the meager public system, the Funders in Richmond transferred school funds to honor the state debt. In 1879, a divisive legislative election concerned with state social services and debt repayments sharply revealed regional and class conflicts. When state appropriations for schools evaporated, Swanson lost his teaching position. [18]

To enhance his career choices, Swanson enrolled for the 1879 to 1880 term at Virginia Agricultural and Mechanical College at Blacksburg. Designed to permit "all classes the opportunity for a new education," the college's creation in 1872 received support from Granger leader Sutherlin, who found distasteful the existing state colleges "open only to the Rich." Perhaps influencing Swanson, Sutherlin, a fellow Methodist and a trustee, proposed to keep rural youth on the farm by an educational atmosphere that favored "manual labor and the common pursuits of industry." Upon arrival, the slender, dark-haired seventeen-year-old discovered an isolated small village, a former Methodist academy promoted to college status by legislative fiat, and its primary building, as a former student recalled, a "classic in its ugliness." The faculty divided over curriculum feuds and suffered from declining enrollment and budgetary deficiencies. Swanson followed a gray regimen that emphasized applied science with a weak liberal arts appendage. The curriculum combined a military officiousness, drawn from southern battlefield nostalgia, with the yearning commercial aspirations of the New South. Cadets challenged institutionalized dullness by staging fake duels, painting professors' cows, and reassembling carriages on roofs. The Lee and Maury literary societies attracted students, faculty, and townsfolk to weekly debates and addresses. Joining Maury, Swanson debated such questions as foreign emigration and whether a lawyer was justified "in defending a bad cause." Initially chosen treasurer, he was soon elected the society's vice-president. Although academically inadequate, the struggling Virginia college strengthened Claude's persuasive talents as he flexed political muscles. [19]

Whether for reasons of personal restlessness or as an economy measure, Swanson did not return to Blacksburg in the autumn of 1880. Avoiding $200 a year in college expenses and influenced by his brother John, he was employed as a grocery clerk at John Carter's store in Danville. With a population of 7,500 (4,300 blacks and 3,200 whites), the town served as the regional mercantile and manufacturing center for Pittsylvania County, which grew from 31,000 to 52,000 within a decade. *New York Times* correspondent E.G. Dunnell found few outward signs of Danville prosperity. Despite "many pleasant residences along its hilly main street," it lacked beauty and "its business streets have a lack-enterprise look," an air "of shiftlessness common to southern cities its size." But, strutting upon uneven cobblestones, energetic entrepreneurs strove to achieve and to acquire. Spurred by profits in bright tobacco, local manufacturers such as James G. Penn turned to the export trade. Sutherlin opened the Danville and New River narrow gauge railroad, financed by local investors and connection with Martinsville and Stuart, the very heart of tobacco country. He and his colleagues also reorganized the town's cotton mills, "without the aid of foreign capital." For two years Claude joined in this commercial ferment, entertaining his customers with knee-slapping humor and promoting his employer's merchandise. His county neighbors, "many of them horny-handed illiterates," noisily cried: "Where is Claude Swanson? Want to see that boy, for I told him when I came here to buy goods, I would call for him." Claude performed before the town's debating society, enrolled in one of the three Danville Methodist churches and enjoyed, with his brothers, the Sunday School picnics and speaking events. Participating in a joint debate between congregations as the Methodist champion, he delivered a memorized speech, and overawed his opponents who attempted to read from fluttering notes. Impressed by his oratory and demonstrating the doctrine of stewardship, four Methodist laymen—Penn, R. W. Peatross, John Cosby, and John Wyllie—offered to finance Claude's ministerial education. After six months of deliberation, he demurred and instead borrowed money from them to attend Methodist Randolph-Macon College.[20]

Only sixteen miles north of Richmond by the heavily traveled Richmond, Fredericksburg, and Potomac Railroad, the college had recently moved to the typical rural Virginia village of Ashland. The courtryside had once sustained groves of great trees, but by 1882 only cutover stands of pines dominated the landscape. Ashland residents still suffered financially from a speculative tourist venture, the Ashland Hotel and Mineral Well Company, a bankrupt victim from the previous decade. Maintaining a brave academic front, President William W. Bennett had reduced professors' salaries and engaged in other retrenchments. A preparatory for Methodist ministers, the college offered a reasonably stong humanities program, but financial exigencies made its sciences more sketchy than substantial. Claude roomed in "cottage no. 1," which provided "very simple" sanitary and heating facilities: water was brought by bucket and smokey soft coal or wood stoves provided heat. Joining the Washington Literary Society and Phi Kappa Sigma fraternity, he edited the *Randolph-Macon Monthly* during his first year. For Claude, college life was composed as much of personalities as of ideas. Ashland's families, members of which continually assayed the morals of college youths, maintained connections in Richmond that Swanson appended. A Richmond physician's widow, Annie Deane Lyons, who rented rooms to students, and her two daughters, Elizabeth and Lulie, attracted him, and he took frequent trips to Richmond for social events. Winning the Sutherlin oratorical and Washington debating medals, he spoke at each commencement while at Randolph-Macon. In June 1883, he delivered "A Nation's Wrongs: Their Causes and Remedies," a truncated history of Ireland that stressed what Swanson interpreted as Great Britain's perfidious role. Frequently applauded, he received "numerous floral tributes [proclaiming] . . . his popularity among those who knew him, especially the ladies."[21]

As a very minor spearholder, Swanson participated during these years in the encompassing drama of Virginia politics. Having created conditions that severed their control, the Funders ceded power to the Readjusters in 1879. A quarrelsome lot composed of rural patriarchs suspicious of industrialization, younger lawyers and businessmen from the undeveloped Valley and Southwest seeking industrial growth, and Granger and Greenback leaders intent upon improving state services and business regulation, they promised to "readjust" the state debt to escape heavy servicing costs. Following his election to the U.S. Senate, former railroad manipulator Mahone added organizing genius and a powerful political personality that gave shape to this broad coalition. Using Republican patronage and black voters, he played upon momentary themes. Preeminent between 1879 and 1883, the Readjusters sought "to expand opportunities within the system, to create a more open and democratic climate for industrial effort," and to make capitalism work for "the men who want money as well as the men who have money." Ten years earlier, the Conservatives had voiced similar if less pronounced sentiments, and their policies had reflected "an eschatological vision of prosperity through capitalist development." The debt issue appeared to be the major division between Funder and Readjuster Conservatives.[22]

Personalities and regionalism composed a powerful factor in these shifting, political coalitions. Swanson's sense of place and his loyalty to Pittsylvania and Danville interests led him to oppose Mahone. Petersburg and Norfolk had long represented commercial threats to Pittsylvania County and Danville. Mahone had crossed in the legislature Danville patriarch Sutherlin. Readjusters sponsored renewed state control of tobacco warehouses and a Mahone-dominated railroad commission. Readjuster legislation, by allowing blacks greater representation, removed Sutherlin and Penn from political control of Danville's city council. To give coherence and organization to anti-Readjuster elements, a railroad competitor of Mahone, Culpeper congressman John S. Barbour, in the summer of 1883 aligned the remaining Conservatives with the national Democrats. Assisted by detail-conscious Thomas Staples Martin of Scottsville, Barbour thoroughly reorganized every precinct and district in Virginia. Also, major Readjuster improvements from tax reforms and debt readjustment through increased support for public schools were accepted. Not to be outdone, the next year Mahone joined the Republicans. Two vast political organisms had been created, one nourished by national Democrats, the other by national Republicans. As a member of a family with strong political foundations in pro-Funder Pittsylvania, as a protégé of Danville entrepreneurs, and as an associate of Richmond Democrats, Swanson naturally favored the restructured Democratic party after 1883.[23]

At Randolph-Macon, a future Methodist bishop, James Cannon, Jr., of Maryland, pleaded with Swanson to bow to his Danville sponsors and declare for the ministry, because he could render "a great service as a Methodist preacher." Instead, twenty-seven-year-old Richard F. Beirne, owner of the *Richmond State* and a classmate of Swanson's patron Wyllie, recruited him for the Democratic cause. Cannon recalled that Beirne, who lived in Ashland, "stimulated Swanson's political aspirations." In the autumn of 1883, Democrats regained the Virginia legislature by accusing Mahone of "boss rule"—Mahonism—and by drawing the color line. A race riot in Danville, incited by a scurrilous pamphlet, contributed to the victory. With Beirne observing, Swanson delivered his first public political speech in 1884 at Hanover Court House in behalf of Grover Cleveland. So thoroughly involved were Virginians in that campaign that 85 percent of the eligible voters cast their ballots. The Democrats survived by 6,000 votes of 284,000. Federal patronage now flowed to slake Democratic thirst for office. From 1884 to 1885, Swanson also edited the *Hanover and Caroline News,* a weekly published in Ashland. Benefiting from Beirne's Richmond advertisers and his journalistic advice, the *News's* layout and contents advanced beyond ordinary Virginia weeklies. Swanson made it a Democratic mouthpiece.[24]

Graduating in June 1885 with majors in Latin, German, and chemistry, Swanson decided to study law at the University of Virginia. After a "pleasant and profitable summer" in Swansonville, he visited Randolph-Macon "to see the boys and other friends" en route to Charlottesville. The twenty-three-year-old graduate expected that he was "in for some hard work." The editor of the college *Monthly* wrote: "Some of the Washington Hall boys are betting on you for a future governor. Don't disappoint them." From October 1885 until graduation on July 4, 1886, Swanson absorbed the convivial academic world of the Grounds, joined the Jefferson debating society, won its coveted medal, socialized in the Phi Kappa Sigma fraternity, and faced "Old John B." Minor, resident senior law professor. He performed well in the "daily recitations accompanied by close searching interrogatories" and in the written exercises. Increasing his course load to graduate in one year rather than in the recommended three years, Swanson undertook an "immense amount of work" but "was thought to have no superior in his class." Dark, swarthy Henry De La Warr Flood from Appomattox became, as Swanson later professed, "in every way" his college chum." From a politically and socially prominent family, he associated with Swanson "in class and college politics." Francis "Frank" Rives Lassiter from Petersburg also became a close friend.[25]

The rough egalitarianism of Virginia Agricultural and Mechanical College and Randolph-Macon was rarely present at the University of Virginia. Despite reforms by a Readjuster board of visitors, the university still served the sons of "the professional and mercantile classes of the cities and towns" as "training grounds for the state's economic and socially elite." Crack-knuckled Pittsylvania County farmers, ambitious Danville entrepreneurs, the marginally acceptable gentry of Ashland, and fleeting glances of the "sham generally about the society of Richmond" failed to prepare Swanson for the sons of the truly wealthy and socially elect who based their opinions of classmates on family lineage, material wealth, and class prejudice. Despite attractive personal attributes, Swanson may not have surmounted the social deficiencies caused by his growing impecuniosity. Rumors circulated that he had won the debator's medal in a suit borrowed from Flood. Through his public career he would encounter these men, comfortable in their exclusivity, place, and privilege. Often he would be in conflict with them. Wiser socially and professionally, he departed Charlottesville in summer 1886 to establish his law practice at Swansonville.[26]

Financial necessity placed his office at home rather than at a more lucrative site in Danville. The young lawyer moved in 1887 to Chatham, the county seat, twelve miles north of Danville. He assisted lawyers too remote from county records, searched land deeds, collected past-due bills, and handled suits for Richmond fertilizer companies. He appeared before courts in nearby Henry,

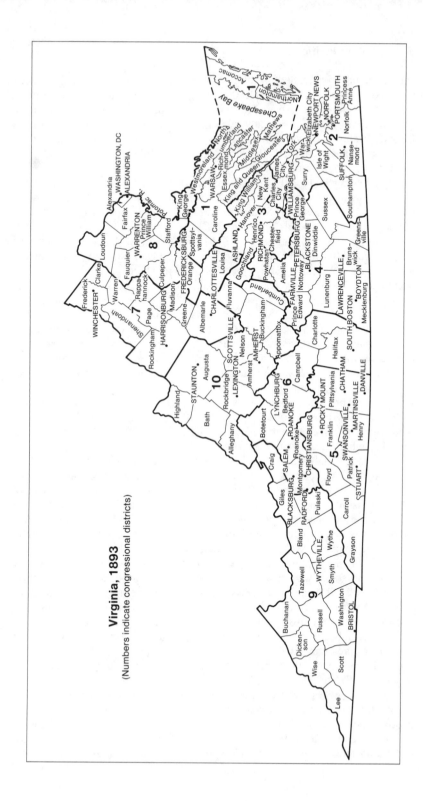

Virginia, 1893

(Numbers indicate congressional districts)

Halifax, and Franklin counties and before federal and state benches at Danville and Richmond. Furnishing the lead article in the *Virginia Law Journal* in January 1887, he estimated that in two years he had achieved "a phenomenal success in the practice of law." In 1888 he earned $4,000, which enabled him to invest $2,500 in Sutherlin's Riverside Cotton Mills in Danville and to pay off his remaining college debts.[27]

In early 1889, Swanson intended law as his "chosen profession," anticipating the time when he would be able "to go to [a] large city," where he would have "better and more extended opportunities." Yet, he could not escape the courthouses that propagated local politics and a rough-hewn acceptance of human foibles. There, one lawyer recalled, one practiced the necessity of "getting on with one's fellowman." The courtroom crowd appreciated displays of wit, repartee, and magniloquence. It was but a short route to campaign rallies and political debates for ambitious young lawyers. Swanson followed such a path. He and his family rejoiced as Democrats rewon the governorship in 1885 with Fitzhugh Lee and, at Mahone's expense, four years later with Philip W. McKinney. Swanson aided each canvass. In 1888, during the Cleveland campaign, he spent a week in Henry County "making one or two speeches a day." These contests shattered the Republican organization, which proceeded in 1890 to lose every Virginia congressional district. Appearing invincible, Democrats attracted many young men, thereby acquiring contrasting world views, conflicting interests, and vaulting ambitions.[28]

At the Democratic state convention in Richmond in August 1889, Swanson gained statewide attention for the first time. He seconded the thirty-three-year-old Beirne's unsuccessful nomination for the Democratic gubernatorial candidacy. Beirne ran behind McKinney, Danville's choice and a two-to-one favorite of Pittsylvania County. Swanson's efforts for the Richmond publisher stirred critical comments among the delegation, but he probably planned to transfer his law practice to Richmond. There, under Beirne's aegis, he would dabble in politics and await developing opportunities. Beirne fell ill, however, and died in February 1891. Had he lived, he would have been the leading candidate for the governorship. Swanson obviously had been Beirne's protégé; his death altered Swanson's career considerably. He now retreated to his own resources in Pittsylvania. In March 1892, as he passed his thirtieth birthday, he gained election to the state Democratic convention, obtained a place on its resolutions committee, and was listed as a prominent person among the party membership. By then Swanson had decided to seek the Fifth District congressional seat.[29]

The district was composed of seven counties of 161,000 persons along the North Carolina border. Slipper-shaped, it pointed westward with its largest county, Pittsylvania, and town, Danville, forming the eastern heel. Paired and stretching toward the mountains, Henry and Franklin Counties preceded the more remote Patrick County and three plateau counties of Floyd, Carroll, and Grayson. Over 160 miles from the Atlantic, the district depended upon inadequate, rutted pikes fanning from the railheads in the eastern counties. Western district residents lacked any easy exit eastward. No direct telegraphs connected Floyd and Carroll Counties with Danville. Patrick until "very recently . . . was cut off from the world." In the early 1880s, Pittsylvania and Carroll Counties exhibited Funder loyalties. Floyd County voted continually Readjuster. The remainder moved from party to party. In the 1889 gubernatorial election, Henry and Floyd Counties favored unsuccessful Republican Mahone.[30]

Prominent Funder, former Confederate colonel, lawyer, and Danville editor George C. Cabell had represented the district from 1879 to 1887. Martinsville mayor, Republican, and former Confederate private John R. Brown replaced him. In 1888, district Democrats elected Posey G. Lester, thirty-eight-year old Baptist evangelist and Floyd County editor. Mahone's defeat so demoralized Republicans that Lester overcame weak and scattered opposition in 1890. Representative of an emerging Methodist-Baptist majority, Lester was a potent speaker, but his congressional record derived from "his religious faith [that] dominated all other things." Lester did not run again in 1892. By then, prayer alone had not cured the district's marketplace miseries.[31]

District economic activities consisted of traditional subsistence farming, commercial agriculture in tobacco, timber, and grains, and nascent manufacturing. In the plateau counties, grains, fruits, and livestock dominated. Virgin stands of timber were harvested for the ninety sawmills that shaped and planed primal giants of oak, poplar, and pine. Iron mining and a Saltville soda and bleach works exploited mineral resources. Patrick County farmers grew grains and potatoes and worked thirty-two grist mills to accompany the plateau's seventy-five. Claiming to be almost "free of malaria," Henry County enjoyed a railroad boom. After rail connection with the rest of Virginia, Martinsville, its county seat and Danville rival, had grown from three hundred to three thousand persons in five years. Tobacco, corn, and grasses encouraged livestock raising—especially mules—in the county. Tobacco processing increased. "Nearly all" of Franklin County's farmers raised bright leaf. Large and small distilleries consumed a large portion of the district's grains and fruits. Pittsylvania County and Danville led the way in manufacturing and growth. Given the emphasis on tobacco products and distilled fruits and grain, citizens were sensitive to federal taxes on both items.[32]

In the early 1890s, rain followed by floods damaged crops, forcing commercial farmers into debt and punishing black and white tenants. The latter group was further harmed by unstable pricing structures. Having increased numerically since the Civil War, small growers were stung by debt payment as costs increased. A farmer of some means in Cumberland County revealed succinctly that "a short duration of existing conditions [would] reduce all Virginia farmers to serfdom . . . [E]ither he must go into debt [if he can] or become a day laborer." The modest rural tobacco processors fell before market fluctuations brought on by urban warehousemen and larger manufacturers, the American Tobacco Company combination, increasing and costly mechanization, and changing consumer tastes. Surplus manpower guaranteed low wages and marginal poverty. Only Danville in the district could boast of more than $100 per capita property evaluations. Blandishments of promoters and exploiters had raised tobacconists' expectations. Their unrest now arose not from ideological dissent, but, like their fellow Nebraska agrarians, from the "temporary desperation of . . . frustrated, pragmatic" capitalists. As hard times continued, their worries passed beyond economic considerations to preservation of their human dignity.[33]

Following the National Grange, Greenbackers, and the Virginia Farmer Assembly, the Texas-born Farmers' Alliance had been initially designed as a rural social and educational organization. Economic adversity spurred political and class antagonisms and promoted deeper distrust between farmers and city residents. Virginia Farmers' Alliance leader Edmund R. Cocke could "not discuss the important issues" with "a city man for [their] points of observation" were "totally different." By the spring of 1889, the Alliance established chapters in Pittsylvania, Henry, and Franklin counties and formally resolved "to make the growing of tobacco more profitable." Pittsylvania's Chapter planned a cooperative cigar factory in Danville and established the Danville Alliance Warehouse. At its state convention, refusing to support "for office the representatives or paid attorneys of railroads," the Alliance would broaden the railroad commissioner's powers. Widely supported by commercial groups, such a bill passed the House of Delegates, but railroad interests in the Senate diluted it. Encouraged by the Alliance and smaller tobacco companies, the same legislature refused to charter the American Tobacco Company, but the Alliance failed to gain a general bill outlawing trusts. The erratic legislative response convinced some farmers that the Virginia Democratic party could not furnish "much relief" and that they "must look mainly to Congress."[34]

Organized in Chatham in August 1890, the Pittsylvania Central Alliance and Trade Union first tried cooperatives. Stockholders, including an S.A. Swanson in Swansonville, lived throughout the county. Their purchasing cooperative would benefit them by cash dividends and lower prices. A self-conscious community challenging the economic order not by revolutionary but by competitive means, the union collected more than $6,000 to purchase goods, to secure quarters, and to hire employees to initiate a retail and fertilizer business. Operating through September 1892, its property and stock were then sold at auction when good intentions failed to stave off inexperience and misappropriation of funds. Inflationary measures at the federal level became more attractive to Southside and Piedmont farmers who endorsed free and unlimited coinage of silver. These agrarians and small businessmen, both those in debt and those who wished to be, argued that they would then be free from Wall Street credit domination.[35]

"Shall money continue to rule?" agitated one Alliance leader. "That is the naked, undisguised not to be silenced question before the country." In response, Virginia Democratic Senators Barbour and John W. Daniel, several congressmen, and the *Richmond Dispatch* spoke and wrote kindly of the need to inflate the currency. The party continued to use 1880s defenses: low tariffs and white racial solidarity. Seizing upon Henry Cabot Lodge's force bill to regulate federal elections provided momentary unity, but, in October 1891, party chairman J. Taylor Ellyson of Richmond noticed that the Alliance had recruited "some of our, hitherto, most reliable party workers, [who] . . . have caught the infection of this new movement." Mahone instructed his Republican leaders to encourage Alliance candidates, where strong, to attract disgruntled Democrats.[36]

Unfocused social grievances motivated many rural residents in the Fifth District. The touted charm of country life, sustained by commercial farming, proved ephemeral before the credit shortage. Energetic Methodist and Baptist ministers condemned inexpensive liquor flowing in rowdy rural barrooms and the attendant vices of prostitution and gambling as evidence of evil and declining times. Racial animosities and a near-frontier environment of shootings and family feuds contributed to a sense of unease. Mahone observed: "A good many hungry farmers . . . want to have something to say about their affairs. They want a great many things and can't tell what they are." Each year a federal or state election disturbed further the Fifth District electorate.[37]

Democratic presidential candidate Senator David B. Hill of New York, visiting Virginia in March 1891, came to embody agrarian inflationary hopes when he endorsed equal coinage of gold and silver. The Fifth District delegation to the Richmond state convention in May 1892 was committed to Hill over Cleveland by ninety-two to fifty delegates. With Pittsylvania County nearly evenly split, Danville went to Hill. Preparatory to his congressional campaign, Swanson had earlier committed to him. Party factionalism threatened division as Cleveland delegates, 891 strong, would override the "Hillite" minority of 652 delegates to secure a solid Cleveland delegation to the national nominating convention. The convention immediately became embroiled in a regional contest. Counties west of the Blue Ridge favored Cleveland; those south of the James River, Hill. North and east of Richmond, a Cleveland stronghold, Hill did well also. Senator Barbour's recent death created a leadership vacuum, but Senator Daniel, an inflationist and Hill advocate, worked for a compromise. Congressman Charles T. O'Ferrall, a man with gubernatorial prospects and Cleveland loyalties, cautioned his side of the aisle to be moderate. Virginia Board of Agriculture president Sutherlin favored Hill and conciliation. Swanson helped compose an innocuous platform each group could endorse. Martin mollified both sides to avoid "arousing antagonisms which would hereafter be prejudicial to his" planned senatorial campaign. Barbour's nephew, Basil B. Gordon, became state chairman and moved party headquarters to Charlottesville. The rancor was not forgotten, however.[38]

For some months, as he combed courthouse greens and crossroads for delegates to the Fifth District nominating convention, Swanson would avoid these potential divisions. He faced favorite sons and other well-known Democrats. Franklin County state representative Edward W. Saunders, two years his senior, and Judge D. W. Bolen of Carroll County posed specific local problems. In Danville, former congressman and city attorney George C. Cabell hungered still for congressional privileges, but his fellow townsman and distrit Democratic chairman Harry Wooding provided the most pervasive threat. A few days after the state convention, the district committee replaced Wooding with James L. Tredway of Chatham. Wooding encountered Swanson support throughout the district. One Wooding organizer reluctantly confessed the popular Swanson to be a "good fellow." After the death of incumbent W.P. Graves, W.E. Boisseau convinced Wooding to seek the mayor's office in Danville. Later, Boisseau admitted his Swanson loyalties. Saunders stepped aside a few days before the district convention in Martinsville. Bolen withdrew on the first ballot and

Swanson won by acclamation. He pledged his loyalty to state and national platforms, but his personality and gift of oratory would be as important as the issues he upheld. His identification with Hill would also prove beneficial. The Democratic press stressed that harmony had prevailed, favoring the "brilliant and gallant Swanson." Tied to the 1892 Democratic platform, he subscribed to the repeal of the Sherman Silver Purchase Act and to coinage of gold and silver "without discrimination." But Cleveland's presidential nomination did not ease his way.[39]

In June, Democrats named Cleveland for a third time at a rowdy, vindictive Chicago convention. Virginia Hill delegates had been handled roughly and their Senator Daniel booed. The earlier, fragile Richmond compromises shattered. Upon this news, Cocke, within an hour, departed for "the People's Party Convention in Richmond." Elected state chairman of this new party, he attracted other Alliance leaders. First appearing in May in Mecklenberg, the Virginia third party organized to send free-silver delegates to its national convention in Omaha. State chairman Gordon wrote Democratic headquarters that the original anti-Cleveland sentiment spread from the "eastern, or poorer, section of the state" into the third-party organization that, Gordon believed, received financial comfort from the Republicans. As silver agitation increased, in September he hoped that a growing antitariff wave and "the healthy portion of the state" would offset defections. One Democrat expressed the general attitude among the leadership: "I feel on tender hooks of anxiety on account of this silver agitation." Former Hill delegate Carter Glass of Lynchburg labelled Cleveland supporters "mugwumps and political hermaphrodites," but he remained loyal after his return from Chicago. He vowed to renew the Hill campaign in 1896. Martin observed that the Populists were "much strengthened by Cleveland's nomination."[40]

In addition to the third party, squabbling Republicans, divided for a decade over Mahone, opposed Swanson. Benjamin Harrison's federal appointees fell out with precinct and district organizers in Pittsylvania County. Danville postmaster J.H. Johnston feuded with Pittsylvania chairman C.T. Barksdale, a deputy U. S. Marshall and Danville realtor. District chairman W.S. Gravely of Martinsville died in March, creating further turmoil. In April, county Republicans purged Barksdale and elected "a county man," J.H. Pigg of Chatham. Some Southside Republicans advised Mahone to abandon Harrison's reelection campaign and, in coalition with the Populists, to concentrate upon four or five key congressional races. The Fifth District furnished an opportunity. Newly elected Republican district chairman William H. Gravely met in August with Populist leaders and agreed to follow them for the time being.[41]

Populists held emotional and economic arguments that could cost Swanson votes. More class conscious than the Readjusters, their campaign, one journalist concluded, pitted "class against class" and assumed that "sections of the country are arrayed against sections." Blaming a Cleveland-endorsed tobacco tax for an ominous decline in one year of two million pounds on the Danville market, they claimed a deceitful Democratic-Republican national coalition prevented circulation of free silver up to fifty dollars per capita, prohibited easy loans, banned rail rates at cost, and avoided a heavy tax on accumulated wealth. Editor

Charles H. Pierson of the Populist *Virginia Sun,* rumored to be financed by
Mahone, assailed Cleveland Democrats. He censured New South promoters
who, in wooing northern capital, bartered "away Virginia's birthright for a mess
of pottage."[42]

On September 1, with five of seven counties represented, the Populist
district convention praised the national ticket of James B. Weaver and Virginia's
James G. Field, the force bill, and the Populist Omaha platform. As suggested
by their Republican sympathizers, they condemned the Anderson-McCormick
law that allowed Democrats to control Virginia elections. Former Commonwealth's attorney George L. Richardson of Henry County offered the crowd of
Alliance members and Republicans a chance to salvage sound logs from the two
"old rotten parties" to build the Populists. A Franklin County farmer and "liberal
Democrat," Calvin Luther Martin accepted the congressional nomination but
withdrew a week later. A People's Party committee then named Henry County
clerk of court Benjamin T. Jones. Five days later in district convention Republicans in larger numbers than expected approved the McKinley Silver Purchase
Act and denounced the Anderson-McCormick law. They also favored the force
bill and adjourned without naming a congressional candidate. Holding prior
Republican attachments and backed by former Republican congressman John
R. Brown, Jones and his candidacy apparently harmed efforts at Populist-
Republican cooperation. Martin returned to be a candidate. Not until the first
week in October did he resign again in favor of Jones.[43]

Revamping 1880s organizational techniques, district Democrats ordered
more meetings, parades, and piles of food, but Populist leaders instructed
agrarians at rallies to withdraw to avoid Democratic orators. In late September,
Democrats tried to canvass each voter in every precinct to determine areas of
strength and weakness. Speaking with Swanson, ex-Confederate cavalryman
and Clevelandite Congressman O'Ferrall campaigned in the district as did New
Yorker and Hill devotee James F. Grady. Young Democrats such as Danville
lawyer Andrew Montague traveled the seven counties for Cleveland and Swanson. Acompanied by files of marching Democrats, vice-presidential candidate
Adlai Stevenson addressed five-thousand persons in Danville. Swanson published a campaign newspaper, *Alliance Democrat,* and collected district funds
to employ carriage drivers, to purchase train tickets for voters, and to obtain
frequently alcoholic refreshments for election day. Tobacco-wealthy Democrats
such as Oliver W. Dudley contributed to overcome financially strapped Republicans and Populists.[44]

With some pride of authorship, Swanson proposed that the Democratic
state platform, stressing "conciliation, concession and compromise," held cures
for the district's marketplace ills. Removal of federal taxes upon state bank paper
issue would augment currency to meet commercial and agricultural needs. He
opposed the Internal Revenue Service' use of informants and would reduce the
protective tariff. He abused the force bill and echoed Democratic claims that its
passage would "seriously imperil the peace of our homes and safety of our
society." The color line was drawn in the eastern precincts of the district. The
Danville Register observed at Chatham court day white and black Republicans
and "third party folks" congregating "in such a fashion that it was hard to tell

'tother from which." A "warm, personal friend" of Swanson, *Register* editor W. Scott Copeland cautioned Democrats that they had "no part or lot in such a political mixture." Democrats should "come back to your own people." *Richmond Dispatch* owner Ellyson could discover "no man of prominence" who "exerted or had reason to expect approval or preferment in the Democratic party" in the Populist camp. Swanson warned that Jones was a "wool and dyed Republican. . . , a candidate for delegate" to the Republican national convention. "Everywhere," he emphasized, Jones's nomination was "regarded as a Republican trick." In more elemental political tones, Swanson admonished precinct leaders "to work especially and earnestly" for him. "You know I would do any[thing I] could for you."[45]

By 14,112 votes to 12,006, Swanson won his first political office. He carried by 150 votes or more six counties but lost Henry, Jones's home county. In Virginia, Cleveland accumulated a 35,000-vote majority, leading Harrison by 50,000, while Populist Weaver drew but 12,274. Democrats maintained control of every congressional district, at least one by fraud. Richmond celebrated the largest Democratic victory since the Civil War with a massive parade. Democrats had appealed to racial and class pride and prejudice, campaigned for a low tariff, condemned threatened federal intrusion into elections, and assaulted excessive federal excise taxes. They used the Mahone and Republican endorsement of "fusion" with Populists to hamper transference of Alliance members into the People's Party. Control of election machinery made Democratic judges "the absolute jury as to the qualification of the voters." In his district, Swanson won owing to his exhaustive canvassing, adept organization, and personal charm. He did not increase significantly, however, the total his predecessor had accumulated in 1888. Throughout the state, Populist-backed congressional candidates received 90,000 votes. Had Republicans more campaign funds and the Populists better organization, Virginia Democrats would have encountered far greater difficulty in maintaining the loyalties of credit-shy entrepreneurs and farmers.[46]

The 1892 campaign marked one of the last triumphs of the Barbour-reformed Democratic party of the 1880s. Populist proposals for electoral purification, state constitutional changes, and state ownership of railroads stirred great publicity in debates, newspapers, and oratory. Although sociopolitical programs lacked a system and reliance upon personal relationships and emotional sloganeering was epidemic, a new set of definitions in Virginia politics had emerged. Regionalism and hostility toward bankers, railroad managers, and industrialists had been sharpened. The New South vision of manufacturing and commerical development had grown dim in the eyes of poverty-stricken farmers of Southside Virginia. Consistent with tradition, however, voters continued to treat government as an instrument to an end: their economic and social improvement. If Democrats opposed the force bill and federal intervention in elections, they observed no inconsistency in legislating federal currency ratios to benefit their credit-starved citizenry. If Populists condemned centralized power of railroads and Wall Street, they favored centralizing the power of government to control both. Swanson's promises carried an implied commitment to use agencies of the federal government to aid and expand services.

2

Faith with the People
1893-1898

Thirty-one-year-old Claude Swanson led a resurgence of youth within the Virginia Democratic party. One University of Virginia classmate remarked to Petersburg's Francis R. Lassiter that "the Young Democracy" now advanced to the forefront of state affairs: "You and [Andrew] Montague and Swanson have secured big plums under the Federal Government and Hal Flood helps to run the State as a Senator." To advance his political standing, Swanson avoided a stern, implacable ideology and used his personal affability while repeating generally acceptable political slogans. Eventually this would not suffice, and he emerged as an agrarian spokesman who proposed more government involvement to resolve social and economic problems.[1]

A portion of Swanson's political strength in the early 1890s derived from the decentralized, ramshackled Virginia government that favored town and country politicians. Although numerous, they derived influence from relationships within the political environments of their locality. State delegates and senators exhibited many of the same propensities. Averaging 180,000 people, the congressional districts bound these communities into viable entities that served as the state's political subdivisions. In normal times, a congressman who brought home the political bacon of patronage and who developed connections at state and federal levels came to be a political duke affecting not only federal but state and local politics as well.[2]

Entering his first term, amid comments of a "new era in politics," Congressman Swanson joined a heavy Democratic majority in the House of Representatives that elected Georgian, English-born Charles Crisp as Speaker. President Grover Cleveland personally prepared to dispense patronage, but one Virginia congressman feared he was "going to be monstrous slow" doing it. In the midst of this plenty, the Virginia delegation fell out as they saw "matters in the light in which there seems to be most prospect of benefit to their own Districts." With Congress out of session, Swanson schemed for "one of the big places"—a district attorneyship—for the Fifth District. In a night-long caucus of the Virginia delegation in Senator John W. Daniel's office, Swanson maneuvered for Andrew Montague, a Middlesex native who had moved to Danville in the 1880s to practice law. Son of Virginia's Civil War lieutenant governor, Montague gained influential Charles T. O'Ferrall's vote by promising to appoint

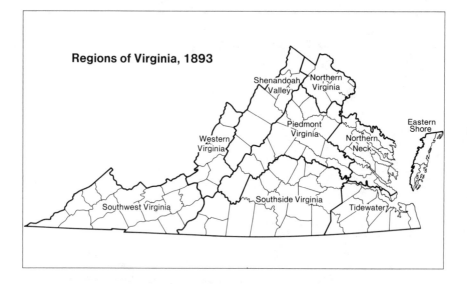

Regions of Virginia, 1893

from his district J.B. Stephenson. On the eleventh ballot, Montague obtained the delegation's agreement. Swanson introduced the young lawyer to other congressmen, the attorney general, and Cleveland. He also attempted to remove rumors that Montague had favored David Hill by labeling the district attorney designee "as an enthusiastic Cleveland man when delegates were [being] elected." Cleveland accepted the Virginia delegation's recommendations.[3]

Swanson instructed his University of Virginia classmate Lassiter to visit Washington in a quest for eastern district attorney. It would be "unexcusable to *miss* this position by a disposition not to go through a few days inconvenience to secure it." Swanson gained additional influence when Cleveland named Lassiter. But, growing sensitive to factional labels and contrary to practice, the president appointed a Cleveland man as Lassiter's assistant, against the latter's wishes. Indicative of the party schism to come, this action led Daniel to confess to Lassiter: "Grover is a law unto himself, and has executed it to suit himself." In Virginia, pressures that had produced the anti-Cleveland spasm increased as the 1893 depression deepened.[4]

The treasury's gold supply had declined for over two years. Backing legal tender, gold was also under assault by the 1890 Sherman Silver Purchase Act that required the Treasury to purchase silver; the circulating medium had increased by $150 million but the same Treasury notes might be and were redeemed in gold. International conditions produced a further gold outflow. Decreased tariff revenue and heavy congressional expenditures led to a Wall Street panic based upon whispered fears that the nation's gold standard would soon be abandoned. On June 30, 1893, Cleveland ordered a special session of Congress to repeal the Sherman Act. The Democratic majority in Congress now needed to undo this earlier Republican compromise. Swanson and other agrarian congressmen faced a difficult choice.[5]

In 1892, national Democrats had endorsed both gold and silver coinage, without favoring either metal, of equal intrinsic dollar values to be adjusted by international agreement. Demanding paper currency be maintained at par with and redeemable in coin, the party branded the Sherman Act a "cowardly makeshift, fraught with possibilities of danger" Presently fearful of Alliance cooperatives and their competition, railroad-spawned mercantile centers as Danville and Martinsville caught in growth economics demanded more credit. Swanson's pledge to "the free and unlimited coinage of both gold and silver" responded to their needs. In the House he voted for repeal but stood grimly with the minority that attempted to pass a silver seigniorage bill similar to the inflationary Bland-Allison Act of 1878. Without evidence of federal aid or Democratic support for credit-starved entrepreneurs and farmers of the Fifth District, Swanson faced a party-rupturing revolt among his constituents.[6]

To enhance his influence in Richmond and patronage opportunities, Swanson earlier had joined the gubernatorial campaign of O'Ferrall, the recognized front-runner and Cleveland favorite. In April 1893, Swanson attended in his behalf county conventions as they selected delegates to the state nominating convention. Danville and its environs found Algernon S. Buford more acceptable as a candidate. Aiding in reorganizing the Danville railway after the Civil War and enabling its subsequent expansion, he was a close business associate of William Sutherlin. Swanson's endorsement of O'Ferrall, despite sound political reasons, smacked of treachery to some Danville partisans. Sutherlin's death in July 1893 created further diversions from older political patrons. Adept at compromise and recognized as a "most intelligent public spirited, and patriotic citizen" of Danville, he left no successor. New personal and political relationships emerged. Swanson led most of the district to O'Ferrall with 102 delegates. Danville and part of Pittsylvania County persisted for Buford.[7]

Aided by Cleveland's patronage and effective organization, O'Ferrall won on the first ballot; the party adopted a popular Populist standard by endorsing a graduated income tax. Sponsor of railway regulating legislation, R.C. Kent received the lieutenant governor's nomination. The convention applauded Swanson's advocacy of the 1892 Chicago platform and the appropriateness of the Sherman Act repeal. Swanson voiced his fidelity to "the silver dollar and gold dollar on a parity and the equality of a dollar in silver or gold or greenbacks." Howls of delight followed his pokes at the Populists, "full of broken down politicians and lawyers," opposing the Democrats, "the integrity and intelligence of the Commonwealth." In attempting to split O'Ferrall delegates, Carter Glass of Lynchburg, following Daniel and his favorite J. Hoge Tyler, raised the question of free coinage of silver that eventually developed into a major issue of the campaign. Its endorsement soon became a necessary part of the campaign catechism of would-be successful Virginia politicians.[8]

Populists nominated estranged Democrat Edmund R. Cocke. William Mahone's Republicans attempted to encourage Democratic disruption rather than victory by Cocke. The silver question intruded; "Sockless" Jerry Simpson, mesmerized Chatham crowds with visions of free silver. Owing to Republican national policies, a national Populist, William H. Gravely of Henry County and Republican district chairman resigned to oppose continuing Democratic

"Bourbonism" by accepting the third party's nomination for attorney general. He boasted: "The Democrats try to get us on state issues, but we keep firing the silver question at them and the people want to hear it." Populists used Daniel's speeches against repeal of the Sherman Act and stressed class differences. O'Ferrall's campaign drew the color line and a convenient race riot in Roanoke reawoke racial antagonisms. Democrats attacked Mahone as much as Cocke for the former's covert aid to the latter. Swanson blamed much of the economic decline upon the disruptive character of ill-founded Populist proposals while O'Ferrall loudly proclaimed his support of bimetalism. He secretly sought unsuccessfully to postpone until after his election the Senate vote on the Sherman Act repeal. He won by 127,490 votes to Cocke's 81,239. For the Democrats, the vote totals and majority compared unfavorably with the previous gubernatorial election. Although Cocke's support blossomed in traditionally Republican black precincts, large numbers of blacks did not vote. One observer estimated that two-thirds stayed away from the polls. While Danville's vote of 1,115 for O'Ferrall and 80 for Cocke illustrated black inactivity, O'Ferrall lost Floyd, Franklin, and Henry counties and carried Pittsylvania county by 500 votes. If blacks had voted in numbers comparable to four years earlier, the Populist Cocke conceivably could have won in 1893.[9]

Concurrently, the election of Thomas Staples Martin to the Senate became a cause célèbre of reform politics in the next decade and held immediate consequences for Swanson. John S. Barbour's death in May 1892 emboldened a gaggle of regional politicians, mostly former or incumbent congressmen, to succeed him, but the youngest contender, fifty-two-year-old Albemarle lawyer Martin, proved the most popular. He first attempted to gain from Governor Phillip W. McKinney an interim appointment but failed despite considerable endorsement by legislators. Besides his work in earlier campaigns, his activities in the 1891 legislative elections in distributing railroad funds to receptive campaigners to defeat the Kent railroad bill had broadened a base of support. McKinney unexpectedly named Eppa Hunton interim senator and refused to call a special legislative session. For the next eighteen months, aided by Flood and dodging between Hill, Cleveland, and O'Ferrall factions, Martin scoured the districts for delegates. Railroad developer and owner of the *Richmond Times,* Joseph F. Bryan contributed to casting former governor Fitzhugh Lee as Martin's primary competitor. In the 1893 autumn legislative campaign, Martin again offered campaign funds to Democrats from the railroads who feared Populist proposals to nationalize the lines. In November, counting his commitments, Martin noticed that "the howl that generally follows defeat" was already "going forth" from his competitors. On the sixth ballot, in the legislative caucus, he won the senatorship.[10]

Myths of the Martin election described him as incapable of election "without the power of railroad money and influence" and characterized him as a sly, unknown manipulator who tricked his way into office. In the *Richmond Times,* Bryan fostered these accusations, and others who favored Lee supported the story. A legislative investigating committee reported, however, that Martin's use of funds was "not different from those resorted to in former campaigns." The committee referred to the continuing presence in Virginia politics of railroad personnel since the inception of the greasy, steaming machines. Politics during the previous twenty years had been at least partially shaped by expansion and consolidation struggles of various roads. Through the statewide lines with their feeder systems, railroad men and their lawyers had become a unifying, centralizing force owing to their knowledge of localities and leaders across the state. Railroad techniques became political techniques. As railroads rationalized their organization, they constantly sought competent barristers, especially those who had won cases against them. Barbour's recruitment of able youngsters to the Democratic party in the 1880s and Martin's similar penchant reflected this basic railroad practice.[11]

Martin symbolized corporate organization rather than corporate ideology. The hundreds of letters he sent over the years reflect a clerk's concern for details rather than an ideologue's. Desiring an "administration senator," Cleveland had made available campaign funds and patronage appointments to Fitzhugh Lee, who held many railroad contacts and claimed Martin would oppose Cleveland policies. Politically inept, Lee mistook parades for precinct organization and no longer could depend upon Barbour's disintegrating Democratic organization. Accusing Martin of fostering a machine overlooks his contributions toward general Democratic success. Of the sixty-six votes he received in the Democratic caucus, forty-one derived from areas where Populists received 40 percent or more of the vote. Only ten Martin-aided candidates had failed to gain election. His opponent's accusation of a Martin machine after 1893 derived from linkage with the Mahone machine and its negative connotations relating to class, race, and region for many white Democrats. As a legislative handler, Flood won his political spurs in this campaign, being "the happiest man in . . . [Murphy's] hotel and . . . recipient of as many congratulations as Martin." Swanson had known Martin since Richard F. Beirne's political introduction in the 1880s. In April 1893, Swanson and Martin had traveled together to New York to attend a four-day review of naval squadrons and probably to hunt for political contributions. In February 1894, escorting the senator-elect to the Senate floor, he introduced Martin to various senators, including Hill. Swanson's commitment to Martin in 1893 was not a result of ideological similarities; rather, as in O'Ferrall's case, Martin had been the most available candidate.[12]

Yet, mere politicking would not guarantee Swanson reelection. Danville lawyer Berryman Green had applied for the district attorneyship Montague received. The old Confederate and former state district judge then campaigned for a U.S. Circuit judgeship. As Martin counted his votes in the legislative caucus, Swanson was in Washington petitioning Cleveland in Green's behalf. The Virginia congressional delegation divided, and Cleveland selected another person. Five days later, the *Richmond Dispatch* carried a letter by "Civis" denouncing Martin as a captive of the railroads and as his accomplice J. Taylor Ellyson, who replaced ailing Basil B. Gordon as Democratic state chairman. Green admitted writing the polemic. Swanson may well have considered Green's moral outrage as generated by the disappointment of an office seeker. Given Sutherlin's death, Democratic failure to expand credit, and the disenchantment of Buford and Lee supporters with Swanson, Green now led the anti-Swanson revolt in the river city.[13]

In 1894, Swanson's involvement in state government appeared more clearly. He discussed with "most of the delegates" from his district an increase in
salaries for state district judges. He assured his friend Judge Stafford G. Whittle
of Henry County: "Martin favors this." Following a tariff debate in the House,
Swanson returned to Richmond "to enlist Martin's services actively." Not until
1896 did Whittle and his judicial colleagues gain a raise, but Swanson had
convinced the prominent judge of his interest. He observed in the tariff class
conflicts, and impressed his listeners with his factual grasp and the clarity and
force of his expression as he fought to reduce tobacco taxes. He attacked again
the force bill, endorsed graduated income taxes, and sought a $10,000 appropri-
ation to study the feasibility of rural free delivery of mail.[14]

Swanson also began to oppose Cleveland. Like other southerners, he spoke
for the Bland seigniorage bill that angered a creditor-oriented president who had
floated a Treasury issue to bolster the gold reserve. Having "always favored" the
coinage of silver rather than storing bullion in the Treasury, the congressman
questioned whether the Democratic party was keeping its pledges. Cleveland's
biographer dismissed this agrarian criticism as the money supply had grown
"more rapidly than in any previous period in American history." Swanson
identified the location of much of this supply of bankable or loanable funds in
the northeastern United States, which made "the rest pay interest and tribute to
it." He labored to repeal the federal tax on state bank issue, gained Democratic
caucus approval, but failed on the floor of the House with only 102 votes in
support. He laid defeat to factional opposition within the Democratic majority.
The Bland bill passed, however.[15]

Despite pleas that party unity required his signature, Cleveland vetoed the
bill. He dismissed a delegation of petitioning southern and western congressmen as men who "pandered to the delusions of the people and voted all
sorts of legislation in order to keep themselves in office." Refusing to be labeled
in factionalist terms, Swanson claimed he was a "platform Democrat," who
would "keep . . . faith with people." Breaking with Cleveland, Swanson
approved overriding Cleveland's seigniorage veto, endorsed Hill for president in
1896, and accelerated his patronage activities. The depression grew worse. The
Richmond Terminal System was reorganized and other railroads failed. In
January, the American Tobacco Company ceased purchases on the Danville
market; the tobacco crop had few buyers.[16]

Swanson suffered from Cleveland's political decline, which dropped lower
than the securities market, identified by one broker as "dull, stale and unprofitable." A Danville Republican gleefully noted widespread Democratic estrange-
ment and Swanson the object of much anti-Cleveland discontent. In Richmond,
the Virginia Democratic legislature rallied, adopting Barbour's 1880s tactics of
absorbing opponents' proposals and grasping more securely voting procedures.
Sidetracking a possible, Populist-inspired constitutional convention, the Assembly amended the 1884 Anderson-McCormick law into the Walton Act that
provided the secret ballot statewide. A voter could consume two and one-half
minutes casting a locally printed ballot that required him to draw a line, at least
three-fourths of the way, through names of candidates for whom he did not vote.
A special election constable would aid illiterate voters. Shenandoah and Page

counties' senator, M. L. Walton, who sponsored the bill, opposed giving them any help. Editor Glass of Lynchburg agreed, because it would allow "virtue and intelligence" to govern. Desperately in need of votes, Democrats in Populist and Republican districts attached the constable requirement. Senator-elect Martin wrote key passages and gained additional legislative gratitude.[17]

In August 1894, at the district convention in Stuart, Swanson's renomination "carried with a whoop." Although outside circumstances endangered his reelection, he controlled in competent fashion the district's Democrats. Refusing to endorse Cleveland, they favored lower tariffs, a new system of state banks, an income tax, a purge of pension roles, and coinage of silver at a ratio of sixteen to one. Although the state bank plank was not popular in the counties, the platform authored by Danville editor Frank S. Woodson marked the first Virginia Democratic congressional convention to favor the Populist silver ratio. Commentaries evaluated Swanson's approval as the same "had he the matter to himself."[18]

Fifth District Populists expected to continue cooperation with Republicans and intended to nominate Gravely as their coalition candidate. But scenting victory and opposition to Gravely among the rank and file led Republicans after eight ballots to select former judge George W. Cornett of Grayson County. They favored the Republican national party, coinage of silver at parity with gold, and removal of the Walton Act. Third-party delegates, sixteen in number, met in Chatham and nominated G.W.B. Hale, a Populist state senator. Failing a union with the Populists, Danville prohibitionists offered W.T. Sheldon for congress as well. Surveying this mixed political scene, state Democratic chairman Ellyson found campaign funds scarce and feared "several districts . . . will be lost unless we can render . . . some necessary monetary help."[19]

As a member of the state executive committee, Swanson tapped party resources directly. Democratic newspapers, such as Glass's *Lynchburg News*, praised Swanson's renomination because he had "made a record that cannot be successfully assailed." Hill, O'Ferrall, Montague, and Beverly B. Munford, spoke throughout the district. At Rocky Mount, Senator Daniel attracted "the largest crowd assembled here in years" and at his elbow Swanson endorsed "everything Daniel said." In Martinsville, Swanson debated Cornett, confused him over the silver issue, and routed him "horse, foot and dragoons." So effectively did Swanson argue against Republican tariff and monetary positions that some Republicans begged Mahone to send a capable speaker to "demolish Swanson on his own dung hill." Swanson also faced Hale despite Populist heckling and what he termed Populist lies "out of the whole cloth." Despite such displays, opponents were encouraged as increased federal taxes on brandy and whiskey soured mountain precincts and prices fell lower on the tobacco markets.[20]

Danville continued to be a barrier against Swanson's reelection. Green, constable of the third ward, admitted that he stood with the "strong element" that opposed Swanson. Resentful of Swanson's boasts that "all the earth and Pittsylvania County . . . [was] for him, except Danville," Green tried to stir opposition among Democrats, claiming Swanson "had not the first idea of Democratic principles. . . . [He was] a creature and servant of rings." His election bid would "overthrow . . . Virginia Democracy" and, if O'Ferrall and Munford could not pull him through, a "fraudulent count" would be needed. Local businessmen Thomas B. Fitzgerald of Riverside Cotton Mills and W.P. Hodnett, a former Swanson employer, worked the wards for him. In the third, John Swanson directed Democrats, and Cornett's handlers accused him of deliberately slowing "the colored [voting] line." Other Democrats were charged with intimidating black citizens by "halloing, running and swearing." Montague's law partner, N.H. Massie, led "almost 150 Democrats" to "yell . . . as soldiers, as if they had won a victory."[21]

Merchants and mechanics in Danville reportedly vowed they "would not support the Democratic party if they could live and . . . support . . . their family against the heavy pressure . . . brought against them by party leaders." A storekeeper, Hugh L. Guerrant, "orated . . . all over town" against Swanson. The congressman interviewed the twenty-three-year-old, asking what "he had done against him." One of Swanson's college benefactors, R.W. Peatross at "Sunday School on the Sabbath" sought to soothe Guerrant, who eventually voted Democratic despite its being "a bitter pill." Montague defended Swanson's second nomination as it was "generally thought [he] . . . has made a good representative." Among Riverside Cotton Mill employees who were Democrats, only "one out of ten" voted for him. In addition to Cleveland and the depression, a portion of their discontent originated, in Montague's mind, from Swanson's patronage "appointments" which had not given "universal satisfaction in his area."[22]

Some of these appointees were black men. In May 1893, sensitive to black votes received in his first election, Swanson sought to place E.N. McDaniel, "a very prominent colored Democrat" from Cascade in Pittsylvania County, at the expense of "the scalp of some Republican negro." In 1894, W.H. Pleasants, a black Danville Republican, was accused of being paid by Swanson to urge his colleagues either to vote for Swanson or to "go home . . . and do nothing." In reality, although he held a federal appointment at Swanson's hand, Pleasants refused to follow Cornett, a mountain Republican spokesman, who in 1888 had opposed "any negroes representing them at national conventions." Pleasants aided a black cigar maker, W.J. Reid, to become Danville Republican chairman, thereby splitting the party as Mahone's appointee refused to step down. Reid proceeded to organize Swanson clubs and the *Danville Register* congratulated Pleasants upon his course. In the rough and tumble of the era's politics, accusers quoted Pleasants as advising, "If Democrats have money to buy negro votes, for God's sake let the negro have all the money he can get." Fewer than 250 black votes in Danville were cast for Cornett. Whatever the case, Swanson appointments had been well placed. At thirty-four of forty-two precincts in Pittsylvania, election officers were federal employees who "owed their respective positions to patronage and procurrance" of Swanson. Others had received federal favors from District Attorney Montague.[23]

The Walton Act determined procedures for the 1894 campaign but it generated as much confusion as control for the Democrats. Both Republicans and Democrats lost votes owing to smeared and incorrectly marked ballots. Some illiterates suspected that they were instructed by election constables to

vote for Swanson when they preferred Cornett. Other voters refused to participate. One shouted: "Come on and less go, cause I can't read and I ain't satisfied
to vote that way." Feuding Republicans failed on occasion to present common
lists for election officers. "A great many" Republican leaders worked and voted
for Swanson while others aided "Captain" Hale, the Populist candidate. Party
lines were so tangled that one election judge admitted that he appointed poll
workers whose political preferences were unknown. Still others were enticed to
stay away by promises of credit of fifty cents or a dollar by Democratic or
Republican merchants. The Walton law did not bring about Swanson's victory:
he won by 10,750 votes to Cornett's 8,417 and to Hale's 1,121.[24]

Complex procedures generated by the Walton law had threatened to over-
whelm election practices. Overcoming these barriers, Swanson gained advantage from his opponent's organizational weaknesses, aid of outside personages,
shrewd application of funds and patronage appointments, a determined loyal
Democratic campaign force, and bipartisan support. While absorbing Populist
platforms and voters, he had moved away from the decaying Democratic
hegemony established in the 1880s toward a yet to be defined new political
order. But Martin's election, Swanson's hard-won reelection, and the rise of
younger politicians perturbed older Virginia leaders. Swanson's willingness to
endorse free silver at a sixteen-to-one ratio advanced beyond a formula for an
entrepreneur's economic salvation. It bid to metamorphize into a symbol of
class revolt.[25]

Placing aside politics, Swanson extended to "only a few friends" wedding
invitations to "a very quiet affair." His marriage to Elizabeth Deane Lyons, an
attractive and socially astute daughter of widow Annie Deane Lyons, had
evolved over an eight-year period. The thirty-two-year-old groom invited Flood:
"We have always been such warm friends, since our acquaintance at the
University." Danville Democratic chairman Ben C. Belt served as a grooms-
man, and William Swanson was best man. The ceremony took place in Mrs.
Lyons's Washington residence in a room decorated with white columns and
illuminated by candles in silver candelabra, a gift of the Virginia congressional
delegation. The newlyweds honeymooned in Florida.[26]

Scarcely had the Swansons departed than the young congressman's office
received Cornett's intention to contest his reelection. The Republican doubted
the constitutionality of the Walton law and use of election judges to instruct
illiterate voters. Republican allegations of irregularities fastened upon four other
of the ten Virginia Democratic congressmen: William A. Jones of the First
District, William R. McKenney of the Fourth, Peter J. Otey of the Sixth, and
Harry Tucker of the Tenth. Claiming "at least 20,000 votes" in Virginia had
been discarded owing to mismarking, the Republican accused 1,300 election
constables of conspiracy. Given earlier success in challenging two Democratic
congressmen in 1890, Republicans would strengthen their party by branding the
faction-ridden Democrats as hopelessly corrupt.[27]

The Cornett case meandered through the first months of 1895. Lawyers
examined witnesses and compiled reports at ten dollars a day. Composed of six
Republicans and three Democrats, House Committee on Elections, number
three, reviewed these depositions. Virginia Congressman Jones presented in

April 1896 the committee's findings, which favored Swanson. During February 1897, he again defended his free-silver colleague. Although the Virginia election code was quite similar to that of other states, Election Committee member Henry F. Thomas censured the Walton law as "the first legislative attempt to invade and overthrow" the secret ballot. The Union veteran maintained that neither Cornett nor Swanson deserved the seat. Blacks, he accused, had been denied the franchise by intimidation and connivance. Jones reminded the House that, should Cornett win all contested ballots he claimed, Swanson would still hold a fifteen hundred-vote majority. Election Committee chairman Republican Samuel McCall of Massachusetts cautioned Thomas against "decorating . . . Southern Democrats with every vice." He questioned "coddling" Southern Republicans through Republican congressional majorities. Although it earlier unseated Petersburg's ill McKenney in favor of Republican Robert T. Thorpe, the House voted 127 to 21 against a roll-call vote and sustained the Election Committee's report on Swanson.[28]

Surviving these partisan blows, Swanson discovered that the "pure elections" issue had become involved in the silver controversy. Having used the issue for years, as reflected in the earlier force bill, Mahone conceived of an "honest elections" conference to be held in Petersburg. After meeting with J. Haskins Hobson, state Populist chairman, he worked to broaden the sporadic Republican-Populist alliance. General Assembly delegates who favored such a reform received their endorsement. Republican William W. Cobbs of Pittsylvania County reported a positive attraction to pure elections as Danville Democrat Eugene Withers denounced corrupt politics. A bipartisan group—the Reform Party of Pittsylvania—tried to recruit Withers but the state Senate candidate demurred. Wither's law partner Green agreed to help. Cobbs doubted his utility but he would take any help from Danville, that "bitter bourbon hole." Populists Cocke and James G. Field attended Mahone's conference in August. Brunswick Democrat Edward P. Buford did also because he regarded "the question of honor in Elections as the most important connected with Virginia legislation." Democrats launched a counterconference at Roanoke attended by Withers but moderated by Daniel who proposed postponing any consideration of a constitutional convention from fear that Republicans and Populists might dominate it. Pittsylvania blacks, sensing a plot to disfranchise them, grew suspicious.[29]

Other interests claimed the pure election issue. In an apparant reactionary mood, in September 1895, Pittsylvania County Democrats in convention reversed their free-silver endorsement and did not approve Daniel's course. Delegate John A. Tredway confessed: "When Major Daniel left his seat in the Senate . . . to advocate the election of Thomas S. Martin, Major Daniel and I parted company." If its proponents' political ethics could be questioned, free silver's appeal might diminish. Cleveland loyalists were rallying behind Fitzhugh Lee who stalked the precincts seeking election of his friends to the new legislature that would either reelect Daniel or determine his successor. The former governor encouraged his pro-tem of the Senate, John Hurt of Pittsylvania, to stand against the "combine" because it was "never too late for anything." In July 1895, he urged sound-money congressman Harry Tucker of

Lexington to prevent renomination of a pro-Martin and free-silver state senator as it was "better in any event to have friends than enemies in the legislature." He again appealed to Cleveland, as did O'Ferrall, to use his patronage power in Virginia for those who "march with the administration for pure elections and sound money."[30]

Lee's efforts generated additional Democratic disruption while Mahone's unexpected death in October muddled Republican tactics. In the autumn Fifth District legislative elections, Withers won a state senate seat, but a Republican represented Carroll, Grayson, and Patrick counties. Voters in Franklin and Floyd counties sent Populist Hale to the senate on an "honest election" platform. Delegate seats went to Republicans in Patrick and Carroll counties. Populist wards in Pittsylvania County voted heavily for two Republican delegate candidates and Henry County nearly sent an "honest elections" representative to Richmond. Voters had not been lured away from free silver, however. In the district and along the North Carolina line to Norfolk, Cleveland Democrats fell from power. Intent upon reforming the election law, Flood with Swanson's advice removed the objectionable constable provisions to prevent congressional Republicans from "turning the Virginia [congressional] delegation out." The legislature also called for a referendum for a new constitution for May 1897.[31]

Swanson anticipated many of these developments. He adopted style and manner that was populistic, notably anticorporation, while his tobacco entrepreneurs continued in their support of him. Although a colleague scolded him for defending the "moonshine vote," he reviled government informers paid on a commission basis to report illicit distilleries. This system was frequently fraudulent, usually expensive, and always resulted in few convictions, he claimed. He opposed reduction of the debt of Union Pacific railroad owed to the federal Treasury, and the *Richmond Dispatch* classified him as the "most outspoken Virginia champion" pressing for financial relief. Unable to unite faction-ridden congressional Democrats for free silver before arrival of the Republican Fifty-Fourth Congress, he criticized another Cleveland bond issue and the president's refusal to follow Secretary of Treasury John Carlisle's plans to expand state bank credit sources. Cleveland had failed to use party machinery "to obtain reasonable harmony so as to secure and perfect legislation," Swanson complained. He mocked gold proponents, saying that they would not respond to Gabriel's trumpet if it were made of silver. As Swanson feared, Virginians now faulted a congress that fiddled "while the country [was] being consumed." At least one voter reported that thousands no longer would follow so-called parties dealing "with the destruction of the classes."[32]

Earlier Virginia Democrats had used class prejudices to discount Populist appeals. In his first congressional campaign, Swanson bragged that Democrats attracted "the best people" and that Populists suffered by comparison. But by the mid-1890s such tactics were politically dangerous. Martin observed privately that the "hopeless condition of [the] people" pushed them from restlessness to desperation: "Their purpose . . ., to make some change, has taken shape in the free coinage movement and . . . nothing can swerve them." As Swanson pursued free-silver voters, he went beyond simply irritating district economic and social conservatives; he appeared to have abandoned them.[33]

Swanson had misled many of the men who in 1883 had patched the party together. A tone of servile attentiveness emerges from his early letters addressed to them. His concurrent public announcements of sustaining the political status quo gave way to anti-Cleveland statements, radical monetary proposals, and patronage appointments to socially unacceptable persons. Revamped election procedures and new political techniques also eroded the older elite's influence. Swanson's style now was as objectionable as his substance. He refused the role of subdued statesman, humbly accepting their advice. As he increased his popularity among the less prestigious economic and social classes, the conservative-minded fell away from this mischief-making congressman. Sound-money journals gave voice to a gnawing class hysteria. The *Richmond Times* blared that, should Democrats nominate a free-silver presidential candidate, "the Democratic ticket will be considered to be that of the communists, the anarchists and the repudiators of debt." Urban-rural divisions also presented themselves. Political opportunists, whether Cleveland Democrats, such as Green, or ambitious younger politicians, such as Montague, circled Swanson's political redoubts, ready to challenge him. He moved to place gnarled, county associates in influential party positions. The public strife and private quarrels over silver bubbled from sources as varied and tangled as the tributaries of the Dan River.[34]

Personalities and propaganda from beyond the Fifth District stirred further the free-silver cauldron. Former Nebraska congressman William Jennings Bryan spoke at the University of Virginia, praised Jefferson, and believed he would now stand with the people against plutocratic wealth. Senator Daniel's throbbing oratory echoed as he moderately led in August 1895 a noisy silver conference in Washington. Some politicians in Virginia adopted silver for camouflage purposes. Others were silent, like Martin, whose course the Cleveland *Richmond State* identified: "Statesmanship becomes reduced to shifty politics, expediency takes the place of courage and cunning has exaltation over frankness." Swanson grasped free silver at least in part from political necessity. He later likened his espousal to "placing his head upon the block." His emphathetic attachment, however, to agrarians and mechanics reinforced his decision.[35]

Creditor spokesmen and Cleveland delegates had denied Democratic inflationists control of the state party in 1892. Four years later they surrendered it at the state Democratic convention in Staunton. Cleveland's political demise, an embarrassing 1895 Democratic legislative campaign, open threats and evidence of party desertion, the Supreme Court ruling unconstitutional a federal income tax, and caustic attacks by a rural free-silver press contributed to their fall. Three Virginia congressmen led the surge. Abandoning Cleveland, Jones rallied the Northern Neck for silver, and, in Lynchburg, Otey organized city and county conventions to elect free-silver delegates. Most militant and outspoken, Swanson directly assaulted in December 1895 Republicans, who "turned a deaf ear to everybody except the greedy and avaricious bond holders." Three months later, he implied that Democrats and Populists should meld to aid "the producing masses to meet their obligations." Creditors should not question how debts were paid, "in silver, gold or greenbacks," but, instead, if they could be paid at all.[36]

The Staunton Democratic convention of June 1896 received an assortment of interpretations. A generally acceptable estimate described it as a disposal of

Cleveland's laissez-faire policies, a move toward greater governmental intervention, and a reply to the Populists. Yet another judged it as a confusion of overlapping interest groups, torn between eastern corporations and southern and western agrarians. Politically, it may have enhanced Senator Martin's move to dominate the party or it may have simply been a harmless diversion to please radicals but leave moderates in control. It could be observed as a removal of doctrinaire, inflexible party leaders in favor of more opportunistic and flexible professionals. It could also be assessed as a distraction that prevented substantial reforms. Another appriased it as the conclusion of agrarian reform in the state. Finally, it might be labeled a seedbed upon which future reforms would sprout.[37]

Above all, the convention drew together endemic parochial interests, organized arbitrarily into congressional districts, that voiced a persistent localism. Indistinctly comprehending the means needed, they were intent upon gaining their various goals. For many delegates representing thirteen hundred precincts over the state, free silver was venerated for more than monetary considerations. Themes of sectionalism and oratory from the growing cult of the Lost Cause filtered through the debate. Armed with free silver, determined this time to conquer, some Virginians would charge the North's golden Cemetery Ridge. Others imagined silver a weapon of class vengeance against wealthy elites. Business leaders divided. Mercantile interests discerned advantages. Corporate railroad managers feared nationalization lurked behind silver curtains. Local entrepreneurs initiating investments in private telephone companies held similar qualms. Literate Virginians who wrote letters, made speeches, and published newspapers only occasionally reflected the diversity of economic, class, religious, and cultural tides flowing through the Democratic party in 1896.[38]

The vote over a unit rule polarized silver and anti-silver delegations. Should it be adopted as a governing requirement for the Virginia Democrats sent to the Chicago national convention, the delegation's vote would be cast by the majority. Local free-silver groups had sponsored its approval and Swanson left no doubts about his endorsement. "Bedecked with badges," he met with each arriving delegation and, apparently, as the *Richmond Times* noted, pleased them with his "silvery speech and . . . satisfactory sophistry." At a preconvention silver caucus, he called for the unit rule and would have no "stopping at any halfway measures or of having halfway delegates" sent to Chicago. Having accepted Cleveland's appointment as United States counselor general to Cuba, Lee did not attend the convention. Joseph Bryan was ill. As a result, the sound-money forces lacked both a symbol and the political savvy to rally. Danville delegate Massie scotched a move to elect delegates to Chicago before the convention approved the platform. Senator Martin broke his silence, accepted free silver, and denounced Cleveland as a "party wrecker." Delegates refused the gold standard 1,276 votes to 371 and approved silver by a similar margin.[39]

Daniel exercised his temperate influence upon the unit rule controversy. He and the executive committee forged a compromise that, while not approved by the gold delegates, passed two to one. When selecting delegates, the editor of the *Norfolk Landmark,* John H. Glennan, announced he would vote against free silver at Chicago should he be elected a delegate, the convention tumbled into

an uproar. Swanson stepped forward and reminded Glennan that he yet remained
to be elected and that the convention should refuse that election to assure silver
delegates at Chicago. Presenting an alternative, absent in earlier drafts by
Daniel, Swanson resolved that Virginia's delegation be instructed "to cast the
entire vote of the state . . . as a majority" of the delegation determined. Nearly
twelve hundred votes supported him to pass the unit rule and he held the
convention in his hand. He had kept his promises and went to Chicago as an at-
large delegate with Daniel, Jones, and Judge Henry S.E. Morison of Scott
County.[40]

During the spring and summer of 1896, Virginia Democrats purged
"goldbugs." The state executive committee no longer contained Cleveland
loyalists and sound-money defenders Joseph Bryan and Harry Tucker. Silver
paladins Jones, Rufus A. Ayers, and Swanson dominated. Its chairman and
Baptist businessman Ellyson kept his position by recanting previous Cleveland
loyalties and speaking for the party's platform, thereby covering his sound-
money attitudes. Governor O'Ferrall was cut adrift from party circles. In district
conventions, incumbent Democratic congressmen fell to silver challengers:
Tucker to Flood, Tazewell Ellett to John Lamb, Smith Turner to James Hay,
Elisha Meredith to John Rixey, and D. Gardiner Tyler to William Young. Only
Swanson, Otey, and Jones escaped the slaughter. Former chairman Gordon, after
the silver Chicago convention, left the party to follow Republican presidential
nominee William McKinley. Other sound-money Democrats bolted to a third
party, the National Democrats, but in truth worked for McKinley. Veteran
Washington Journalist E.G. Dunnell of the *New York Times* wrote that "without
such assistance the Virginia Republicans could have made but little impression."[41]

At Chicago, as a member of the Credentials Committee, Swanson helped
assure seating of silver delegates. He had agreed publicly in May to the necessity
of "having a western man" as the presidential nominee. On the first presidential
ballot, Virginia voted for Senator Joseph S.G. Blackburn of Kentucky, followed
by three roll-call votes favoring Richard Bland of Missouri. As early as the
second ballot, six Virginians moved to Bryan of Nebraska, but the unit rule that
Swanson continued to defend prevented their votes from being recorded. Swanson now openly worked for Bryan's nomination, and, on the fifth and nominating ballot, the Southside delegates carried the majority for him. Swanson also
favored the reform platform that stimulated such misgivings in Glass that he
voted against it. "Brimful of enthusiasm, . . . under the witching spell of
Bryan's oratory," Swanson praised the platform for drawing a line between
"plutocracy and democracy." Three planks he held most vital in attracting voters
were reform of the financial system achieved partially by remonetizing silver,
reestablishment of the income tax to force vested wealth to "pay its just share,"
and negation of the "mugwump idea" of civil service. The latter laws created "a
professional class of office holders . . . out of place in a republican form of
government." Back in the Fifth District, condemning Cleveland's policies, he
secured his third congressional nomination. Swanson gained as well an endorsement from the Pittsylvania County Populists and their twelve hundred votes
owing to his "stand on silver."[42]

The Republicans challenged Swanson with former Fifth District congressman and Martinsville banker John R. Brown. As in 1892, Swanson published a campaign newspaper and appealed directly to farmers, merchants, blacks, and whites. Law partner of Populist Gravely, N.H. Hairston confided that in the Martinsville district "nearly all the Populists . . . voted and worked for Bryan . . . and Swanson." Populist congressional candidate Hale withdrew in Swanson's favor. Individual blacks crossed from the party of Lincoln to the party of Bryan. Despite a strong Republican reputation, "Uncle Tom" Stone declared he would "vote for the silvermen." Other black Republicans threatened William Allen "that any colored man . . . going to vote for Swanson . . . ought to be taken and lynched." Employer Lemon Luck informed black Thomas Hodnett, "You are fixing to put yourself in slavery again" by voting for Swanson. Ben Arrington laughed that he voted for Swanson, although he "swore he voted for Brown and got Brown's money." National Republican boss Mark Hanna sent an estimated $160,000 into Virginia, intensifying party conflict. In Chatham, John A. Tredway and veteran county treasurer John Richard Whitehead joined the gold National Democrats. Chairman of the Pittsylvania County electoral board and brother of Swanson's private secretary, Walter Coles, Jr., could not determine voter party affiliations easily. The parties had been "so mixed up since the last spring elections [1895]."[43]

Traveling upon horseback to keep "appointments night and day . . . to speak," Swanson visited familiar political enclaves and admonished his supporters to action. Twenty-four-year-old W.M. Enright, chief mail clerk in Danville, pedalled by bicycle under John Swanson's orders to arouse the third ward. A Swanson federal revenue appointee in Lynchburg encouraged his brother, R.H. Herndon, to campaign in Danville for Swanson. While many white and black citizens disliked admitting their illiteracy, the Parker law, replacing the Walton Act, opened up voting choices because it did not permit "old party workers to handle the darkies as freely." Veteran Republican C.T. Barksdale complained of $1,200 to $1,500 being spent by the "so-called national Democrats" in Pittsylvania County. He confessed that many otherwise unreapproachable men performed "tricks" that he considered "extremely dishonest." A tobacco hand later swore that Swanson offered him twenty-five dollars to form "a club of boys to vote" for him. He also said Swanson told "the judge of elections to mark out Brown" on the day of election. Swanson did organize clubs in every precinct critical to his election to provide a speaker every Saturday evening. A reordering of political allegiances occurred among some voters; the machinery of politics pushed the remainder into one camp or another. As crude and sharp as rusting barbed wire snagged on oak posts throughout rural Virginia, the 1896 election established a new political order in the state.[44]

Newspapers reflected the upheaval. Editors of the *Danville Register* bolted the Democrats. Ellyson's *Richmond Dispatch* smothered its gold editorials and struggled to remain loyal after Bryan's nomination. Young John Garland Pollard transformed the *Richmond State* into a silver organ only to sell it to Joseph Bryan who would silence it and acquire the *State's* Associated Press wire service. His paper, the *Times*, censured silver, and Martin and preferred black rule to "dishonesty and fraudulent tricks." These developments left a residue of suspicion that the victors of the 1890s elections had won by fraud rather than by shrewd political representation of popular opinion.[45]

Defeated by defecting gold Democrats, millions of dollars from eastern corporate interests, and Mark Hanna's organized machinations, Bryan and his 1896 national campaign had aided Swanson. Escaping some of the anti-Cleveland emotions in the Fifth District, Swanson gave the campaign a partisan Democratic aura. Winning a bobbin's width victory of 551 majority of the 28,151 ballots counted, he depended upon precincts in Danville, Franklin and Pittsylvania counties. Notably he gained 1,400 more votes in his home county than in 1894. Restructuring from ruined remains of earlier organizations, Swanson's associates retained control of the district Democratic party.[46]

Following general Republican strategy, Brown contested Swanson's reelection. The Republican House majority accepted Republican challengers Richard A. Wise of Williamsburg and Robert T. Thorp of Boydton, but not Brown. After parliamentary maneuvers, four members of the nine-person review committee signed a minority report favoring him. A majority report was never forthcoming. Committee member Edgar D. Crumpacker of Indiana in April 1898 called for House consideration of the minority report. Among others, Hay of Virginia and Indiana Republican Robert W. Miers placed roadblocks in his way. Crumpacker moved for consideration three times in nine months. The House refused by comfortable margins. In March 1899, Crumpacker withdrew from further effort. A year later, Swanson resurrected the affair by seeking restitution for expenses beyond the allowable $2,000 for contested election cases. On his feet, Crumpacker complained that Swanson and his friends "succeeded in every instance in denying" Brown a right to be heard. Claiming his integrity had been questioned, Swanson retracted his request. The justness of his case and his popularity may have played a role in this denouement. His influence with the House derived also from his membership on Post Office and Post Roads and Ways and Means committees, both of which dealt with revenue bills and patronage plums.[47]

Swanson increased his role in Virginia's political evolution. He continued to endorse the legislature's call for a constitutional referendum in May 1897. A gubernatorial candidate and free-silver advocate, former lieutenant governor Tyler of Pulaski County sought his endorsement through intermediaries. While "favorably disposed toward Tyler," he excused himself by offering "that the people should be permitted to have their choice in the matter without interference." Danville state senator Rorer James admitted to Tyler: "Swanson is for Swanson." The congressman had also learned from his earlier support of now discredited O'Ferrall that harm could ensue from openly playing favorites. Further, Senator Daniel, with his reelection approaching, intended "to have nothing to do with the fight." Martin would do nothing "to antagonize" Ellyson's candidacy.[48]

Swanson joined Montague's pursuit of the attorney general's office without hesitation. He had accommodated the Middlesex native since 1893, first in securing the district attorney's position, then in upgrading his salary. He had also done much the same for Lassiter, who also sought the attorney generalship. By speaking in the last month of the Bryan campaign, Montague assuaged doubts about his fidelity to the 1896 Democratic platform. Besides a spry, political opportunism, Montague responded to the present through a dour nostalgia for a past, presumed golden age. Such sentiments were common in contemporary Virginia and nurtured the growth of the Lost Cause myth of the Civil War. One Virginia memoir recalled, "We thought that all the terrible wars had been fought, all the great decisions rendered, and all the heroic deeds done." Swanson steered Montague past the candidacies of incumbent R. Taylor Scott and William Hodges Mann of Nottoway County.[49]

No predominating ring or organization existed in 1897 within the Virginia Democratic party. Regionalism formed a primary force in determining nominees for state office. No person might easily be nominated if a neighbor was an incumbent or a candidate for higher state office. Contemporary issues also had their effect. Despite Martin's attempts to refurbish Ellyson's silver image, free silver advocate Tyler won the gubernatorial nomination. Edward Echols of Staunton became his running mate by defeating former Populist Cocke. Montague had earlier skittishly avoided any alliance with Tyler, but Swanson had taken steps to assure that his brother Henry helped the latter's campaign. Addressing the convention, Swanson "brought down the house" by endorsing the 1896 Chicago platform: "We are missionaries for Bryan and the cause." Both Montague and Lassiter attacked Scott for his hesitancy to be "an original silver man" and his description of the Chicago platform "as an incendiary attack upon our institutions." Swanson had earlier endorsed the national document as a loyalty oath. It had removed the "taint of Clevelandism, [had] divorced itself from Wall Street alliances" and had championed "the rights of the producing masses." Montague promised patronage that probably included school superintendencies and Swanson coached him into the lead at the Democratic convention in Roanoke. Scott's death on its eve aided their cause. Hay shifted the numerous Rockingham delegation toward Montague upon promises of a position in the attorney general's office for a person in the county. Despite Congressman Jones's opposition and Flood's move to Lassiter after Mann faltered, the Danville lawyer won on the third ballot. For a second year Swanson had his way with the Democrats in convention. The party carried the general election in "one of the dullest . . . [campaigns] in Virginia history."[50]

Another event in Roanoke has been labeled "the beginning of the Progressive Movement in Virginia." Jones in late June proposed a primary election or nominating convention to select Democratic senatorial nominees. At the August convention, close upon the heels of a debate with Hay, he pushed the issue upon the floor for consideration. While not directly threatened by the implementation date of the resolution, Daniel crossed Jones. Martin's late conversion to silver, his tariff votes, and Jones's previous political proclivities were discussed. The convention then refused Jones his motion by 850 to 609 votes. Allegations blossomed that Martin had used proxies of departing delegates to defeat it. Yet the junior senator lacked the ability to nominate either his gubernatorial or attorney general preferences, revealing weaknesses that probably encouraged Jones to act. Daniel's influence, while more substantial, could not avoid a convention endorsement of the controversial Chicago platform. More to the point, Jones appeared self-serving. One observer claimed his vehement attack on Martin offended enough delegates' sensibilities to refuse his proposal.[51]

Swanson was accused of "conveniently" leaving the debate and thereby standing with Martin and Daniel in support of the status quo. Since his first term in Congress, however, he voted for direct election of senators by the people and had contributed to purging from party leadership those Virginians who had resisted the agrarian reform movements. He had endorsed the constitutional referendum aimed at general election reform that the voters had refused in May 1897 owing to its anomalous goals. Some saw reform to be a restriction of the franchise, following examples of Mississippi and South Carolina. But others, such as Populist Field, complained that the vice of the system "is not illiterate suffrage. It is corrupt suffrage." Swanson knew that election reform in the hands of some Virginians would produce reactionary results.[52]

Impulses for change had been coursing throughout Virginia localities. Methodist, Baptist, and Presbyterian pulpits and organizations dispensed warnings to repent and to reform. Not only temperance, but education, home missions, social reordering, and extended care to the destitute were moral imperatives placed upon their parishioners. Aroused in part by visiting lecturers, secular elements responded to visions of an effective and free public school system. In 1897 state Democratic platform promised greater governmental concern for handicapped and hearing impaired Virginians and that "every child . . . shall be assured of an opportunity for education." Aroused Populists and Bryan Democrats furnished much of the vital base to initiate these reform appeals. Observing reform budding only in Jones's political tactics at Roanoke in 1897 ignores a garden in full bloom.[53]

Between 1892 and 1898, Swanson emerged from a presumed subservience to the 1880s Democratic elite into a major forceful personality in state politics. Incorporating some black and white Republicans, new voters, and Populists, he maintained his congressional office despite two contested elections. But he did more than survive. A technically proficient politician from the first, he now acknowledged, by popular stands and compassion, democratic elements in the Fifth District. He refashioned its Democratic organization to respond to a class-sensitive electorate. By 1898 he and his friends dominated its election machinery also. As the major Democratic spokesman for free silver, the unit rule, and the Chicago platform, he surpassed occasionally the influence of Daniel and certainly that of Martin. His performance at the 1896 and 1897 state party conventions exhibited his strength among many Virginia localities. Nationally, he publicly displayed his Democratic partisanship and regional perceptions by breaking with Cleveland and arguing for an expanded governmental role in the economy. Behind closed doors of committees, his flexibility, shrewdness, and intelligence led him across party lines to ingratiate himself with influential Republicans. The events of 1898, however, would break the gray, threatening decade and furnish new issues and political requirements for Swanson to meet.

3

Platform Democrat
1893-1903

While he assembled a political organization that won seven consecutive congressional elections, Claude Swanson assumed a larger role in the U.S. House of Representatives. In addition to his monetary proposals, the accumulation of his votes, speeches, and statements provide a picture of a reform-bent, partisan, and effective congressman. Relying less on oratory, he moved from formal speeches on free silver and credit famines to becoming a skilled debater and parliamentary veteran. He perfected the use of charm, knowledge, and persuasion to gain his ends from both Democrats and Republicans. Bonding to the Democratic party, he identified himself as a "platform Democrat." Using patronage and popular themes to maintain his office, to serve his constituency, and to expand his political base in Virginia, he also responded in democratic fashion to most issues. In tending the minutiae of the moment that public life proliferated, he had few opportunities for deep speculation. Yet he acquired an astute sophistication in treating the expanding, diverse federal government. As a result, his importance in Virginia grew; Thomas Staples Martin recruited him to aid his reelection.

From 1893 through 1905, as a member of the Post Office and Post Roads Committee, Swanson served rural and small-town interests. For these localities, little change in mail delivery had occurred since the early Republic. Dispensed from railheads to contracted star-route carriers, mail was deposited at fourth-class offices in villages, county stores, or farm houses where residents would call for it. Journeying to these post offices could consume an entire morning; inclement weather and poor roads increased delays. In addition, star-route contracts were subject to considerable abuse. In October 1890, Congress and Republican Postmaster General John Wanamaker sponsored free mail delivery for small towns and villages. Although some opponents accused the Philadelphia merchant of preparing to enter the mail-order business, rural leaders from the Grange, National Farmers' Congress, and Farmers' Alliance, as well as the rural press, encouraged an urban-rural coalition on the subject. As spokesman, Wanamaker argued that the system "belonged to all people" and "no person should be penalized for living in the country." Forty-eight experimental routes were proposed in the summer—four were in Virginia. By Swanson's arrival in March 1893, Congress had initiated the struggle for rural free-delivery.[1]

Although the previous session's post office appropriation bill included $10,000 for further rural mail delivery experiments, a depression, the postal bureaucracy, and a stubborn Democratic postmaster prevented their realization. Suspecting Republican appointees lingered in the Post Office Department, Swanson urged implementation "to get information . . . to know how to act in the future." Since contract carriers transported mail from railroad stations to small post offices, why not, conjectured Swanson, distribute mail along the thirty-mile routes "to everybody who will put up a box." A new postmaster, William C. Wilson of West Virginia, agreed reluctantly to undertake further tests, if funds were available. New Republican chairman of the House Postal Committee, Eugene Loud of California, opposed further financing, but Populist Senator Marion Butler renewed the project. In October 1896, the frequently delayed "experiment" began.[2]

Appropriations increased to $3.5 million by 1901. A new federal employee category appeared. The rural carriers sold stamps, received money orders, and issued registered mail—services not provided by star-route personnel. The carriers also formed a spreading interest group petitioning for higher salaries. In February 1902, a majority of the House Postal Committee members voted to transfer carriers to the politically influential contract system to remove them from the federal payroll and to protect star-route contractors. Swanson and Indiana Republican George W. Cromer proposed continuation of Post Office control over routes and carriers as an adjunct of the Civil Service Commission. He had earlier berated the commission, but now he would use its protection for rural carriers. Although the Post Office had not usually allowed congressional influence, Swanson had a hand in selecting one-half of the "thirty or forty" carriers that now served the Fifth District. He rated the service as "one of the most important . . . that has ever been started by our government." Land values would be raised, rural life made more attractive, and dangerous "congestion of . . . population in the cities" reduced.[3]

Congressmen from the North and the South debated the Swanson-Cromer minority report for a week and voted to oppose the "radical reversal of policy" favored by Loud. Despite the chairman's dismay and opposition by four Virginia congressmen—James Hay, John Lamb, William A. Jones, and John Rixey— Swanson had challenged House tradition. At least one observer was startled: "A Democrat and a Republican are thus seen jointly acting together to overturn the decision of the Post Office Committee, of which they are members." A sectional alliance had preserved the rural free-delivery system. Conveniently, the Civil Service Review Committee included Swanson's former secretary, Henry C. Coles, as a member. Owing to higher literacy rates among other factors, Republican districts received more carriers in the future. But the policy of the rural service to deliver only to literate households helped spur Virginia demands for improved education.[4]

Favorable results required that Swanson become familiar with departmental regulations and also that he become acquainted personally with postal hierarchs. He was remembered as "simply indefatigable in his efforts to thoroughly equip himself for the practical part" of his congressional duties. Yearly, he grew closer to the postal authorities, and they furnished him ideas, arguments, reports, and general support. This close relationship produced some untoward results in 1903. After a series of Republican postal scandals, Fourth Assistant Postmaster Joseph L. Bristow admitted malfeasance by Republican postal appointees. To dilute the issue, Bristow hinted that 190 congressmen had made "illegal" recommendations for postal salary increments. Alone in the Virginia delegation, Swanson was cited as having requested for eleven postmasters and clerks throughout Virginia salary increases beyond established scales. He had submitted them for his Virginia colleagues' constituents as well as for his own. Insisting that every member of the House "should agree to the fullest investigation," Swanson accused Bristow of attempting to "muddy the waters." Congressman Hay of Virginia initiated a review of Bristow's allegations that revealed their politically motivated qualities.[5]

In his exertions to expand rural mail service, Swanson joined another congressional regional alliance. In February 1892, a year before Swanson's arrival in the House, the Richmond Terminal System obtained from Congress a subsidy to underwrite a fast mail train from New York through Washington, Lynchburg, Danville, and Atlanta to New Orleans. The Atlantic Coast Line in Virginia had previously abandoned the unprofitable contract, and a spokesman alleged that considerable political pressure had awarded it to the Richmond Terminal System and moved the terminus from Florida to the Mississippi port. From 1893 through 1903, only one other route received extra sums from postal authorities. Swanson defended the arrangement. The "Richmond and Danville road, or the Southern System, agreed to do this service only when it became evident that withdrawal of the service would operate as a complete derangement of mail matters in the South." The Post Office supported a service schedule that permitted "a newspaper the day it was published" in New York "to be distributed through the system." The federal subsidy compensated the road for loss of passenger traffic that occurred owing to an early departure time. In 1897, pleading for other sections' support, he insisted that it meant "a great deal to us in getting our letters and conducting our business." He observed in 1899 in a losing cause that "every little road that goes to the country and the different cities in the South get their mail on this mainline." In addition to satisfying publishers and businessmen, the southeastern partnership had pleased thousands of constituents.[6]

Other Virginia congressmen agreed. Initially, Jones, Lamb (representing Richmond), and northern Virginian Rixey contacted the superintendent of railroad mail service to continue the arrangement. To discredit Swanson in Virginia and play upon the state's regional divisions, in 1901 Jones accused Danville of being placed before Richmond. Unlike western agrarians, Swanson did not consider local railroads to be antagonistic to the general interest of the electorate. The reorganized Southern Railway, successor to the Richmond Terminal System, was a corporate descendant of the old Richmond and Danville Railroad. Urging federal funds to support such a service, Swanson offered an alternative to the economic shocks produced by the unrestrained capitalism of the era. If the Virginia legislature could partially finance the railroad before the Civil War, the federal legislature could sustain and then expand its services. He continued to seek restoration of the subsidy. Postal chairman Loud complained

fretfully about this "plunder" claimed by "oppressed" southerners who deduced: "Well, this is our country; we don't get our share; let us stand together."[7]

Despite his position as ranking Democrat, Swanson lost his assignment on
the Postal Committee in November 1903. An increase in Democrats, a shift in
congressional leadership, and perhaps his role in the Swanson-Cromer minority
report accounted for his removal. As early as the previous September, party
leaders had been collecting votes for the speakership should Democrats regain
the House majority. Despite Hay's availability, Swanson committed to Democratic minority leader James P. Richardson of Tennessee. In return, Richardson
promised Swanson chairmanship of the Ways and Means Committee. Neither
Hay, Richardson, nor the Democrats won. The new Republican majority leader,
Indiana Congressman and North Carolina-born Joseph Cannon, had earlier
expressed distrust of the Postal Committee, saying some members would "have
to go." Cannon's close friend John Sharp Williams, a ten-year veteran from
Mississippi, became minority leader. Earlier he had tangled with Swanson over
the southern mail subsidy and, although originally voting for rural free delivery,
he opposed Swanson's 1902 defense of the system. Smarting from Swanson's
campaign for Richardson, Williams removed him from the patronage-rich
committee. Cromer also was reassigned.[8]

Razor-tongued, humorous, and sarcastic, Williams represented the first
wave of southern House leadership sent by an electorate reduced by a disfranchising state constitution. Swanson did not fare as well under Williams as
under other Democratic leaders. Williams's successor, Champ Clark, attributed
the eventual revolt against Cannon's arbitrary rule as the result partially of the
"personal animosity" Williams engendered among House Democrats. Cannon
gave Williams "the power of making up the minorities on committees, reserving
to himself [Williams] a sort of superiority in that regard." Swanson's partisan
role in 1908 before the national Democratic platform committee in denouncing
the authoritarian House leadership included Williams in the minds of knowledgeable listeners: "No one can accomplish anything without the consent of the
Speaker," Swanson claimed. Swanson took credit for the eventual plank decrying the Speaker's "arbitrary power" and demanding the House majority "direct
all deliberations and control legislation." Eventually in 1910 in a bipartisan
move, the House sheared the power of Cannon and the minority leader. Reform
legislation passed more easily through the House as a result.[9]

Swanson's presence on the Postal Committee expanded his political prestige in Virginia and assisted his rise within the House. His appointment in
March 1897 by Republican Speaker Thomas B. Reed to the Ways and Means
Committee revealed just how advanced was that standing. The committee
drafted revenue legislation and along with Appropriations was "clothed with
extraordinary privilege" in parliamentary debate. Majority party agreement
usually determined the nature of revenue bills before formal introduction for
committee discussion. Few, if any, effective compromises could be obtained by
minority members, and the committee was one of the most partisan in the
House. Yet, assignment to the seventeen-person committee carried great weight
within the complex power patterns of the House in the late 1890s; Swanson's
membership marked him as one of a handful of representatives composing the

primary House leadership. Not only did these men shape national economic policy through tariff schedules and other revenue bills, they also assumed important roles in molding party programs. As the House was less influenced by the executive than later, they could raise partisan issues that were reflected in national campaigns. The character traits that led Swanson to the center of Virginia politics carried him into the matrix of House leadership as well.[10]

Swanson's internal role among House Democrats grew accordingly. From time to time, he obtained special assignments to rouse to the floor Democratic House members for important votes. He attuned himself to Democratic attitudes and communicated to leaders how legislation and other critical issues might fare. He also used his considerable persuasive talent to forward legislation favored by party leadership. In later Congresses, this duty became an assignment of the party Whip, but in the 1890s this office did not exist; the party battles of the period produced a need for such. Swanson's role with others helped initiate its original definition and functions. An early Republican Whip, James Watson, recalled Swanson during these years as the "Democratic Whip." He formed a friendship with the Virginian, "one of the finest and kindliest men" he had ever known.[11]

On Ways and Means, Swanson defended Fifth District economic interests. The Republican majority continually viewed tobacco and distilled spirits as revenue sources. Previously, the committee had been warned of health dangers in nicotine by Chief of the Bureau of Chemistry in the Department of Agriculture, Harvey M. Wiley. He sought to ban in cigarette packages cards and pictures designed to entice children to purchase tobacco products. One revenue proposal considered by the committee included a prohibition of coupons in merchandising cigarettes. Ironically, small manufacturers favored the reform to protect them from larger, more well-financed corporate competition. The committee considered allowing tobacco growers to sell directly to manufacturers without a licenses. In response to pressure from Virginia, Kentucky, and Tennessee, the membership reviewed possible tariff discrimination against American tobacco by foreign countries. The industry's needs for cheaper Cuban tobacco for wrappers and inexpensive foreign sugar for tobacco processing reinforced Swanson's low tariff principles. During his nine years as a member, he sharpened his understanding of the American economic scene from the complex matters before the committee.[12]

The tariff served as a major political issue of the era. Swanson's election to Ways and Means was seen as a "well deserved recognition of one of Virginia's brightest and ablest young men" and as the result of his reputation as "one of the tariff experts on the Democratic side." He was expected to be a Democratic foeman of the new tariff schedules suggested by President William McKinley and demanded by Speaker Reed. Swanson and his Democratic committee colleagues also interpreted the tariff proposals to party members throughout the House. Depressed world trade and lower tariff collections from the 1894 Wilson tariff led Republicans to endorse a high tariff. In the spring of 1897, Swanson set to work, confessing that he was "busy night and day . . . on the tariff." Local politicians complained that he partially neglected them as his national priorities took his attention.[13]

In drafting the 1897 Dingley tariff, the Republican majority on Ways and Means turned to the 1890 McKinley tariff for inspiration. Speaker Reed allowed only two weeks' debate on the committee's proposals. Despite opposition from American soap manufacturers, Swanson successfully prevented a rise in rates on glycerin, an elemental finishing component for tobacco. Furnishing figures to indicate American steel corporations enjoyed an almost absolute barrier against foreign competition, he moved to reduce the proposed tariff on steel. The lower Wilson tariff had produced only $745 in tariff revenues from foreign steel. Post road expansion would be stimulated if foreign steel could force domestic manufacturers to withdraw from pricing pools. He and his fellow Democrats failed on this and other occasions. Maintaining strict party lines, Republicans pushed for more protectionism. Upon receiving the House bill, the Senate leisurely debated the legislation, amended 872 articles to the bill, and returned to a conference committee to resolve House and Senate difficulties. By mid-July, the House once more had an opportunity to compose the list of government protection for a mosaic of American economic interests.[14]

The House Democratic leaders viewed the conference report as an opportunity for lowing manufacturing interests to grow fat behind protectionist fences. A notable increase removed raw wool from the free list to mollify western agrarian silverites. Swanson delivered two major thrusts at the emerging high-tariff majority. First, he defended tobacco growers and exporters who, under a low tariff "could get better [tobacco] prices in an open market and then purchase cheaper European" consumer goods. Export of 9 percent of the corn crop and 27 percent of the wheat crop did not compare with over 60 percent of the annual tobacco production sent overseas. Dependent upon foreign trade, tobacco might be the target of foreign retaliation if the tariff legislation passed. Concerned also over existing foreign duties, he and other tobacco congressmen passed a resolution encouraging McKinley to pursue reciprocal trade agreements. Swanson also derided a refusal to place sugar on the free list as class legislation. The "object of this bill is to make the rich richer and to trust that they will permit a little increased wealth to leak through on those beneath." Opposing such trickle-down economics, Swanson knew that 1.8 million pounds of sugar were used annually in Virginia's tobacco processing factories. The Dingley tariff passed, but his partisan performance typified exchanges between Democrats and Republicans in the McKinley Congresses. Democrats intended now to use the tariff issue in the 1900 presidential campaign, but, unexpectedly, war intervened.[15]

During the decade, Spain's colony Cuba had become a quagmire that entrapped both the United States and Spain. After the explosion of the USS *Maine* in Havana harbor in February 1898, humanitarian concern for Cubans gave way to threats of war against Spain. Upon its approach, Ways and Means could expect to accumulate greater legislative authority. As a contemporary analyst discerned, in wartime the committees on War, the Navy, and Ways and Means were "a ruling triumvirate." Rumors and then journalistic accusations featured McKinley's plan to purchase the island. He would soon approach Ways and Means for necessary funds. Swanson questioned if McKinley's concerns were "simply furnishing food to the starving people of Cuba." The president should be permitted to relieve the causes of famine, but his true intentions should also be unveiled. Swanson opposed Cuban "autonomy of any kind which will not be acceptable to the Cubans." Before appropriating a "single penny," Congress "ought to know the plans of the Executive." Swanson and other House Democrats responded to McKinley's long-gestated war message by attempting to force "recognition of the Republic of Cuba." They favored his use of American land and naval forces to achieve independence and extending "immediate relief to the starving people of Cuba." Following a strict party vote, the resolution failed but became a basis for the Teller Amendment that eventually provided for Cuban independence.[16]

Virginia appeared thrilled by war preparations in the spring of 1898. From the small towns, citizens crowded excursion trains to Norfolk to view the assembling white vessels of the fleet. Owing to his incendiary statements, Consular General Fitzhugh Lee returned to the United States at the request of Spanish authorities. Virginians grew so enthralled with the ex-Confederate that Swanson, attuned to the moment, excused him as having been "discreet, judicious and resourceful." Identified with the growing Lost Cause cult of the Civil War, Lee appeared before an investigating congressional committee and spurred visions of armed men seated upon galloping, heavy-breathing war horses. With war, Virginia received a quota of 3,000 volunteers, but over 15,000 white and black Virginians answered the bugles within two days. The Fifth District also carried a large share of the war burden. Placing much of the expense of war upon the small consumer, Ways and Means doubled excise taxes on tobacco and distilled spirits. Swanson fought fiercely the tobacco taxes, seeking a vote by item in the House. Owing to parliamentary barriers, he lost and during the debate old sectional animosities flared. Swanson and Ohio Republican Charles H. Grosvenor exchanged remarks so intense that they were removed from the *Congressional Record*. Agrarians, however, were startled, then pleased, as the war-time treasury inflated the currency by placing $100 million of certificates of indebtedness into the money markets while minting a half-million silver dollars a month.[17]

After the war, the new American empire created controversy, and Democrats in partisan forays censured Republicans who struggled to develop a coherent colonial policy. At the onset of peace, in allowing annexed Puerto Rico "free access" to American markets, McKinley aroused interest groups. They pushed Ways and Means chairman Sereno Payne in February 1900 to propose a revenue act that would impose tariffs at a rate of 25 percent of the Dingley schedules. Swanson accused the Republicans of surrendering to sugar and tobacco corporations who feared that free trade with Puerto Rico would produce the same for the Philippines. Expressing a desire to leave the latter "as quickly as we can with honor and safety," he cited constitutional and historical arguments against the proposed revenue bill. Swanson mocked that King George III of England would have approved it. Should it pass, denying Puerto Rico equitable admission to American trade, it would mark the "end of the history of the Republic, . . . open the history of the Empire", and be a forerunner "of countless other bills to follow . . . to inaugurate the new imperialistic regime."[18]

The Payne proposals formed, in Swanson's mind, a "practical concrete illustration of what imperialism means." By destroying Puerto Rican cigar manufacturers under the proposed tax, the only alternative left islanders would be to export tobacco to the United States to benefit American cigar manufacturers and to harm, among others, Virginia farmers. McKinley directed Puerto Rico as if it were a corporation, using an appointed board of directors, "having no connection with the interests of Puerto Rico." Not only were special corporate interests protected at home but overseas as well. Forcing a "vicious system of colonial government" upon the Filipinos was typical of an administration that permitted growth and domination of trusts within the United States. The flag, Swanson observed, does not follow the Constitution, but follows the contributors to the Republican party. McKinley compromised and obtained a revenue collection rate at 15 percent of the Dingley levels. By the summer of 1900, Swanson was regarded as "one of the foremost opponents of imperialism."[19]

The approaching presidential campaign gave impetus to Swanson's role. As a "platform Democrat," he favored the 1900 document that pledged unending struggle against "private monopoly" in all its forms. Proposing monetary and political reform while endorsing the 1896 Chicago platform and direct election of senators, the Democrats objected to McKinley's foreign policy. An anti-imperialist plank held that the Constitution follows the flag. Despite its being an "able and progressive" set of national priorities, neither the platform nor William Jennings Bryan could defeat McKinley.[20]

After McKinley's assassination in September 1901, Theodore Roosevelt's administration proposed a "temporary" revenue act for the Philippines. Government and business interests in December 1901 decided to continue the colonial tariffs by maintaining the high Dingley tariff upon Filipino products entering the United States while charging very small entry fees for American exports to the islands. Swanson labeled it a program determined "to enter into a system of colonial conquest and government" resembling the action of the British Parliament in the 1760s. An "irreconcilable, dual position of subject and stranger" was in the offing. He urged that the Philippines be given independence. If the annual $100 million spent to control restless Filipinos was used instead "in building and maintaining a navy," the nation could launch one "superior to any." The legislation passed, nonetheless.[21]

Economic conditions in the Philippines deteriorated. To provide revenue to operate the government and to stimulate trade, the Roosevelt Administration requested a 75 percent reduction of tariff charges upon Filipino exports to the United States while maintaining the earlier schedule on American imports. Swanson complained that the Philippine reduction bill had been "railroaded through [Ways and Means] without any certain information being possessed by a single member . . . and no study of the previous two years experience." In December 1902, he submitted an amendment that there must be "free trade between this country and their so-called colonies." The House refused his and Democratic colleagues' similar objections. Cuban tariff reciprocity had created even greater furor over imperialism.[22]

Owing to General Leonard Wood and the War Department, the Roosevelt Administration proposed in January 1902 tariff reciprocity with Cuba to strengthen its wobbly economy. Convening two weeks of hearings, the Ways and Means Committee heard a variety of interests from Puerto Ricans who sold their tobacco to Cuba to gain the advantageous label of "Cuban Tobacco" to Pittsylvania County farmers, enjoying a banner tobacco year. American cigar manufacturers complained, but Swanson apparently observed no threat to Fifth District interests. The reputation and quality of Cuban tobacco and cigars would not be altered by tariff increases. His central emphasis and that of other Democrats focused upon the "sugar trust" and its monopolistic control of refined sugar. The House passed the reciprocity bill only after "a coalition of beet sugar congressmen and Anit-Trust Democrats" forced in April 1902 acceptance of Cuban refined-sugar rates at raw-sugar rates. After considerable haggling, intervention by Roosevelt, fear of foreign trade advantages through Cuba, and sugar trust incursion into the sugar beet industry, the House considered the bill as a conference report in November 1903. While Swanson accused the whole tariff system of encouraging retaliatory measures by European nations against American farm products, he, Williams, Clark, and George B. McClellan offered a minority report still insisting that no increase in refined sugar schedules be permitted. Eventually, they accepted an amended reciprocity act in late 1903 that increased tariff charges on the Cuban export.[23]

Swanson turned to his benefit these and other controversies during his attendance in the House. The growing rural mail system cast thousands of his tariff and anti-trust speeches throughout the state. Swanson considered them a "service to the party" and to him. He maintained successfully a woman as postmaster in Chatham after "the President [McKinley] and Post Master General acted very nicely about it." Having promised her advocates that "I generally land on top in my fights . . . ," he cautioned after victory not to "brag around about it." The postmaster and her supporters forwarded campaign donations, and he thanked them for their "kindness and liberality in the matter." He also directed his postal friends to dole out the bounty of the Department of Agriculture. To a postal employee he instructed 200 packages of vegetable seed be given to Chatham "negroes wherever you think they will do good" and "to white people whom I have failed to send to."[24]

Returning farm propserity (caused in part by wartime inflation), increased gold supplies, small Eurpoean harvests, and abundant credit sources directly affected Swanson's political course. Class bitterness subsided, and, in 1898, he ran again for Congress against Republican state senator Edmund Parr of Patrick County. Parr held several lucrative star-route contracts throughout the nation, and Swanson's free delivery proposals threatened to overturn his livelihood. The congressman called upon Attorney General Montague, who responded with alacrity, and benefited from South Carolina Senator Benjamin Tillman's visit to the district. But in the end he took up this "most desperate fight . . . with practically no one but himself to do the fighting." Of 23,000 votes cast, he won by a 3,600 margin over a disorganized Republican party.[25]

The dimensions of his victory complemented Swanson's continued rise in the House of Representatives as well as in Virginia. The 1880s Barbour Democratic party system of precinct captains, lists of voters, and centralized party organization had collapsed. Many Populists had become Democrats, but their allegiances were more issue and class-oriented than focused toward the party. One Southside Democratic leader complained in 1898: "We are in worse shape than we ever have been." Surveying growing party disjunction, J. Taylor Ellyson as party chairman labored to obtain funds, speakers, and local workers. Virginia's nine Democratic congressmen endured generally with the most efficient state political organizations. U.S. Senators Martin and, to a lesser extent, John W. Daniel intruded in local politics to guarantee legislative support for their reelection. They encountered there congressmen and other influential regional politicians and, when possible, favored alliances.[26]

A growing list of conflicting reform proposals required responses from these incumbents, as revealed by Swanson's actions at the federal level. One reform, direct election of senators, transgressed economic and social lines and offered an opportunity for political exploitation. Since his first days in Congress, Swanson had voted for resolutions favoring direct election, and he used this record to defend himself in Virginia. In 1897, Congressman Jones from Warsaw discovered the issue in his attempt to implement a binding senatorial primary election or state nominating convention. It appealed to idealists, disgruntled reactionaries, Populists, and gold Democrats, as well as to those who matched his disdain for Martin. After Daniel's reelection, Jones approached newly installed Governor Tyler and Attorney General Montague as well as Congressman Lamb of Hanover County to discuss the legislature's refusal to create a senatorial primary. In early 1899, the year of Martin's reelection campaign, Jones initiated a series of meetings; other politicians also gathered. One meeting held in Washington included Eppa Hunton, Jr., son of Martin's predecessor and a Warrenton resident; John C. Parker, a state legislator from Southhampton; N. H. Massie; and Montague from Danville. Congressmen Lamb and Rixey of Culpeper also attended. Hearing of these events, Martin linked those in attendance with Lee and R. Walton Moore of Fairfax who would "unite to strike" at him. Over fifty persons signed an invitation to Virginia Democrats to assemble in May 1899 to endorse popular election of United States senators. The so-called May Movement had been launched.[27]

What other impulses there may have been, the primary motivation of the founders was to remove Martin. Jones had earlier admitted that he would "ruin the power of the [Martin] machine" by an "organized and effective movement set on foot to secure the defeat of Mr. Martin." Moore agreed: "I am one of these who are interested in the principle not only in an abstract way, but in its application to Mr. Martin." Co-author of the 1884 Anderson-McCormick law, William H. Anderson joined because of resentment over Martin's election at Lee's expense. Clevelend supporters and former congressmen John Goode, Jr., of Bedford and James W. Marshall of New Castle represented the older order of Democrats as well. Regionally oriented, J. Hoge Tyler's Southwest, Lamb's Richmond area, and Northern Virginia furnished much of the movement's leadership. The *Roanoke Times* considered it "too grand and noble" to be used as a mere device to oust Martin. Carter Glass identified it as devious and factional, "a humbug." The claims against Martin repeated anew accusations made by Joseph Bryan in the *Richmond Times* during the earlier free-silver furor.[28]

Preferring to keep his position in Cuba, Lee withdrew from consideration as a Martin opponent. By April 1899, Tyler, Montague, and Jones remained as the most likely to oppose the senator. Effective in his clerklike way in organizing a campaign, Martin now needed to depend upon local and regional politicians to persuade legislative candidates and members of the Democratic state central committee to oppose the movement and thereby favor his reelection. Owing to the 140 legislators that would reelect him, he was by necessity driven to involve himself in legislative elections. Many politicians he sought had risen to prominence within the decade and were either from the Bryan wing of the party or had abandoned Cleveland as a party wrecker. Swanson became essential to Martin's reelection. By 1899, the thirty-six-year-old Swanson had established a political organization in the Fifth District, fronted by espousal of popular issues, reforms, and personal attractiveness and based upon political savvy. Swanson could deliver the votes and acquire necessary campaign funds. Knowledgeable of the district's political enclaves, Swanson leaders fetched voters to the polls. Wealthy tobacconists, the state party, local and state candidates, and federal patronage accounted for much of his funding resources. Apportionment gave the district one-tenth of the legislature's voting strength; Pittsylvania County and adjoining Henry and Franklin counties housed large numbers of Virginia Democratic votes. Swanson had attracted also many Populists and Republicans by 1899. To gain Swanson's commitment, sometime between January and April 1899, the senator agreed to help Swanson should he "decide to be a candidate for Governor."[29]

Such arrangements were common in Virginia politics. The May Movement organizers had not consulted Swanson despite his having "voted each time in Congress for the election of senators by direct vote of the people." He admitted his friendship with Martin in the past and that probably explained why he had not been invited. One Botetourt Democrat warned Anderson that his county had tried Democratic primaries, and Republicans had voted in them. He opposed its reintroduction and the May Movement, as did "the body of true democratic voters in [his] county". Given its shaky organization and condition, the Democratic party would be further weakened, observed Francis R. Lassiter, by Jones's factional movement. One politician identified a source of its origins when he studied its regional characteristics. He would watch with "utmost interest this fight between our leaders of the Southside Democracy and the 8th district [Northern Virginia] people and their allies." To Swanson, direct elections were acceptable; when applied to Martin for factional reasons, dubious. After all, the Democratic 1897 convention and then the legislature had rejected Jones's earlier, similar appeals.[30]

Meeting in Richmond in May, the movement attracted between 450 and 800 persons, depending upon which newspaper one read. Observing in a more precise manner, Martin estimated that attendance "outside of the 1st [Jones's] district was nominal." Given this failure, would-be-candidates fell away. Even before the Democratic central committee refused handily to accept a nominating primary or convention, Attorney General Montague declined to serve on the movement's governing committee, citing his busy schedule and unwillingness "to co-operate in name only." Anderson and Jones dropped out. Montague then promoted Governor Tyler, who recalled that no one "was so insistent as Mr. Montague. He often sought my office, at the mansion and elsewhere." He offered to make forty speeches, "painted in glowing colors what the future held" for the governor. Once Tyler announced, Montague cooled; the promised "forty-three voluntary offers of support from school officers did not materialize." As the governor and the attorney general directly influenced superintendent appointments, Montague used this state patronage for himself. Some months before, the *Richmond Dispatch* had reported "whispers of Mr. Montague aspiring to the office" which Tyler occupied.[31]

Swanson performed the paramount role in Martin's election. Showing considerable skill, he indexed campaign issues for Martin, drafted statements for legislative contests, and advised the senator on tariff matters. One journalist reported: "When a serious phase of the campaign arises, Mr. Swanson always turns up in Richmond." He would appear at Martin headquarters, leaving his congressional duties in Washington or traveling by rail from Pittsylvania County. He and incumbent state senator Rorer James campaigned among Fifth-District voters "to elect Martin delegates . . . on the grounds that he will aid him for Governor." Jones spoke at rallies over the state where he censured Martin as little more than a railroad lobbyist who misled the people by appearing to favor direct elections. Local Democratic committees ruled on the means to legislative nomination: by primary vote, by a mass meeting, or by local conventions. The great variety furnished further fuel for controversy, but legislative candidates favoring Martin generally won nomination.[32]

In the autumn 1899 election, "independent" candidates tried their hands. Endorsing Martin, Glass of Lynchburg, in his freshman state Senate campaign, faced rural Populist opposition. Former Populist William H. Gravely won a delegate seat in Henry County. At the Democratic convention in Pittsylvania County, the 1896 Chicago platform and direct elections received endorsement, while senate and delegate candidates favored Martin. Swanson reduced appearances beyond his district, and Lassiter chided him that more than telegrams were needed "if he wanted the people of Southside Virginia" to sustain his gubernatorial ambition. But both Martin and Tyler forces had, as Danville party chairman Eugene Withers reported, produced "almost universal dissatisfaction in . . . [the] district with one or more of our candidates as the means by which they were nominated." By mid-October, Swanson was considered a gubernatorial candidate who would have "the backing of Senator Martin" despite many of his friends favoring Ellyson. In December, the Democratic caucus in the General Assembly renominated and thereby elected Martin by 103 votes to 27. The voting pattern replicated earlier regional patterns of the May Movement.[33]

The new General Assembly contained only one-fourth of the members who had attended its previous session. Despite allegations by editor W.C. Elam of the *Norfolk Virginian Pilot* of the presence of a Martin machine, voting blocks were difficult to discover. In an unsuccessful Senate vote on an employer liability law opposed by railroads, four senators close to Martin in the Tyler campaign cast conflicting votes: Henry D. Flood voted for it, Richmond City's Henry T. Wickham of the Chesapeake and Ohio against it, and two others, J.L.

Jefferies of Orange and William B. McIlwaine from Petersburg, paired their votes. The legislature passed a call for a constitutional referendum for May 1900, a racial segregation law for railroads, additional local prohibition regulations, and a pure-food law without enforcement funding. It defeated election reform, a bill to incorporate Virginia Telephone and Telegraph, and a child-labor law. In the last instance, officials from Danville's Riverside Cotton Mills spent three months fighting it and were supported by Pittsylvania County senators Rorer James and Jospeh Whitehead, "both of whom were financially interested" in the mills.[34]

During the legislative session in early 1900, Swanson visited Richmond for short intervals. He interviewed legislators and examined issues for his gubernatorial campaign. Other candidates received attention as well: Lieutenant Governor Edward Echols of Staunton, Democratic state chairman Ellyson, Richard C. Marshall of Portsmouth, and Attorney General Montague. The congressman also repaired relationships frayed by the Tyler-Martin campaign. Representative Epes's death in March opened the way for Lassiter to become his successor. Hay and Martin, but especially Swanson, structured a campaign strategy for the strikingly handsome Petersburg lawyer. Most important, Governor Tyler needed to call an early election to prevent opposition to Lassiter from developing. Fearing Tyler was "being influenced to some extent by the other side," Swanson appealed directly to the governor in personal and political terms.[35]

Initially, Tyler resisted an early election. To Lassiter, Swanson suggested "to make it so hot for [Tyler] . . . that he will abandon" those who counseled otherwise. Swanson's arguments were telling: Lassiter's vote was needed now in Washington to aid William F. Rhea's contested election by William Walker, a long-time Republican foe of Tyler. If the election were postponed, it would be entangled in the anticipated constitutional referendum in May, at "a time when all the negroes will be brought in full force to vote against a constitutional convention." He concluded by urging Tyler to prevent further factional tiffs and to recall the past: "At a time when you needed friends, I proved myself to be a warm and efficient one, while some who are now claiming to be were not." Swanson aided Lassiter in his preelection activities and, in doing so, outflanked William Hodges Mann of Nottoway. A note from national Democratic chairman, Senator James K. Jones, further strengthened Tyler's resolve, and he ordered the special election for April that contributed to Lassiter's victory.[36]

Upon the edge of a new century, Virginians who viewed change as harsh and unsettling scrutinized the past hundred years for reassurance and inspiration. For the next few years, politics would abound with references to past ideals, traditions, and myths that could inspire contemporary Virginia society and heal disruptions. These motifs reinforced a sentimental atmosphere grown heavy with nostalgic resumes emitted by members of the Lost Cause cult. Shrewd and aspiring politicians spoke of shaping the future from the past's virtue and honor in terms quite notable for their vagueness. During the 1899 autumn legislative campaigns, Attorney General Montague had ignored "independent" reform candidates, praised Democrats in all their parts, and approvingly observed "the revival of the older and better spirit of the Commonwealth." Montague projected a personality, as one historian has noted, sincere, idealistic, calm, and reserved. In effect, he resembled a statesman of the old school, a gentleman. He spoke for maintenance of state employee salaries, endorsed the silver standard as "a democrat [sic] of the old hard money type," favored improved public schools and legislative control of trusts, and censured McKinley for his imperialism. The South, he said, knew imperialism well; after the Civil War, the region had received a considerable dose. He added, "Our civilization and the civilization of the black man had been set back many generations by the enfranchisement of the negroes." While citing well-established reform proposals, Attorney General Montague became one of the first elected Virginia state officials to link the growing sentiment for constitutional revision to disfranchisement of black Virginians.[37]

Swanson's candidacy also forced Montague to run for governor. Swanson had been instrumental in advancing Montague's political career and apparently had gained Montague's acquiescence in 1897 for Swanson's gubernatorial try in 1901. But the attorney general, bound by the regional imperatives of Virginia politics, wrote to Anderson: "If [Swanson] . . . be strong enough to nominate himself, I cannot be taken as Attorney General from the same county. . . . Self preservation seems to require that I myself shall be a candidate for the . . . nomination." To another, he saw Swanson as intent upon succeeding Martin or Daniel and "anxious to defeat me" even for the attorney-generalship. Swanson and "other friends of Senator Martin wish to eliminate me by the geographical scissors." Sooner or later the two young politicians would have to match political wits. The 1901 gubernatorial campaign apeared to be the chess board upon which they would play. Montague would take such issues as pure elections, "the Martin machine," distressing election irregularities, and possible black disfranchisement through constitutional means to win his way to the governor's mansion.[38]

In March 1900, the legislature called for yet another referendum on a constitutional convention, the third in fourteen years. The Democratic convention in May made it a party issue by adopting an endorsement. Flood, Daniel, and Montague led in its acceptance that provided the resulting draft be submitted to the electorate for approval. Others, Martin and Congressman Rhea, had questioned its being made a party issue. William Jones opposd it being even held. Swanson had earlier endorsed a call but now grew silent. What had been begun by Republicans and Populists to break Democratic control of elections had been considerably warped by time, events, and personalities. The movement had blossomed into a pure-elections issue that required no agreement on fiscal or monetary public policies or further government regulatory activities. The senatorial primary had been aimed against Martin and his so-called machine, but, by 1900, the issue had broadened into proposals for constitutional disfranchisement of blacks and threatened to become a general antidemocratic movement. Swanson also was sensitive to efforts to reduce southern congressional representation based upon disfranchising action by other states or through federal intervention as earlier stated in the Lodge force bill. But, as important, the threat to his electoral base, composed of many whites and some blacks who faced disfranchisement, led him to restraint. Montague campaigned over the state for the referendum's success, however, vowing to submit the results for popular approval.[39]

Voting against a convention 6,056 to 5,246, despite Danville's favoring it 1,266 to 140, Swanson's district reflected its congressman's opinion in May 1900. By a total of 77,362 to 60,370, the statewide vote called for a convention, supported primarily "by the [white] votes of the black counties and cities, as opposed to the white counties." Although Anderson, speaking to the state bar in July, called black enfranchisement "an atrocious blunder, a moral crime and a degradation of citizenship," six months later an observant journalist could detect "no great popular movement" in the state to disfranchise blacks. Earlier having warned of a possible loss of white votes, the *Norfolk Virginian Pilot* opposed such radical action: "Are white men so sure of each other than none need watching?" Current events may have pushed acceptance as much as any. A double lynching in Nottoway—the hanging of black and white tramps—led Mann, Walter Watson, William A. Land, and Joseph W. Bryant to issue the Nottoway platform which condemned the current Reconstruction Underwood constitution as the source of contemporary social vicissitudes: "Unrestricted suffrage has been and is now a serious menace to the peace and prosperity of the state." Heavy rains on election day may have allowed its passage.[40]

Despite distractions, the tide of Bryanism still ran high in the state in 1900. The Virginia Democrats had endorsed his second presidential nomination and favored reenactment of the 1896 platform. Swanson declined to go to the national convention in Kansas City, remaining instead to gain his fifth congressional nomination before the district convention. He attended the state bar meeting and planned to be "near by to consult about matters" when the Fifth District Republican convention met. He hoped to "arrange it" so that he would have no opposition in the autumn general election. He would then be free to campaign about the state, to assist colleagues such as Flood and Lassiter in their congressional bids, and to prepare the ground for his gubernatorial race. But illness struck and he had "to go off to the spring and rest up." Republicans nominated John Richard Whitehead, a Cleveland Democrat and father of Swanson's law partner, Joseph Whitehead. Swanson's secretary discovered the "the Republicans and gold bugs" had combined and there were "signs of treachery in the camp." Swanson returned to the Fifth District, where he remained for most of the autumn campaigning. In September, Lassiter pleaded: "Montague is to speak here . . . , while Sussex clamors for Swanson at big meetings . . . and I can get nothing from him." Whitehead accused Swanson of being in league with the American Tobacco Company. In typical style, Swanson overcame Whitehead by rallies, organization, and speeches and convinced voters that Whitehead's leaping from party to party deserved the confidence of neither Democrats nor Republicans. He won 14,293 to 10,292 votes, a thousand above Bryan's district vote.[41]

Concurrently, Swanson was victimized by partisan journalists. In the 1899 autumn legislative campaign in Augusta County, he was quoted as having said, "Virginia Democrats are fit only to be led." If for no other reason, Swanson's astuteness would have prevented such an unpolitic statement. He protested Editor Elam's sly attempt to link him to William Mahone's tactics by replying that such a quote was an "absolute false statement." No reputable person who attended the meeting "would make such an assertion." In June 1900, in the heart of his district, Henry County Democrats in convention supposedly endorsed Montague for governor. After strong protests by Swanson supporters, the report was withdrawn. Linking Swanson to a Martin machine also was a favorite pastime of some Richmond and Norfolk journals. His relationship with Martin was a typical, contemporary political alliance; no machine in lock-stop fashion commanded Swanson. Other alleged Swanson statements and supposed occurrences harmful to his candidacy floated through the political atmosphere and have been repeated by some historians.[42]

In December 1900, Swanson gathered his energies for the gubernatorial struggle. Elected in the partisan popular elections of the 1890s, he was not apprehensive about the dozens of local elections and mass meetings that would select delegates to the nominating Democratic state convention. His record made him as reform bent, as responsive to popular issues, and as capable of realizing platform goals as any practicing, elected official in Virginia. But he would have to parallel his campaign with dozens of local elections that would also choose delegates to the constitutional convention. Montague, an able and wily opponent, was pushing ahead in his two-year campaign. Swanson would find 1901 difficult.

4

Middle of the Road
and Stepping High
1901-1906

Between 1901 and 1906, Claude Swanson moved from being an influential regional politician in Virginia's factionalized Democratic party to becoming a commanding personality known throughout the state. He was unable in 1901 to secure the governorship through the nineteenth-century nominating convention, but, upon its replacement by the party primary, he applied in Virginia techniques perfected in the mass politics of the Fifth Congressional District. His gubernatorial nomination and election in 1905 confirmed his political prowess and established patterns other candidates would follow to gain future nominations.

In 1901, Swanson first approached local leaders in the quid pro quo manner of Virginia politics and then appealed publicly to voters by his dashing personality and reform proposals. Events intervened, however, and distorted his gubernatorial campaign. During January 1901, while the Virginia legislature met in special session, Swanson traveled back and forth to Congress to prevent reduction of the state congressional delegation by Republicans using 1900 census data. As senior Ways and Means minority member, he also contributed to reducing the federal tobacco tax. J. Taylor Ellyson's withdrawal from the race brought Swanson hurrying to Richmond to court the Baptist businessman's supporters. Andrew Montague apparently promised Ellyson he could continue as Democratic state chairman, but Swanson allies attracted some Ellyson voters. A published sample of the hundreds of Swanson letters petitioning local leaders reminded them "I am grateful and stand loyally by my friends." He also noted that Virginia's two senators and a majority of congressmen "are warmly advocating my nomination," but Montague ward workers cited the letter as typical of "bossism." Rumors circulated from Swanson sources of Montague's 1897 pledge to Swanson "to abstain from the [1901] gubernatorial race." The attorney general countered that "my political life is a protest against such promises of combinations."[1]

Endorsed by Samuel Gompers, president of the American Federation of Labor, Swanson gained the machinist union's accolades as one of "the greatest labor advocates in the House of Representatives." Montague manipulated the Richmond Central Trades and Labor Council for an endorsing resolution upon a claim of Swanson opposition to a 1900 Virginia employer liability bill. Swanson denied the charge and Trades Council president John Krausse testified to his popularity with labor and revealed that the pro-Montague statement passed during Krausse's absence. But the fabricated accusation followed Swanson through the campaign and harmed him especially among railroad employees.[2]

Filling an appeals court vacancy revealed more clearly the nature of the gubernatorial race and Virginia's decentralized, regional politics. The legislature would select in January 1901 from among four candidates: William Hodges Mann of Nottoway, William A. Prentis of Norfolk, Archer A. Phlegar of Christiansburg, and Stafford G. Whittle, a Henry County judge. While claiming to have "no individual axes to grind," Montague recommended that Governor Tyler appoint Whittle to the unexpired term while awaiting the legislature's decision. Tyler named instead his neighbor Phlegar, despite the latter's belief that "Whittle would do better . . . because of his experience" and youth. Phlegar also thought Montague "would naturally incline to Judge Whittle, because of locality." House of Delegates Speaker Edward W. Saunders considered Mann and Phlegar so closely affiliated with railroads that "the corporation people stood to win" with either man. Tyler also received warning that Whittle, "a good judge and lawyer, . . . fought with a great deal of relish and vigor" Tyler in the recent senatorial contest and remained "an ardent supporter of the Martin-Swanson faction." Swanson tried to enlist Thomas Staples Martin in Whittle's behalf, but as early as August 1900 the senator sent telegrams to Assembly members "making personal appeals . . . to support Judge Mann."[3]

Mann and Whittle emerged as primary contenders. On various occasions, Swanson had aided Whittle in obtaining salary increments, a Martinsville post office, and other government projects. He resisted consolidation of the judge's district and now sponsored his advancement, although Senator Martin and Congressmen Francis Lassiter, James Hay, and Henry Flood took Mann's side. Swanson also collected Prentis's associates in Portsmouth and Norfolk when their candidate faltered. Obtaining second-choice commitments from legislative friends of Mann and Phlegar, Swanson, owing to Martin's efforts for Mann, approached Congressman William A. Jones. But the First District congressman would do "nothing either way as usual where his own interest is concerned." Regional bias prevented Swanson from exerting "personal influence" in Jones's district: "It usually goes against all those I am associated with in politics." In January 1901, Swanson caucused with legislators and emerged with Whittle's nomination. Montague believed Swanson was forced to aid Whittle, but a more considerate observer found Swanson's course "most admirable." He "took risks . . . in order that he might serve a friend." Swanson had chanced irritating followers of regional judicial candidates within a few months of electing delegates to the state nominating convention. Some office seekers would have lacked courage, but Swanson's response refuted "the ungenerous suggestion" that he was a "machine politician." Succeeding to Whittle's judgeship, Speaker Saunders agreed, having earlier written Whittle: "We have no organization in this state that makes and unmakes candidates." Ironically, the *Norfolk Virginian Pilot* announced Whittle's election with headlines: "Machine Defeated."[4]

To gain the gubernatorial nomination, Swanson required a majority of 1,468 convention delegates apportioned by the 1900 Democratic presidential vote. Some localities preferred a "precinct primary" that permitted registered Democrats to vote, the winner gaining all of the delegates. Others adopted a "minority representation" plan that apportioned delegates to candidates on the basis of votes received. Each Democratic city or county committee selected as its voting format either viva voce voting, secret ballot, or a shouting "mass meeting." Swanson announced a platform providing a statewide primary for governor, improved roads, and a renovated school system, but Martin's role in Swanson's campaign became the major issue.[5]

In early March, Swanson protested Montague's attack upon Martin's alleged cozy relationship with corporations and accusations of Swanson's subordination to him: His opponents had "cried combinations, corporations, sin, rule, and all that" until he was "sick of it." In speeches and pamphlets he emphasized Democratic services to Virginia and his role in composing that record. Montague could not easily censure these accomplishments. Swanson toured the state in April, surveyed his opportunities, and met local partisans. While his Richmond headquarters issued a heavy correspondence directed at specific groups, he gained time to reduce Montague's lead in delegates by convincing the Democratic state committee to hold its convention in early August. In late April and early May, Montague openly accused Martin of being a second Mahone and cleverly phrased innuendos that reawoke racial tones of the 1880s campaigns. Similar themes were present in parallel local elections of delegates to the constitutional convention.[6]

Had Martin rescinded his earlier agreement with Swanson, the former would have had nowhere else to go. He was convinced that the "organization . . . promoting Montague's candidacy is inspired by the sole purpose of breaking down what they see fit to call 'The Martin Organization'. . . . Swanson is the strongest man to make the fight." Although a majority of the state Democratic executive committee usually supported his contests, Martin had been unable to elect Ellyson, Mann, or Flood, while Swanson had achieved considerable success in backing victorious candidates for state office. Martin had been more elected than electing and he feared Montague turning "the power" of the governorship against him. The incoming governor would leave office in 1905, the same year Martin's current term expired. His motives were self-serving, but Swanson accepted his aid nonetheless.[7]

Edward Echols needed a viable campaign in the Valley and tactics necessitated either Swanson or Echols delegations, with second choices favoring the remaining candidate. The clerk of court at Buena Vista complained, "We can't get a Swanson delegation. It is mainly hatred [for] Senator Martin that hurts Swanson here." In Winchester, Richard E. Byrd feared that "Montague's friends . . . seem to have plenty of money." Publicity, refreshments, payment of delegates' expenses to the convention site in Norfolk, and similar expenditures consumed funds. Martin warned Echol's manager Flood of affairs in the central Shenandoah Valley: "Matters are completely at sea and drifting in the wrong direction." On May 10, Swanson agreed with James Hay and Flood to raise with Martin one-half of a $20,000 common campaign fund. Echols would provide the remainder, but only he met his pledge; he contributed an additional $2,200, as well. The attorney general drew upon a bountiful treasury. Some funding came from his wealthy Fairfax relative Joseph Willard, a candidate for lieutenant governor, and probably significant contributions from publishers, seeking to place their texts on the state multibook lists. The great lever of the Montague effort rested upon the fulcrum of state patronage in appointments to the court and public-school systems.[8]

For nearly four years, Tyler, Montague, and state school superintendent Joseph Southall had named or reappointed 118 district school officers. The promise of favorable school superintendents had encouraged Tyler to engage Martin for the senatorshp. In May 1901, incumbents and aspirants contested for sixty positions and, owing to their earlier appointments, remaining superintendents were unusually susceptible to political influence from Montague. At least fifteen new persons were named. Pleading with Lassiter to sway Tyler and Southall in his behalf, Frank Massie still fell to a "Montague man." In Franklin County, a popular official who "was for Swanson" lost to a brother of the local Montague manager. Siding with Montague, Carter Glass sutained his brother's continuation as superintendent in Lynchburg and, to Montague's benefit, opposed the Campbell County chief school executive. As announcements of selections came late in the campaign, Swanson had little opportunity to organize friends of defeated candidates. He did question Montague's objectivity, but the "Red Fox of Middlesex" protested that he would not manipulate the school system for mere political gain. His proposal for additional funding for public schools enticed other school personnel as well.[9]

By mid-May, Swanson had carried elections in Petersburg by a wide margin, in Alexandria by a more narrow count, and in Pittsylvania County by a rout. Assisted by Echols and Richard C. Marshall groups, Swanson secured a minority representation plan for Richmond. A riotous delegate selection meeting in Henrico County received wide newspaper coverage that blamed Swanson partisans for malodorous behavior. He repudiated these excesses, but Montague added the event to his list of accusations. Swanson questioned "snap primaries" at Manchester, Fredericksburg, and Goochland. In the latter case, "many farmers, not having daily mail, did not know" of the election. Editor F.O. Hoffman of the *Franklin Times Democrat* complained that heavily outnumbered Montague supporters attempted to disrupt the mass meeting, then withdrew and nominated a separate delegate list. At Roanoke and elsewhere, Swanson spoke for improved government made responsive by his governorship and for providing better schools and roads. In the rain at Boydton, he cornered the "Red Fox", who accepted his challenge to debate. Before three hundred astonished observers massed in a tiny, damp courthouse, the two staged one of the more colorful events in modern Virginia politics.[10]

Initially "very calm and dignified," Montague regretted that "two candidates for the Democratic nomination should . . . debate," declared that the government of which he was a prominent part was "never more corrupt than now" and vowed to sponsor "a people's government—not a government by clique." Face flushed, hair ruffled, Swanson cited his independence from Martin, urged a gubernatorial primary, and questioned the platitudinous attorney general's past political actions. Where was Montague in the 1896 Cleveland-Bryan fight? "Did you attend the primaries that year? Did you go to the Staunton convention?" There, despite Martin's wishes, Swanson had put his head "on the block" for free silver. Against Martin opposition he had electioneered in 1893 and 1897 for Montague and in 1901 for Whittle. Pointing a finger at an increasingly distressed opponent, he asked, "What about school superintendents, Jack?" How did Montague stand on the school contest in Boydton? "Tell us, Jack." Vexed and angry, Montague claimed he had won public office by his own merits, but thereafter, despite appeals from Swanson, he refused a second debate. Swanson two weeks later published letters revealing aspects of Montague's political maneuvers in the 1890s."[11]

Leading Montague in delegates on May 26, at the zenith of his campaign, Swanson stood with John W. Daniel at Lynchburg while the senator attested to his gubernatorial qualities. But time was short and one Daniel informant considered it "a shame that [Montague] . . . [used] his position as Attorney General to further his candidacy" through superintendent selections. He distracted attention by "crying out 'ring, machine, etc.' " The informant added, "The newspapers are helping him—some . . . with a full knowledge of the conditions as *they are*." Conjecture had Martin withdrawing because he was "doing the congressman more harm than good" by his continuing advocacy.[12]

Fittingly, shaped by local circumstances, the denouement of the campaign occurred in Danville. Since 1892, many of its citizens had opposed Swanson and his partisan Democratic platform commitments. Although a Cleveland stronghold bobbing in an inflationist Bryan sea, however, the town had voted Democratic. Previously careful organization had derailed factional opposition, but in 1901 labor unrest at the Riverside Cotton Mills defeated Swanson's plans. Textile workers had struggled for a ten-hour work day and management had agreed to test the proposal, but later gave notice that on April 1 the eleven-hour schedule would return. House of Delegates member George C. Cabell, Jr., son of the former congressman, local lawyer, and "sole honorary member of the Union," became involved in the threatened strike. Probably at Swanson's suggestion, Gompers met company and civic leaders but failed to reach any agreement. While quoting Bryan's cry opposing crucifixion of labor, Gompers and southern organizer Prince Greene cautioned strikers to avoid politics and to consider means for a successful strike. But workers allowed "outsiders to influence them to dabble in politics. After politicians used them on election day and told them to work under an eleven hour system, they realized who their friends were but too late." Apparently citing Swanson's alleged opposition to the employer liability bill, Cabell convinced them to vote for Montague, who on May 28 carried Danville by 77 of 1,841 votes cast. Swanson headquarters blamed "troubles in the cotton mill" for defeat while citing Cabell as "an active Montague man." News of Glass winning Lynchburg for Montague by 800 votes deepened the gloom.[13]

These triumphs and partial victories in Richmond and Norfolk gave Montague by June 15 over 500 delegate commitments while Swanson claimed 237. Local politicians paused in their efforts to avoid backing a losing candidate. Closing his capital headquarters, Swanson moved to Chatham, and Echols with but sixty-seven delegates withdrew to avoid embarrassing "the future action of those" who had given him their "cordial and loyal support." Swanson's error in citing endorsement from Martin provided Montague, who had spoken for black disfranchisement and had benefitted from concurrent elections of constitutional convention members, with the Democratic gubernatorial nomination.[14]

In August, the thirty-nine-year-old Swanson traveled to the Norfolk state convention amid predictions that a "complete revolution" was at hand and "almost a complete change" of the executive committee would follow Montague's nomination. Swanson considered allowing his name to be nominated and then to acquiesce to the convention's will. But this ploy had about it a stubborn factionalism and, unlike previous conventions, he might face a hostile reception. Upon arrival, he abandoned nomination plans, stressed Democratic unity, and presented a brave front. His hotel rooms opened to receive backers, some still adorned with his campaign buttons. So bright and jolly did he appear it was as "though he and not the 'Red Fox' were to be the victor." Even an admiring Montague delegate told a reporter that he preferred "Swanson's pluck than any office he could think of."[15]

In the evening of August 14, young Cabell nominated Montague, who won by acclamation. Delegate demands brought Swanson forth from the Fifth District delegation. Abandoning his assertive campaign style, he coated his speech with conciliation. He had rarely referred to the coming constitutional convention and did not now. Swanson claimed no one deserved success "who cannot graciously and manfully bear defeat." To his 250 delegates, he pledged to follow Andrew Jackson's dictum: "He never failed a friend." Swanson predicted continuing Democratic success as long as the party based its strength upon "the great masses," resisted "demagogues who promise much and do little", and counted "party fealty and party service . . . as badges of honor and not causes for disfavor." Turning, he met Montague and exchanged a handshake that, with his speech, brought the convention cheering to its feet. In taking his opponent's hand, he reached also toward the 1905 gubernatorial primary.[16]

Following a six-week European trip with Elizabeth and Thomas Martin and his wife, Swanson joined the campaign against Republican J. Hampton Hoge. Taking advantage of Theodore Roosevelt's dinner invitation to Booker T. Washington, Montague branded Hoge's party as one that loved "a negro better than a white man." The winning Democrat did not carry the Fifth District and some critics faulted Swanson, but the gubernatorial candidate's close identification with the constitutional convention and rough handling of their congressman made him less than popular in the county precincts. Montague gained fewer votes than Tyler four years earlier; the "Red Fox" ran even in major white counties, carrying cities and black-belt districts. Voting patterns did not reveal him as representative of any vast urban reform movement, as only 18 percent of the state's population lived in its cities. His strongest vote developed in the First, Second, Third, and Eighth districts, from the Tidewater through the Northern Neck to Fairfax and to Loudoun. Swanson spoke in areas that he had previously neglected. Secretary of the May Movement and constitutional convention member John S. Barbour, nephew of the former senator, praised him for his

"As the Game Is Being Played in Virginia." Cartoon by Clifford K. Berryman, *Washington Post*, June 20, 1901.

work in Northern Virginia, saying he "covered himself with glory . . . and rendered valuable service to the state ticket."[17]

Montague took the oath of office in January 1902 before the assembled constitutional convention rather than the incoming legislature. Many of the leaders of the May Movement and the 1901 Democratic and constitutional conventions were the same and a vast reform wave appeared building to contemporary commentators. During the recent gubernatorial campaign, Montague headquarters claimed that May Movement advocates who were delegate candidates had been elected to the convention. Molded by Jones, John Rixey, and Montague and joined by Lieutenant Governor Willard and Attorney General William A. Anderson, this new spirit would embrace Glass, R. Walton Moore, Julian Quarles, and Caperton Braxton. Led by John Goode, they and their colleagues would rally to purify Virginia politics in the constitutional convention. Most of the reformers claimed ancestral homes within a vast sickle-shaped pattern, beginning in the Northern Neck at Warsaw to Fairfax, along the Blue Ridge to Rockbridge and Bedford through Danville. Primarily Funder strongholds in the 1880s, these areas presently contained closely balanced racial divisions, the borderlands between predominantly black and white Virginia counties. Class similarities were present. Jones, Eppa Hunton, Jr., Anderson, Cabell, Moore, and Goode were Episcopalians. Glass and Willard were Methodists but the latter had attended Alexandria's Episcopal School. Quarles, a Presbyterian, and Montague, a Baptist, were the only members of their congregations among reform leadership.[18]

In addition to personal, political, regional, or reform motivations, an antidemocratic sentiment united these men who considered a politician's conduct and manner as substantial an issue as his politics. Sleeve-soiling, boisterous mass politics linked with latter-day, painstaking political coordination integrating business management techniques offended these reformers. Former Northern Neck resident Braxton complained: "These degenerate days, . . . merit counts for little. . . . [O]nly push and organization . . . , as a rule, carries the day." Goode listed decorum and courtesy as necessary qualities for acceptable public careers and expressed considerable enmity toward the ungenteel Underwood constitution that had unleashed upon the state not only black voters but mass politics as well. In making executive appointments, Governor Montague revealed a prejudice in favor of "prominent men," despite advice to avoid that "Virginia idea of distinction" and select instead "useful men," known or otherwise. Contemporary Virginia patriarchal tendencies reinforced by a heavily mythologized past peopled with statesmen and warrior heroes reinforced the elitest bent of the reformers.[19]

In the 1893 Lee-Martin senatorial contest, the reformers had generally favored Lee and several maintained close relations with the general. Willard had served as his aide-de-camp in Cuba, and Lee, a Fairfax native, campaigned for Montague. In recent national elections, none endorsed Bryan's presidential candidacy to the degree that Swanson had. Despite his free-silver advocacy, Jones had remained loyal to Grover Cleveland until the last months of his second administration. As a delegate to the 1896 Democratic national convention, Glass refused to vote for its platform. Swanson recalled that Montague in 1892 played both Hill and Cleveland sides, and "split himself between the two." Four years later, he "took to the woods" and until the last days of the canvass avoided identification with Bryan Democrats. Years later, Montague would admit to a life-long admiration for Cleveland. Although the Great Commoner would soon visit the state, the 1901 constitutional delegates defeated a motion to invite Bryan to address them.[20]

These men subsequently produced in June 1902 a document that would avoid an active state government, that refused a combination of services in Richmond, and that preserved a weak chief executive. A powerful board of education and a state corporation commission, reduced judgeships, and enhanced tax revenues for the University of Virginia were subordinate to disfranchisement of black Virginians and, as events would prove, a considerable number of white citizens. On items affecting local government, localism prevailed. Although the "members of the Convention were well aware of the weaknesses of county officials . . . , not only was the structure of county government unchanged but the details as well," wrote one authority. A majority opposed centralization, whether in politics by the Democratic state committee, in business affairs by distant corporations, or in government through efficient state agencies. Drafted by Braxton, the corporation commission might appear contrary to the trend, but local patriarchs profited from it and the legislature retained control of appointment. Coupled with anticipated lower state expenditures, the commission would raise corporate tax assessments. There would follow less need for local property taxes and a stabilized tax base for Virginia bonds. A purified franchise should reduce social and political upheavals and encourage northern capital to invest through local banks. Demonstrating their antidemocratic impulse, the delegates voted forty-seven to thirty-eight to proclaim the constitution rather than to submit it to the electorate. Despite earlier pledges to the contrary, Governor Montague acquiesced.[21]

Franchise sections and proclamation of the new organic law provoked an uproar in the Fifth District. Swanson associates D.W. Bolen of Carroll County, T.C. Gwyn of Grayson County, and young J. Murray Hooker, commonwealth attorney for Patrick County and state Democratic committeeman, voted against proclamation, as did the district's three Republicans from Franklin, Henry, and Floyd counties. In Pittsylvania County and in Danville, all four delegates endorsed proclamation, including Berryman Green and Eugene Withers. Evaluated by a later historian, the new fundamental law, "generally believed then and probably true . . . , would have been defeated" had it been submitted to the voters. Under the guise of reform, reaction to the previous generation of Virginia politics had carried.[22]

Swanson discovered a harmful political residue in his 1902 congressional campaign. Opposed to proclamation, convention delegate Beverly A. Davis of Franklin County, thirty-five-year-old graduate of Georgetown University and former commonwealth attorney, described himself as a Republican elected by Democrats who feared the revised law would shut "out white voters as well as black." Swanson detected "more dissatisfaction" than he had thought "concerning the new constitution and the suffrage provisions" in August 1902. He had also to oversee a new registration, to prepare for his first congressional primary, and to face possible redistricting.[23]

To fund registration and mailing expenses, Swanson suggested that Flood approach his former contributor, Edward P. Meany, counsul for the American Telegraph and Telephone Company. Now a New Jersey resident, Kentucky-born Meany forwarded aid to Flood, Swanson, and William F. Rhea to enhance Democratic opportunities in the House of Representatives. Swanson instructed his Chatham friend and banker Edwin S. Reid to lobby in the legislature to redraw his district by either dropping Floyd County or by adding Halifax County so that he would "not have such a hard time next time." He encouraged Judge Whittle to turn out Henry County Democrats to guarantee "a good registration," and from Withers he received Braxton's arguments defending the new constitution "to reply to any assaults that Davis may make upon the convention." Claiming constitutional prohibitions and because it most adversely affected Glass and Jones, Montague vetoed the redistricting bill. In November, however, Swanson won his sixth congressional election, defeating Davis by nearly four thousand votes of seventeen thousand cast.[24]

After the election, Norfolk legislator and railroad lawyer Alfred P. Thom, Hay, Flood, and Martin met to ponder Virginia politics. Independent of the senator's control, Swanson attended, and his advice, whether about the new primary law, further congressional redistricting, or Montague's governorship, was valued. Lassiter was missed. In 1901 and early 1902, Swanson had aided the Fourth District congressman in a contested election case. Intervening with the lawyer of Lassiter's opponent, he negotiated a postponement of the contest hearing and confided to Lassiter the inclinations of Swanson's "Republican Friends" on the congressional election committee. Narrowly renominated, Lassiter became distraught in September by his sister's death in a carriage accident and was unable to campaign. The physical and mental price paid by participants in turn-of-the-century Virginia politics was sometimes high. As for Martin, he surveyed a state whose politics he had been unable to dominate, the most recent example being Swanson's failed gubernatorial candidacy.[25]

A recent constitutional delegate, Joseph C. Wysor of Pulaski County, conjectured that Martin "has no great hold on Virginia. Whether justly or unjustly, he is looked upon as crafty and scheming and as the head of a ring surrounded by unworthy satellites. . . . It clings to him like the shirt of Nessus." Having helped create the Martin myth, Virginia journalists continued to define politics in simplistic alignments. A Richmond columnist proposed that person-alities more than ideas predominated "the weird conglomeration which goes under the name of Democracy in the Old Dominion." It was full of "ardent protectionists and earnest tariff reformers, dyed in the wool silver men and red hot gold bugs, enthusiasts, expansionists and moss backed kickers, strict constructionists, and zealous Populists and socialists." Amid such fluidity and contradictions, the politicians who gave the party structural integrity were skittish. Martin supposedly was considering a "combination" with Lieutenant Governor Willard. Swanson partisan Walter Coles joined with Jones to suggest to Harry Tucker that he oppose Flood in the 1902 congressional primary to prevent the latter from entering the 1905 gubernatorial race. Swanson objected strenuously to a *Richmond News Leader* reporter who identified him as favoring a Braxton senatorial quest. Admitting Swanson's distinctiveness from Martin, Montague estimated him to be "impulsive and when desperate quite indepen-dent."[26]

Two years before the 1905 senatorial primary, Swanson carefully avoided entanglements in the Martin-Montague feud. Although one report from the Fifth District claimed Swanson and Rorer James were at work so that "Cabell . . . and others would be squeezed like a lemon and thrown aside," Swanson muted vindictiveness, if present, toward the governor. Cabell abandoned Danville and soon moved to Norfolk. Securing as many alternatives as possible, Swanson knew James to be committed to Martin while state Senator Joseph Whitehead of Chatham was for Montague. Both men were a part of Swanson's cadre of leaders.[27]

During the winter of 1902, the congressman suffered a second severe respiratory infection within three years that revealed symptoms of emphysema: breathlessness, chronic bronchitis, and lung pressure upon the heart. Yet his sinewy, angular body, often enshrouded in tobacco smoke, would resist for a generation the enfeebling disease. A contemporary report described him as "nervous in his manner and active as a humming bird. . . . But he is not surpassed in politeness and cordiality. His speech is brisk and gracious, and when he tackles a proposition it is with vim and fire." Following a two-month trip to Europe, in November 1903 he and Elizabeth hosted at their home near Chatham the marriage of her sister Lulie, "said to be the most beautiful woman in Virginia," to Richmond businessman-politician Cunningham Hall. Swanson continued purchasing stock in Dan River Mills, formerly Riverside Cotton Mills, and acquired real estate in the county and in Washington. As an adjunct of Dan River Mills, Swanson Brothers in 1904 contributed to the organization of Park Place Mercantile Company, holding sixty-nine of the seventy-six $100 par value capital stock. Park Place prices were "in most cases considerably lower," and coal and wood sold for 20 percent less than the Danville average. In 1909, Dan River Mills disposed of its shares to Swanson Brothers, while retaining the fuel business. The Swansons also developed lumber resources, established a branch in Greensboro, North Carolina, and bought sawmills and timber tracts.[28]

After 1901, Virginia Democratic leaders tilted toward northeastern party interests seeking to reassert control after two, faction-ridden Bryan campaigns. Various presidential possibilities, from former president Cleveland to novice congressman William Randolph Hearst, paraded past southern politicos. Martin, Flood, and Hay committed themselves to Senator Arthur P. Gorman of Maryland, who favored repressing the "Wild People" of the Bryan wing. Whether attracted by David B. Hill, other Tammanyites or Virginia-born Wall Street financeer Thomas Fortune Ryan, Swanson joined with Ellyson, Glass, and Jones to favor Alton B. Parker of New York. Hawking Parker in early 1903, Ryan invited Virginia and the South to return to the ways of their fathers so that "there be the least possible interference by the state with private rights" and to avoid the "new follies of budding state socialism." Among his recruits, he welcomed Montague who feared Gorman "would use the patronage of the state to build up Martin." In May 1904, Swanson introduced Ryan to Flood who, with Montague failed by a narrow margin to control an instructed Parker delegation and yielded to a coalition nominally led by Martin.[29]

The Virginia delegation at St. Louis voted for a triumphant Parker who immediately dismayed them by favoring the gold standard and by subordinating the tariff issue. Swanson could but lamely praise his personality. An attempt by Democrats to swing to the right of Republican Roosevelt, to unify the party, and to win in 1904 went awry and permitted Roosevelt to prevail easily. The *Norfolk Virginian Pilot* railed that "the leaders who have stood by it [the Democratic party] for the past eight years surrendered control at St. Louis to the men who had done their best during the same time to destroy it." Parker's nomination did aid in seating Ryan, assured of Virginia residency by his Nelson County vacation home, upon the Virginia Democratic executive committee. By shifting to Parker, Martin had gained at Montague's expense, the latter becoming increasingly isolated and unable to establish effective communication with Jones. Lacking many of his former allies, the governor announced his senatorial candidacy in the autumn of 1904.[30]

In the previous December, Swanson had determined to succeed him. But before concentrating upon this task, he faced in a congressional election J.B.

Stovall, formerly of Halifax and previously a member of both houses of the Virginia legislature. Stovall questioned Swanson's fitness following the Bristow report and his activities on the postal committee. The congressman listed benefits from rural delivery and defended increasing salaries of hard-working Virginia postal clerks who "were not paid as well by one half as a lot of sweet scented dudes who were department clerks in Washington." Stovall admitted a rough-hewn justice at work, and, despite the deadweight of the Parker candidacy, Swanson won nine thousand votes to Stovall's forty-seven hundred. Surprisingly, Republican Roosevelt came within four hundred votes of carrying the Fifth District as many young Democrats were attracted to his "strenuousness."[31]

The disfranchising sections of the constitution had their effect. In 1896, Swanson's opponent collected eleven hundred votes in Danville; in 1904, Stovall received eighty-four, and the total vote was the lowest of Swanson's seven campaigns. But an active Republican party, organizing the black vote and making use of divisive class issues, was absent in 1904. The Virginia Republicans implemented tactics designed to capture white voters from the Democrats, now increasingly devoid of the race issue in elections. Glass estimated that, of the 146,000 eligible black Virginians in 1900, only 21,000 had registered by 1905 and but half had paid their poll taxes. White voting had declined as well, but presently Democratic candidates would register much of it for duty in primary elections. The Democrats lost sixty-six thousand votes and the Republicans sixty-nine thousand between the presidential elections of 1900 and 1904. According to the *Richmond News Leader*, "The new constitution has done its work well. . . . [A]ll future fights in Virginia will be white man's fights, with only the very best and most intelligent negroes voting."[32]

Swanson initiated his gubernatorial campaign by applying the same talents he had perfected in the previous democratic decade at the very moment of reduction of the electorate. Using accomodation within his broad and inclusive politics, he soothed local and regional hostilities, standing apart from Martin while courting Montague elements. A former legislator from Russell County, Jacob C. Gent, informed Montague, "No antagonism now exists between the Montague and Swanson people." He added, "We are to a large extent agreeing to supporting Mr. Swanson for Governor." Swanson hinted of a "break in relations" with Martin while the latter sent similar signals. Swanson spoke for legislative candidates and bolstered Democratic precincts by registering additional white voters. The western white counties had become more significant in state politics, and, in the autumn of 1904, he campaigned there with Braxton. Through the year he spoke to such diverse groups as the state bankers' association and Virginia's organized labor councils.[33]

Potential Swanson opponents received press attention throughout the year. Lieutenant Governor Willard, state Senator Mann, and former Attorney General Rufus A. Ayers posed as regional candidates typical of recent Virginia gubernatorial politics. Willard based his political appeal in Northern Virginia, Mann in the Southside, and Ayers in the Southwest. Anderson, Harry Tucker, and Braxton, all from the Valley, tended to cancel one another out. Swanson was one step ahead having recruited an "active man" in each of the state's counties intent upon "getting up a good organization" He reminded colleagues such as Flood to "touch all the influence you can in my behalf."[34]

Performing perhaps as a stalking horse for Willard, Ayers dropped from the race. The lieutenant governor, as identified by the press, held attachments to the Montague faction and had been a coleader of the 1901 reformers, but he had created considerable confusion in chairing the state Senate. In laying foundations for his campaign, the Fairfax millionaire spent $13,000 in postage alone, but his lack of political luster, non-Virginia birth, regional conflict, and abandonment by earlier allies worked against him. Mann represented an entirely different Virginia. Born in Williamsburg in 1847, since his early teenage years he had earned his own way. By 1867, he secured a Nottoway County judicial appointment that he held through the Readjuster years. He gained notoriety by refusing applicants liquor licenses, forcing them to appeal to a higher court. Serving upon the state Democratic executive committee during the 1890s, his political ambition increased with his law practice, a principal client being the Norfolk and Western Railroad. He failed to achieve an attorney general nomination in 1897 and an appeals court judgeship in 1901, despite the aid of Flood and the concern of Martin. Becoming a state senator in 1899, Mann, a Presbyterian elder, closely identified with black disfranchisement and the organized, aggressive prohibitionists.[35]

Gifted at organization and self-advertisement, a classmate of Swanson's at Randolph-Macon and now a Methodist minister, James Cannon, Jr., had become "in matters pertaining to moral and educational work of the state" indispensable to Mann. In 1901, Cannon and eighteen prohibitionists met in Richmond to establish the Virginia branch of the Anti-Saloon League to coordinate religious and secular efforts at liquor reform. Although dry, Mann assumed a conservative stance on the prohibition issue; he preferred local option elections rather than sweeping statewide or national referenda. In 1903, the Mann liquor law and additional amendments permitted local electorates to close rural saloons. While the law respected Virginia's localism, it followed tactics proposed by the national league. The Virginia drys certified candidates for local, state, and national offices who were committed to prohibition. Urban newspapers by 1904 had grown restless over the divisive potential of yet another rural-inspired reform.[36]

Calling for active government involvement to improve society as well as individuals, the Anti-Saloon League approached Swanson, who replied in 1905 that he would, if governor, enforce "the Mann bill, as I will every other law upon the Virginia statute books." Cannon commented that if one could "divine whether Mr. Swanson favors the law or disapproves of it, he deserves the gold medal due the chief of cryptogramists." The Women's Christian Temperance Union, evangelical Protestant groups, and the league followed a Fabian process that would eventually dry out the state.[37]

Like Cannon and Mann, many drys favored reform of public education. Democratic platforms had proposed educational advance since 1880, and, after conferences in the late 1890s, church and secular reformers announced plans for rural and mountain areas as well as black neighborhoods. The Southern Education Board in 1901 began using propaganda techniques not unlike those of the

Anti-Saloon League to awaken local consciences. The same year, Swanson, then Montague, had voiced traditional Democratic calls for educational improvement, and the latter publicized the board's efforts. Outside philanthropists like Robert Ogden and John D. Rockefeller helped finance the movement. Formed in 1903, the Virginia Cooperative Education Association launched the May Campaign two years later. An intense state speaking tour to reinforce rural interest in better schools, this surge of activity served as a preliminary to the Democratic gubernatorial and senatorial primaries in August 1905.[38]

Whether presenting appeals for improved roads, modernized penal institutions, or practices for advanced agricultural and social services, other reformers resembled in their zeal the prohibitionists and school promoters. They filled primarily educative roles that awakened the reduced electorate and local and area politicians. Candidate for the state school superintendency in 1905, Joseph D. Eggleston, Jr., of the Prince Edward County schools noted "the people were flocking to our meetings" and the politicians "came on the run, begging that they might be permitted to take part." Their increased presence signaled the May Campaign's victory, for only through the politicians could means be discovered to realize the goals of the reformers. With rural leaders predominating in these educational activities, Swanson spoke again for education; while benefiting his campaign, his words reflected a common theme: invoking government to ameliorate social and economic adversity.[39]

Published in 1905, Swanson's campaign platform contained seven specific planks. Committed to "a progressive and efficient system of public education," he would subsidize with state funds inadequate teacher wages, extend the school term, and obtain less expensive schoolbooks. Virginia could not secure good schools with "high priced books and low priced teachers." As the campaign progressed, he demanded a single book list, selected by the state board of education, to replace local lists of 118 districts. Improved roads stood second in emphasis. Increased expenditures at all levels of government were needed for roads to "make country life more desirable and delightful" and to hasten the growth of trade. He invited white immigration and encouraged investment to complement existing shipping, mineral, commercial, and manufacturing resources. He particularized the necessity for "cheap freight rates to the seaboard" that must be accomplished "through the great powers of the corporation commission." He suggested that both the Board of Education and the commission had operated in clumsy fashion since the revised constitution of 1902. The labor commissioner's office should become a source for reliable statistics and proposed legislation. Virginia's first industry, agriculture, deserved generous attention, and increased pensions for Confederate veterans and their widows should also be forthcoming. He pledged that the quality of his appointments would win for him a reputation for attentive, businesslike administration. Candidly, he claimed no promises of offices had been made to individuals, but he added, "Things being equal, I will stand with my friends."[40]

His opponents produced similar gubernatorial goals, and Swanson scoffed that "Captain Willard had been in the legislature ten years and Judge Mann six and neither had introduced a bill on these subjects." A Richmond editor recognized that Swanson's 1905 platform, as had that of 1901, dealt "frankly with the people and boldly announced his position. . . . [His] example now has become part of the unwritten political law of Virginia." Editor of the *Petersburg Index Appeal,* R.P. Barham, recalled that in 1901 Swanson "failed only as vicarious sacrifice to a factional cry of reform." He had been "shamefully misrepresented." While a composite of collected proposals of the previous two decades, his platform reflected a consistency that collided with the views of Ryan or Joseph F. Bryan, publisher of the recently combined *Richmond Times-Dispatch.* After Swanson announced his goals, Bryan wrote Daniel that some Democrats "have been so saturated with Populism that many who call themselves Democrats haven't the faintest idea of what fundamental principles of the party are."[41]

In his confident manner, Swanson thrust at a reporter on a winter-bright day in early February 1905 "a batch of 32 letters all of them touching on the contest." A large number were from "many of those [persons] who were opposed" to his candidacy in 1901. Montague could not realistically have expected Swanson partisans to join the governor's senatorial candidacy. Swanson, however, expended considerable effort to scour away easily revealed associations between himself and Martin. A Martin-Montague debate in July featured a blistering personal assault by the governor upon the senator that released acrimony similar to that of 1901. Swanson avoided being either a subject or a participant in these exchanges.[42]

Concern that Swanson might falter led agents of Virginia's senators to make careful observations of his campaign. In May, Martin's secretary, R.C. Kilmartin, wrote recuperating Lassiter that Swanson was "in the middle of the road and stepping high." Kilmartin did not think there was "a particle of doubt about his election." In June, a former legislator, James D. Patton, confided to Daniel, "It now looks to me that Swanson is going to be the nominee of the party." James passed additional information to Patton obtained by the former's news sources as president of the Virginia Press Association. Swanson again denied his opposition to the 1901 Virginia employer liability bill and repeatedly recalled that Gompers "has stated my record in Congress shows I have always . . . advocated legislation favorable to the working man." The candidate added, "I am standing by and with the masses, where I have always stood."[43]

Class issues did arise; the gentility of Swanson's supporters and his own gentlemanly qualities were questioned. Alexandria commonwealth attorney Crandal MacKay reissued charges of the "postal scandal" on the eve of the Swanson speech in Roanoke. Claiming Swanson lacked "delicate instincts," MacKay argued that John Sharp Williams had removed Swanson from the Postal Committee owing to his dishonesty. In an interview MacKay asserted that he fined and imprisoned more friends of Swanson than those of any other official. Allegations surfaced that the candidate had failed Montague in 1901 by not campaigning. Responding in Roanoke before a crowd, "the largest of its kind in years," Swanson countered that he elected to remain on Ways and Means rather than on the Postal Committee. He referred to Willard's negative votes on the 1901 employer liability bill and the Jim Crow passenger law. Minority leader Williams reinforced Swanson by appearing in the state to substantiate his explanation. After William's statement, the *Norfolk Virginian Pilot* considered Swanson vindicated.[44]

Winning the nomination by a majority of 42,634 votes of the 83,202 counted, Swanson led his adversaries in 71 of Virginia's 100 counties and in 10 of 23 cities. Mann and Willard each captured twenty thousand votes. The former's strength centered in prohibitionist Valley counties and his neighborhood Southside ones, especially in those precincts through which the Norfolk and Western Railway passed. Willard secured Richmond and Northern Virginia, former Funder outposts along the Potomac River, and several counties in the Southwest. Swanson held eight of the ten congressional districts, losing the Third and Eighth between the capital and Washington. With the exception of Glass's Bedford and Campbell counties, his tallies increased the closer he came to the Fifth District. By 46,991 to 36,307 votes, Martin retired Montague to a law deanship at Richmond. Having never run an election of his own, Montague suffered from a poor record with the General Assembly and ineffective use of state patronage. A superficial similarity in totals between Swanson and Martin reinforced journalistic notions concerning the presence of a powerful Martin machine.[45]

Composing the backbone of Swanson strength, his rural constituencies, many from the old Alliance and Populist areas, may have voted against Montague as much as for Martin. In the southern third of the state, Martin rode Swanson's coattails, in the middle third each received equal support, and in the northern portion Martin outpaced him. Had Swanson faced but one opponent, his margin would have surpassed Martin by at least ten thousand votes. Both men benefited from regional allies, particularly Rhea in southwestern Virginia. Flood aided Martin but contributed to Mann as well. In 1905, rather than receiving it as bounty from a Martin machine, Swanson won his election as a "man of unusual force . . . who makes and keeps friends."[46]

An active Republican since 1869 and former judge of Virginia's court of appeals, Lunsford Lewis, a native of Rockingham County, led his party's slate. The Richmond lawyer, a member of the lily-white branch, claimed the Republicans were now cleansed of the black voter while the Democrat-inspired election laws continued to bulge with "rotteness." Lewis stimulated concern among those Democrats who believed that only race had bound the party together. Glass accused Lewis of acquiescing to thirty-five years of the "unspeakable crime" of the black franchise and branded him a scalawag. Jones accused Lewis of advocating miscegenation owing to some remarks in 1877 that questioned the constitutionality of a legislative proposal prohibiting interracial marriage. Lieutenant governor candidate Ellyson scattered racially slurring pamphlets across the state. Swanson warned that a Republican victory might return the "negro as a voter," to his harm and the general distress of the state. Opening his campaign at Hanover Court House, where twenty-five years earlier he had delivered his first campaign speech, he now spoke for a program of Democratic continuity and growth, keyed to aspiring middle and lower economic classes.[47]

In the autumn campaign of 1905, Swanson received cooperation from a broad spectrum of Democrats—from Montague to such former Populists as W.H. Gravely and Calvin Luther Martin. Voting their strength, Democrats elected Swanson governor over Lewis by 83,544 to 45,975 votes, the total being some 70,000 fewer than that of the 1901 general election. Lieutenant Governor Ellyson and Attorney General William A. Anderson joined him as the primary executive officers of the state. Three fundamental challenges awaited Governor-elect Swanson: to construct viable and realistic programs to match and to fulfill his broad platform promises and campaign oratory; to command the General Assembly to appropriate action; and to survive politically the constitutionally weak governorship.[48]

5

Concur and Cooperate 1906-1910

Governor Claude Swanson conducted one of the most effective terms of executive leadership in the history of the commonwealth. Nourished by a national reform mood that some historians have labeled the Progressive Movement, Swanson utilized his organizational skills, personal attractiveness, astute politics, and a broad and flexible intelligence to realize the greater number of his campaign promises. He gave direction to the General Assembly that enacted proposals accumulating since the Readjuster era. No "swashbuckling lieutenant" of white-thatched Thomas Martin, Swanson recruited the senator's friends and minions to strengthen his own political hand. Upon the conclusion of his tenure, Swanson gained praise from Carter Glass's *Lynchburg News:* "In the discharge of an exalted trust he has earned the 'well done' of his people and that they give him without stint." In January 1910, Virginia's citizenry witnessed the phenomenon of a Virginia governor leaving office more popular than upon entry.[1]

Swanson presided over a state whose recent past was fraught with a destructive war and debilitating economic convulsions. Largely rural, Virginia experienced a restless move to the cities by whites after 1898 as urban employment opportunities reappeared, but many black Virginians apparently fled the countryside and the state. From 1890 through 1920, census reports cited an increase of 15 percent in the white population; the black counterpart grew by only 2 percent. During Swanson's governorship, four-fifths of the 1,854,000 inhabitants of the Old Dominion lived in nonurban areas, marking this decade the apex of the yeoman farmer. Virginia staples—corn, wheat, truck, tobacco, and fruit—advanced; only cotton faltered, losing to fresh Texas fields. Between 1900 and 1920, more Virginia acres were under cultivation than at any previous time.[2]

City population from 1900 to 1910 rose by 40 percent, a pace maintained except during the 1930s. Throughout the state, eight thousand firms registered with the census of 1900 and, while businesses decreased owing to combinations and momentary recession, manufactured products' value doubled by 1910 and wage earners increased by 30 percent. Agrarian attitudes and culture predominated as city slickers in yellow shoes and dark, woven suits carried rural habits into the mean streets and ranked, urban warrens. In the high noon of agrarianism, however, the urban age had dawned.[3]

After his election, Swanson enjoyed a two-week respite, added several pounds of flesh, visited Washington to conclude congressional obligations, and addressed the Elks convention in Richmond. The remainder of December he spent in Chatham, before a Christmas visit with his brother-in-law, Cunningham Hall, in the capital city. There he contacted legislators, wrote his inaugural address, and composed a personal staff that featured his campaign manager Edwin S. Reid, a close friend Pannill Rucker of Martinsville, and Ben P. Owen, Jr. Swanson's private secretary, Owen had trained in journalism, had served J. Hoge Tyler as secretary, and, most recently, had managed Swanson's campaign office in 1905. Owen used his professional associations and speaking talent to Swanson's advantage as both men cultivated Virginia editors. Favorable placement of news items and positive editorial support resulted, especially in the copy-hungry smaller journals.[4]

For his inauguration, Swanson declined "a parade or any ceremonies of consequence." Interviewed by a reporter at the state library, he admitted "private reasons for not wanting a display on that occasion." He resigned from Congress in late January and formally visited Governor Andrew Montague and legislative leaders. On February 1, 1906, he rode in a sparkling, new carriage "without flourish of trumpets" to the recently refurbished Capital. He met Montague in the state corporation commission courtroom and walked to the crowded Hall of Delegates to take the oath of office. Swanson's striking figure stirred memories of Richard F. Beirne's prediction that the young Randolph-Macon student would be governor before his hair silvered. Some observers must have noted an irony concerning Montague, as he, more round and plump than his 1901 opponent, ceded authority. Smiling and nodding, Swanson wore upon his lapel a tiny boutonniere of violets that matched those in his wife's bouquet.[5]

Following a prayer by Reverend J. Sydney Peters of Richmond's Trinity Methodist Church, Swanson in his inaugural address admitted that difficulties faced his administration, but he intended to mark it "by the moral, educational and material progress" of Virginia. In the federal legislature he learned that "the best result of legislation, the best administration of government, are obtained when the executive and legislature fully concur and cordially co-operate." He promised "to communicate with the General Assembly frequently and fully" to reduce factional disharmony and partisan politics. Government's full potential would develop natural resources, regulate railroads, sponsor immigration, rework bank regulations, control insurance corporations, increase teacher wages, emphasize primary education, imporve the school system, sponsor libraries, build highways, employ convicts on state roads, enforce pure food laws, and preserve state records. The state treasury surplus could finance many of these projects and continuing economic growth would provide additional tax revenues. After receiving from Judge Stafford J. Whittle the oath of office amid circling applause, he turned to greet the congratulatory crowd in the bright chamber. That afternoon, he and Elizabeth met officers of government, and in the evening Lieutenant Governor J. Taylor Ellyson entertained in his richly appointed home Governor and Mrs. Swanson.[6]

Richmond had grown upon hills of the James River valley and presently provided a paradox between old South tradition and new South ambition. Civil

War scars throbbed persistently in its collective memory; fresh from foundries, idealized, bronze Confederate statuary now ennobled intersections and vistas while the Confederate Soldiers Home housed many of the living comrades of the sixteen thousand buried at Oakwood Cemetery. Prospering from railroad technology, epitomized by a triple-tiered iron bridge that carried Southern, Chesapeake and Ohio, and Seaboard Air Line railways, by 1906 the city had doubled its Reconstruction population to 112,000 to become the fourth largest urban center in the South. Early extension of telephone and electric lines and the nation's first interurban electric trolley line stimulated real estate and commercial development. Opportunities among interrelated channels of lawyers, bankers, investors, wholesalers, educators, retailers, and manufacturers spawned dreams in many country youths to scheme, to grow wealthy, and to build mock colonial mansions. Riding on horseback, in a carriage, or a new snuffling automobile, meeting for meals at the Commercial or elsewhere, striding over the twelve-acre plot before the Capitol on Shackoe Hill, Swanson became a focal point of Richmond's social and commercial world.[7]

He entered an executive office little altered by the 1902 constitution. Former governor and constitutional delegate William E. Cameron defined the governor as little more than a figurehead, "a man to make speeches at tournaments and reunions, and with no power to enforce discipline upon those who are put under him." Besides appointing members of state boards, the executive nominated to the General Assembly the three state corporation commissioners and held item veto privileges of appropriation bills but lacked strong administrative powers to enforce laws. Beyond removal for misadventures, the governor had but weak control over bureau heads who could be indifferent to his wishes. In 1906, authority was decentralized and maintained so by a predominating and suspicious localism, shaped by clashing parochial attitudes, agrarian discontent, and crusty governmental doctrines. One observer wrote that, lacking substantial reform, to operate effectively "a political boss or clique" must arise to dominate the government.[8]

A foundling home for future congressmen, judges, and other state officials, the Virginia General Assembly since the 1880s had biennially prevailed over governors. Recently having shackled an impolitic Montague, it brimmed with ambitious local politicians, conscious of their prerogatives and powers. Even Senator Martin's senatorial elections at their hands had been difficult and punishing affairs. Emphasizing seniority, elected to staggered four-year terms until 1907, the forty-member Senate contained nearly independent political barons, legates of dozens of local political enclaves. Composed of one hundred representatives, the House of Delegates bubbled in an exuberant, frothy manner, an untutored democracy that required firm handling and carefully structured, restraining parliamentary devices. Few legislators had long-term plans or projects and most were tied to momentary issues; their world view derived from the great matrix of Virginia white Anglo-Saxon Protestantism.[9]

The new governor eagerly embraced necessary politics. During the autumn of 1905 and before the General Assembly convened, he searched for available entries into the legislative pit. He interviewed influential members and drew them into a closer, personal relationship by appealing to their particular inter-

ests. Former state senator Bland Massie christened the tall governor the
"gamecock," the rooster being the Democratic symbol and representative of
Swanson's plucky ways and partisan Democratic stance. His personality held
sufficient breadth to be comfortable in a drawing room or in a tobacco warehouse, but he drew his emerging legislative strength from the loyalty of the rural,
"country" delegates.[10]

Swanson influenced the 1906 House of Delegates to an exceptional degree
through a new Speaker. A consistent opponent of Martin, John F. Ryan of
Loudoun County retired in 1904 after nearly a decade in office. Son of a former
Speaker and present appeals court judge, William D. Cardwell of Hanover
County defeated Fairfax County's Robert E. Lee, Jr., Montague's former aide-
de-camp and, despite support from Henry D. Flood, John Churchman of
Staunton. A friend from Swanson's college days and participant in his gubernatorial campaign, the tyro Speaker held several priorities that influenced
committee appointments. In naming chairmen, he followed internal hierarchical
patterns and subordinated ouside influences. He gratified first senior members
with records of close association with Cardwell and Swanson, then newly
arrived persons who displayed influential political credentials and, finally,
Cardwell's opponents and their supporters. Illustrative of the process, Flood's
brother-in-law, first termer Richard E. Byrd of Frederick County, desired the
chairmanship of General Laws, but Cardwell "could not refuse to give [Edwin
P.] Cox [of Richmond City] the position." Cox "ranked first" and had been "a
very warm supporter" of Cardwell. At Swanson's suggestion, Cardwell awarded
Byrd the Judiciary chairmanship, which bumped Lee from the Committee,
creating a flap that senior members and other committee assignments mollified.[11]

But Byrd found difficulty in securing judiciary appointments for persons
favored by Flood. After district revisions, the congressman preferred Edwin
Hubbard of Buckingham County but Bennett T. Gordon of Nelson received
legislative approval. Owing to their role in the "recent battle for life contest,"
two Swanson candidates won appointments to eight-year terms: William W.
Moffet of Salem and Claggett B. Jones of King and Queen County. Cardwell
retired unexpectedly in April 1907, and, while Martin toured Europe, Flood
urged Byrd to announce his candidacy for the speakership. During the legislative primaries in May, the brothers-in-law contacted district judges Walter
Watson, Jones, and others to align their local delegate candidates for Byrd.
Deputy insurance commissioner Jacob N. Brenamen judged Byrd's hopes also
dependent upon unopposed, incumbent legislators. Promises were exchanged
and, although seniority was a factor, the great majority of these legislators either
maintained or improved their committee assignments in the next Assembly. Five
months before it convened, Byrd correctly predicted his election.[12]

The Cardwell and Byrd elections resulted from cautious politicking, not a
"word" going forth to some "tribe" of Martin legislators. Furthermore, residues
of bitterness over these speakership maneuvers could produce for Swanson
legislative irritations that might blister normally smooth-handed manipulation
of the delegates by the leadership. Flood's district had produced a speaker
candidate in Churchman, and Robert W. Withers of Nansemond made a

determined run. While they increased their legislative influence, both Flood and Byrd suffered aftereffects. In addition to seniority, internal trades, external pressure, and factors as frivolous as alphabetization of membership lists determined many committee assignments. The most powerful committees, however, provided calm harbors to offset tidal changes among the delegates. In both sessions of Swanson's governorship, despite different Speakers, the same men sat on the Finance Committee and kept their collective fingers on the state's purse strings. Chaired by Alfred M. Bowman of Salem and with a predominance of membership from beyond the Blue Ridge Mountains, the committee welcomed in 1908 only two new members who represented the same districts as their predecessors. Among its membership, Swanson held personal associations with his classmate from Virginia Agricultural and Mechanical College, John J. Owen of Prince Edward County, and Pittsylvania County's Samuel Wilson. [13]

The state Senate tottered toward transition. During the 1906 session, Richmond lawyer and director of the Chesapeake and Ohio Railroad Henry T. Wickham had been Senate pro tem since 1897. In 1907, his rural constituents denied him reelection in part owing to his overt involvement in railroad matters. Another senior senator, Democratic floor leader George S. Shackleford of Orange, chaired in a frequently independent manner the Privileges and Elections Committee. He, too, did not return in 1908. Further uncertainties resulted from a new constitutional requirement that each senator face election in 1907. Flood nervously wrote Swanson of potential defeats for legislative friends. "The first thing we know we will have the Virginia Senate organized in the interest of the opposition." Soothing him and revealing his detailed knowledge of legislative races, Swanson refused to be frightened by the "opposition." As governor, he dampened many factional fires in both houses, and, to the tenacious factionalist Flood, he replied, "The situation in the state is very good." He traveled often across the Old Dominion and scattered letters encouraging favorable election results for "our friends". Twenty-four new senators took seats in 1908; sixteen incumbents returned. Reluctant Staunton lawyer and land developer Edward Echols, a former lieutenant governor, narrowly won, over Frederick W. Sims of Louisa County, the pro tem position to lead a body containing many members who were "strangers". Echols reported, "I am ignorant of any views or ideas they may entertain."[14]

Returning from Europe, Martin supported for the chairmanship of the Democratic caucus William Hodges Mann, a 1909 gubernatorial aspirant. Martin and Flood believed incorrectly that his ascension would allow them "to organize the Senate" as they chose. Urban elements and those senators dissatisfied with the Nottoway County lawyer's prohibition proclivities fought his candidacy. A labor representative, E.C. Folkes, proposed unavailingly to reorganize the Senate along lines of "new men versus old." Swanson maintained a covered position, but Mann eagerly placated his former opponent by placing upon the Steering Committee George T. Rison, a "man from his county." A new committee on nominations appeared, chaired by Echols, with Mann, Rison, T. Ashby Wickham of Henrico County, and forty-year-old John A. Lesner of Norfolk County who, in addition to an interest in road building, was president of the Virginia Liquor Dealers Association. The Finance and Banking Committee divided; Saxon Holt chaired the new Insurance and Banking Committee and George B. Keezell became Finance chairman. Chairman in 1901 of the Swanson for Governor Club in Newport News, merchant-banker Holt promoted better roads, improved education, and opposition to prohibition. Judged as "possibly the most influential member of the senate," Keezell represented populous Rockingham County, and Swanson counseled him on steering favored bills through the legislature. Another Tidewater politician and close Swanson associate matched Holt in influence: William W. Sale of Norfolk, who in 1908 replaced Shackleford as floor leader and chaired the Privileges and Elections Committee.[15]

Swanson's relationship with Charles T. Lassiter exemplified how he obtained cooperation and concurrence with an individual legislator. Brother of Congressman Francis R. Lassiter, the younger man's interest in better roads originated in part from enlightened self-interest—his family possessed quarries that produced crushed stone and cut granite spalls. He had entered civic activities as chairman of the Petersburg Roads and Streets Committee in a city eager to build "farm to city" highways. Lassiter joined Swanson in 1905 not only because he was his "personal and political friend," but also because he had put Lassiter's "city and section under profound political obligations." In February 1905, Lassiter helped found the Virginia Good Roads Association in Danville to expound advantages of competent highway construction and to induce "the Federal Government . . . to contribute aid for public roads." Lassiter knew of county efforts at road building and wanted more information and expertise through state-supported topographical surveys and engineering advice. Elected to the state Senate in 1905, he received from Swanson an invitation to meet before he wrote his inaugural address. "In reference to public roads . . . you seem interested . . . and well informed." Lassiter and Delegate Withers of Suffolk forwarded the governor-elect drafts of road bills defeated in 1904 and anticipated a "heart to heart talk" so that they could "agree on their final form." The new governor welcomed these eager boosters and incorporated their reform energy.[16]

Since the 1890s, Swanson had become accomplished in funding post roads from federal sources and knowledgeable of Department of Agriculture road-building experiments. Created in 1905, the Federal Bureau of Public Roads was an information agency Swanson also consulted "before determining the best policy in reference to roads" in Virginia. Not only had agrarians, commercial interests, and urban developers turned to more permanent roads as an answer to growing transportation necessities, but the railroads agreed as well. Roanoke City resident, Illinois-born Lucius E. Johnson, president of the Norfolk and Western Railroad, warned in 1904 that "railroads . . . have about reached the limit of economy" in extending feeder lines. Public thoroughfares must carry "the products of the farms, mines and forests" to existing railheads. The matter, attested the gold Democrat, of "good roads" seemed to "rest upon the Federal Government." Gathering local reformers and various interest groups, Swanson directed road legislation through the 1906 Assembly that created a state highway commission and the office of commissioner, permitted counties to expand issuance of bonds, and employed convicts for road construction.[17]

Civil engineers composed the new four-person commission. Three came, respectively, from the Virginia Military Institute, Virginia Agricultural and Mechanical College, and the University of Virginia faculties. As the commissioner and fourth member, Swanson selected Phillip St. Julien Wilson, a thirty-nine-year Powhatan County native, graduate of Virginia Military Institute, and Richmond assistant engineer. Despite continuing friction, the commission began to centralize and rationalize Virginia's road building, increasing state influence over localities. In the autumn of 1907, preparing for additional legislation in the 1908 session, Swanson invited Bowman, chairman of the House Finance Committee, Withers, Charles Lassiter, and "one or two other leaders of the two Houses" to formulate "a bill looking to direct appropriation of money from the state treasury in the interest of good roads." Swanson specifically favored the "New Jersey plan of the state appropriating a sum of money contingent upon the county raising a similar sum." Forcing the issue and giving it coherence, Swanson emphasized that over $1 million in taxes eroded annually from Virginia dirt roads. Making the first direct appropriation of Virginia revenues for road building, the Assembly established a $250,000 annual fund to be matched by county expenditures and supervised by Commissioner Wilson. The governor utilized his office to publicize road conferences. The most notable occurred in 1909 in Richmond, attended by Virginians from town, hamlet, and cove, presided over by president of the Virginia Good Roads Association Charles Lassiter and joined by Virginia's Automobile Association leader John Lesner.[18]

Postponement until 1908 of major state contributions to road construction resulted from a primary emphasis given schools by Swanson. In 1906, school reformers from the Cooperative Education Association, newly elected Superintendent of Public Instruction Eggleston, and individual legislators seeking popularity and public school boosters produced fifty-two different bills that crowded the session's agenda. Swanson cut through this tangle by insisting that "the first great need of this state" was the "improvement of our primary schools." Thereafter followed enactments authorizing local school trustees to borrow up to $3,000 from state funds, consolidation of one-room schools into more substantial buildings, doubling state primary teachers' salary supplement from $200,000 to $400,000, and increasing the number of traveling libraries. The Mann County High School Act provided $50,000 in matching funds for construction of rural high schools that complemented urban high school growth. By 1910, state appropriation reached $500,000 and its universities raised their admission standards to require high school standing. The Carnegie Foundation for the Advancement of Teaching reported that "probably no educational development in any State . . . is more remarkable." Lobbyists such as William and Mary professor Bruce R. Payne and Superintendent Eggleston made fundamental contributions, and Protestant leaders encouraged the General Assembly as well. Methodist minister James Cannon, Jr., took pride in advising Presbyterians Mann and Eggleston.[19]

Swanson and his legislative leaders harnessed frequently divisive forces of rural localism in advancing public education by requiring matching funds, publicizing surrounding areas success, and incorporating local patrons. North

Carolina-born and recently installed president of the University of Virginia Edwin A. Alderman believed Swanson and the "present regime" intended to "excel Montague and his regime in devotion to the [educational] work." Unlike Montague, they would "appeal to one of the rooted characteristics of our people, namely, local pride." Earlier efforts by "outsiders" of the Southern Education Board had mishandled local prejudices and raised racial hackles, and its leaders had assumed partisan positions for Montague in the 1905 senatorial primary. One educator recalled Swanson's successful tactics as the "term 'free school' was forgotten. People everywhere talked with pride of ownership of 'our schools.' "[20]

"Surpassed by no state board in the union . . . with stronger powers," the Board of Education served well Swanson's intentions. Despite Eggleston's claim that annual $200,000 campaigns by publishers produced "indirect and . . . direct forms of bribery," the board persisted in sponsoring multiple book lists for selection by individual school boards. In February 1906, two new ex officio members, Swanson and board chairman Eggleston, joined incumbent Attorney General William Anderson. Also, three experienced educators were elected for four-year terms by the state Senate from a list of faculty furnished by the individual boards of trustees of the six state-supported colleges. Once constituted, the board then named two more members, a county and city superintendent. Swanson would remove the board's tendency to bow to local authority and harmonize it with the legislature by requiring each educator candidate to reveal to the Senate his attitude toward a single book list; the governor and senators would then winnow holdovers and fashion a new board.[21]

By March 1907, Swanson controlled the board with Eggleston, J.L. Jarman of the State Female Normal School at Farmville, and H. Beverly Tucker of Virginia Military Institute standing with him on most issues and superintendent appointments. These votes permitted selection of S.R. McChesney of Bristol, nephew of William F. Rhea, and M.M. Lynch of Frederick County as new superintendent members. Louisa native Charles W. Kent of the University of Virginia followed more slowly. Restructuring required the removal of J.T. West of Norfolk County and multiple book list adovcate E.C. "Ned" Glass, Lynchburg superintendent and Carter's brother, leaving the Glasses "pretty sore." Flood had pushed Beverly Tucker, a devotee of the multiple list, but, upon discovering the "new test oath" of the single list, he ordered state Senate clerk Joseph Button to destroy Tucker's original statement and substitute a single list declaration. Tucker's conversion arrived in time. Once the board's majority favored a single list, Attorney General Anderson did also. Swanson from time to time used local politicians to nudge board members and, in 1908, a single list for primary schools was adopted, followed two years later by one for the high schools. One estimate considered that book costs were reduced by 30 percent.[22]

Suspicion continued toward centralizing authority in Richmond. In 1908, the state Senate postponed indefinitely a bill mandating board approval of school building plans, but, citing benefits to pupil health and eyesight, leaders managed to require board certification of new schools' sanitary features. To pool funds and hire full-time professional supervisors, the same legislature grudgingly granted authority to the board to select one superintendent for two or more smaller counties. In this "most terrific fight" faced by the board, the Assembly conceded owing to Swanson's "wisdom and experiece [that] moderated hasty action." Eggleston recalled: "He stood by us to the end."[23]

In June 1909, after a closed-door, three-day session that admitted "delegations from all parts of the state" to plead their case, the board announced superintendent selections. Postponing a dozen critical appointments, its choices revealed "many incumbents fallen by the wayside." Younger, better-educated persons, attracted by increased salaries, were appointed and, as in Richmond, they were not always endorsed by local school boards. The published list awoke "terrific howls." Accusations that he played politics with public schools fell about the governor, but a week later the remaining positions were filled. Echols and new Commissioner of Wildlife and Fisheries McDonald Lee failed to secure their choices, but, descending from Cub Run, Keezell had his way. Finally, one appointee resigned owing to local protest; a Norfolk man had been placed over Newport News schools and he received another assignment. Sixteen new school districts were created, consolidating small counties and towns under professionally qualified superintendents.[24]

Edwin Alderman praised Swanson: "You and the State Board of Education have done one of the largest pieces of constructive educational work during the past week that has been accomplished in any Southern State in the last decade . . . [by improving the] supervisory phase of educational life in Virginia one hundred per cent." Swanson had "set an example and given a model to the people of the need for expert supervision." Appreciating "difficulties, practical worries and troubles of such a revolution," Alderman prophesied, "You and those who believe in you . . . will be as proud, if not prouder of your share in this thing than in almost any single act of your career." He credited the "enormous power" of the board that Swanson, he knew, had reinforced to exercise such authority.[25]

In 1907, Swanson had argued that "the success of every school is dependent upon the teacher. . . . It is folly to spend thousands of dollars in the erection of a handsome building to be occupied by worthless teachers." Improved salaries to attract college-trained instructors and summer normals at the University of Virginia and elsewhere enhanced instruction. At Harrisonburg, Fredericksburg, and eventually Radford, teacher training schools were established. To build the facility at Harrisonburg, the other two institutions represented necessary political compromises. An agricultural high school in each congressional district was authorized and a scientific farmer from Burkville, T.O. Sandy and a staff were hired to direct farm demonstration work for white and black children. The latter development followed at Eggleston's request a conference with Seeman Knapp, a New Yorker and Department of Agriculture pioneer in southern rural education. Also at the meeting were Alderman, S.C. Mitchell, and Agricultural Commissioner George Koiner. Two other representatives of influential families were present, publisher John Stuart Bryan and Mary Cooke Branch Munford whose husband had been an old Swanson acquaintance from his early lawyer days in Chatham. The 1908 legislature broadened availability of rural libraries and inaugurated a teacher pension fund. It passed the Williams Building Act, which permitted a more liberal interpretation of local school board financing powers and earlier cited state regulations upon school construction. While acquiring the College of William and Mary, the General Assembly provided state colleges with increased appropriations. As Swanson appointed trustees, he experienced campus politics as well. For example, in naming a new superintendent for V.M.I., he received heavy pressure from alumni and regional interests. He masterminded a financially viable *Virginia Journal of Education* and selected a qualified editor, J.A.C. Chandler, and a reliable board of directors.[26]

Persistent discrimination appeared in dispensing state educational funds. Many southern educators considered manual or technical training as proper for blacks along with the restricted suffrage. In Virginia, had that vote remained active, a more positive governmental response would have issued from such an accommodating politician as Swanson. In an earlier, more democratic age, the Readjusters attempted to answer not only white but black demands for educational improvement. Now Swanson pursued a paternalistic approach and, while he and the General Assembly refused separation of appropriations based upon tax receipts paid by each race, they left fund apportionment "according to the best judgment of the [local] board." Generally, the dual, segregated system provided vastly inferior black facilities; black teachers, however, may have been better prepared than their white counterparts.[27]

Swanson skirted racial issues to gain school improvements. He disagreed with Reverend John E. White of Atlanta who proposed a southern interstate racial commission to study and recommend policies to improve black-white relations. Factors in the governor's decision were established legal segregation, a general quiet along racial frontiers, and an apprehension that such a commission "would precipitate . . . a discussion and a division" on the race question that might provide an "excuse for Federal authority to intervene." An equitable settlement "cannot be accomplished all at once, but only through years of patient, persistent, and patriotic endeavor." The burden was heavy, leadership skittish, and time and history worked against black children who would grow old before adequate educational adjustments were initiated. State sponsorship, however, of road improvements, rural libraries, demonstration education, public health, industrial regulations, penal reform, and railroad rate reductions benefited black Virginians as well as white.[28]

Remembering tension-fraught and sometimes bloody racial politics of the previous thirty-five years, Swanson also avoided heated rhetoric along the racial frontier. Public passions were still easily stirred. During his governorship, a feuding family in his former congressional district invaded a courtroom and shot the judge. In his first two years in office no lynchings occurred. In the last two, a mob provoked by alleged sexual outrages victimized one black and two white males. On at least two other occasions, prompt action by Swanson prevented similar tragedies. In August 1907, stirred by pleas of local authorities to avoid a race riot in Onancock on the Eastern Shore, he entrained from Richmond to Old Point Comfort within two hours and took a police launch across Chesapeake Bay. Arriving at noon the next day, he ordered in state militia and addressed 200 restless citizens from the porch of the local hotel. He vowed to use judicial procedures and to "stay a week, a month, or even spend the summer . . . to keep the peace." Order was restored. While not ideal, racial conditions had improved beyond the previous two decades.[29]

By law, Swanson stood more distant from the state corporation commission than from the Board of Education. The governor appointed members with state Senate approval to the potentially powerful commission. After some difficulty, upon its creation in 1902, Montague had first nominated commissioners to staggered six-year terms: Chairman Beverly T. Crump, a lawyer from Richmond; Henry Fairfax, a former legislator and engineer from Loudoun; and Henry C. Stuart, a millionaire land developer and cattle baron from Wytheville. Author of the constitutional article creating the commission, Caperton Braxton evaluated these men as representatives of groups and individuals unfriendly to the regulatory concept. In 1904, the commission placed tangible value of railroads and canals at $63,269,632, thereby increasing state tax receipts from $277,329 to $583,406. City and county revenues from these sources rose to $658,598.[30]

The 1906 General Assembly disagreed with the commission's evaluations. They discovered that federal authorities estimated Virginia railway property worth $211,315,000, a figure more than three times that of the commission. By combining various taxes, the commission replied that the railroads paid taxes on an adjusted base of $164,461,977, or 70 percent of the federal appraisal. Probably at Swanson's behest and noting that these corporations were publicly chartered monopolies, Attorney General Anderson petitioned for an increased evaluation. Citing unstable business conditions and unknown effects of propsed new rate schedules, the commission in October 1907 refused to alter its original estimates.[31]

By then the commission faced massive legislative displeasure. In 1906, the General Assembly had established a Bureau of Insurance and selected state Senate clerk Button as first commissioner. Since 1896, the former editor and secretary of the state Democratic executive committee had chaired Flood's Tenth District committee. Ascribing to its constitutional authority to regulate the companies, the commission insisted that it appoint the insurance officer. Chairman Crump held ideological objections to the bureau and personally disapproved of Button. Stuart and Joseph Willard, whom Montague had appointed to replace Fairfax, agreed. In August 1906, the Court of Appeals upheld the legislature; Button gained an appointment that put "the other people in the hole."[32]

The commission continued to resist legislative interference. Despite a rising demand for further railroad regulation and Swanson's campaign and inaugural pledges to secure "just and reasonable rates" for disadvantaged localities, the commission moved slowly. Emboldened by the governor's leadership, the 1906 legislature passed the Churchman Act, which placed Virginia in the vanguard of southern states in lowering passenger rates. Drafted by Delegate John Churchman of Augusta County and Senator Camm Patteson of Buckingham County, the legislation that Swanson signed required the commission to establish rates for intrastate passenger service and instructed the railroads to offer ticket books for five hundred miles or more at a rate of two cents per mile. The Atlantic Coast Line Railroad refused to obey the law and Anderson initiated court proceedings. The railroads' lawyers assigned the commission as the sole constitutional authority to establish transportation rates and accused the legislature of ignoring the federal Fourteenth Amendment relating to due process. Also the commissioners refused to concede to the legislature and, trying to avoid any appearance of connivance with the railroads, considered the reduced rate tickets as unconstitutional as well. In November 1906, the Court of Appeals agreed with both the railroads and the commission and set aside the Churchman Act. The designers of the new constitution had apparently succeeded in placing regulatory power apart from popular opinion.[33]

The commission did undertake an inquiry concerning the two-cents-per-mile rate and expended months in debate over uniform charges. In 1905, Swanson had demanded freight schedules that would erase intrastate discrepancies between rail shipments east or west and those north or south. Lacking coherence, the prevailing system affected adversely the Fifth Congressional District. Entering into the rate maze, one investigator discovered great difficulty in "determining just what the exact rate on a specific article between points was." In April 1907, the commission proclaimed rates that were somewhat lower and made freight schedules uniform. Some rumors circulated that Commissioner Stuart had arranged rates to benefit his cattle business. New passenger schedules proposed a maximum rate of two cents per mile for the ten most financially secure roads and a graduated scale of up to three and one-half cents a mile for the remainder.[34]

Evidence developed in 1905 that Chairman Crump held interest in a company that drafted charters for the commission's clients. Delegate Richard Byrd chaired a legislative investigating committee that recommended dismissal, but a minority report critical only of Crump's conduct passed, owing, Byrd believed, "to the tremendous pressure on the part of Judge Crump's friends." In April 1907, contemporaneous with the publication of the new freight and passenger scales, Crump resigned. Swanson's role is obscure, but, given his later actions, he actively favored rate reduction and probably gave direction to the General Assembly's censure. He now prepared to make his first commission nomination.[35]

Swanson named District Judge Robert W. Prentis of Suffolk, a decision that filled columns of newspapers with comment. A long-sequestered promise also surfaced when Swanson admitted his first choice to be William F. Rhea, who had refused, claiming business conflicts. Some persons whispered that Martin and other Rhea friends had influenced Swanson, but, more importantly, regional politics also prevented Rhea's acceptance. Commissioner Stuart resided near Rhea's home in Bristol. The General Assembly accepted Prentis who became chairman, and the passenger rate controversy continued.[36]

The commission under Prentis mandated schedules for lower passenger rates effective July 1907. Facing renewed railroad objections, Swanson strengthened the courage of the commissioners, Attorney General Anderson, and special counsel Braxton at a two-hour meeting on July 21. Five days later he added Senator John W. Daniel to the Virginia legal team. The railroads obtained a federal injunction enjoining action until the bench could rule upon the constitutionality of the new rates. Fleeing a heat wave, Swanson received this news while on Chincoteague Island. Returning quickly to Richmond and primed for battle, he demanded that the commission publish its rates and announced he would "exercise all the powers possessed by me as governor" to ascertain that the "right and the dignity of the state [would] be maintained." From various hollows and hills of Virginia's political landscape echoed support for the governor who threatened a special legislative session. Counter moves by the roads, formulated by Alfred P. Thom, now general counsel of the Southern Railroad, included a petition to Martin "over the phone." Former West Virginia senator and presently railroad lawyer Charles J. Faulkner wrote his nephew Flood to restrain Swanson, who had been "trying to gain a little popularity and to make capital by very wild declarations of what ought to be done."[37]

Swanson received similar corporate appeals but refused to retreat. After a day-long session that lengthened into night, a resolute governor, state officials, and disgruntled railroad lawyers agreed to a Swanson memorandum that required the roads implement the commission's mandate on or before October 1, awaiting a court ruling. At least one legal authority labeled Swanson's proposal as prudent, permitting the companies to petition for rate adjustments should a ruling in their favor be reached. Eventually, in a decision "very much involved and far from satisfactory either to the railroads or the state," the Supreme Court ordered a new hearing before the commission. In 1909, after a diligent investigation, the commission settled upon passenger fares of two and one-half cents per mile and allowed coupon books to be sold for two cents per mile. Both freight and passenger rates by 1910 had been reduced and tax revenues increased owing in part to Swanson's actions. Virginians had enjoyed nearly two years of reduced rates, a situation that realized the intention of the Churchman Act of 1906. The 1909 decision had been reached with a majority of members being Swanson's appointments.[38]

Commissioner Stuart resigned in 1908 and, by choosing Rhea, Swanson triggered a partisan and factional uproar. Republican Senator John C. Noel of Lee County accused the Bristol politician, now a Richmond resident, of "nearly everything possible in the political calendar." Led by the *Richmond News Leader's* denunciation of Rhea as "an unscrupulous politician," the capital press heightened Noel's charges. In the investigative circus that followed, witnesses included a reluctant Stuart, Rhea, and Swanson, who would "stake the future" of his administration "on Judge Rhea's ability." As one journalistic cliché summarized, Speaker Byrd handled Stuart so roughly he "set Richmond agog." A majority opinion recommended appointment while Richmond's Ashby Wickham authored a negative minority report. In a commotion-filled joint session, the General Assembly sustained the governor and his nominee by eighty-six votes to forty-six. Opposed legislators included twenty-three Democrats, some of whom were outraged at Rhea's record, others represented other candidates, and sixteen lived between the James and Potomac rivers in Jones's congressional district. Localism, gubernatorial aspirations, and Democratic factionalism had driven to a marked degree oratorical winds, but railroad interests may have encouraged the debate. Flood alerted county newspaper editors to offset the Richmond press and counseled Swanson to "take some [similar] action." As in the Judge Whittle case in 1901, Swanson had again exhibited a loyalty to political allies. Rhea served until 1925 on the commission and, as is frequently the rule, yet another partisan politician proved to be a competent judge.[39]

After the Rhea affair, noting the legislative authority of the commission, Swanson favored a proposal for popular election of commissioners: "In all free countries legislative bodies . . . are elected. I believe this is best for Virginia". The reduced electorate could "safely be trusted." The state Senate accepted election but it failed by two votes in the House of Delegates. The governor also approved and may have initiated a legislative investigation designed to remove Judge John W.G. Blackstone. A close associate of Martin, Blackstone had been reversed in numerous decisions by the Court of Appeals and behaved personally in a questionable manner. In the Onancock affair of August 1907 Blackstone had denounced the governor's actions and the "boy soldiers" fulfilling the mission. Swanson responded curtly, and petitions arrived in the legislature seeking Blackstone's removal. After a publicized hearing, the General Assembly removed him despite some dissent by a few senators and Noel's observation that Blackstone's fate resulted from his "audacity to criticize Governor Swanson." After a dazzling denunciation by Byrd that the state librarian had sold "some of the most valuable manuscripts that the State" had owned and had pocketed the proceeds, the library board dismissed the incumbent in July 1907, hiring forty-three-year-old Hampden-Sydney professor Henry Read McIlwaine, a Johns Hopkins University graduate. Swanson also reorganized the Eastern State Hospital at Williamsburg, as "perfect disorder and chaos" threatened.[40]

The General Assembly of 1908 continued systemization of state services. Augmenting a campaign to establish standards and increased appropriations for poor relief, child welfare, state prisons, mental health care, and epileptics, Superintendent William F. Drewry of Central State Prison at Petersburg proposed successfully to the legislature the creation of the Board of Charities and Corrections. Following a meeting with Hastings H. Hart of the Russell Sage Foundation, who displayed for the inquiring governor "the splendid purposes of the legislation," Swanson appointed an informed board and resisted office seekers to name as its secretary Reverend Joseph Thomas Mastin, director of the Virginia Methodist Conference Orphanage. Concurrently, an overhaul of public health agencies produced a new state board of health, designed to centralize through Richmond various county efforts, and directed by Enion G. Williams, a brother-in-law of Charles Lassiter. The state also constructed hospitals and sanitariums for epileptics, tuberculosis victims, and blind, deaf, and mute Virginians. Strict regulations for cocaine were proclaimed, and electrocution was substituted for hanging as capital punishment. Professor W.P. Saunders of Virginia Polytechnic Institute, brother of the Fifth District congressman, became dairy commissioner. Requiring that federal sanitary standards be followed, Swanson ordered Saunders to indict reluctant bakery owners who failed to meet them. In Richmond, he joined the efforts of W.T. Sedgewick, the Civic Improvement League, and labor unions to better city sanitation facilities. Not since the Readjuster era had Virginia's elected leaders been so responsive to social concerns.[41]

Swanson had gathered nearly every advowson available to the governor's office to structure a responsive legislature and bureaucracy. Until midnight or later in the mansion, he evaluated during Assembly sessions proposed legislation and so influenced its final form to his satisfaction that he did not veto an enactment. He used social occasions and dinners to advance his legislative agenda and expanded greatly his contacts with the socially prominent. Yet, as the *Charlottesville Daily Progress* observed, at his term's conclusion he was "less spoiled than any man in public life." The newspaper hailed him as "plain, approachable, direct and positive, fair and just, without haughtiness or show." A Swanson legislative address revealed his ties to "country" legislators. Upon return of a committee to inform the governor that the Assembly stood prepared to receive him, its spokesman brushed aside a decorum-conscious doorkeeper, waved his hand at the Speaker of the House of Delegates and bellowed "Hi, Thar, Mister Speaker. We just seen Claude and he said it was all right and he'd be down in a minute." Swanson's authority within the legislatue led Speaker Byrd to admit that Swanson was "in complete control of legislation here and especially financial legislation. [Finance chairmen] Bowman and Keezell do nothing without his consent. . . . They and the Governor have apportioned out the [Treasury] surplus." Inescapably, the legislative progeny of the 1906 and 1908 General Assembly carried Swanson's imprimature.[42]

During his four-year term, Swanson's personal life featured short trips to Chatham and retreats to the valley or to coastal resorts to disengage from politics. In the summer of 1906, he could not rest in Swansonville, "being called back" to the capital. He anticipated an autumn visit with his seventy-seven-year-old father and attending sisters. Swanson asked them to "see that Papa has every possible comfort [and] luxury . . . he desires. Send the bills to me and I will pay them. Don't let him want." Swanson also spoke at the Jamestown Tercentennial celebration at Norfolk and his speech on Virginia was widely distributed. He convinced Washington bureaucrats to build a federal demonstration highway that served as a main artery to the exposition grounds. He sent funds to his sisters to pay the expenses of their Jamestown trip. Both Swansons were alert to opportunists who might manipulate a friendship for unfair advantage; one of Elizabeth's female escorts was carefully investigated as to her reputation and intentions. After the 1908 legislative session, Swanson took in Chatham his first vacation of any length while in office. During 1909, Elizabeth suffered from tonsillitis, which reduced her social activities. Swanson continued to invest in stocks and real estate, on occasion teaming with Flood, Flood's nephew Harry Byrd, and others to purchase warehouse property in Washington by jointly borrowing $75,000.[43]

In January 1910, he addressed the General Assembly for the last time before the inaugural of his successor Mann. No substantial increase in taxation had occurred but revenues during his last two years had exceeded by $916,000 those of his first two. The "expenditure made for progressive policies have more than paid for themselves." State debt had been significantly reduced. He listed schools, roads, and the first modern geological survey of the state as part of the government's contributions to prosperity. He noted a continuing lack of uniformity in taxation as each locality determined its assessments that produced uneven state revenues. His office had not improved, in his mind, state regulation of banks. While Virginia was one of the few states that derived any "considerable revenue" from income taxes, Swanson as one of his last acts endorsed a proposed federal income tax. Answering some complaints that the state treasury would encounter a $250,000 deficit, he contended that the "enormous increase in the cost of living" and a $100,000 excess in operations of the courts had caused a temporary dislocation. No member of the Finance Committees was recommending cutbacks of the new projects. Concluding before a standing ovation, he summarized that it was not "either the wish or to the interest of the people of Virginia to check the splendid progress the state is making along educational, moral and material developments." Superintendent Eggleston testified that many of the education achievements "would not have been possible of accomplishment" without him.[44]

On January 27, 1910, the General Assembly of Virginia presented to the Swansons a silver water set amid a scene, according to one journalist, that "stirred the souls" of those present, leaving the governor "much affected by the presentation." The *Norfolk Virginian Pilot* assessed his accomplishments: "He has failed in no case to give zealous attention to his public duties. . . . Virginia will be fortunate if all the governors to come . . . should measure up to the official standard he has achieved." Similar praise bubbled from the Richmond press, the *Roanoke Times,* and other newspapers across the Commonwealth.[45]

6

The Latest Successful Comeback 1906-1911

Concluding his gubernatorial term, Claude Swanson faced a recent Virginia political habit that precluded governors from additional elected office. Few Virginians expected, however, the vital and adroit politician to retire to squiredom in Pittsylvania County. Journalists speculated that Swanson might be appointed to the state corporation commission, take a "trip of four months to Europe," or devote "time to his private affairs." A more realistic conjecture placed Swanson in the House of Representatives. Expressing no interest in a commission chair, he declined to discuss a renewed congressional career. In the Fifth District, associates anticipated his return to a House seat while being groomed for the U.S. Senate.[1]

In 1906, circuit court judge Edward W. Saunders of Franklin County had succeeded Swanson, but was too hard pressed with problems of voter registration and payment of capitation taxes to defend himself against Republican opposition. By April 1907, impolitic Saunders had "made a bad bull in his treatment of James, Reid and others of the boys in the Fifth." To bolster him, a redistricting bill placed contrary Floyd County in Carter Glass's underpopulated district. Saunders won by a margin of ninety votes in 1908. Officially, he stated that district Republicans were "awake and vigilant," but privately his friends complained that Swanson partisans withheld votes because "returns came in slowly and the election . . . was in doubt for several days." While Swanson made "speeches at every part he could reach," the Richmond press speculated that Saunder's narrow margins would allow Swanson an easy return to his old seat. The *Richmond News Leader* admitted that he carried "many of the republicans . . . when he was a candidate for Congress." Rorer James would welcome his candidacy in 1910, having "been trying to whoop [Saunders] in the past two elections" with diminishing results.[2]

Swanson had also considered succeeding John W. Daniel, nor was he bound to concede Thomas Staples Martin another election. A binding factor in Democratic politics for fifteen years, Daniel had displeased disfranchisers in the 1901 constitutional convention because he had been "willing to do no effective thing on Suffrage." In 1904, gaining a fourth term and still popular, he turned his attention to his generation's essential experience, the Civil War, and conjectured that he "had largely thrown his life away by being" in politics. In Lynchburg, he continued to note a "growing feeling against him in his own county. . . . The question asked is 'What has Daniel done?' " Swanson encouraged him to defend his flanks and backed Don P. Halsey against a dissident state senator, A. Frank Thomas. Swanson agreed with Henry D. Flood that if Daniel "lost his home District he would certainly have opposition in the [1909] Senatorial primary." Halsey won, but Thomas continued to harass Daniel.[3]

The governor's relationship with the battle-lamed Daniel may have been closer than with any other contemporary politician. In October 1906, he wrote, "I feel towards you an affection almost [of that] entertained for my father, and you can call on me freely and fully." In the summer of 1909, sixty-eight-year-old Daniel won renomination and, in January 1910, was reelected by the legislature for a fifth term beginning in March 1911. In his middle sixties, Martin faced another election in 1911. Swanson's successor might well appoint the next Virginia senator.[4]

As early as 1906, regional candidates mulled over the Democratic gubernatorial primary three years distant. Nottoway County's William Hodges Mann used the state Senate as a staging area and tightened his connections with the Anti-Saloon League. At Charlottesvile, fifty-three-year-old lawyer, investor, and state Democratic committee member Richard T. Duke, Jr., gained endorsement from his fellow townsman Martin. Across the Blue Ridge, at Lexington, former congressman Harry Tucker, more recently legal educator and president of the American Bar Association and of the Jamestown Exposition, expected to enter the race. One year his junior, fifty-six-year-old corporation commissioner, wealthy Southwest Virginia business man, and 1901 constitutional convention member Henry C. Stuart tested his corporate ties in Richmond. Lynchburg editor and congressman Glass would play upon a reputation as a debater and disfranchiser won in the constitutional convention.

Swanson held varying affinity for these eager claimants. Mann and his political entourage remembered that on more than one occasion he had thwarted Mann's political ambition. Flood, however, sought to settle differences between them. Swanson knew Duke by way of Martin, who admitted, "As long as Judge Duke is a candidate for Governor, I will, of course, support him." Despite Tucker's past alliance with Andrew Montague, Swanson in September 1905 visited the Cleveland Democrat; he later told Tucker, "I enjoyed your kind hospitality. . . . Your mint julip was fine and kept me going for a week." As a member of the corporation commission, Stuart had managed to lower freight rates at his Honaker shipping station from $82 to $50 per car and, as reported by Flood's young nephew Harry Byrd, "was greatly benefited by this reduction." Swanson, however, continued to campaign for Stuart in the Ninth District congressional elections.[5]

Few men of the era would as consistently oppose Swanson as forty-eight-year-old Glass. Not beyond misquoting Swanson, Glass privately branded him a crook, an attitude that may have derived from Swanson's alleged unethical electoral activities in the Fifth District. Glass believed that "a man who would steal his fellow citizen's vote would, in exigency, pick his neighbor's pocket."

On the two occasions that the diminutive Glass broke openly with Martin (1901 and 1911), slender Swanson was the cause. The governor's close friendship with Daniel helped also to turn Glass away from Swanson. In 1908, Halsey, Daniel's nephew, considered opposing Glass in the congressional primary, indicative of the growing tensions between Glass and the Daniel family.[6]

Democratic organizational instability also made Swanson's way to the Senate difficult. The governor fell into a series of congressional elections that eventually influenced the senatorial selection. In the Fourth District, recovered Francis R. Lassiter depended in 1906 upon Swanson to regain his congressional office. Mann assisted him in repelling a prohibitionist assault in 1908, but Lassiter died the next October. His brother Charles narrowly failed to succeed him. John Rixey of the Eighth District fell victim to tuberculosis and a mishandled surgeon's knife in February 1907. Swanson postponed a special election until Alexandria lawyer and publisher Charles Carlin, although not preferred by Martin, developed a successful organization. In the Tidewater Second District, Swanson probably contributed to incumbent Harry Maynard's defense of his seat against two challenges by George C. Cabell, Jr., who claimed he had made peace with Martin's "state organization." The governor was not as fortunate in pushing Otho Mears in a contest against William A. Jones in the First District, however. Overspreading these events were problems in the state chairman's office where J. Taylor Ellyson continued to be less than efficient. Lacking a centralizing order, the party continued to deteriorate and individual politicians such as Swanson grew in command.[7]

Precinct level complaints vaulted to the top of the agenda of the state Democratic committee. Regional spokesmen Duke, Alfred M. Bowman, and John Whitehead of Norfolk brought cheering committee agreement by their censure of the party primary. Some members may have wished to avoid popular elections, but primaries also encouraged the party's increasing disorganization. Local, county, and state conventions had been "practically" abandoned, depriving the party of the enthusiasm generated by such occasions. A local politician in Frederick County recorded lingering resentment toward the new disfranchising constitution and considered the black vote eliminated at the cost of "thousands of old white voters [who] were offended by the provisions and have become indifferent to the results." Other organizations—school groups, good roads associations, religious denominations, and the Anti-Saloon League— vied for attention. The league had attracted in Frederick the "discontented," while Democrats "lost ground which is being occupied by the Republicans." Some analysts feared that the Republicans prepared to vote their full strength and to absorb dissident Democrats. Reflecting wide agreement, Flood suggested, for example, that voting be made less restricted: an amendment should remove the poll tax, and the constitutional convention's minority report on suffrage should be adopted to allow franchise qualification based upon armed service or property tax payment and satisfactory comprehension of the state constitution. Nonetheless, the political status quo of 1902 was maintained.[8]

The 1908 presidential contest opened new rents in the flimsy Virginia Democratic party. Thomas F. Ryan marshaled influence to recruit Flood and Martin for another crusade against William Jennings Bryan. From his large estate in Nelson County, he contributed to party congressional candidates and used Flood to secure tax relief for his Virginia holdings. Congressman James Hay required "the necessary adjuncts of the campaign," and Flood obtained funds from Ryan. Swanson also advised Ryan on his tax problems, and John Swanson of Swanson Brothers may have held business contracts with Ryan and his Virginia land companies. In January 1908, Ryan probably encouraged Flood to contact anti-Bryan leaders such as "Jeffersonian Democrat" James M. Guffey, a wealthy Pittsburgh oil and mineral developer and national committeeman. In Virginia, to blunt Bryan fervor, Daniel was projected as a favorite-son candidate, or, failing that, the state convention would send an uninstructed delegation. Another tactic featured a late May 1908 trip by Governor John A. Johnson of Minnesota as a potential alternate to Bryan; the *Richmond Times-Dispatch* compared him favorably with Grover Cleveland and editorially prayed for a revival of the "true democracy." Having distributed Johnson literature as part of his plan, Flood influenced the state committee to delay the Democratic state convention until further anti-Bryan organization could occur. But Swanson had by then endorsed Bryan to the perturbation of Martin and Flood.[9]

Often visiting the state, the Nebraskan kept alive rural Virginia loyalty, and J. Hoge Tyer stoked the old Bryan themes. Congressman John Lamb was startled in the autumn of 1906 by the cheers that Bryan's name evoked among his rural constituents. Swanson initially declined to join this reawakening enthusiasm and, claiming a heavy schedule, turned down an invitation from Tyler to introduce Bryan at the Radford fair. Thomas wrote Tyler, however, that the governor had found time "to attend Ryan's picnic in Nelson County", and Glass later recalled for Bryan that Swanson told him he had planned "to have a 'previous engagement,'" saying he would be damned if he would countenance" him, being "bitter" toward the Nebraskan. Swanson went to Radford, however, being "whipped" by the state press into doing so, claimed Glass. Whatever the cause, Swanson's appearance in Radford resulted in a photograph of himself with Bryan, which soon occupied "a prominent place in the Governor's Mansion." The trip so aroused Swanson's political sense that, in January 1908, he refused to participate in the northeastern cabal against Bryan. A poll of the General Assembly taken the next month revealed a majority, including George T. Rison of Pittsylvania County and Speaker Richard Byrd, favoring the prairie politician for president.[10]

The "ultra Bryan people" launched a cleverly arranged effort to defeat Daniel's favorite-son candidacy and to force instructions for Bryan upon Virginia's delegation to the national convention. At the end of March, Bryan visited Richmond, escorted by Swanson and greeted five thousand Bryanites. Thereafter, Daniel's candidacy evaporated and Martin gambled on an uninstructed delegation, but he found Swanson's "conversation with us . . . so unsatisfactory that I do not expect the slightest let up on his part" in "propagating Bryanism." Martin also speculated that he would join Jones, Tucker, Stuart, and Tyler for Bryan instructions to the detriment of Mann's gubernatorial candidacy. On May 6, the governor united openly with the Bryan movement, considering him to be "not only the strongest, but . . . the most available man for the nomination." Martin tried again to silence Swanson, urging Flood to join him: "It would not be best for me to take it up with him alone." Meeting in Richmond they petitioned the governor to favor no instructions, but they failed and the anti-Bryan campaign floundered in Virginia.[11]

In Lexington, Bryan leaders worked "up the farmers and the clerks," and, at the election of convention delegates, "the Bryan forces generally voted down Daniel and William A. Anderson without ceremony." Washington and Lee president George H. Denny complained that "they had typewritten slips with the names of delegates and the alternates, and the slips were voted. Everything was done *secretly*. They held caucuses." He added, "We knew nothing of it whatever." Dispatched to the Fifth District to impede Bryanism, Congressman Saunders discovered a "crowd . . . determined on Bryan, and ready to take any sort of action that would be considered in his interests." Martin could not fathom the Bryan leadership. He surmised that Bryan and Tyler had an "understanding . . . that the latter [was] in charge of his interests in Virginia." Martin conjectured, "Swanson, perhaps, thinks he is in charge." But, wondered the senator, could "Bryan [be] . . . relying on William A. Jones?" William F. Rhea claimed he misconstrued Flood's directions for an uninstructed delegation at the Roanoke convention, and Swanson guided the assemblage into Bryan's camp. Flood failed to secure a seat for Ryan among Virginia delegates to the national convention in Denver. Martin's "statewide organization" proved to be a phantasm when forced to oppose public opinion, well-directed and led by Swanson.[12]

Symbolic of their party standing, Swanson went to Denver with Daniel, Tyler, and Martin as "Big Four" at-large delegates. Bryan invited Swanson to present a seconding speech and he quickly accepted. He speculated that the Republican nominee William Howard Taft "will find it impossible to cling both to Roosevelt policies and the Republican platform. . . . He will be compelled to repudiate one or the other . . . [as he] will find it impossible to be one and the same time a reactionary and a reformer." Swanson also helped place a section in the Democratic document that demanded reduction of the power of the Speaker of the House. Nominee Bryan's subsequent behavior, however, appalled him. The prophet of reformers proved politically inflexible toward former Democratic opponents; he claimed that he had "always been right" on fiscal policies and refused to compromise with southerners such as Daniel. Remnants of the Bryan-Cleveland schism surfaced when the convention refused Alton Parker's resolution memorializing the recently deceased former president. Although devoid of a practical political effect, Bryan forces roughly handled Guffey and a portion of the Pennsylvania delegation under contest by Bryan delegates. The Virginians under wiser hands vainly voted to seat Guffey's group. Dejected, Swanson muttered to a reporter: "What's the use? Bryan is sure to be nominated and sure to be defeated. Let us hope that will end him and that we can elect another man four years later."[13]

Swanson's political sense led him to submerge this realistic assessment, and he painted a party more united than at any time since 1892. He admitted a need for a "well planned and well coordinated" canvass for nominee Bryan, but in mid-October he had shifted to emphasizing congressional elections. Speaking in Ohio and Indiana, he concluded the autumn season in Richmond, recipient of a "great ovation." Martin revealed his weakness in reporting to William F. Sheehan, Parker's 1904 manager, that "the current of sentiment in Virginia was so strong for . . . Bryan that it was manifestly impossible to check it." He felt the necessity of an interview with Ryan "to have him understand if possible the conditions." Lured by a possible judgeship, Montague nearly joined Republican Taft's camp. James scoffed, "Jack is about to go over to Taft for a mess of pottage." Another Virginia elitest, University of Virginia president Edwin A. Alderman, wrote Walter Hines Page; "Hurrah for Bill Taft!"[14]

Virginia gubernatorial candidates dodged through the 1908 presidential election with varying results. Tom Duke withdrew and went to work for Tucker, but, owing to his "too conservative" image, Tucker lost Jones who preferred a candidate "to run on a platform somewhat similar to that which enabled [Robert] La Follette . . . to beat the . . . railroad combination" in Wisconsin. After considering a possible candidacy, Jones combined with Glass to favor Stuart, who encountered personal obligations that forced him to abandon the race in late January 1909. Glass then pushed forward, faltered, and failed to enter, leaving the field to Mann and to Tucker. Directed by fractious James Cannon, Jr., the Anti-Saloon League both helped and hindered Mann's lusterless campaign. The *Richmond Times-Dispatch* censured the Methodist minister, "Religion may appropriately use prohibition as a handmaiden but it seems hardly suitable for prohibition to seek so to use religion." The league's endorsement of local option boosted Mann in mid-February 1909 and avoided a more disruptive and controversial statewide dry referendum. Thereafter, Mann's dry colleagues and urban liquor interests entered into a de facto alliance. Rural areas would vote dry "while Norfolk, Newport News and Richmond would countenance the open saloon and [perhaps] force the liquor traffic, via the jug trade, on the prohibition counties." The broker in this compromise was Senator Martin.[15]

Having selected Mann in May 1907 as his candidate, Martin discovered in the next winter that his candidacy was moribund. Prohibition crossed class lines, regional loyalties, and political friendships. Congressman Carlin became so "timid that he is afraid to work for his friends for fear of alienating people who may be friendly to the other man," reported Flood. James informed Martin as early as July 1908 that "Swanson was doing nothing whatsoever for Judge Mann." He thought Mann should inspire Swanson with a promise "to appoint him to the Senate in case a vacancy should occur" while Mann was governor. Suspicious that Swanson had suggested James's mission, the senator refused any agreement, preferring to consider Swanson in Mann's camp. But little that was constructive emerged from the Fifth District. Swanson informed his associates that Mann's candidacy "was no occasion for a general policy among our friends." Swanson did advise Martin on Mann's organization and, at Martin's request, Mann conferred with the governor "as frequently as possible" to recruit "Swanson's special friends." Although some progress was made in the spring of 1909, Martin condemned those "inherently wet" people of Pittsylvania County who were not only slow to support "Judge Mann but were actively for Tucker." Such an observation corresponded to Tucker's reconstruction of a Swanson conversation in which the latter admitted that he would vote for Mann, but beyond that "his hands were off the fight." As a result, many of "Swanson's closest friends" followed Tucker, who in the primary carried five out of seven Pittsylvania magisterial districts. [16]

Lacking Swanson, Martin moved deeper into dangerous political trenches to rally allies. In March 1909, Richmond reporters saw on one day the political syncretist conferring with Cannon at Mann headquarters and on the next receiving in his hotel room at Murphy's state senator John Lesner, who was "closely affiliated with the liquor interests in Norfolk," and Samuel L. Kelly of the Virginia Liquor Dealers Association. Martin probably warned Cannon to avoid rhetoric about statewide prohibition because it would defeat Mann and elect Tucker who would then veto any such legislation by the General Assembly. He ostensibly reminded the reverend that a two-thirds vote was needed to override the governor. He most likely pledged the liquor dealers that Speaker Richard Byrd and Mann would not advance beyond existing local option laws. The Mann lieutenants grew more irritated with Swanson, however, and, near the eve of the August 1909 primary, Flood telephoned the governor and intimated that he would stand a poor show for senatorial appointment should Mann lose the Fifth District. Apparently agreeing to endorse Swanson for the Senate, at some future date, Flood persuaded the governor to pack "his grip" and leave on the next train. Four thousand votes gave Mann the victory over Tucker from the low total of seventy-three thousand. Based upon his regional Southside support, Flood's and Swanson's districts, wet Norfolk's vote and, of most importance, the Southwest returns, Mann increased his 1905 vote by nineteen thousand. Yet Tucker may have lost owing to his ineptitude, an earlier anti-free silver bias, arousal of former Readjusters by attacking Mann's affiliations with Mahone, identification with "outsiders" in the Ogden educational movement, and his administrative failure with the Jamestown Exposition and corporate associates. Mann, Flood, and Martin won as much by default as through effective organization. [17]

Swanson had reason not to be attracted to Mann's candidacy. As a lawyer for the Norfolk and Western Railroad and a proponent of prohibition, Mann posed a serious problem for many Democrats. A large number of wet Democrats refused to vote in the primary from a conviction that, should he win the nomination, they would be bound to vote for Mann in the general election. In Danville, Eugene Withers discovered opposition to Mann among them to be so "intense that they could not be inclined to go into the primary at all." Had those who favored Tucker voted, a very decisive majority in Danville and the surrounding area may have helped to defeat Mann. Although Swanson voted for Mann, he may have encouraged wets to sit out the election. He campaigned for Mann in the autumn election against Republican William P. Kent, but he also responded to widespread requests from localities wishing to hear him. He spent considerable effort knitting together party fragments and making appointments that satisfied Democratic factions. Swanson concluded his duties on February 1, 1910, by escorting Mann to the inaugural ceremonies. [18]

Commentaries during the autumn and winter of 1909 which claimed a closed, efficient, methodical Martin machine lacked considerable substance. In March 1910, Stuart announced his candidacy against Republican congressman C. Bascomb Slemp. Glass spent considerable time in the Mann-Kent election and expected Martin's approval of his gubernatorial aspirations in 1913. Tucker initiated friendly conversations with Flood concerning the next governor's race. William Jones remained in factional opposition and Montague represented Republican John M. Parsons against Saunders in a contested Fifth District congressional case. The Swansons attended Mardi Gras in New Orleans and visited Mexico and California. They planned to return by mid-March to discuss various real estate investments with Martin, Flood, and Harry Byrd, now a Winchester newspaper editor, land developer, and fruit grower.[19]

In December 1909, Daniel appeared briefly in public and then illness confined him to his Lynchburg home. Concerned relatives took him to Florida to recuperate. As Martin concluded a European visit and as Swanson prepared to leave the state, Flood busily established liasons with local politicians to assure his selection should a senatorial vacancy occur. Daniel suffered a minor stroke on March 7, and three days later Swanson returned as intended, confessing he was "out of touch with affairs of state." He arrived late in the evening of March 14 at Washington's Willard Hotel, expecting to discuss business matters. The following day news arrived from Florida that Daniel was in a deep coma and near death. The real estate deliberations expanded into a political showdown. Swanson discovered Mann was preparing to appoint Flood to the Senate.[20]

Swanson informed the enlarged meeting that he would be a Senate candidate whether Mann selected Flood, Cannon, Richard Byrd, or any other Virginian. Standing for reelection in 1911, Martin recognized immediately that his prospects could be seriously impaired by a Flood-Swanson contest. At home with the Bryan wing of the party, Swanson stood apart from Martin and, with a recurrent, sprightly independence, the former governor held a vast popular base beyond registered voters that crossed party lines. He had established an effective newspaper network favorable to his candidacy and a great number of citizens felt they had benefited from his governorship. Through his public career, he had "sounded the tocsin of advance" for aspiring Virginians who outnumbered considerably their more established fellow citizens. Personable and responsive to popular causes, he had a "hold on the people that seem to grow stronger each year." His appointees were still loyal and, only a few weeks earlier, state legislators had risen to their feet in salute, demonstrating that had the General Assembly been in session, he would have easily been the members' choice to succeed Daniel.[21]

Mann would follow Martin's desire in the senatorial appointment as evidenced by some of the new governor's nominations. Commentaries then and later pictured Flood graciously stepping aside on Martin's behalf and allowing Swanson the office. In fact, considerable strength had moved to the latter. Speaker of the Virginia House Richard E. Byrd doubted whether Flood could withstand an electoral challenge featuring Swanson and some third person. More important, fifty-six-year-old Hay, Seventh District congressman first elected in the Bryan year of 1896 and currently candidate for House speaker, sided with Swanson as did Carlin of the Eighth District and corporation commissioner Rhea. Given these circumstances, political reality, a commodity he held in abundance, led Martin to favor Swanson.[22]

"The Latest Successful 'Come Back.'" Cartoon by Clifford K. Berryman,
Washington Star, August 1910.

   Daniel recovered, however, and returned to Lynchburg. Gossip circulated through Virginia that a compact between Swanson and Governor Mann had been sealed. Attempting to void such an agreement and misunderstanding the political realities of the moment, Tucker and other critics publicly condemned the "premature scramble for John Daniel's place" and relayed to Mann examples of Swanson's tepid advocacy of his gubernatorial candidacy. Objection to Swanson continued within the Flood family and Harry Byrd insisted that Flood not step aside: "Many people believe [Swanson] . . . is not a big enough man, to be Senator." Two days later, having returned from Washington, he telegraphed his father to run if Flood "should give way to Swanson." In April, Tucker discussed with Flood the senatorship. Daniel died on June 29 and conjecture reappeared. Searching for a partner to oppose Swanson and Martin in the 1911 primary, Tucker called for "a meeting of the best men in our party." Fishing for aid in his gubernatorial quest, Glass interviewed Martin and Flood, informing them that he favored the latter's appointment. By mid-July, Flood admitted that opposition to Swanson by "a number of prominent men" had "some effect" upon him, but he also knew what awaited him should he run. On August 1, 1910, Swanson received the short-term appointment from Mann and advocated popular election of senators. Receiving Daniel family congratulations, he wrote to Edward Daniel: "Outside my immediate family, there was no one for whom I entertained a greater affection [than Senator Daniel]. . . . He encouraged me and aided my every ambition."[23]
   Nationally, Taft's failure in 1910 to overcome his innate resistance to reform resulted in a feud with Theodore Roosevelt which produced Republican distraction and Democratic opportunities. Political insurgency became popular initially among the more reform-minded and then opportunistic Republicans and spread into Democratic ranks. Swanson concluded as early as April that the Democrats should win control of the House of Representatives for the first time since 1895. Owing in part to swift increases in living costs, anticorporate attitudes gained momentum and turned against incumbent politicians. Popular journalistic treatments inclined to favor those who made the accusations. In Virginia, an experienced political observer detected a "feeling of unrest over the entire state [that] is more pronounced even than it was when Montague was elected over Swanson. A man who identifies himself with this movement openly is going to . . . benefit."[24]
   As in 1901, Swanson risked being hitched to Martin's political plow, but not until November 1910 did vague, scudding opposition precipitate into overt resistance to his Senate appointment. Campaigning for Saunders, he found the Fifth District "in a wretched condition," and secured from Ellyson fifteen hundred dollars in funds. As he worked the dusty Southside precincts, he met Flood on a similar mission who predicted that Glass would oppose him—a proposition that spread throughout the state. Glass, however, telephoned Martin to reassure him that there was "nothing to the talk of Jones running" against him. Glass's gubernatorial candidacy depended upon Stuart's success in the Ninth District congressional race. If Stuart lost, various sources hinted that he would join a coalition with the Martin machine to secure the governorship in 1913. Glass's *Lynchburg Daily Advance,* as late as November 7, praised Swanson for

"doing noble work" in the Virginia congressional campaign. Two days later, Stuart failed by two hundred votes against Republican Slemp. During the next six weeks, Jones and Glass approached first an ailing Tucker then Stuart to run against Swanson, but both refused. At a meeting in late 1910, Glass, Tucker, Jones, and others decided upon a combination race: Glass and Jones against Swanson and Martin. An informed legislator, upon hearing their intention, wrote Tucker that Glass was "especially strong in the attack," a man who could "righteously arouse" the people for "political reform" as had Montague in 1901.[25]

Announcing their intentions in January 1911, both congressmen attempted to affix to their candidates national reform sentiments and initially called for political morality. Viewing their opening statements, the *Richmond News Leader* conjectured that the "public interest can scarcely be sustained by means of vague charges directed at no particular individual or essays on the beauties of purity in politics." The newspaper at the time was influenced by Flood and Richard Byrd, an adept editorial writer, but the statement held considerable validity. Richmond lawyer and publisher John Garland Pollard, preventing Martin from dominating the *Richmond Evening Journal,* directed it in behalf of Jones. After a joint session, the challengers and Tucker, Montague, and Anderson proclaimed establishment of the Virginia Democratic League, an organization similar to the 1899 May Movement, dedicated to the "supremacy of Democratic insurgency in Virginia over the present state organization." The league's leadership also reflected the regional bias of the earlier group; Jones's congressional district furnished its principal officers, state Senator Charles V. Gravatt of Caroline County and Pollard from King and Queen County. League secretary was managing editor of the *Richmond Times-Dispatch,* J. St. George Bryan, son of recently deceased Joseph F. Bryan. Operating by March, the league sought a legalized primary apart from the state Democratic party, popular election of senators and state corporation members, abandonment of the fee system for public officers, and economy and publicity in public office. In April, Glass was critical of Swanson's governorship for "extravagance and mismanagement" and questioned his congressional record.[26]

Locating specific issues to use against Swanson had proven a hardship for Glass. He did, however, produce two: as governor, Swanson allegedly bankrupted the state and, as congressman, he had been a confidant of the the tobacco trust. The first evolved from unanticipated expenditures in judiciary operations. The second accused Swanson of using confidential information, Glass argued, to purchase several hundred shares of American Tobacco Company stock as tobacco taxes were being reduced after the Spanish-American War. Admitting to buying on margin and then selling the shares, Swanson also told of obtaining more in 1901, but on both occasions Congress was not in session. To replace the junior senator, Glass offered himself as the "true representative of the people." Swanson suffered a serious stomach disorder in May and June that required recuperation in Atlantic City. Postponing open electioneering until the last month of the primary, Swanson dispatched thousands of letters while depending upon intermediaries and pro-Swanson newspapers to carry much of the fight to Glass.[27]

While influencing public opinion, Virginia journalists formed a most productive network of information-gathering. Drawn to politicians because of their news value, the journalists became ensnared in the political groupings of the era. An editor in his youth, Swanson worked to form lasting bonds with them. However, even a lifelong associate such as W. Scott Copeland, *Norfolk Ledger Dispatch* editor, expected to be courted at every election. Editor James admitted that "every paper" in the Fifth District except his "made [Swanson] pay tribute constantly." Cannon launched the *Richmond Virginian* in 1909 and, during its ten-year existence, Swanson signed at least one $1,000 note that he eventually paid. Recent purchaser of the *Petersburg Index Appeal*, Walter E. Harris obtained financial support from Tucker, but refused editorially to endorse Glass, owing to his silence during the Tucker-Mann primary. Concurrently, Harris had held since 1905 connections with Flood and Martin. Editor and part-owner of the *Roanoke Times* Alfred B. Williams and the implacable James of the *Danville Register* immediately opposed their fellow-editor Glass's candidacy. Labeling both indecent, he condemned the editor of the *South Boston News* of having sold out to the "political machine in Virginia" upon reception of several large Swanson advertisements. Martin complained that the *Lynchburg News*, a Glass paper, had perhaps harmed him more "than any other . . . in the State," but the senator could request Richard Byrd of the *Winchester Star* to "write an editorial for the Washington *Post*" and be certain that it would appear in print. In January 1911, Jones regretted that "quite a number of newspaper propositions" had been made to him; he said, "I only wish I was in a [financial] position to consider them."[28]

Swanson and other candidates purchased extra copies of local papers for distribution, and favorable editorials resulted in county papers. A Pulaski correspondent for the *Roanoke Times, Lynchburg News,* and *Richmond News Leader,* who did not "pretend to bind these papers to anything," offered Tucker in the 1909 campaign that, by his "numerous communications to them," he could do Tucker "a large amount of good" for a twenty-five dollar service fee. The owner of the *Strasburg News* would help him "for a consideration." F.O. Hoffman, *Franklin Times Democrat* editor, petitioned Tucker for financial assistance because Hoffman was a Democrat faced with a "Yankee" competitor "who is a menace to our party." Early in the 1911 campaign, neither the *Richmond News Leader* nor the *Times-Dispatch* favored Glass or Jones. In July, the latter published letters placing Martin in close relationship with railroads during the elections of the early 1890s. Under John Stuart Bryan, the *News Leader* moved "good and fast" to the challenging candidates, but a more difficult problem occurred at the *Times-Dispatch* where editor John C. Hemphill cited his contact and refused to alter editorial policy to favor the two congressmen. Considered a "damn fool" by George Bryan, Hemphill eventually left for a three-week vacation immediately before the election; the *Times-Dispatch* then certified Glass and Jones. Similar understandings were established with the *Norfolk Virginian Pilot* under its editor, former governor William E. Cameron. The Virginia Democratic League publicized widely the "change of editorial attitudes" of the Richmond press.[29]

William Jennings Bryan had congratulated Swanson upon his elevation to the senatorship and later observed that the "case between Swanson and Glass is not so one sided, for Swanson has had an abundance of training." Glass tried to convince Bryan that Swanson "was intimately connected with the railways," referring perhaps to the railroad postal subsidies that Swanson had obtained in the 1890s. Bryan denounced Martin in April 1911 in an unsuccessful attempt to prevent his election to the minority leadership in the Senate and continued to harass Martin in his *Commoner.* He declined to censure Swanson, however. Westmoreland Davis, publisher of the influential *Southern Planter,* resident of Loudoun County and president of the Virginia Farmers' Institute, approved the candidacies of Jones and Swanson. A Norfolk politician claimed that Glass and Martin could stand comfortably upon the same platform, but "could Glass and Jones?" Early in the campaign, Jones called for direct election of judges, a statement Glass greeted with silence. Unable to agree upon a common platform, the congressmen abandoned their moral campaign and concluded with a vituperative, personal assault against the senators. Shallow journalistic froth continued to describe a contest of "progressives" and "conservatives" or "independents" versus a "machine."[30]

Swanson remained in the Senate until a few days before the primary. At Lawrenceville, near the tracks of the Atlantic and Danville Railroad, he opened his campaign replying directly to Glass's wildly thrown accusations. His speech explicated state financing so as to reduce the issue of state bankruptcy to a sham. He "willingly shared with the General Assembly responsibility and credit" for the record of his gubernatorial term: "None has advocated the abolishment of any of the hospitals, schools and road improvements." He accused "the People's Champion" of opposition to the 1901 employer liability bill and to the corporation commission, of prevention of speedy publication of the 1901 constitutional convention debates, of advocacy of gubernatorial appointment of judges, and of conflict of interest. As a bank director and member of the House Banking and Currency Committee, how could "he serve the people in their desire for currency reform?" Swanson attested that his investments were mostly in real estate, following Bryan's example, and the balance was "almost entirely in . . . Danville and Pittsylvania county." Alfred Williams revealed that Glass had used confidential information as clerk of the Lynchburg city council to accumulate real estate profits. Speaking there, Swanson accused the "Saintly Statesman" of conducting along with Jones a campaign of "stolen letters." Both senators concluded their campaign in Danville amidst "wild enthusiasm" and plates of barbecue. Having written local leaders to "be active and alert and see that the full vote is polled," Swanson knew on the eve of the election that everything was "most encouraging."[31]

Swanson gathered 67,497 votes to Glass's 28,757, and Martin did nearly as well against Jones by 65,218 to 31,428. Swanson held 70 percent of the vote to Martin's 68 percent. Before the franchise for women was legalized, ninety-six thousand Virginians had cast the largest Democratic primary vote between 1901 and 1921. More votes were available, but, as one local leader recorded, "nearly all the voters considered Martin and Swanson safe and would not take the time from their work." Winning 89 of 100 counties and every city but Lynchburg,

Swanson embarrassed Glass in his congressional district by collecting 57 percent of the returns. Swanson also led Martin in all but eleven counties but trailed in twelve of nineteen cities. In fifty-eight counties and eleven cities, a difference of less than thirty votes occurred between the two. In addition to Flood's, these counties were in the Second, Fourth, Fifth, and Ninth districts. For the most part, they had been centers of Swanson' strength in the 1905 primary and had been sites of intense contests between Democrats, Republicans, and Populists in recent years. In these localities, Democratic regulars held their allegiances to proven incumbents. A commanding influence of adept regional leaders appeared in the election; Flood, Rhea, Charles Lassiter, William W. Sale, and a host of sidekicks encouraged Swanson majorities to vote for Martin. Within Jones's First District, far removed from his home precincts, Glass received two thousand more votes than in his own bailiwick. Former Populist boxes continued to contain large majorities for Swanson who swept to new gains in Richmond and northern Virginia.[32]

Swanson had earned the Senate by his governorship, willingness to progress, party loyalty, political sagacity, and massive rural support. Martin profited from these circumstances and contributed his own entourage of friends and associates to the 1911 primary victory. Jones and especially Glass descended to demagogic depths to represent themselves as legates of the people. The election proved that an effective coalition of localities and regions had been fitted together, departing from a decentralized, nineteenth-century order into a twentieth-century condition that increasingly promoted centralization and authority in Richmond and eventually in Washington in the hands of the two senators. The power was used to gain consensus among the coalition members and only later would it become a more inflexible authority. Before this election, Swanson had engineered a structure to win elections; afterwards, he evolved into a patriarchal figure seeking to avoid controversy and party dissension. Yet, scarcely had the returns of September 1911 disappointed the owners of the *Richmond Times-Dispatch* than national and state developments provided ingredients to project the novice senator into the inner workings of the federal government.[33]

7

Both Ears to the Ground
1910-1917

As a senator, Claude Swanson continued the political habits that he had practiced since 1893: he responded quickly and positively to Virginians ranked in their regional interests, he gathered and awarded patronage, he favored expansion of government services, he maintained his allegiance to the national Democrats, and he infiltrated to the center of political and bureaucratic Washington. In these years he passed his fiftieth birthday, consolidated his political position, and facilitated a generation of agrarian demands into legislative reality.

In his initial committee assignments, he worked for federal contributions to vocational high schools, preferred a more advanced workers compensation law than the Senate would pass, defended a new cabinet position for labor and rural free delivery of mail, while proposing that federal naval subcontractors be included under the federal eight-hour work day. A member of the Public Buildings and Grounds Committee, he seeded federal buildings throughout Virginia and aided colleagues in their pork barrel projects. Generally, he counseled for lower tariffs, federal aid to highways and vocational education, and direct election of senators, including federal oversight of senatorial elections and party primaries to regulate corporate contributions.[1]

Assigned to the Post Office and Post Roads Committee in March 1911 and drawing upon his House experience, Swanson guarded rural delivery appropriations and requested $20 million for rural roads. Contesting northeastern interests, he claimed great federal sums had been spent "to encourage . . . cheap railroad and water transportation," and now financing should aid the hinterland's road construction. These debates bred over sixty bills, and Swanson was appointed to a joint House and Senate review committee to consider additional federal post road subsidies. He and his nine committee colleagues developed a plan for a fifty-year, three-billion-dollar expenditure to be initiated by $500,000 of pilot road projects. Pushing Virginia counties to match federal dollars, he recorded complaints of county supervisors objecting to the unaccustomed, federally mandated eight-hour day. Eventually in 1915 the committee produced a complete, major report that shaped future federal highway legislation.[2]

Replacing Thomas Martin on the Naval Affairs Committee in March 1911, given the commercial and naval interests converging at Hampton Roads, Swanson was considered a "yard senator." From his earliest days as a congressman, his interest was drawn to the Norfolk area; as governor he sponsored its growth through the Jamestown Exposition. Regional interests—coal, tobacco, timber, grain, ship building, and railroads—lobbied for its development. When channels and facilities were improved for military reasons, civilian interests were served as well. In June 1912, Swanson previewed one of his future roles by calling for an increased navy "without hesitation, without interruption." Wary of German and British construction, he claimed the "best guarantee of our peace and [that] . . . of the world is a strong American Navy."[3]

An opportunity to elect in 1912 a Democratic president emboldened Swanson and his party to compose a legislative shopping list to attract voters. They also hunted for a nominee to bind Democratic factions into a winning force. House Speaker Champ Clark was Swanson's choice. Both men had arrived in Congress the same year; by 1904, as desk mates in the House, they were "very chummy." In 1906, Governor Swanson had approved of the Virginia delegation backing Clark for minority leader to defeat incumbent John Sharp Williams who had refused to fill Swanson's vacant seat on the Ways and Means Committee with another Virginian. In October 1910, a would-be-candidate, James Hay, thought it "wisest for us to suggest Clark" as Speaker in the new Democratic House. Possessing a "more consistent 'reform record' than any other Democratic candidate could claim," Clark opened his presidential campaign headquarters in February 1912. Swanson admired his political talents and agreed with his opposition to high tariffs, corporate concentration, and railroad improprieties.[4]

New Jersey governor Woodrow Wilson, a Staunton native and a Presbyterian minister's son, accumulated a mixed group in Virginia advocating his nomination. Maintaining connections in the state through academic admirers of his political writings and scholarship, he had been offered on three occasions the presidency of the University of Virginia, but he preferred Princeton instead. Swanson probably first met him as a speaker at the Jamestown Exposition. Its president, Harry Tucker, was attracted to Wilson and, after the former's unsuccessful 1909 gubernatorial campaign, he visited Wilson in New Jersey. William A. Jones, Carter Glass, John Garland Pollard, and chairman of the Virginia Democratic League, Charles U. Gravatt fell in with Wilson's presidential effort in October 1911. Earlier having praised Wilson's antimachine activities, Andrew Montague joined with House of Delegates speaker Richard E. Byrd who was enthralled that his University of Virginia classmate might achieve the presidency. Lacking ideological coherence, Virginia Wilsonites adopted tactics similar to Wilson's suggestion to Josephus Daniels for North Carolina: accuse state opponents of machine politics. Such maneuvers required no clear definition of goals and fitted contemporary attitudes. Swanson maintained his Clark commitment, despite Henry Flood's sponsorship of a third candidate, Kentucky-born congressman Oscar Underwood of Alabama.[5]

Wilson's search for western delegates led him to advocate the initiative and referendum, a move that chilled some of his Virginia supporters. The owners and editor of the *Richmond Times-Dispatch* accused him of "insidious vagaries." While he disagreed with Wilson's political course, stronger reasons led

Thomas Staples Martin to oppose him. Having voted for William McKinley in earlier elections, Wilson had come late to party honors, and Martin's 1911 adversaries now congregated about his candidacy. Influenced by George H. Denny, new president of University of Alabama, and probably Thomas Fortune Ryan, Flood adopted the candidacy of Underwood, a former president of University of Virginia alumni who had "a pronounced hatred of Bryan," who preferred a moderate tariff and who opposed the initiative, referendum, and recall. Martin was not visibly moved, and, given the differences of opinion, a strategy emerged for an uninstructed delegation to the national convention.[6]

Despite Clark's defeat of Wilson in several crucial western state primaries, Swanson still shielded his preference for the Missourian from the public. Martin's ailing wife required the Charlottesville politician's attention and, while agreeing to an uncommitted delegation, Flood searched for commitments to Underwood. Despite his brother-in-law's activity for Wilson and his criticism of "the organization," Flood also wished "to treat Dick [Byrd] nicely." By the end of May, a Flood correspondent surmised, "All along . . . Swanson might be for Clark, but I believe if you and Senator Martin agree on Underwood you can get him in line."[7]

At the Norfolk state convention, outward harmony prevailed. Clark and Underwood elements accepted eight at-large delegates divided evenly between Wilson and non-Wilson men. Of the twenty-four Virginia votes, Richard Byrd claimed twelve for Wilson, and Tucker counted nine and three-quarters—other estimates gave him only six and one-half. Although an absent Martin had reservations, Flood proposed that Thomas Ryan be named a delegate. Such a prospect had caused Swanson to clash "with Flood when the proposition was . . . first broached," but to no avail. Speaking for party harmony, Swanson favored no instructions, but interruptions came from unfriendly delegates "who rode him for wanting [instructions for] Bryan four years earlier." He replied with heat that he was "first, last and always for the interest of the Democratic party." Editor Walter Harris of the *Petersburg Index Appeal,* a lonely Wilson paper in the Southside, noted that "Swanson . . . caught it pretty heavy" as he "made the mistake of losing his temper." After refusing a preferential presidential primary and adopting a unit rule to be enforced by two-thirds of the delegation, the convention sent a potentially divided deputation to the national convention in Baltimore.[8]

The city's proximity to Virginia encouraged Virginians to attend. Calling upon his uncle's influence, correspondent Harry Byrd joined the Virginia newsmen recording with varying accuracy the consequential convention. Corporation commissioner William F. Rhea sat with the Virginia delegates and Edwin A. Alderman squeezed into the spectator gallery. Not leaving on one occasion until five o'clock in the morning, Elizabeth Swanson stayed through the extended nominating activities. Her husband, chairman of the Virginia delegation, agreed to follow temporarily the Virginia Underwood majority through the first few ballots. Except for opposing Wilson, Martin remained "inclining passively to Underwood," owing to his friendship with Flood, reported correspondent K. Foster Murray.[9]

After William Jennings Bryan polarized the convention in a series of divisive statements that censured "any candidate for president who is the representative of J. Pierpont Morgan, Thomas F. Ryan or August Belmont," Flood angrily responded that Virginia delegate Ryan had been elected by a thousand honest Virginians and accused Bryan of seeking to "destroy the prospect of Democratic success." Swanson had correctly anticipated what followed. Telegrams of protest and dark headlines from state newspapers condemned "the multi-millionaire Ryan" placed upon the Virginia delegation by "trickery." On the tenth ballot, a shift of ninety New York votes to Clark pushed his total to a majority of 556, although a two-thirds vote was needed for nomination. Swanson now called upon Flood to release the Virginia Underwood delegates, but, having seconded Underood's nomination and suspecting that Clark was Bryan's candidate, the congressman refused. Only three Virginia votes moved to the Speaker on the thirteenth ballot. Before the next role call, Bryan denounced any candidate preferred by New York and a distraught, noisy deadlock settled upon the convention. Swanson could hardly bring himself to speak to Flood.[10]

After a recess, Wilson's total mounted and, on the thirtieth ballot, he passed Clark. More composed and probably influenced by an alarmed Martin, Flood now permitted most of the Virginia Underwood vote to switch to Clark, giving him twelve of the state's share. During another recess carried by anti-Wilson forces, the Virginians, as reported by the *Richmond Times-Dispatch,* decided to shift to Wilson, and "if he dropped back the whole delegation under the unit rule would swing to Underwood." Swanson had no intention of voting for Underwood. He explained later to South Carolinian Bernard Baruch: "I saw that my man Clark was dead. I wasn't going to lay down on that ice and get political pneumonia. No sir! I got up and cut some fancy didoes and came out for Wilson." On the next ballot, leaping upon a chair to be heard, Swanson cast the state's twenty-four votes for him. Professional politicians in the Indiana and Illinois contingents, "led by so-called bosses," also moved to Wilson, who achieved the nomination "by a traditional bundle of bargains and compromises that defied ideology."[11]

Swanson had cautioned Virginians about party priorities in 1912. "If the Democratic nominee is too radical, he will split the [Democratic] vote for Taft," or "if reactionary, he will drive many of the progressives to Roosevelt," a soon-to-be, third-party reform candidate. What was needed was "a man with moderate views of a [reformer] . . . with conservative tendencies as it were." Reassured by Wilson's presidential campaign, Swanson quickly pledged his efforts and suggested means to crystallize current sentiment favoring Wilson. Predicting that the contest between William Howard Taft and Theodore Roosevelt would be "extremely bitter," he also advised successfully that the Wilson convention manager, William McCombs, be named national committee chairman, owing to his "tact, political sagacity and wisdom." Swanson soon thereafter became a member of the national Wilson election committee. Wilson ignored the Democratic platform's advanced proposals and campaigned "backward instead of forward," securing the middle ground between Taft and Roosevelt. In November, he won the presidency by a plurality. Virginia gave him more than seven thousand votes above Bryan's 1908 state total.[12]

Correctly anticipating Democratic control of Congress, Swanson and James Hay had conferred in July 1912 to frustrate last-minute Republican patronage appointments. After party victory, Swanson discussed appointments with Martin, Flood, and Richard Byrd. They decided to be "careful about any agitation [over] . . . patronage control," so not to "turn Wilson in the wrong way." Assurances at the end of December 1912 that each congressman "will control [postal] appointments," and that "Mr. Wilson will adhere to this course" pleased Swanson who remembered Grover Cleveland's patronage debacles. Virginia Wilson leaders, however, attempted to foster factional divisions of the nominating campaign by advertising a presumed animosity between the senators and Wilson. Speaking at Staunton and intending to be jocular, Wilson had his remarks taken out of context by journalists who made them appear to censure Flood, Ryan, or Martin. Both senators were absent and a boycott was mentioned. In reality, Swanson had been in the president-elect's party until called home by the death of a relative, and Martin continued to attend his seriously ill wife. From the first, Swanson and his Virginia friends dedicated themselves to party harmony and soon convinced the president that they were not reactionaries. Flood learned in May 1913 that Wilson appreciated "the way the Va. Delegation in both Houses are standing by the policies of the Administration." The congressional Democrats were intent upon making "a Democratic record, and Wilson, the prime minister, prepared to provide leadership." Swanson had espoused most of Wilson's first-term programs before the president had entered national politics, and no major opposition to them appeared on his record.[13]

In March 1914, Wilson appointed six of seven of the Swanson and Martin nominees to major Virginia patronage posts, including Richard Byrd as western district attorney. Fifteen years later, Wilson's postmaster general, Albert S. Burleson, claimed practical politics motivated the president to accept the nominees of professional politicians over those of reformers. More complex reasons moved Wilson, however. Initially, Wilson requested cabinet secretaries use a common form for appointments, cataloguing factional affiliations with "groups or wings of the party." Campaign aide Walter Wick prepared a Virginia "Pre-nomination Friends" list for Burleson. But Wilson investigated the "anti-organization" office seekers in Virginia and, in at least one major instance and probably others, found them wanting in ability. Cabinet applicant Tucker, he discovered, had a spotty administrative record with the Jamestown Exposition and had edited inadequately his father's constitutional law textbook. He refused to appoint Tucker attorney general or secretary of war. Wilson even had evidence to question recently-elected Congressman Montague's choice for Richmond postmaster. In 1914, seeking federal patronage to defeat Flood, Tucker encountered Secretary of State Bryan's misleading counsel that Wilson was "not at liberty to disregard the representatives whom the people have sent to Washington as his co-laborers."[14]

In searching for patronage, Swanson appeared untiring. Vice-President Thomas Marshall, presiding officer of the Senate, recalled "Claude Swanson . . . can get more things done and secure more offices than any man I ever knew." By letter, interview, and telephone, he harried cabinet officers and bureaucrats and incorporated Wilson's secretary, Joseph P. Tumulty, into his designs. On one occasion he instructed Tumulty to intercede for him as he was "very busy in the Senate, [and] it is impossible to come to the White House." In another case he reminded Tumulty of a promise "that you would do all you could to aid me." Not only would Swanson join in major decisions that determined Interstate Commerce Commission members, but, after a two-year campaign, he delighted in restoring a dismissed constituent to civil service employment. While not always successful, Swanson presented his arguments with verve. Wilson admitted to Burleson that Swanson, who had been "in the other day and [felt] deeply about the case of the Danville post office," had made "a great impression" on him. In this instance, Burleson did not follow the wishes of Swanson who then convinced the Senate to refuse the postmaster's nomination. Careful not to rent his property to the government, as chairman of Buildings and Grounds, Swanson obligated other Democrats who, by his actions, replaced Republican landlords.[15]

Wilson's first Congress encountered a junior senators' revolt against the seniority system that determined chairmanships and committee assignments. Approximately twenty-five to thirty of fifty-one Democratic senators favored Indiana's John Kern for majority leader and prevented Martin's being elevated to that office. Ideological tags such as "progressive," "conservative," and "reactionary" were bandied about, but ten of Kern's insurgents were freshmen; nine more had just arrived in 1911. Not having the votes, Martin compromised, allowed Virginia-born Kern the victory while obtaining a seat on the Steering Committee that nominated senators to their assignments. He also gained chairmanship of Appropriations. As Kern proved "slow and lacking in alertness," senior senators absorbed much of the leadership duties. Swanson advised Martin, and, of the senior members, only Benjamin Tillman of South Carolina did not gain his first choice. He was somewhat mollified by chairing the Naval Affairs Committee. Swanson gained an advantage in the tussle. On major committees, beyond chairing Buildings and Grounds, Swanson ranked third on Education and Labor, Naval Affairs, and Post Roads, and joined the prestigious committee on Foreign Relations. With Martin's senatorial authority, and that of Virginia colleagues in the House, the junior senator within three years came to hold sound relationships with members of Congress, prospering his projects and expanding his influence.[16]

Swanson's memories of lost Democatic opportunities intensified his search for congressional party harmony with the executive. Contemporary politics suggested a similar effort since the minority Democrats won the presidency in 1912 by a plurality and required stronger coalitions to secure a majority in 1916. Swanson's talent in formulating regional alliances proved valuable in the passage of agrarian proposals on tariff reduction, graduated income tax, currency reform, antitrust legislation, rural credits, vocational education, demonstration work, better roads, and prohibition.[17]

The Democratic pledges to remove artificial trade barriers and to reduce living costs materialized in the House of Representatives as the Underwood tariff, a moderate downward revision that included a graduated income tax schedule. Upon its reaching the Senate, interest groups and their lobbyists threatened to nullify it, but Wilson demanded an investigation of senators' financial holdings to uncover any conflict of interest. Swanson endorsed this tactic that attracted reform-minded westerners to rally around the tariff. Over six hundred Finance Committee amendments further lowered the House version. From July into September 1913, Swanson voted in over 110 roll calls and, except for his absence to vote in the Virginia primary, he continued into October to stand with the majority to sustain the committee and final passage. The Underwood tariff reduced income tax exemptions from $4000 to $3000 and approved rates that shifted more revenue burdens to northeastern states. No Virginia special interest unduly influenced Swanson, although lower, complicated textile schedules may have favored southern looms, such as those in Danville, rather than northern counterparts. [18]

Lessons from the panic of 1907 and the 1912 platform pledge helped House Democrats propose a reordered banking system. Wilson and Treasury Secretary William G. McAdoo accepted many of Louis Brandeis's ideas and convinced House Bank and Currency chairman Glass to include Bryan's plan for federal control of the currency and banking structure. The Glass bill provided regional public reserve banks that reduced partially the dominance of banking centers such as New York, Chicago, and St. Louis. Swanson found the administration-backed plan, when it reached the Senate, "wise, prudent and constructive legislation" as it did not seek "to satisfy the extreme radical . . . nor the predatory reactionary." The new system, Swanson posited, would oversee banking in the same way the Interstate Commerce Commission regulated railroads. Specifically he referred to Wall Street actions in 1907 when northern capitalists froze Richmond bank deposits and denied a source of credit at the very moment when crops were marketed. But the legislation's specific nature engendered deadlock as Republicans and maverick Democrats joined to defeat the reform. [19]

Reminding Swanson of Cleveland's party-destroying performances, Wilson's exasperation grew. Opponents introduced a plan for a controversial, highly centralized banking system under federal authority which threatened Democratic unity. On November 8, after being closeted with Wilson, Swanson activated authority granted him by absent majority leader Kern. Incorporating earlier suggestions, he requested a party caucus to bind Democratic senators to the administration bill. His proposal attracted twenty-seven Democratic signatures, a necessary majority endorsement, which dismayed Republicans who had infiltrated their ranks. In Democratic conferences on November 26 and 28 which voted to sustain the administration, Swanson served as an instrument of the White House. Wilson and his executive aides revealed to Glass that "effective caucus action . . . was chiefly due to the skill and unmatched persuasiveness of the junior senator from Virginia." In Senate debate, Swanson emphasized forcefully the observation that "when power is given, platform promises should be transferred into legislative enactment." The result was the Federal Reserve System. [20]

During the spring and summer of 1914, Congress passed two additional reforms: the Federal Trade Commission Act, which gave federal authority to the generation-old wish of agrarians to control "trusts," and the Clayton Antitrust Act, which loosened earlier restraints against labor organization and further codified illegal corporate practices. Swanson contributed to Democratic majorities in both instances. He followed Wilson rather than Samuel Gompers, who requested a more complete labor section. Supporting Democratic floor leaders, he answered roll-call votes in August and early September. On one occasion, he opposed prohibition of common carriers owning mines and other businesses beyond their actual needs, following the general pattern in the Senate of leaving to the judiciary precise definitions of monopoly-restrained trade. Both pieces of legislation advanced beyond earlier congressional and presidential proposals and, taken with the Federal Reserve and the Underwood tariff, many agrarians believed they would "strengthen the posture of the United States in its competition in world markets." Entrepreneurial activity would benefit from government action, an old theme of Southside politics familiar to Swanson.[21]

A series of brutal strikes in the West Virginia coalfields in 1912 and 1913 prompted the Senate to investigate possible abridgment of postal laws and immigrant statutes. Over objections of states rights-conscious southerners, the Senate ordered the Education and Labor Committee to report on the affair. Setting a precedent, Swanson and four colleagues, John K. Shields, James E. Martine, William S. Kenyon, and William E. Borah, went forth to inquire into "the official acts of a state and the conduct of justice by its Governor and courts." The committee visited the mining camps by special train, "leaving . . . men and women, with their children about them . . . startled and awed . . . by the sudden appearance of the Senators." Following hearings in Charleston, West Virginia, and Washington, the committee concluded that, although peonage was not in evidence, postal service was not intentionally interrupted, and immigration laws were not ignored, the miners' constitutional liberties had been abridged. Swanson's signature appeared on the 1914 report that stated in part the strike had resulted from "attendant human greed" of the mine owners.[22]

Speaking in July 1913 to the Richmond and Newport News metal trade councils, Swanson praised organized labor and its impact upon government. To the senator the great issue was "to bring about fair distribution of wealth resulting from labor" and government must assure such a goal. Labor had contributed to public education, pure food, child-labor and safety appliance laws, and "a generally more progressive attitude toward life." Having helped establish the new Department of Labor, he favored combining various statistical and labor agencies to strengthen its role. Following reduction of the Virginia electorate in 1902, the remaining voters might be expected to defend the status quo. Yet, organized labor exerted political leverage for change, and Swanson considered seriously their proposals during the years of Wilson's New Freedom.[23]

In the same summer, Swanson welcomed resolution of the Virginia Democratic gubernatorial nomination. Henry Stuart announced plans to run in 1912, and Richard Byrd, quickly leaping upon the bandwagon, vowed he was "first and last for Stuart." After several meetings Martin endorsed the Southwest Virginia businessman. Tucker, chasing an elusive cabinet appointment, and Glass, burdened by his chairmanship of the Banking and Currency Committee, declined. Without serious opposition, Stuart in August won the nominating primary. J. Taylor Ellyson was reelected lieutenant governor, but a dry Richmond Baptist, Pollard, upset incumbent Attorney General Samuel W. Williams by a plurality of one thousand votes. Directing a "progressive" campaign, "anti-Machine" Pollard benefited from unfortunate school superintendent appointments by Williams, his close residence to Stuart, and Pollard's allegations of political misdeeds that permitted "many ignorant and corrupt negroes" to be registered to vote. Swanson avoided primary endorsements by saying, "When I was governor of Virginia, I gave my attention to Virginia issues, now in the United States Senate I give it to federal issues."[24]

One issue resounded at both levels: prohibition. Deprived of a dry referendum by the previous two legislatures, James Cannon, Jr., in 1913 insisted that legislative candidates state their views on such enabling legislation. To protect incumbent Fifth District state senators William A. Garrett and George T. Rison, Swanson successfully waved aside potential Cannon interference. Local optionist Stuart could not prevent the 1914 General Assembly from passing referendum legislation, now endorsed by Swanson and Martin. Given the privilege to break the Senate's tie vote, Ellyson prevented a political bonding between Pollard and Cannon. The latter also carried to Washington Virginia prohibitionist attitudes by lobbying for the Webb-Kenyon bill that prohibited interstate liquor shipments in conflict with local laws. Elements of the movement reflected a rural suspicion of the urban, distrust of the wealthy, racial animosities, and moralistic superiority. Yet, it was also a broadly based reform in the Methodist-Baptist culture that used scientific, economic, and social arguments to combat what was interpreted as a vast and destructive increase in alcohol use.[25]

Opponents stressed local rights arguments against the centralizing, regulatory mandates of the prohibitionists. The Virginia Association on Local Government included Charles Lassiter, Ben P. Owen, Jr., Alfred B. Williams, and Westmoreland Davis, all of whom had voted for Swanson, as well as William Anderson, Eppa Hunton, Jr., and Edward Randolph, who had not. With Jones abstaining, Martin, Carlin, and Montague voted for local option, but the remainder of the Virginia congressional delegation opted for the dry referendum. Rumors circulated that Swanson had voted against the prohibition referendum that carried every city but Williamsburg, Norfolk, Richmond, and Alexandria and swept the state in September 1914 by ninety-four thousand to sixty-three thousand votes. Attending the funeral of his eighty-five-year-old father in the Methodist churchyard in Swansonville, Swanson did not vote. Marked by an "unusually large gathering of relatives, friends and neighbors," the occasion also permitted discussion with local leaders. Topics reviewed included Glass and his senatorial aspirations, the problem posed by the new Internal Revenue Service collectors, what role Cannon would play in Virginia politics, and the fate of politicians tied too closely to the "brewing interests." But, above all, the European war that had blazed into consuming strife a month earlier and its effects upon an agrarian people's overseas markets dominated conversation.[26]

Swanson had warned the Senate that the war's course was "almost as disastrous financially and economically, in this country, as we were ourselves engaged." Agrarians and their suppliers suffered a credit famine following liquidation of European assets and consequential transfer of gold to Europe. The crisis produced by a scarcity of transportation and a resulting cancellation of orders led to rapid deterioration in crop prices. Tobacco plunged from 12.8 cents an average pound in 1913 to 9.7 cents in 1914. Swanson believed the crop suffered disasters "equal to those inflicted upon the cotton industry." The Farmers' Union and other agrarian groups unearthed earlier demands for government warehouses to store crop surpluses to cure the cotton crisis. As European powers operated state tobacco monopolies, Swanson added tobacco to the proposal since its growers held "a large portion of tobacco . . . without a market." Urban and rural interests united on the warehouse issue. A member of the government's emergency agricultural advisory board, S.T. Morgan of Richmond, boasted that his firm—The Virginia-Carolina Chemical Company—could build a warehouse unit for $500 to $1000. Other earlier agrarian plans to increase credit peppered Secretary of the Treasury McAdoo's desk. Swanson again suggested removal of the federal tax of 10 percent upon state bank issue that would be closely regulated by federal authorities. Eventually McAdoo approved emergency currency to southern banks based upon cotton and tobacco stored in the warehouses, but absence of other regional concurrence, inadequate planning by McAdoo and Wilson's hesitancy produced uncertain market conditions not resolved until 1916 by a rush of Allied war orders.[27]

More startling to many conservative Democrats, Wilson's administration, following conferences with congressional chairmen, proposed a federal subsidized merchant marine to alleviate the shipping crisis. Old-line Virginia Democrats considered the proposal as "undemocratic as it was bad politics to make concessions to particular classes of citizens." Congressman Edward W. Saunders labeled the measure a "dash into the unknown," as it would "constitute a distinct movement toward general Government ownership and operations." Undeterred, Swanson listened to Dan River Mills spokesmen, who could not obtain overseas dyes, and to complaints by tobacco exporter G. Stallings and Company of Lynchburg that transportation charges to neutral Holland had tripled and had increased by five times to Italy. One timber exporter using Norfolk and Newport News had "no assurances of being able to forward our timber overseas" and incurred surcharges on trackage and storage.[28]

Democratic indecision and Republican filibuster held the bill over until 1916. In August, another party caucus bound Democrats into a majority vote and Wilson signed legislation creating a shipping board funded with $50 million to construct, to charter or to purchase merchant vessels. Swanson performed a valuable role; Secretary McAdoo considered him one of eight Democrats who aided in overcoming sectional differences to accomplish "the rebirth of the American Merchant Marine." Swanson, as McAdoo observed, with other colleagues had discarded outworn political philosophies to meet new necessities, being "moved by a sense of immediacy and . . . constructive needs of the hour." His agrarian constituents and ship construction trades at Hampton Roads anticipated direct benefits.[29]

Swanson also persisted in directing federal funds to rural Virginia. In March 1914, he, Wilson, and Secretary of Agriculture David F. Houston discussed selecting a common road bill from the diverse ones being proposed.

Impressed by Swanson's road building achievements, Wilson named Virginia highway commissioner Phillip St. Julien Wilson as assistant and eventually director of the Office of Public Roads and Road Engineering. As a member of the committee evaluating road subsidies, Swanson reasoned that the states should initiate projects funded up to one-half by the state and approved by the Secretary of Agriculture. States would maintain roads at acceptable levels or lose any future federal subsidies. After regional compromises, Swanson argued against sectional discrimination and desired the federal government to "pay as it went, and then permit the states to supplement that and pay their part." Five million dollars were initially appropriated until a total of $75 million would be attained in 1921. As floor manager, he also gained permission in March 1916, if Federal Reserve banks were not nearby, to deposit postal savings funds in local state banks in "the county where invested." He aided small rural banks such as Chatham's by reducing urban banking influences and by increasing available rural credit.[30]

Swanson's 1916 reelection campaign began in the spring of 1915. Moving his efforts to Chatham in July, his secretary, Archibald Oden, working in the Swanson residence, Eldon Hall, found himself "busier than when in Washington . . . working night and day." Through letters and personal contact, Swanson sought to discourage the candidacies of Glass and Tucker. Perhaps to remove Glass as a potential gubernatorial candidate, Attorney General Pollard importuned the Lynchburg congressman to repeat his 1911 campaign against Swanson. Despite petitions from "a recent conference in Washington of anti-Swanson men in Virginia," Glass hesitated. Flood and Martin in behalf of Ellyson approached Glass who agreed to replace Ellyson as Virginia's national Democratic committeeman upon the latter's announcement for the governorship. As reported by the press, Montague and Stuart refused to tilt with Swanson. Tucker came much closer to doing so than anyone else.[31]

Through John R. Crown of the *Baltimore Sun,* the Virginia Republican party chairman, Congressman C. Bascomb Slemp, offered Tucker fifty thousand Republican votes in early January 1916 if he would run as an independent against Swanson. Tucker went to Washington to "talk matters" over with Glass and instructed associates to converse with Republican leaders Slemp, Alvah Martin, and Robert Fulwiler. They advised Tucker that he would be counted out by "the Ring" in the Democratic primary, but if he waited until the last moment to announce his independent candidacy, Republicans could pay their poll taxes "while Swanson doesn't know it" and win in November. Speaking in Florida, Tucker began to prepare for his candidacy by censuring women's suffrage, nationwide prohibition, and anti-child-labor legislation. In addition to his bitterness toward Wilson, Tucker responded to a reaction in Virginia against the president and administration Democrats.[32]

One Virginian lamented, "The less Congress does for a few years the more it will commend itself to the conservative sense of the country." "Tired of having [Wilson] exact everything against the grain," Congressman Walter Watson wrote in his diary that "Wilson is at bottom a Hamilton," favoring centralized government. He feared the Democrats were placating "socialistic elements." Unable to obtain a Supreme Court appointment, Montague winced when Martin and Swanson first preferred another Virginian and then did not object publicly to Wilson's choice of Brandeis. Montague censured a contemplated women's suffrage amendment as a "rude overturning of many fundamentals." Local optionists also feared nationwide prohibition. Tucker edged closer to candidacy in June 1916, encountered Swanson's preparations "for a hard fight," and turned away at the last moment. The former Wilson organizer of 1912 then worked quietly in behalf of Republican presidential nominee Charles Evans Hughes.[33]

Swanson's solid support for Wilson and his own popularity prevented Tucker's candidacy. The president's marriage to Virginian Edith Bolling Galt brought him, as Swanson noted, "closer to our people," and Wilson's course in foreign affairs reflected "patience, courage and tact." Responding to rural distress through national legislation that strengthened government's role in the economy, Swanson courted the six thousand-member Virginia Farmers' Union; he suggested to Flood that he visit state Secretary-Treasurer D.M. Blankenship of Amherst, "a warm friend." He added, "I think he can be very valuable." Realty developer Egbert G. Leigh, Jr., of Richmond did not think Swanson could be beaten: "Repudiation of party principle carries no penalty, where the act is in itself popular."[34]

Impressed by the dry referendum of 1914 in Virginia, the junior senator endorsed prohibition as the "expressed will of the people of his state." Some wets, such as Alfred Williams, now editor of the *Richmond Evening Journal,* condemned the senator's stand as "an abject and humiliating surrender" to Cannon. But, by November, 1915, both Virginia senators discovered the Methodist minister to be "very satisfactory in most respects" on Virginia's legislative races. Flood gathered aid from Reverend J. Sydney Peters of the Anti-Saloon League to convince legislators to place recently elected Harry Byrd on state Senate committees of his choice. One Southside editor sighed: "Claude has got the prohibitionist vote pretty well sewed up, owing to his eagerness to vote for every measure which squints at any sort of prohibition."[35]

Swanson also in 1916 won for Rorer James the state party chairmanship. The earlier agreement with Martin and Flood to name Glass national Democratic committeeman unraveled when James expressed his interest in the office. Swanson hailed James as one of his "closest friends, . . . an unusually fine and splendid man." Martin then attempted to secure Glass's withdrawal, but he refused. A party brawl appeared imminent. Ellyson, however, resigned not only his position on the national committee, but his office of state Democratic chairman as well. Deftly incorporating local politicians and judicial aspirants, James and Swanson informed Martin that the Danville editor would withdraw his committee candidacy in exchange for the party chairmanship. The agreement was sealed one week before the state convention. Campaigning undercover for the position, Flood was forced to step aside. Viewing Swanson's unopposed reelection and the resulting tranquil state convention, a dismayed Glass, in his subjective fashion, professed illness at the thought of "six more years of the common crook who now disgraces the State in the Senate."[36]

Sharing a drawing room with Martin, Swanson traveled two weeks later to the Democratic convention that renominated Wilson and that accepted one of the more significant political platforms in modern American history. Partially composed by Martin, party pledges would commit the United States in foreign affairs to internationalism and, domestically, projected a daring utilization of federal authority in the marketplace. Swanson sensed that the national temper would not accept election of a "stand pat" candidate, and the platform pushed Wilson beyond his previously announced constitutional limits. Swanson also saw the need to repair the party in Congress. In 1914, margins had been so reduced that Hay observed, "We came near to losing our chair at the head of the table." Tillman complained that Democratic disorganization was "a vice of all committees I serve on," and Republican Henry Cabot Lodge concurred privately that there was "every sign of a disintegrating party." Wilson needed reform voters who had followed Theodore Roosevelt's third-party campaign in 1912. Sensitive and astute Democrats in the Senate tried to convince him to sponsor and then to use his prestige to pass popular legislation. To test Democratic cohesion, Republicans endorsed a federal workers' compensation law favored by organized labor and a controversial child-labor law. Swanson found no great difficulties with the former bill; he had frequently stated that "government should be a model for all employers of labor." Democratic leadership, however, quailed before the child-labor proposition.[37]

In the previous session, Lee Overman of North Carolina had postponed its consideration, and Ellison D. Smith of South Carolina and Thomas Hardwick of Georgia berated it. A campaign to convince Wilson to intervene surfaced, and personal interviews were conducted with him. He visited the Capitol on July 18 to lobby for the federal workers' compensation bill and to speak formally for the child-labor legislation. The Democratic caucus still refused to endorse the latter. The Senate Steering Committee, however, arranged the agenda to allow consideration of the bill. Aware of negotiations proceeding within the Democratic caucus, Republicans moved on July 21 to consider by unanimous consent the child-labor bill. Seeking additional time, Swanson prevented passage of the motion, and on July 25 Democrats determined to pass the legislation. With no further delaying tactics by objecting Democrats, Swanson and Martin on August 8 voted with the majority for its passage, but southern colleagues, including Hoke Smith, John Sharp Williams, and Duncan Fletcher, still opposed it. A few days later, in carefully planned succession, the Senate accepted the compensation act.[38]

Swanson's vote for the Keating-Owen child-labor law derived from several sources. First, as a component of the Democratic platform in an election year, it attracted his favor. Reformers such as Virginian Alexander McKelway and labor lobbyists helped convince him. Virginia contained fewer textile mills than more southern states and objection to "competition of the child-employing industries" came from a large number of Virginia businesses. Despite opposition from Dan River Mills and Lynchburg interests, over the previous fifteen years the state had tightened child-labor laws. During Swanson's governorship, fourteen had become the minimum working age, with few exceptions. A superior law passed in 1914, but enforcement proved difficult. Federal legislation appeared the most efficient solution, but Swanson's favorable vote reflects his convictions as well.[39]

War in Europe altered Swanson's parochial role of husbanding appropriations for Hampton Roads into one of planning national defense policy. In

Wilson's early administration, confusion over Senate committee assignments, refusal by the Democratic caucus to increase naval expenditures, Wilson's emphasis on domestic reform, Bryan's opposition to armaments, and internecine Democratic conflict over division of naval funding reduced party unity on naval affairs. From 1913 through 1915, previous patterns of the Taft administration continued as naval legislation lacked coherence. Satisfied with a fleet "second to Britain," small-navy Democrats, midwesterners, and some southerners argued against naval increases. Secretary of the Navy Daniels, however, rearranged the navy's General Board and brought it under his control. Scarcely two weeks after the new administration had begun, the Swansons were entertaining socially the Daniels family. Soon the secretary initiated a general review of continental navy yards, visiting the Hampton Roads area and making his first descent in a submarine. The House Naval Committee inspected the facility in July 1915. And in the Senate, Swanson continually reinforced the secretary's attraction to Norfolk Navy Yard, which employed a large number of his fellow North Carolinians.[40]

Hampton Roads advocates and Swanson were not only being politic but realistic. Despite Naval Affairs Chairman Tillman's desires to strengthen Charleston yard, the Roads offered superior harbor facilities over other sites on the Atlantic seaboard. Former Republican secretary and Bostonian George Meyer had recognized it, and maritime theoretician A.T. Mahan, aware of the "political grounds," stressed the Chesapeake Bay's high priority in drafting defense plans for the East coast. Balanced between the privately owned yards at Newport News and the federal yards at Portsmouth across the harbor, Swanson linked extremes in the Senate and recruited young Assistant Secretary of the Navy Franklin D. Roosevelt in his gossamer threads of political alliance. Convinced of Swanson's loyalty, the ailing Tillman increasingly granted him more influence with the Naval Affairs Committee. By 1916, Tillman purred: "Swanson is very busy about the Navy Department and I presume he is looking after Norfolk. He can not do too much for Norfolk to suit me."[41]

As narrowly partisan as Tillman, Massachusetts Republican Senator Henry Cabot Lodge was "very adroit." He always attended committee meetings, and "with his experience . . . can manipulate things." As a member of Foreign Relations and author of the controversial Lodge force bill of the 1890s, he was more leery of Swanson, noting the Virginian to be "normally one of the most flexible of men—very quick and very active." The Boston yard advocate enjoyed recounting a jesting accusation made by Alabama senator John Bankhead: "I have heard of men with their ear to the ground; but Swanson, you're the only man I ever saw who kept both ears to the ground." Having lost his accustomed influence and connections within the Navy Department and distrustful and spiteful toward Daniels, Lodge gradually entered into a cooperative relationship with Swanson.[42]

In January 1915, war preparedness threatened to become a major issue in the 1916 national elections. Preferring 1914 levels for the fiscal year beginning in July 1915, Wilson sought a sixty-million-dollar reduction of budget projections and Daniels opposed increased naval appropriations. Swanson badgered Daniels to abandon such a conservative stance and, in part to muffle Republican Lodge, give positive support to naval preparedness. But Daniels saw no justification for "the present hysteria about the Navy. . . . [W]e ought not to go too fast." Originally opposed to a general increase in naval funding, Tillman tried rousing the navy but found it permeated "with egotism and self-sufficiency enough to sink it." When the 1915 navy bill reached the Senate, Naval Affairs unanimously increased requests, using new powers granted in recent committee reorganizations. In February debates, during the shipping bill disturbance, Swanson proposed government manufacture of large-caliber naval projectiles to avoid the high prices of private manufacturers. He censured them for the "main idea" that prevailed—"the profit made in the sale." He applauded a naval reserve, opposed a Taylor time study system in navy yards, backed a government armor plate factory, and aided Daniels with a reorganization of the Navy Department that featured a new office, the Chief of Naval Operations. For protection of trade, Swanson ranked expensive battleships above cheaper submarines. After a March 1915 conference committee that abandoned the armor plate scheme, Lodge, feeling "bound to say that I think the conferees have done extremely well," congratulated Swanson on his funding accomplishments. Pushing Daniels and Wilson beyond their initial intentions, a significant bipartisan Senate alliance shaped the administration's first major preparedness bill.[43]

Motivated by his Virginia political priorities and his strong nationalism, Swanson did not agree with the next draft for navy development forwarded to him in October 1915 by the administration. Daniels had reduced a projected six-year plan for construction and improvement of facilities to five years, but Swanson preferred more rapid development. Augmented by career anxieties of naval officers, hesitancy predominated in the administration. While he emphasized the Atlantic fleet and stressed speedier fighting ships, the secretary refused "being stampeded" into larger requests for shipbuilding. He also studied ways to prevent corporations from cornering the vital metals markets.[44]

By early 1916, entangled in Virginia politics, skirmishing in the Senate over the merchant shipping bill, and carefully moving to gain renomination, Swanson was unable to attend seriously to Naval Affairs business. The committee renewed debate over the government armor plate factory, and Tillman ordered Swanson to "follow the example of some members who are always on time and be in the room promptly at ten o'clock." Delaying further committee consideration and representing private steel interests, Boies Penrose of Pennsylvania fulminated against the armor plate project. Again the Senate Steering Committee discovered a means to circumvent procrastination, and Wilson aided them. In April, committee considerations were hindered anew by the illness of Congressman Lemuel Padgett, chairman of the wrangling House Naval Committee. By the middle of June 1916, spurred on by the immense sea battle at Jutland, by Democratic political strategy, by fears over Pacific developments, and by a rapidly concluding fiscal year, Tillman created a subcommittee of himself, Swanson, and Lodge to review the inadequate House bill that requested no new battleship construction and a total of only seventy-seven new ships for the next five years. Tillman, frequently ill, left the major drafting to the two senators. A Navy Department clerk recalled reading out items for inclusion with "Lodge stretched out on a sofa and Swanson nervously pac[ing] the room." They made their decisions "on the spot."[45]

Freed from previously engrossing events, Swanson provided another example of his characteristic ability to respond to a crisis by intense application of energy following a period of apparent lethargy. He convinced Wilson and Daniels to accept original requests of the General Board report that they had diminished: increased ship construction, sixteen new capital ships, and a large augmentation in manpower. Despite the House's contrary actions and Daniels's hesitancy, he warned the president that Lodge chafed to incorporate Democratic naval preparedness timidity in the autumn presidential campaign as a major issue. Wilson acquiesced and accepted the Senate Naval Affairs recommendations as administrative policy. Swanson also encouraged Daniels to sponsor a three-year rather than the early proposed five-year construction timetable. The committee unanimously bound itself to the Swanson-Lodge subcommittee recommendations that favored an additional $45 million over House figures and increased ship construction to 157 vessels. Provisions for small private yards and Charleston were included. Swanson then prepared to fashion a majority from distressed Democratic elements to pass the bill in the Senate.[46]

Opening debate in July 1916, Swanson supported the construction as necessary for an adequate navy. "For weal or for woe," the United States and its navy "are united in indissoluble wedlock" and "naval supremacy ultimately means national pre-eminence and triumph." A strong navy would convoy around the world the agricultural, manufactured, and mineral products of the nation. Profit from foreign trade, made possible by the European war, "has given us wealth almost unspeakable" and upon its conclusion "this nation will be rich beyond the wildest dreams of avarice." The United States should not be "foolish enough to suppose that this aggressive spirit of the European Powers has been satisfied and will cease at the termination of this war." Although he claimed sponsorship of a navy second only to that of Great Britain, his proposals in reality would bring the fleet to near parity with its British counterpart. He explained the necessity of naval oil reserves, supported naval reorganization, and endorsed an experimental laboratory staffed by Thomas A. Edison to perfect less expensive naval weapons free from private patents. He resisted assignment by Congress of specific ships to the Pacific as contrary to presidential prerogatives and continued to argue for naval manufacture of shells and armor plate. Committing the United States to expend $588 million for naval armaments within the next three years, the bill passed on July 21, seventy-one votes to eight.[47]

House small-navy advocates issued such a barrage of opposition to 250 Senate amendments that the *New York Times* feared the preparedness program was awash. At Swanson's suggestion, Wilson interviewed House conferees at the White House. On July 27, the president reported to his fellow Virginian that he had seen them "on the Naval Bill" and was "hopeful of very satisfactory results." Wilson congratulated Swanson for "the successful work" he had done "in this great matter." The conference committee still squabbled over forty-nine items, particularly those treating personnel realignments, increased shipbuilding, and improvement in harbors to accommodate deep drafts of battleships. A second committee became necessary. Penrose replaced Lodge on the Senate side, but Daniels believed correctly that Swanson's "skillful piloting" would assure funding for the armor plate factory. Compromises floated and the bill passed as amended. While admitting to Daniels his small role in its passage, on August 29, 1916, surrounded by military officers and House and Senate committee members, Wilson signed before motion picture cameras the army and navy appropriation bills. The president proclaimed, "Never before by one single act of legislation has so much been done for the creation of an adequate Navy."[48]

Swanson steered advantages for Virginia into the heart of naval priorities. Demands for modern facilities at the Norfolk yard had surfaced in the Tidewater press, and area journalists stressed the "hard fight" that Swanson conducted to insure that at least one of the new capital ships be constructed at Hampton Roads. From a total of $1.4 million in appropriations, Norfolk Navy Yard would be virtually rebuilt. Swanson bragged that the new, large dry dock would place it at the apex of United States naval installations. Additional facets of the act led him to obtain a naval research facility in Virginia. By November 1916, Daniels had instructed the General Board, judging sites for the new armor plate mill, to consider four Virginia locations. Parallel to the reworked navy bill, the Hay army bill met Swanson's approval. Opposed to a large standing army, Swanson also was sensitive to the effect such a force might have on naval appropriations. He agreed with local Virginia National Guard units, some on duty at the Mexican frontier, who disliked complete federalization. Both the 1916 Navy Act and the National Defense Act, however, expanded the federal presence in the Commonwealth.[49]

As one of the administration's primary senatorial advisors, Swanson drew closer to the inner Democratic leadership focusing on national finances, naval preparedness, and the 1916 presidential contest between Wilson and Hughes. He advised McAdoo, his Washington neighbor, as early as June to attract as many "independent and progressive people as possible" by publishing in critical states pro-Wilson interviews from known Progressives. Pennsylvanian Vance McCormick, who had replaced McCombs as Democratic chairman, and South Carolina publicist and former House Ways and Means Committee statistician Daniel C. Roper, now campaign headquarters director, also tapped Swanson's political acumen. A typical relationship was that established between the Virginia senator and the director of campaign publicity Robert W. Woolley, which grew out of the latter's desire for federal office and Swanson's practice of having friends in proper places. As his influence grew, the more secondary and tertiary politicians and office seekers sought his favor, producing a consequential growth in the network of his acquaintances, which defied any single ideological grouping and assured him of increasing influence.[50]

After Wilson's 1916 election victory, Swanson obtained naval acquisition of the Jamestown Exposition tract and construction of capital ships at Norfolk, but lost Radford as the site of the armor plate factory and Richmond as the location of the projectile plant. He probably masterminded the Helm Commission, a special investigation of naval facilities south of Norfolk. In December, Newport News Shipbuilding and Dry Dock Company obtained two of the four battleships allocated. Commanded by Captain William D. Leahy, the Atlantic Fleet converged at Hampton Roads for inspection by delegates to the Southern Commercial Congress; Norfolk and its environs vibrated under boom conditions. Swanson contracted a serious illness, and his absence provided additional proof of his worth to Tillman and the Senate. On two occasions in late January 1917, Tillman complained, "Daniels is not helping me at all." He went to the Swanson home on R. Street only to be turned away, first by Elizabeth, who "seemed about as 'bad off' as I imagine you are," and second by "your nurse and the butler." An abscessed throat, requiring a most painful lancing, afflicted Swanson, but Elizabeth's illness initiated a two-year decline. Recuperating, Swanson helped draft and defend the 1918 navy appropriations bill and, in conference committee, mollified Tillman by constructing compromises necessary to approve the legislation.[51]

Foreign relations enveloped Swanson as international events precipitated war. He enjoyed cordial relationships with Secretary of State Bryan and his successor Robert Lansing. On the Foreign Relations Committee since 1913, he served under two chairmen, Georgia's Augustus O. Bacon and, following his death, William J. Stone of Missouri, Clark's 1912 campaign manager. Swanson cordially assisted Secretary Bryan during Bacon's illness and, upon inception of the European war, he participated in a subcommittee reviewing existing treaties to determine international obligations. During the Mexican crisis he aided in drafting in April 1914 a narrow, guarded Senate response to Wilson's call for intervention in Mexico while advising him that "if he was going to do nothing, he ought to say nothing." Swanson watched after Virginia interests when revolutionary Mexican elements threatened seizure of the Virginia and Mexico Mine and Smelter Corporation or when tobacco brokers Dibrell Brothers experienced increased storage costs while awaiting time-consuming trade licensing required by Great Britain. As war approached in April 1917, Stone, who had been more deliberative than supportive of administration policies, broke with Wilson over arming merchant ships sailing into war zones. Gilbert Hitchcock, the second ranking Democrat on the committee, agreed with Stone; next in seniority, Swanson increased in value to the president.[52]

Prosperous overseas trade and a dearth of military preparedness originally dissuaded Swanson against war with Germany and its Central Power satellites. As late as November 1916, he praised Wilson's avoidance of war. The next month, House chairman of Foreign Affairs Flood told Lansing that he favored war but would wait until a decisive voting majority appeared in the House before advocating it. Swanson's actions indicated a similar mind set and, in the first three months of 1917, occurrences such as the Zimmerman note removed his hesitancy. During his illness in January, he sorted priorities and returned to labor for party unity on defense measures. The armed ships debate crossed party lines and tensions between Wilson and key Democratic senators grew to politically damaging proportions. On March 20, the cabinet sanctioned war. Three days later, having been informed of the cabinet's decision, most likely by Daniels, Swanson told Lodge. Lodge confided to Theodore Roosevelt that Swanson, approving intervention, now "feels as we do." Once Wilson decided, Flood in the House and Swanson in the Senate were chosen to handle the war resolution, and both Virginians advised Lansing upon its drafting.[53]

Wilson's war message in April 1917 carried an emotional and ideological current affecting Swanson as much as had Bryan's 1896 silver speech. Swanson accepted war without any wide or deep support among Virginians. Speaking to the war resolution, he cited German infractions against American sovereignty. To Swanson, the aim was not "peace or war." "War has already been wantonly and lawlessly prosecuted against us." Maintenance of open seas and defense of American citizenship were coequals amid the entrepreneurial themes of his oratory. German submarines presently limited American trade. "If we acquiesce . . . about three-fifths of our entire export business will cease at once." Economic distress would then surpass that of war itself. Citing Lansing, Swanson would "defend our rights upon the seas at whatever quarter violated, . . . at any cost." This new challenge required the "cultivation of the stronger and sterner virtues." Following passage of the war declaration, Swanson emerged as an even more useful and versatile advocate of Wilsonian war and foreign policies.[54]

8

Neither Hesitate nor Halt
1917-1921

A mainstay of Woodrow Wilson in the Senate, Claude Swanson contributed his opinions in war councils and fell heir to mustering legislative majorities for the administration. Encumbered by partisan congressional preparedness and anti-war debates, Wilson entered the conflict with a precarious political advantage in the House of Representatives and a divided Democratic party in the Senate. Swanson and other Virginia congressional leaders, including newly elected majority leader Thomas Staples Martin, were soon entangled in programs for military expansion. Following the armistice, defending Wilson's wartime course yielded to struggling to forge support for the president's peace proposals.

In the first few days of war, Swanson and Martin met with the president. A month later, twenty-five legislators including the Virginia senators and Flood discussed with Wilson means to consolidate and unify ship construction. That afternoon, Swanson returned to the White House to converse with the president alone. Partially incapacitated by illness, Tillman ceded to Swanson the chairmanship of the Naval Affairs Committee and commented that the Virginian could handle "everything connected with the Navy." In the first five months prescedential war plans were cast and Swanson's committee became a congressional focal point for continuing development of America's war fleet. [1]

From spring through autumn of 1917, Swanson with other loyal Democrats shielded Wilson from partisan Republican criticism. In doing so, he earned a greater appreciation in the White House. At the beginning of the war, the Virginian circumvented Daniels and appealed directly to Wilson for advantage in naval policies. Wilson reinforced his secretary in matters of "really capital importance," but the increasing pace of war led him more frequently to acquiesce to Swanson's suggestions. For example, an often postponed enlargement of the Norfolk Navy Base became a reality in June 1917, owing to Swanson, to his Virginia colleagues, and even to Henry Cabot Lodge, whom he had recruited. Aware that the House naval committee opposed acquisition of the Jamestown Exposition property, the Virginians attempted to bypass it by substituting an emergency deficiency bill to the House Appropriations Committee. That committee balked, and as conferee on the conference committee Martin toiled to accomplish their goal. Eventually, the prestige of Wilson, Daniels, cabinet, and General Board members were required to break a two-week deadlock. In addition to bailing out Exposition sponsors by purchasing 440 acres, the appropriation of $3 million was used to improve the site for navy use. War emergencies became a powerful argument to pass legislation that peacetime congresses had denied.[2]

Swanson dealt with other issues that also raised sectional hackles. Private interests implemented stratagems to develop drilling sites on western oil lands reserved for the navy and found allies among such Democrats as Nevada senator Key Pittman and Secretary of Interior Frank Lane of California. After hearings before Naval Affairs in January 1917, Swanson proposed to Wilson that the government lease only existing wells and allow no further drilling. Following a series of telephone exchanges, the compromise withered. By the autumn, oil interests also pleaded that war requirements demanded immediate action. Josephus Daniels warned Swanson that a projected bill to exploit the naval reserves was being shifted to the more receptive Senate Public Lands Committee. Still seeking middle ground, the Virginian gained Pittman's agreement to allow leasing of public lands except for those set aside for the navy. In the Senate, praising Daniels, Swanson would preserve $100 million in public resources from the grasp "of a few individuals." Christmas recess intervened and Lane attempted to gain the advantage, but Wilson refused to "go an inch farther than was embodied in the proposals of Senator Swanson."[3]

In January 1918, in concert with Daniels and Attorney General Thomas Gregory, Swanson promoted legislation "to take over all the lands on the three oil reserves and give authority to the Secretary of Navy to operate them." Braced by Wilson's endorsement, Swanson moved in the Senate that Naval Affairs proceed with condemnation procedures and avoid the prodevelopment Public Lands Committee. After four days of sporadic debate, he won by a vote of forty to fifteen. During the remainder of the war, Daniels and Gregory, in Swanson's words, resisted "the long standing fight to take away from the Navy" its oil lands. In 1919, although legislation failed to pass, Swanson again agreed with Pittman for some development of public lands while reserving the navy's fields. Upon passage of the Navy Act of 1920, Swanson believed he had contributed to the protection of the public interest through federal authority to maintain competitive fuel pricing. In assuring low fuel prices for the navy, he, Daniels, and other leaders furnished price comparisons with the private sector. For his efforts, he was commended by the National Conservation Association. The political effect within the Democratic party, however, probably widened sectional fissures between East and West, though they might have been worse without Swanson's parliamentary touch.[4] But a new administration in 1921 made a shambles of these Wilson policies.

In January 1918, Swanson "heartily approved" Wilson's Fourteen Points address and explicated it on the floor of the Senate. The Virginian blamed filibustering senators during March 1917 for having encouraged German aggression, and detailed reasons for American entry into the conflict. He anticipated a new democratic world order in which American citizenship would be respected throughout the world as had once that of Rome. As this "widely extended conflict will greatly change the map," the United States will be called upon to defend domestic freedoms on foreign fronts. Treasury Secretary William

G. McAdoo congratulated him on "a bully speech" with "the right ring to it."[5]

As chairman of the Public Buildings and Grounds Committee, Swanson obtained massive appropriations for government housing for employeesin national defense work. Warning of an impending loss of states' rights, Albert B. Fall heckled him, but Swanson held that the Executive, not Congress, should determine details of the housing agency. "Speed, speed, speed, is what is needed in this matter." He also gave Wilson advice during these months on munitions procurement, officer appointments, and operation of the War Industries Board.[6]

Not only did Washington assume an atmosphere of a "boom city . . . rushing, shouting, building and hurrying," but Swanson saw Virginia erupt in war-borne prosperity. From the day following Wilson's war address when the battle fleet drew up the York River until peace eighteen months later, the state became a forge and granary. Petersburg, Roanoke, and other Virginia towns and farms bustled; the Tidewater cities expanded so that one citizen exclaimed, "The pressure in Norfolk is getting too great." At the navy yard, employee walkouts occurred owing to a lack of ice water, ventilation, and sympathetic supervisors. For years, workers' accusations of an unfair wage scale had drawn Swanson into debates over yard working conditions. Now, Samuel Gompers visited and urged immediate wage increases, and even Wilson suggested that supervisors who could "better understand the temper and attitude of the men" be hired. A central argument in maintaining modest salaries at Norfolk emphasized the area's relatively low cost of living. Daniels hesitated to raise wages also because it would inflate department budgets. Other Virginia businesses complained of being at a disadvantage in competing for labor should navy yard wages escalate. Farmers protested when labor agents sought rural workers by advertising wages of twenty-three cents per hour. Swanson agreed that recruitment efforts in the hinterland did "great injustice to the farmers," but federal wage standards for the navy yards operated as a de facto minimum wage, placing local employers in a national wage structure. As local and federal authorities wrestled over jurisdiction, Swanson also regretted wartime street riots, increased racial antagonisms, and persistent prostitution in the area.[7]

During the winter and the spring of 1918, Swanson endured some of the most demanding months of his public career. Earlier, Elizabeth's failing health necessitated a trip to the Mayo Clinic in Minnesota for surgery and treatment. She was operated on again in October 1917. Seventy-one-year-old Benjamin Tillman's physical condition had worsened; he initiated a reelection campaign in South Carolina which drained his remaining physical resources. During critical Appropriations hearings, he abandoned his Naval Affairs responsibilities to Swanson, who alertly placed the complete bill on the legislative calendar so as "not to be blocked by the Post Office and Army Appropriation bills." Typically, Swanson and his senatorial colleagues increased by $202 million navy funding requests over those of the House. After meeting with Daniels, he reassured the public of the navy's competence in overcoming the growing German submarine menace. In May, he was moved to the Rules Committee but continued to chair Public Buildings until Tillman's death in July elevated him to chairmanship of Naval Affairs. He found respite from the rigors of wartime to ride and hunt in the nearby countryside or in the familiar terrain of home. Swanson occasionally sent pheasants to the White House larder; for more substantial services, the president's secretary placed his name upon a select list for patronage preference.[8]

Wilson's presidential course antagonized vested interests. Former Virginia resident, Wilsonian, and dabbler in state politics, historian William E. Dodd feared that reaction would come in the Senate from so-called corporate spokesmen such as Martin, "the quiet shrewd agent of big business," and Swanson, "a small potato rolling along the way Martin marks out." Adverse response, however, came partially from former 1912 Wilson sponsors in Virginia. Harry Tucker committed his energies to forming states' rights clubs and to recruiting for the National Association for Constitutional Government. He continually censured women's suffrage proposals, prohibition, and federal child-labor laws. Congressman Andrew Montague warned Tucker in January 1919, "If we can prevent socialism and bolshevism I will be surprised and satisfied." But, while privately accusing Wilson of being "an irresponsible egotist," aging majority leader Martin doggedly followed the president's leadership. Dodd awoke to this situation nine months later when he discovered Montague as bitterly opposed "to the President as any Republican."[9]

Daniels remembered that Wilson came to office intending to oust "men regarded as machine politicians." But "Martin piloted through every appropriation Wilson recommended" while "Hoke Smith and [Thomas P.] Gore and others, who had been strong advocates of Wilson . . . [were] unwilling to cooperate unless they could call the 'figgers.' " Even friends of Swanson spun doubts about the direction of the presidency. In the spring of 1918, Congressman Walter Watson praised the Supreme Court's negation of the child-labor law as the "greatest victory for the Constitution in many years." Yet, despite the "precedent set," he voted for the prohibition amendment because his "constituents would have it so." Whether or not constitutional questions arose in Swanson's mind, his inclination to accept change as adjustment and not revolution prevailed.[10]

His "very cordial relations" with railway director-general McAdoo and Treasury Comptroller John Skelton Williams provided patronage sources among the war regulatory agencies and successful nominations for managers in the nationalized railway system. Both Virginia senators obtained federal subsidies for heavy military use of Virginia roads. These and other plums aided Swanson in standing with the administration's refusal to raise the federal ceiling on the price of wheat. Alertly, Republicans continued their attack against Wilson's war policies by claiming the president played favorites among the regions. Although Virginia grew considerable amounts of wheat, tobacco and cotton were exempt from regulation. Despite an ill-advised October 1918 call by Wilson for a vote of confidence in the congressional elections, Democrats lost control of Congress by narrow margins. Yet, the election represented no massive retreat from the president, and persistent Democratic strength revealed itself outside of the Midwest.[11]

Swanson attended the Senate irregularly in the autumn of 1918 owing to "an illness in the family," that of Elizabeth, who had not recovered. Also, he aided extensively the Democratic congressional campaign, and, after November

1918, he struggled to pass Democratic legislation in the lame duck session of the Sixty-fifth Congress. Apprehensive of the approaching new Republican Congress and effects of the November 1918 armistice, he schemed with Daniels to pass a naval appropriation bill when "the psychological moment to put it through" occurred but feared the odds were "against it." Lodge and Penrose debated each item in committee, and Swanson's pessimism proved correct. He withstood Republican criticism of Wilson's armistice terms and similar censure for the presence of twenty-five hundred troops in northern Russia. He underlined that their presence there resulted from concern that the "Bolshevik" government might have allowed Archangel to become a German submarine base and U.S. troops were needed to protect large amounts of supplies.[12]

Sectional issues in the last weeks of the war congress intruded to the extent that some Wilson advisors opposed selection of any more southerners to federal posts. Joseph P. Tumulty advised against any more such appointments, especially from Virginia. In the list of new appointees appeared Carter Glass, elevated to secretary of the treasury after McAdoo's resignation. But Swanson continued in the Senate in support: Wilson's food relief program for Europe was not only charitable but wise as starvation "produces anarchy, . . . conditions that are opposed to order and the best interests of humanity." In attempting to reunite wavering westerners, he asked for a rural network of roads funded by state and federal appropriations. Western support accumulated as Swanson reseamed the western-southern alliance with such legislation. To be successful with these ameliorating tactics, he needed stability in the executive and majority leader to anchor his projects. Wilson, however, left Washington in early December 1918 for European peace conferences, and Martin evidenced a general physical decline.[13]

Republican and anti-Wilson Democrats pursued Wilson's peacemaking in the same manner they had censured his war efforts. From February 1919, extraneous speeches upon foreign matters littered Senate debates. By Monday, March 3, the Senate had been in continuous session for several days, and, to clear the agenda, Swanson intended to call for a recess on Tuesday. Exhausted from the previous day's debates, he overslept. Fearing defeat for the general deficiency bill, Martin objected to an improperly placed proposal on the floor. Advised to withdraw his motion, he angrily refused despite being informed of an agreement to permit debate of the item. No one, Martin rasped, could commit him to any agreement without his knowledge. Since Swanson had participated in the compromise early Sunday morning, he rose and stated that he "did not bind the Senator from Virginia and had no desire to do so." Republican Wesley Jones backed Swanson's statement. In the past Swanson may well have used Martin's authority to gain hold of parliamentary advantage, but Martin's public anger unnerved him. Within a few moments, Lodge introduced a resolution concocted to embarrass Wilson; it contained thirty-seven names of senators and senators-elect opposed to the Wilson draft of the League of Nations. They could form a minority large enough to defeat any peace treaty in the next Congress. Martin rose again and objected, as did Swanson, to debating the motion out of regular order. Lodge conceded and entered the names into the Senate record.[14]

Lodge used the "Round Robin" affair to illustrate his slyness in parliamentary maneuvers. The Virginians have been criticized for voicing opposition to Lodge's motion for unanimous consent to discuss his resolution, since without objection the Democratic majority could have debated and then defeated the item. In reality, a long and divisive contest would have followed, and the thirty-seven nay sayers would have had their names revealed in either case. A special session, as Lodge desired, with Republican majorities probably would have been necessary, and Wilson, in Paris, would have been doubly embarrassed. Either choice for the Democratic leadership was distasteful, but the objection was a sound parliamentary response.[15]

As Democrats fought "to make a record" for the 1920 presidential election, Swanson subscribed to Wilson's League of Nations draft. Privately, he searched for compromises to assure passage of the broad outlines of the League and the emerging peace treaty. This required a bipartisan majority to maintain any semblance of the Wilson League. Lodge and his fellow Republicans needed to amend the Wilson proposal drastically to make it a Republican product or, failing that, to defeat the League entirely. In the new Senate, as majority leader, he structured the Foreign Relations Committee, preparing to review the peace treaties, to respond to his will as its chairman. Wilson contributed also to an alienation between himself and the Senate. Foreign Relations Committee Democrats had suggested he take members of the committee to the Paris peace conference. Pittman proposed Democrats Swanson and Lee Pomerene of Ohio and Republican William E. Borah. Wilson refused and left the Democrats on the committee to ensnare Republican votes.[16]

From March to July 1919, Wilson adjusted final drafts in Paris in part to meet advice from Democratic senatorial leaders and pro-League Republicans. By May 19, Swanson evaluated senatorial attitudes and discovered two primary objections: the revised covenant's Article XXIII, "to secure fair and humane conditions of labor for men, women and children" through international organizations, and the more encompassing Article X, requiring collective security agreements for League members. He urged modification because some Republican senators held "conscientious objections" toward the two clauses. Through the State Department, Swanson advised American delegates, upon signing the document, to reserve in writing "that labor unions was a domestic question." As for Article X, he thought it should "be limited to five years with the privilege of renewal." Wilson wrote Robert Lansing to inform Swanson that his compromises were "out of the question. . . . [We] must fight it out" along present lines. By June, Wilson also spaded groundwork for the 1920 presidential campaign by consulting, among other cabinet secretaries, Glass, William B. Wilson, and Newton Baker, as well as Democratic chairman Homer Cummings. Sustaining this political motif, he planned a speaking tour across the nation to obtain passage of the League.[17]

Swanson warned against a wide speaking campaign and suggested appearances in carefully selected states whose senators were most easily influenced by public opinion. He knew, for example, that Knute Nelson and Frank B. Kellogg of Minnesota "could be influenced by their constituents." By the end of June, Swanson heard that Wilson planned immediately to go to the public upon his return. He attempted to telephone Albert S. Burleson and then hurriedly penciled a note to the Texan to caution Wilson that he should "first deliver his address to the Senate in Congress fully covering the treaty and League." Then, he should allow it to permeate the political atmosphere for two or three weeks before initiating a national appeal. Otherwise, the president would leave the impression he was going "to the country over the Senate." Many senators, Swanson warned, "agree with me." Swanson also motored to the White House to admonish Tumulty in similar terms. The president's secretary claimed Wilson "never had an intention of making his tour immediately upon returning." He postponed his trip until September, two months after his July 10 speech that presented to Congress the Versailles Treaty and the League covenant.[18]

On the same day, Wilson conferred for over half an hour with Swanson on Capitol Hill. He was the first congressional Democrat to converse with the president upon his return from Paris, and reporters learned that Swanson emphatically warned him that Article X "would be the center of the struggle in the Senate." Few, if any, reservations would be offered on other articles, and the president must mollify the Senate. Thereafter, Wilson interviewed in the White House senators individually or in groups of twos and threes. To the press, Swanson boasted that Republicans did not have the votes to place reservations upon the treaty; on July 16, Swanson informed Daniels, however, that "there must be some reservations to secure ratification of the League," and Wilson should accept those that would not destroy its effectiveness. Swanson and other administration senators sought a forty-nine-vote block to place favorable interpretations or reservations, if necessary, upon the treaty. He was identified as having been chosen by Wilson "as spokesman in the Senate on the League of Nations," but Swanson quickly denied replacing Gilbert Hitchcock, acting minority leader and ranking Democrat on Foreign Affairs. Swanson did open debate on the League with a three-hour speech that furnished a campaign document that opponents needed to answer.[19]

Swanson interpreted moderately Article X. American territorial integrity, Panama Canal security, and Philippine independence were protected. If the common defense pledge was given, no potential aggressors would challenge League members. The mere presence of the Monroe Doctrine with intent to enforce it had prevented past incursions in the western hemisphere by other powers. So would the League's Article X affect the world. Before Wilson began interviewing senators in the White House, Swanson and Pomerene pressed him to soften his views on reservations, but the president refused. On July 24, William Howard Taft's role at compromise was revealed, and Swanson maintained contact with the former president during the Senate League debates. On August 19, the Foreign Relations Committee met with Wilson in the White House. Swanson tried to resolve controversy over the treaty's award of Shantung to Japan, but four days later, over his objections, Lodge forced a resolution through the committee by a partisan vote of nine to eight that favored Shantung's return to China.[20]

Except for a brief junket to Chatham to vote in the Democratic primary, Swanson attended tedious hearings before the Foreign Relations Committee. Arguing that quick acceptance of the treaty would lead to resumption of trade, he, Senator John B. Kendrick of Wyoming, and other Democrats very nearly obtained an understanding that would have united Wilson committee members with three others favoring mild reservations. Lodge intervened and apparently broke such an agreement. Swanson convinced Bernard Baruch to prepare and circulate an acceptable list of treaty revisions for the president and to seek some understanding with Lodge. By August 16, twenty Republican senators appeared ready to accept the treaty with "mild reservations." Ten days later, Hitchcock being absent, Wilson telephoned Swanson to meet him at the conclusion of the afternoon session in the latter's Capitol Hill office. For forty-five minutes, as his wife waited in the presidential limousine, he received the junior senator from Virginia's counsel on the Shantung imbroglio, on the parliamentary situation, and on possible compromise solutions. Swanson, begging for political compromise, told the president, "What difference does it make if a baby is tied with blue ribbons or pink ones—as long as we get the baby." Other administration senators counseled accommodation, but Wilson did not agree.[21]

Swanson presented his case at the White House for over an hour on the eve of Wilson's transcontinental tour. Press reports indicate he advised Wilson that Lodge's Shantung amendment would fail on the floor of the Senate, but an unamended Article X still formed the major barrier to any acceptance of the League and of the treaty. "An appreciable drift toward other than interpretive resolutions" had occurred, but an ailing Wilson stood "unalterably opposed." Some years later, Swanson correctly recounted to anti-League senator George W. Pepper his last-minute interview with Wilson and remembered the president's careful attention; he had "refused to commit himself, but promised to think the matter over." A few days later Wilson spoke against any reservations, and Swanson "knew the battle was lost." The president then suffered irreversible damage to his health, and, upon return to Washington, Swanson and other administration Democrats hesitated to advise him further for fear of "the effect upon him."[22]

Exertions continued to gain senatorial approval of the treaty, and Hitchcock became involved to a greater degree. While sporadic conflict occurred between Swanson and League opponents in the Senate, he still searched for accommodation. He wrote Taft on October 1, praising his "splendid assistance in this fight." Swanson would soon see Wilson, and it was "impossible to say what settlement" could be reached. The Virginian added, "Matters in connection with the League will reach a crisis next week and the final outcome can be determined." Blocked by Wilson's intransigence, Swanson failed to meld Wilsonians and Republican mild reservationists. Faulting Democratic "subjugation to the President," Lodge may have softened his attitude in late October, willing to concede some points, but the moment passed. On November 19, the Senate Wilsonians could not secure the votes to pass unamended the League and the treaty. Wilson bound his administration senators to a League without reservations and the Republicans held ranks sufficiently well for reservations. Swanson was forced to withdraw in December 1919, "owing to the necessity of taking Mrs. Swanson away to recuperate from her recent illness."[23]

Swanson also was concerned over the drift of Virginia politics since the 1917 selection of Governor Stuart's successor. Progressive Attorney General

John Garland Pollard and Martin's old friend, Lieutenant Governor J. Taylor Ellyson, had been considered the front-runners, both being dry candidates. Another aspirant, wealthy lawyer and local optionist Westmoreland Davis only recently had resigned his presidency of the Virginia Farmers' Institute and used his *Southern Planter* to attract rural admirers. Settling in Loudoun County, since 1903 he had advocated scientific farming and lobbied before the General Assembly for farm programs. By 1916, he was heavily involved with Farmers' Union activities and would later appoint union secretary A.B. Thornhill dairy and food commissioner. Every agriculture extension worker save one was "running over the country working for Davis." Regional loyalties and an anti-urban bias attracted other rural voters to Davis; but, most importantly, he benefited from a state reaction against prohibition. A congressional "bone dry" law prevented even mailed spirits throughout the state and one politico evaluated: "Thousands of men who voted for [state] prohibition voted more against the open saloon than against proper distribution of liquor and they resent very much being cut off entirely." Former bastions of wet strength, eastern Virginia cities cast large pluralities for Davis "as a sort of protest." Davis won nomination by a plurality of 11,500 votes over the two Richmond Baptist candidates.[24]

National events distracted those politicians who normally would have joined Ellyson's campaign. The Nelson County treasurer complained, "Our people are so busy talking about the War that it is a difficult matter to get them interested in politics." Charles T. Lassiter deduced that "on account of the war," there was "almost no talk of politics." State Senator Harry Byrd discovered that developing cold-storage facilities in Frederick County to answer the demands of a war economy "so fully occupies my time that it is nearly impossible to leave home for even a day." A food control bill that would award the administration broad powers to control crop pricing vexed farmers, and controversy reached its peak during the last few weeks before the primary. As Martin was visibly weakening, senatorial succession also contributed to Ellyson's defeat. Deputy insurance commissioner and secretary of the state Democratic executive committee, Jacob N. Brenamen, confided to Henry D. Flood that Governor Henry C. Stuart's "only hope [for appointment] . . . is in Pollard. . . . There is no question he is supporting Pollard." Flood's hope was Ellyson. Stuart and Glass publicly favored Pollard while Montague and W.A. Jones apparently did nothing in their districts to stem pro-Davis sentiment. Even Rorer James only slowly alerted voters for Ellyson in Pittslyvania County.[25]

Swanson retreated from any active statewide involvement for Ellyson. Pollard had usually opposed Swanson in past elections, while Davis had favored him in the 1911 senatorial campaign. In Washington, Swanson voted on August 1, 1917, for the prohibition amendment, resisted formation of a congressional war oversight committee, and participated in delicate parliamentary stratagems to protect tobacco and cotton from federal price-fixing. Had he not gone to Virginia to vote in the primary, Swanson would have voted aye on the far-reaching food legislation, the Lever Act. The *Washington Star* described Davis's success as more of a disaster for Cannon and the Anti-Saloon League than as a direct slap at Martin. Further, the gubernatorial nominee and Swanson held common friendships among agrarian leaders, and he, Flood, and Martin campaigned with Davis against his unsuccessful Republican opponent. State Democratic chairman James and Secretary Brenamen, however, carefully maintained their positions within the party apparatus.[26]

Congressman William A. Jones, whose health had been deteriorating for three years, died in Washington in April 1918. He was succeeded, after a sprawling First District primary, by S. Otis Bland of Newport News, sponsored by Swanson's General Assembly associate Saxon Holt. A Tidewater editor eulogized Jones as "having extreme loyalty to his convictions" and as "intensely partisan and exceedingly aggressive in controversy." Jones "may not have always been just, but he was always honest." Charles Carlin resigned his congressional office in the autumn, and R. Walton Moore of the U.S. Railroad Administration fell heir to it. James P. Woods of Roanoke replaced Glass upon his elevation to the cabinet. Ellyson succumbed to illness in March 1919, and Congressman Watson died at the end of the year. Charles Lassiter's law partner, Patrick H. Drewry, then claimed the Fourth District seat. Elected to the Virginia Court of Appeals, Edward W. Saunders gave James opportunity to become Fifth District congressman in December 1920. Most consequential of these transitions was the death of Martin.[27]

In July 1919, having "been on the sick list since last January," Martin left the first session of the Republican Sixty-sixth Congress and returned to Charlottesville. Although in December 1918 he had informed Swanson that he would not accept any "League of Nations that had teeth in it," he pledged to Wilson later that he would return to vote by "getting in a drawing room on the train." But Martin died in Charlottesville seven days before the League vote and was unable to keep this final vow to his party leader. Having visited him a few weeks earlier, Swanson described Martin's demise as "a sacrifice on the altar of public service and public duty." A special train of fifty congressmen and other friends made the trip from the capital to attend the Episcopal services, and journalistic hyperbole rose to the occasion. One editor labeled him "the foremost public figure the state has produced in half a century." Guilty of misstatement, Glass observed the highland splendor of the funeral as the "stalwarts, the old guard of the Martin clans," coming "from city and . . . countryside" to pay their last political obeisance "to the man who had led them to victory in every political battle that has been waged in Virginia for nearly three decades." Having lost his "best and staunchest friend," Swanson remembered Martin's clear, clerical mind, "never incumbered with subtle distinctions nor beclouded by vague and far distant deductions." He wrote to Martin's daughter in March 1920: "I cannot say how much I still miss your father. The Senate does not seem the same place without him."[28]

Martin's decline and death augmented political chores for Swanson. He heard reports throughout 1919 of Davis's intention to oppose him in the 1922 senatorial primary. In January, Richard E. Byrd observed the governor using his *Southern Planter* to pave his senatorial course, and Joseph Button related in February that Davis had instructed a meeting of school trustees to "go back home and send the right men to the legislature." Button considered Davis to be "bending every nerve to build up an organization." Another observer detected that "the forces of the 'Old Guard' " were "badly scattered." To fill Martin's seat, Davis dismissed claims by Montague, Tucker, and Flood and selected Glass. During a driving rainstorm at his Loudoun estate, Davis interviewed Glass and extracted a pledge from him to "fight the machine for the rest of his life." Political columnists hailed the appointment as a masterstroke. Although no election returns offered evidence, some editors considered Glass to be the most popular living Virginian who would contribute much to Davis's senatorial campaign. In the Senate, the divided Democrats were unable to select a minority leader until April 1920 when the ineffective Oscar Underwood gained the position with the aid of Thomas F. Ryan. Glass's vote in the Senate Democratic caucus helped elect Underwood.[29]

Swanson saw Elizabeth growing weaker. Absent from the Senate from December 1919 until late February 1920, he was perhaps ill also, "unable to attend to any business" or to furnish a major contribution to the last efforts at a compromise League settlement. He resumed in April his committee assignments, legislative role, and patronage activities. On April 22, speaking in the Senate for an amendment to fund a survey of a Virginia creek, he fainted. After "taking a little ammonia," he recovered, walked to his desk unassisted, and assured his colleagues he was not seriously afflicted. Younger Virginia politicians anticipated another vacant Senate seat, but in May, the fifty-seven-year-old senator alerted "his friends . . . that he desired only delegates sent to the Roanoke [State] Convention who were friendly to him." The composition of the Virginia delegation present at the national convention in San Francisco indicated their success. Although a delegate, he did not attend. On July 13 in Washington, Elizabeth died while her husband sat by her bedside.[30]

Beyond his personal grief and the curtain-dimmed windows of his Washington home, Swanson knew of the reaction to Wilson's faltering administration. Through the states a "red scare," a nearly hysterical nativism, furnished evidence of heightened wartime emotions spilling into the postwar era. Strikes and riots reawoke memories of the 1890s. The Sedition Act, passed during the war and dutifully supported by Swanson and Martin, founded a massive repression of civil rights of radicals and other reformers. Turmoil continued over the women's franchise amendment, and Virginia Assembly delegates campaigned against it. In the summer of 1919, the Henry County Democratic convention adopted formal resolutions of opposition. These sentiments bolstered Swanson's vote against the amendment, but upon Wilson's request, he released his pair in the Senate and suggested to the president persons in the Virginia legislature who could lobby for the amendment's acceptance.[31]

In Virginia, social change blew in from the war fields. A Norfolk resident believed he saw "the whole world in chaos . . . . Conditions that used to weigh count no more." The citizens of the Tidewater were "all crazy, money mad and going to the Devil as hard as they can go." In Danville, Henry C. Swanson's partnership in the Union Tobacco Warehouse flourished, and Swanson Brothers emerged as the largest wholesale grocers in the area. Farmers, adopting "motor trucks," choked the city's streets. Farm prosperity broke after July 1920, and tobacco values fell to one-half of their 1919 averages. Raising the largest crops in their history, Virginians now suffered from increased costs, postwar trade dislocations, and inflation. Government sponsorship of wartime production gave way to a government-stimulated credit famine, in part owing to Treasury Secretary Glass's actions. Farmers once more translated their unrest into organized protest. A renewed call for marketing cooperatives fomented instant conflict with tobacco warehousemen, and class antagonisms rippled over the Southside. Sampling these political winds, Tucker set his political sails to catch advantage of the reaction and determined to be a candidate for governor in 1921. The Cleveland Democrat would trumpet the call "Back to the Constitution."[32]

Should Governor Davis, Senator Glass, and candidate Tucker combine against him, Swanson would encounter very difficult obstacles in the 1922 Democratic senatorial primary. In responding, the senator created the foundation of a political apparatus that would dominate the state for the next generation.

9

The Principle of
Local Self-Government
1920-1930

Between 1920 and 1930 Claude Swanson rewove the Virginia Democratic organization to strengthen his senatorship. Women's suffrage, prohibition enforcement, controversial road financing and construction schemes, ambitions of rising politicians, and colliding regional interests presented barriers that only arduous work and subtle adjustments surmounted. In his personal life, he recovered from Elizabeth's death, suffered a series of illnesses, and regained his health. Swanson married Lulie Lyons Hall, Elizabeth's sister and the widow of Cunningham Hall of Richmond, on October 27, 1923. His spirits were boosted by his stepson Douglas Deane Hall, and his new family provided a safe haven from the burdens of public life. [1]

An absent Swanson controlled the Virginia delegation at the 1920 Democratic national convention in San Francisco, where his friends isolated delegate-at-large Westmoreland Davis and nominated his senatorial appointee Carter Glass for president. Voting for Glass for thirty-one ballots, Virginia delegates moved to Wilson's red-baiting Attorney General A. Mitchell Palmer and then to the favorite and Glass's predecessor at the Treasury, William G. McAdoo. Virginians endorsed the eventual nominee, James Cox of Ohio, on the forty-first ballot. Resolutions chairman Glass included in the platform a Virginia-sponsored plank that approved of Wilson's leadership, the League of Nations, and its immediate ratification. He wrote to Rorer James of his pleasure at the "fine spirit towards me which you manifested at San Francisco" and, forwarding voter addresses to Henry D. Flood, greeted him as "Dear Hal." [2]

Swanson further eroded Glass commitments to Davis for the 1922 senatorial primary. On the Senate Democratic Steering Committee, he surprised Glass, committed to Harry Tucker for governor in 1921, with superior assignments: "He is bigger than I thought when it comes to forgetting and forgiving." His loyalty to Wilson had also softened Glass's attitude and, in September 1922, at a Democratic meeting, Glass confessed in Swanson's presence, "since I have been associated with [him]. . . , I have learned to appreciate him more than ever in my life." In December, Swanson promised "We will stand together Glass and if anybody wants to break this combination, let them try it." Past differences held no priority over practical politics that led both men to an easy, if not warmly devoted, relationship.[3]

Despite his recent dry record, Swanson knew his vote against the women's suffrage amendment harmed him with some of the new female voters. Staunton mayor William A. Pratt disliked placing women on party committees simply to placate them. "Few of them are interested. . . . A small number of so-called women's rights enthusiasts have forced this matter." But a presidential and congressional election year stirred Republicans to register women that prompted a similar Democratic enterprise. In the Seventh Congressional District in the lower Shenandoah Valley and Albemarle County, organizers paid poll taxes to enroll white women while registrars determined their voting preferences. An inexperienced official claimed, "This was a new thing to us, this women's franchise business, and they came there and wanted to register, and they did not know how." Republicans successfully contended that large numbers of district voters, mainly women, had been illegally registered, thereby removing from office Congressman Thomas Harrison, a law partner of Richard E. Byrd.[4]

Running for Thomas Staples Martin's unexpired term, Glass encountered no opposition from Republicans who concentrated instead upon western Virginia congressional districts. Richmond lawyer Joseph R. Pollard, considered by one Republican as "one of the most violent negro leaders in the state," taunted the party's lily-white cast. He ran a "lily-black" senatorial campaign that so embarrassed "the regular organization" that it lost two congressional districts targeted for victory. In the Southside, these events favored Democratic handlers. Pollard's angry challenge and Republican registration of black women stirred racial antagonisms. Democratic party chairman James suggested Glass "touch up the negro issue and the colored sister vote. . . . Rap the 'nigger' hard is the easiest way to stir the Charlotte people." But requirements that disfranchised blacks also could remove white voters and as a result were unpopular especially in white Southwest counties. A voter registrar had become, one complained, "a punishment rather than a position." In November, despite a national landslide for Warren G. Harding, Virginia remained Democratic.[5]

Campaigning in the Southwest, Swanson suffered another fainting spell. He assuaged concern over his health and encouraged local politicians in his political outposts; he knew another episode might prove politically disastrous. An owner of the *Norfolk Virginian Pilot* who "frequently joshed" with him, asked him "how 'his machine' was running these days." "Machine?" he answered. "I have never been connected with anything but an organization," being "utterly opposed to any 'machine' in politics." The publisher came away convinced that "Swanson and his closest political followers" considered Harry Tucker "was unbeatable and the clear choice" for governor. Having successfully neutralized Glass, Swanson now attempted to mollify Tucker.[6]

Swanson first persuaded aspiring potential candidates to abandon the gubernatorial field to the sixty-seven-year-old Lexington attorney. Ailing G. Walter Mapp of Accomack County and Lieutenant Governor Frank Buchanan retreated; after a meeting with his law partner Samuel Ferguson, Mapp, and others, Flood agree to withdraw in the last week of August 1920. Probably, Hanover County Democratic chairman William D. "Billy" Cardwell predicted

Tucker would win and that, if an associate of the senator had contested Tucker, he would oppose Swanson's reelection. Swanson preferred an amenable Tucker rather than a faction-breeding gubernatorial primary a year before his reelection. At the conclusion of the 1920 general elections, Swanson representatives approached Tucker's camp.[7]

Judge William F. Rhea of the corporation commission interviewed Tucker's son, J. Randolph, an employee of the court, and commented that "the organization leaders had . . . a general impression that a combination" between Tucker and Davis existed "to defeat Swanson." Rhea concluded that "if Mapp could be taken care of, he was sure Flood could be handled" to benefit young Tucker's father. A "50–50 proposition" on Virginia patronage appointments was offered, and Tucker must remain neutral in the senatorial primary. Cardwell talked also with the younger Tucker, but he refused any solicitations. James went to meet Harry Tucker in Lynchburg, but the latter failed to appear. Given this cool reception, Swanson decided to try another candidate. When this news reached Tucker, he sped to Washington to meet Congressman James, who informed him that "he could not discuss the matter" and "that it was now too late."[8]

To defeat Tucker required a candidate with a large white following; his political personality should fit the times and should be able to attract a large number of newly registered women voters. A lawyer from Wytheville, forty-four-year-old E. Lee Trinkle, had earlier tested the political atmosphere, and, in December 1920, Swanson and Rhea were reported "bringing all pressure to bear that is possible to get Lee . . . as candidate for Governor." To convince area residents of his invincibility, Tucker barraged the Southwest with favorable reprints from Norfolk, Petersburg, and Richmond newspapers. Consulting with Swanson and Flood, Trinkle endorsed the "many progressive movements now on foot" and declared his candidacy on December 30.[9]

Tucker's past record stood contrary to many persistent themes in Swanson's public career. The Cleveland Democrat had also abandoned Wilson in 1916, condemned child-labor legislation, women's suffrage, and the League of Nations while continuing to speak against prohibition and William Jennings Bryan. Owing to Tucker's wet proclivities, his campaign slogan "Back to the Constitution" was translated by one journalistic wag as "Back to the bar-room." State Senator Trinkle had avidly voted for temperance legislation, supported equal suffrage, public schools, and improved roads. In comparing attitudes, Trinkle generally surpassed Tucker as a more forward-looking and accommodating politician.[10]

Structuring his senatorial campaign during 1921, Swanson would publicly avoid having his "candidacy dependent or connected with any other person's." He admitted his preference for Trinkle and would aid him as far as he could, but he concentrated his own "fight for return to the Senate" based on his "own record and merits." Remembering the past, he refused to "make public utterances that would create any impression of dictation from Washington" While issuing flurries of letters, he invited numerous local leaders to the Capitol and sampled public opinion through interviewers. A poolroom clerk attested: "Swanson is always on the job. A couple of weeks ago I wrote him . . . about my Spanish War pension. In two days, I got a letter from Swanson and he got

[me] the pension." A machine-shop foreman commented that the senior senator, "like old wine, gets better with age." From a traveling salesman Swanson learned that he had "a wonderful lot of friends in the state of Virginia." Long-time editor W. Scott Copeland wished that his editorial endorsement would "do something for [Swanson's] candidacy." Two weeks before the August 1921 gubernatorial primary, Swanson wrote his brother John for Fifth District estimates and potential difficulties. If Trinkle was elected, he reasoned that his path would be "an easy one" As for Tucker, Swanson believed he "has never to my knowledge supported me in any of my fights and I do not think he ever will."[11]

The Trinkle-Tucker campaign exposed traditional irritations among Virginia's localities. Trinkle had not only urged that women be awarded the franchise but every person who paid taxes. In the legislature he regretted that too long had the "old slave owners of eastern Virginia" been "a millstone about the neck of" Virginians. In the Southside at Blackstone, Trinkle clashed with state Senator Louis Epes: "Here is the difference between us: you insist upon laws that keep some white men from voting in order that you may keep your negroes from voting, and I am not willing to stand for it." Trinkle endorsed state compulsory school laws that would result in a heavy increase in predominantly black counties' educational budgets. Southside leaders looked desperately for "cooperation from other portions of the state" to avoid disrupting local social and political practices.[12]

Tucker attempted to capitalize on Southside unease by citing recently introduced federal legislation that promised to give "power to control 'Jim Crow' laws" and "lynching in the states" to the federal authorities. Should the federal government force "white and black to occupy the same cars, the sleeping cars, that same power will . . . require the State of Virginia to educate its white and black children in the same schools." Laws forbidding interracial marriage would crumble next. A Victoria resident told him he appreciated his speech, especially as it would "be of great advantage to your interest" in the black counties[13]

Trinkle's prohibition record offset partially these racial appeals. Dry enforcement heightened tension between Virginia's prohibition commissioner, J. Sydney Peters, and local lawmen, some of whom were displeased with the dry statutes. Following an acrimonious 1920 legislative investigation, Governor Davis backed Peters's removal while Trinkle sought to retain the former Methodist minister and Anti-Saloon League activist. A dry counterattack appeared in 1921 and congregated around Trinkle's candidacy. In Halifax, veteran politician and former Baptist General Association president Judge William R. Barksdale was assisted in Trinkle's behalf by "the white ribbon gang and every preacher in the county," but one. Mapp claimed Trinkle meant "much for the cause of prohibition in this State," which encouraged delegations of women to canvass door to door for Trinkle. Contention over enforcement jurisdiction would continue, however.[14]

Good roads in Virginia bred further controversy. State authority met local opposition owing to the 1916 Federal Highway Act, sponsored by Swanson, that required each state to submit a comprehensive highway plan to gain federal monies. Davis and the Assembly had agreed upon a state road system that would centralize state authority over road construction. Highway commissioner George P. Coleman, Tucker's distant cousin, also approved the legislation. In 1920, voters had accepted handily by 111,306 to 48,949 votes a constitutional amendment permitting state road bonds, but tributary roads remained a primary concern. Aware that the projected system would but skirt Pittsylvania County, president of the Chatham chamber of commerce Edwin S. Reid complained of Coleman's sixty-million-dollar plan and expressed "deep misgivings . . . at the proposed distribution of these [road]funds." His counterpart in Danville, Henry B. Watkins, similarly defended the river city. In the vast postwar agricultural recession, J.T. Clement of Chatham expressed agrarian fears that the expenditures would be controlled "by the State Highway Commission and the counties, having no control over it, may be discriminated against; in other words the principle of local self government applies" to road building.[15]

These issues of localism—race, prohibition, and roads—were interspersed among censure of Tucker's past record. James used his *Danville Register* to reopen the scars of the 1909 Mann-Tucker campaign and repeatedly cited Tucker's 1896 abandonment of Bryan. Henry C. Stuart incorporated his regional popularity for Trinkle as well. Although endorsed by the *Richmond Times-Dispatch* and *News Leader* and the major Norfolk dailies and aided by Glass, Tucker could not attract county and small-town journalists to his side. He believed that a two-hundred-thousand-dollar fund given to James by aged Thomas Fortune Ryan contributed to these difficulties, but his defeat was the result of his unpopular stands on prohibition and women's suffrage which overcame his urban strength in former wet centers and his racial appeals in black counties. Typical Tucker organizers' reports emphasized that women "played havoc here," that "the women terrified us," and that "the women have gone nutty on" prohibition and suffrage. Former Norfolk mayor Barton Myers certified Tucker's weaknesses: "Suffrage, prohibition and the sensitiveness of Swanson's supporters throughout the state, because of the apparent close association between your organization and . . . Davis." A 22,500 margin of votes nominated Trinkle as the Democratic gubernatorial candidate, and Swanson savored a "glorious" victory.[16]

In the 1921 general election, Republicans snubbed black members by proposing reform of the state's electoral procedures and revision of schools laws while opposing mingling of the races and a road bond issue. Sensitive to white Southside concerns, Trinkle attacked Republican candidate Henry W. Anderson, a former Democrat from Richmond, who apparently menaced "the white man's supremacy in the 'black belt' of our state." Swanson forwarded to Trinkle headquarters for distribution a quickly composed letter warning that the Republicans bid to inject "the negro into politics in Virginia again." The Democrats must continue to stand for "white supremacy, political and otherwise." Addressing the League of Municipalities in September, he advocated a new optimism in state and national affaris: "We have too much pessimism, morally, economically and financially at this time." Trinkle swept aside the Republicans.[17]

While Swanson contemplated an easy reelection 1922, two deaths jeopardized his candidacy. A few days following Trinkle's triumph, James in Danville died unexpectedly of a heart attack at the age of sixty-two. A replacement for either his congressional seat or the Virginia Democratic chairmanship would be hard pressed to match him. J. Murray Hooker of nearby Stuart, a brother of Swanson's campaign manager Lester Hooker, received serious consideration for state chairman, but certain members of the state Democratic committee felt him "not as well qualified by experience, or possessed of the finances necessary to conduct a campaign." Thereafter, Hooker gained James's congressional seat. Trinkle's manager, William W. Sale, lacked majority support as did Henry Stuart, another potential nominee. A rosy-cheeked youth among these grizzled warriors, state Senator Harry Byrd discovered Julian Gunn of Henrico County petitioning in his behalf. At a meeting in Washington one week after James's funeral, Glass favored Byrd, but Swanson preferred Flood. Swanson wrote letters informing the fifty-person state Democratic committee, and in Richmond, on August 30, he led in certifying fifty-six-year-old Flood chairman. Physically consumed by Trinkle's general election campaign, Flood then fell ill to a respiratory infection that produced a fatal heart attack in Washington on December 8, 1921.[18]

Intending in 1925 to conclude his public career with the governorship, Flood inadvertently prepared for his nephew Harry Byrd to claim the party chairmanship a decade before normal expectations. A spokesman for younger Democrats, carrying his uncle's name, and acquiring his political allies, Byrd petitioned for his uncle's chairmanship; however, he was not popular in every section of the state. A month passed before a final decision was made, as earlier chairman candidates were deemed unavailable. After interviewing Ninth District party leaders in Washington, Swanson conferred with Cardwell, met with Byrd in Winchester, and, in early January 1922, wrote to Jacob N. Brenamen, secretary of the state committee, "Everybody seems to be for Byrd." At January's conclusion, without formal opposition, Byrd became Virginia Democratic chairman.[19]

The 1921-1922 recession, regional antagonisms, urban-rural conflict over funding priorities, and personal pique coalesced into a state Senate coalition opposing contemporary Virginia road construction practices. Echoing Flood's earlier censure, state senator Harry Byrd and Delegate Thomas Ozlin of Lunenburg County criticized the centralized state highway commission, and they eventually succeeded in dividing the commission into five districts headed by a weakened commissioner. Byrd was suspicious of persons with technical expertise and preferred businessmen as commissioners. Because his own section benefited from the existing Valley Pike and, unhappy at the prospect of road bonds for other localities, he constructed a regional coalition from the Valley, the Southwest, and the Southside. A bipartisan flavor resulted with Harrisonburg Republican John Paul and Lexington Democrat A. Willis Robertson in leadership roles. Addressing the General Assembly visiting at Norfolk, Trinkle, however, sponsored a bond issue and Swanson stood by his side, summoning legislators to abandon "governmental and economical cowardice." Swanson observed, "It takes as much effort to mark time as it does to march." Despite Byrd's intrasigence, the Senate pssed the bond issue, but the House of Delegates posed a referendum before acceptance. The Assembly adjourned, unresolved in its deadlock.[20]

Many persons concluded that Swanson had endorsed road bonds, but he retreated before the ensuing uproar. Claiming he was misquoted at Norfolk, he promised to continue his work at the federal level for road improvements. Trinkle's suggestion that a special legislative session resolve the road question brought from Byrd predictions of dire effects upon Swanson's reelection campaign and Valley congressional elections. The senator's mail reflected similar sentiments and, through personal interview and intermediaries such as Cardwell, he convinced Trinkle to postpone consideration until after his election. He also refrained from endorsing any candidate to succeed Flood in the Tenth District, a contest that Tucker won.[21]

The same Assembly session that had muddled road financing saw the Senate approve a compulsory education bill, sponsored by outspoken proponents of good roads, Fredericksburg's C. O'Connor Goolrick, Charles U. Gravatt of Caroline, and Mapp. To Epes's contention that the thirty-one counties with black majorities would encounter excessive financial strain should compulsory legislation pass, Gravatt countered with "local conditions must occasionally be sacrificed for the good of the course of education in Virginia." The House of Delegates, however, amended the compulsory feature to permit governing bodies of counties or cities, in conjunction with local school boards, "to vote to except that particular locality" from the law. Apparently Southside's Epes, "looking for cooperation from other portions of the State," had found additional votes in the apple orchards of the Shenandoah Valley as legislative voting patterns against both road bonds and compulsory education were similar. At the conclusion of the session, Senator Goolrick condemned the House as a "leaderless and incompetent body of men who would wreck any constructive legislation if caprice demanded."[22]

Swanson enlisted other younger, active politicians to blend with his redoubtable phalanx of regional leaders in their sixth and seventh decades. He sent printed speeches, one mailing totaling 80,000 copies, and a final campaign letter that went to 127,000 voters. His past attainments attacted women voters who supported prohibition, normal colleges, improved education, social welfare and, most recently, state and federal funding for maternity and dependency legislation. The business manager of the National Federation of Federal Employees responded to his organization's instructions to "do all within my power and judgement in your behalf" by alerting locals in Virginia cities. Organized electricians in the Tidewater, wrote one union man, "are with you to a man and the officers . . . are doing everything we can for you" and Swanson incorporated Gompers's willingness to endorse the senator's labor record. Superintendents of schools and teachers, as well as Jewish and Roman Catholic leaders, joined the Swanson effort. Newspaper editors Copeland, Harry Byrd, Norman Hamilton, John Slover, Rorer James, Jr., Junius C. Fishburne, and others industriously reprinted mailings from his office and furnished their own encomiums. Among congressmen, Patrick H. Drewry of Petersburg led the Swanson effort. Saxon Holt of Newport News bragged, "Citizens feel deeply grateful to you for your services in Washington in the interest of the Shipyard." Local officials, such as Roanoke city treasurer Lawrence S. Davis, assured Swanson, "Everything is O.K."[23]

Bereft of public office, Westmoreland Davis collided with an "extraordinarily powerful State organization," assessed the *Richmond Times-Dispatch,* one of the few newspapers endorsing him. Davis censured the sixty-year-old senator for his vote for wheat price controls during World War I. But, ten days before the primary, Woodrow Wilson testified that Swanson was "at all times most loyal and helpful in his support of me, . . . always active and energetic in rallying the forces of the party in the Senate to support administration measures." Soon Davis stood accused of opposing the League of Nations. He hunted with woefully amateurish workers for the women's vote only to be preceded by Swanson organizers. He talked of new blood in the Senate but Lester Hooker recited in pamphlets and letters Swanson's presence in the Senate's bipartisan "farm bloc" committee and his accrued senatorial influence. While Davis barnstormed, shaking available hands, Swanson pursued a course "similar to that of Senator Martin of remaining in Washington when Congress was in session, attending to official duties." In Virginia, he deployed skillfully a variety of persons by congressional districts from clerks of court to a governor and a former governor.[24]

Securing 73 percent of a light vote, he defeated Davis by decisive a margin of 102,045 to 37,671. Many Virginians declined to vote, owing to a "too sanguine" attitude by Swanson's friends. Capturing every city—even Richmond—Swanson lost only four counties: Davis's Loudoun, Tucker's Rockbridge, deceased William A. Jones's Richmond, and Rockingham, peeved over Trinkle and road bonds. After the August primary, he went to Canada on a fishing trip with Charles Carlin, and overcoming a throat infection, returned to campaign vigorously. He enjoyed the "relief of mind" when he discovered he "could speak and campaign as formerly." In November, he defeated Republican J.W. McGavock in a contest similar to his conquest of Davis. One campaign worker concluded, "The men [who] for a generation formed the habit of voting for you were . . . escorted to the polls by their wives and daughters, who voted with the 'old man' for the 'Old Senator.'" Although Swanson cited the "great tax on me, as many of my old friends have gone" he earned through his shrewd intelligence and attractive personality a public endorsement few Virginians in public life ever received.[25]

Although Democratic chairman Harry Byrd later claimed considerable credit for the 1922 Swanson primary victory, he had been used in the campaign as a junior partner. Lester Hooker, Swanson's secretary Archibald Oden, and more tested regional politicians handled the significant chores. Swanson assigned Byrd the latter's home district, the Seventh, where the young apple grower harassed Davis through the *Winchester Evening Star* as his predecessor James had censured Tucker. In the autumn campaign, by raising the issue of black women registering Republican, Byrd helped purge his district and the Ninth of Republican congressmen. He also opposed successfully a constitutional convention referendum, thereby preventing any electoral reforms. Having known Byrd since his early years—rumors told of young Byrd in 1906 riding in Swanson's inaugural carriage—Swanson graciously praised Harry to his father. Following the November election, Swanson sailed off to Panama, enjoying a postelection respite while Byrd developed the road bond issue.[26]

Economic adversity proved a valuable weapon for Byrd. In the bright tobacco lands, two years of crop prices had scarcely paid expenses. Farmer discontent was symbolized by the Tri-State Tobacco Growers Cooperative, which Swanson had joined. The 1922 General Assembly responded to their pressure by passing favorable marketing legislation. Some of the tobacco district's rancor focused upon paying additional property taxes for roads based upon a presumed unequal property assessment over the state. State Senate Finance Committee Chairman William A. Garrett from Martinsville had favored road bonds in 1920 but, by 1922, had reversed his stand. Shrewd observers noted a growing rural-urban split and class antagonisms over the road issue. Harry Byrd in November 1922 played to these attitudes. Despite a suggested three-cent gasoline tax in lieu of bonds, the General Assembly in a special session ordered a referendum. After an extended, vituperative campaign, the road bonds failed 127,000 votes to 81,000. A regional coalition, embodying distinctly different local ingredients, produced a victory for the antibond faction. Eastern cities and far western counties favored the bonds. The black counties' propertied leadership lacked registered white voters to carry the election, but Russell County clerk of court Everett R. "Ebbie" Combs instructed county leaders to "eliminate all ideas of the road bond issue being a factional question." As a result, white Republicans were heavily recruited in the Valley and the Southwest. A large vote in Byrd's Seventh District and in the Southside tobacco counties proved paramount to victory.[27]

Whether Swanson actively opposed road bonds in the November referendum is unknown, but in a Richmond meeting during the week of November 20, 1923, a group of Southwest Virginians, aware that their section had profited recently from a string of home grown governors, advised Harry Byrd to pursue the governorship. Stuart, state corporation commissioner Alexander Forward, Bolling Handy, Combs, and Rhea discussed how he might broaden his regional base. A few days later, he proposed a legislative ally in the antibond campaign, forty-year-old Thomas Ozlin, a railroad attorney from Lunenburg for election to Speaker of the House of Delegates. Swanson wrote Ozlin of his admiration for Byrd and expressed interest in his gubernatorial candidacy, but in Washington a few days later he recommended the incumbent speaker, fifty-nine-year-old Richard L. Brewer, Jr., who secured a third consecutive term. Byrd in January 1924 discovered also that gubernatorial candidates abounded: Attorney General John R. Saunders, Lieutenant Governor J. E. West, state Senators Mapp and Buchanan, as well as Goolrick and Congressman R. Walton Moore.[28]

A presidential election, one bane of local Virginia politicians, intruded. Outspokenly opposed to the Ku Klux Klan and a wet, Alabama senator Oscar Underwood again sought in 1924 presidential orders. He served perhaps as a blind for eastern business interests who preferred West Virginia governor John W. Davis, a Washington and Lee graduate. Urban, wet, and Roman Catholic, Alfred E. Smith of New York commanded strong ethnic and sectional loyalties. Admired by Wilsonians, labor unions, and reformers, Wilson's son-in-law and former treasury secretary William G. McAdoo appeared again the front-runner. Now a California resident, McAdoo planned to hinge together a southern-western alliance and hesitated to condemn the Klan directly. In Virginia, both

Swanson and Glass favored McAdoo. "Utterly opposed" to an Underwood nomination, Swanson believed it would be "fatal to the Democratic party."[29]

Congressman Harry Tucker, who considered McAdoo "a disaster," agreed in June 1924 with his father's former student, John Davis, that he and Charles Bryan, brother of William Jennings Bryan, would make "a good ticket." Covertly sponsoring Underwood, Carlin of Alexandria used funds furnished by Ryan, who performed a reprise of his 1912 role. Harry Byrd leaned toward Underwood but probably shifted to Davis. Glass suspected that Byrd so strongly oposed McAdoo's election owing to his distress at McAdoo's administration of the railroads during World War I and commitment to minimum wage laws. Another publisher and opponent of Byrd in the road bond referendum, Hamilton of the *Portsmouth Star,* was McAdoo's campaign manager and cultivated strong support in central and southeastern Virginia. Bryd then shifted to Glass as a favorite-son candidate. At the Norfolk state Democratic convention, Swanson composed compromise bylaws governing the delegation, and both senators believed that the Virginia delegation might be "relied on to go to . . . [McAdoo's] support at an opportune moment." The Democrats adjourned, "leaving a note of harmony peculiar for Democratic conventions."[30]

The national party convention in New York required two weeks to nominate a presidential candidate. Wounded by revelations that he had been legal counsel to discredited Edward C. Doheny, McAdoo fell open-armed upon the Klan issue. A minority proposal to censure the Klan missed passage by the narrowest of margins; without unit rules of various delegations, it probably would have passed. McAdoo's southern and western coalition proved flimsy in surmounting Smith's eastern, urban delegations pursuing the Klan for principle and politics. Virginia delegation chairman Swanson replaced tardy Edwin A. Alderman to nominate Glass who joined eighteen other presidential nominees. During 103 ballots, his delegate total hovered about the twenty-four votes from Virginia. On an anti-McAdoo motion to permit Smith to address the convention, the Virginia vote of fourteen "yes" and ten "no" revealed other delegation preferences. After seventy ballots, Swanson suggested a "complimentary vote" for McAdoo and artfully argued, should he falter, that McAdoo delegates would then move to Glass. The delegation refused despite damage to Glass's nomination hopes. Meeting with managers of other favorite sons who controlled two hundred votes, Swanson proposed a release of their delegates. More a pawn than a principal, Glass wrote a letter requesting that Virginia vote for McAdoo or withdraw his own name, but he could obtain only ten votes for McAdoo. Harry Byrd persisted for Glass as advised by Glass's manager John Stewart Bryan of Richmond.[31]

On the 103d ballot, Virginia helped win a useless nomination for Davis who selected Charles Bryan as his running mate. Upon return to Portsmouth, Hamilton cited the delegation's refusal of a complimentary vote for McAdoo as evidence that some members "hated McAdoo more than they loved Glass." He observed, "If . . . left to Senator Swanson I am sure Glass would have been named." McAdoo's candidacy had been closely identified with anti-Byrd groups; most important, Southwesterner Stuart probably positioned himself against McAdoo, giving Harry Byrd considerable delegate leverage. Norfolk journalists wrote of an emerging contest between Swanson and Byrd for party control. Quickly appointing two persons Swanson had requested to the state Democratic executive committee, Democratic state chairman Byrd pledged Swanson his continuing friendship and other Byrd allies sent the senior senator similar assurances. Swanson continued to give no offense and hid his possible resentment behind friendly expressions.[32]

Swanson in 1924 served as chairman of the Speakers Bureau for the Democratic National Committee and a member of the Democratic senatorial Election Committee. In a Republican year, Senate Democrats lost only four seats but could not furnish a cohesive national program for the stricken Davis campaign against incumbent Calvin Coolidge. In Virginia, Swanson prevented third-party candidate Robert La Follette from attracting labor support, especially among the railroad brotherhoods, and instructed Glass, running for a full term: "Get your clerks active with your friends in the various counties in Virginia." Eschewing the national Democratic campaign, Virginia chairman Harry Byrd concentrated on two western congressional districts, the Seventh and the Ninth, for future benefit. With the lowest number of eligible Virginia voters in the twentieth century participating, the state remained Democratic with nine others, eight of which were southern.[33]

Virginia experienced persistent economic problems. Increased mechanization and improved techniques in railroads and construction trades fathered a decreased need for manual workers. Norfolk and surrounding manufacturing and commercial clusters fared better than inland counties facing depressed agricultural conditions. Enjoying a sprawling building spurt, Richmond continued as Virginia's mercantile and manufacturing heart. Beside educational enrollments, support, salaries, and facilities, the cities advanced in health care, transportation, and other social services. Accumulating banking resources in Richmond and the Tidewater served to sponsor some growth. Yet, the cities were but islands in a vast rural sea; Virginia's counties and incorporated towns accounted for 70 percent of the state's 2,300,000 population.[34]

In the rural areas, isolation bred localism as communications still depended upon post office and newspaper; newfangled radios were in short supply, and poor feeder roads prevented easy extension of telephone lines into the countryside. The *Waynesboro Valley Virginian* in Augusta County reflected a provincialism that feared the "gnawing and ever increasing menace of Labor Organizations," a racism and a sexism that viewed women's suffrage as "a scheme of pernicious Republican political cussedness," a nostalgic stance that favored Harry Tucker's gubernatorial campaign to bring back "a flavor of old and better times," and a parochialism that branded road bonds an urban scheme because "all the city newspapers are for it." The era was marked by memorialization of now historic Civil War battlefields, initiation of the Williamsburg restoration, agitation for government purchase of Monticello, and intensified ancestor worship. Harry Byrd praised a proposed reduction of elected state officials as a positive, "reactionary step, for it reaffirms the wisdom of our fathers." Blacks continued to flee the state; the agricultural population grew less than one-tenth of 1 percent during the decade. Despite an average annual birthrate of nearly 60,000, only 100,000 more persons resided in Virginia than ten years earlier. Many in the lower economic classes turned away with an indifference that political campaigns, cooperative movements, the Farmers Union, or the Ku Klux Klan succeeded only partially in rousing. The mass politics of the 1890s had withered in the mid-1920s to a narrow, local consciousness and a greatly reduced electorate.[35]

Sensitive to accusations of boss rule and machine politics, Swanson assumed a restrained seigneurial role. The editor of the *Norfolk Virginian Pilot* described political Virginia as dominated "by the Royal decrees of half a dozen leaders—when these half-dozen agree—and the agreement is always negotiated in Washington." In April 1925, the senior senator presided at a brisk, forty-four minute session of the state Democratic committee that elevated to chairman his former private secretary Hooker to replace Harry Byrd who had resigned to run for governor. Postponing a scheduled summer trip to Europe, Swanson sent his wife Lulie ahead and joined Byrd's campaign. His preference for Byrd rested upon the later's ingratiation of the older man, promises made to Flood in 1921, and Swanson's attraction to the most available candidate. Stuart contributed his imposing influence in the Southwest for Byrd who faced a reduced candidate field: Orange County resident and auditor of public accounts C. Lee Moore and state Senator Mapp. Congressman Moore considered candidacy until the Fairfax native asked Glass to honor earlier agreements only to discover that he followed Swanson and Stuart "with the same sort of gentle willingness which marked the demeanor of Mary's Little Lamb." Mapp fell heir to similar problems. In June, Lee Moore resigned from the race, leaving only Byrd and Mapp,.[36]

Swanson could appreciate Mapp's campaign platform, which endorsed improved schools and highways, increased voter registration, and statewide property tax equalization that implied a maturation of an efficient state government in Richmond. Mapp had disappointed Swanson, however, by failure to aid actively his 1922 senatorial candidacy. Mapp courted also the Anti-Saloon League and politically active ministers by calling for improved prohibition enforcement but received only lukewarm support from James Cannon, Jr. The bishop refused a maximum effort owing to Harry Byrd's "perfect record" on prohibition. Able to mount only a regional campaign, Mapp failed most grievously in heavily populated Norfolk and its environs. Pledging "progressive, efficient and business-like" government, Byrd authored a vague campaign document. Narrowly educated and provincial, he depended upon the Democratic party organization that he had chaired the previous two years. Glass campaigned widely for Byrd, but Swanson's participation assured the younger man's success. The great, white voting counties of the Fifth District, the Southwest, and the Shenandoah Valley leaned heavily toward Byrd, who collected 107,317 votes to Mapp's 67,579.[37]

After Harry Byrd's defeat of Republican S. Harris Hoge, Swanson labeled Byrd the most "capable of meeting the present situation," and expansively offered the governor-elect assistance "at all times," given "in such ways as to avoid the criticisms of your enemies." Swanson advised Byrd to compose his mind "as to what is the best and right thing to do," then do it. Swanson presented his condolences upon Richard E. Byrd's death, and his son replied that, a few days before his passing, "he and I were discussing the great assistance that you had been to me in the campaign." Because there was "more unrest over the state with respect to the state government" than he had ever witnessed, Byrd planned to consult Swanson in Washington. The latter immediately recommended that a recent ally of Mapp, state Senator Cecil C. Vaughn, representing Suffolk, be appointed to the state Senate Finance Committee. Having known Vaughn since his teenage years, he considered the fifty-seven-year-old bank cashier a highly useful addition to Byrd's legislative support. Byrd complied.[38]

During his gubernatorial term, Byrd requested Swanson's aid with important legislators, but as progressive reform, the governor dismantled a considerable portion of the centralized authority that had been invested in state government since 1900. The Assembly convened on three occasions during his tenure and appeared to resolve the divisive localism, partially inspired by Byrd, that had erupted during Trinkle's faction-ridden term. Senate caucus leader Ferguson and new speaker Ozlin, who overcame a challenge by Richmond's James H. Price, escorted Byrd recommendations through the legislature. The 1901 constitutional convention furnished Byrd ideological impetus and localism triumphed in the "segregation" of taxes. Rather than accept a proposed standardization of property assessment, Byrd abandoned property taxes as a state revenue source and replaced it with increased taxes on gasoline and incomes over $5,000. This produced relief principally for "rural landowners . . . , acutely demanded by the unprofitableness of their calling in recent years." Large rural landowners saved hundreds of dollars while urban centers assumed a larger portion of state financing. Had Byrd incorporated contemporary business trends, he would have consolidated governmental authority in Richmond by following business patterns that stressed efficiency, concentration, and combination.[39]

Approved by the General Assembly, Byrd used special study commissions headed by Judge Robert W. Prentis and Richmond tobacconist William T. Reed to avoid a constitutional convention and to adjust the constitution through a series of referenda. The legislature pruned further state activities in its 1926 and 1928 sessions. Byrd pampered the recently decentralized road system, ignored generally requests for study and additional funding of the public schools, reduced sharply higher education budgets, and refused to consider suggestions for more responsive and less wasteful local government. Continuing a widely criticized fee system for local public officials, he proposed that local school boards appoint superintendents and that local commissions establish tax assessments. The governor should also select the Superintendent of Public Instruction, removing control of that office from the electorate. Although he did not sign the bill, local pressure from black counties convinced him, despite opposition from urban newspapers, to allow a law segregating the races at public assemblages. A treasury surplus developed, not so much from governmental efficiency as from reductions or freezes in state services and, so claimed Virginia tax commissioner C. H. Morrisett, movement to Virginia of wealthy persons attracted by "the state's liberal tax laws."[40]

The Ku Klux Klan objected to the "short ballot" proposals that would reduce the number of elected officials and increase appointments by the governor. Symptomatic of a declining agrarian culture, the hooded order became "second only to the Church as a source for both social and ethnic expression" for those "relocated rural folk living in belts around the industrial cities" in the Tidewater and the tobacco belt. Appealing to nativism and religious prejudice, battening upon economic adversity, a revitalized Klan in 1925 also opposed election of Roman Catholic state treasurer John M. Purcell, appointed by Trinkle to fill an uncompleted term. He encountered primary opposition from Methodist Archie H. Williams, a member of the state Democratic executive committee, native of Pittsylvania County, and resident of Wytheville. A Mason, Williams enjoyed a close friendship with Swanson, for whom he had named his youngest son. Purcell's majority was "so small as to keep his nomination in doubt until two days after the primary" in August. A furniture manufacturer and Henry County banker John D. Bassett challenged Purcell in the general election where the Republican obtained the Klan's endorsement as the "100 percent candidate" and carried majorities in nineteen counties and five cities, including Pittsylvania County by 1,324 to 471 votes. In the 1925 general election, other Republican candidates received an average of thirty-seven thousand votes, but Bassett's total ran twenty thousand votes beyond that.[41]

In 1928, the Klan supposedly threatened to flog Governor Byrd and burned crosses at Covington while he spoke nearby for his proposed constitutional reforms. Byrd collected rumors in 1931 that the Chatham bank had discounted in 1928 Klan paper under the signature of state grand dragon J.L. Baskin, thereby providing funds to oppose Byrd's referenda and Democratic presidential candidate Al Smith. Byrd wanted to blame Swanson, who owned considerable stock in the bank, but no evidence surfaced tying Swanson to the loan, made in 1927, as revealed by Edwin S. Reid, not 1928. For the senator to have agreed to finance a campaign against a Democratic presidential nominee would have marked a gross deviation from his earlier political career.[42]

In evaluating Byrd's reforms, editor Louis I. Jaffe's *Norfolk Virginian Pilot* objected to removal from state control real estate and tangible taxes. Mapp debated with his former supporter Pollard who favored Byrd's proposals. Superintendent of Wise County schools and president of the Virginia Educational Association predicted a disruption of the state's educational system, condemned Byrd's censure of teacher political activity, and warned of the dangers that might arise "from having the public school system become a tool of the politicians." The latter observation derived from a proposed selection by local school boards of superintendents and gubernatorial appointment of the superintendent of public instruction. Senator Glass approved of the short ballot, but congressmen Joseph Whitehead of the Fifth District, Joseph T. Deal of the Second, and Patrick H. Drewry of the Fourth opposed it. Byrd suspected that the latter spoke "for a higher authority."[43]

The "higher authority" was Swanson. In March 1927, Swanson questioned the governor's intention to alter the state literary fund traditionally designated for the lower grades. Now it would be appropriated through the General Assembly who might be strongly tempted "to divert the fund for higher educaton." He objected also to local school board appointment of superintendents. He would reduce the period between the payment of poll taxes and voter registration from three years to an experimental one year. Swanson suggested that the Court of Appeals retain its present seven-person membership and believed that the governor's salary should be standardized rather than subject to legislative whim. Despite these disagreements, Swanson did not publicly differ. The referenda barely passed in June 1928, and districts long loyal to Swanson did not easily accept the constitutional amendments. Pittsylvania County and Danville voted heavily against all five proposals, three of which, gubernatorial appointment of the Commissioner of Agriculture, the Superintendent of Public Instruction, and the Treasurer, won statewide by only 3,000 out of 133,000 ballots cast.[44]

The referenda purposely preceeded a potentially divisive 1928 Democratic state convention. To enhance his national influence, Swanson preferred that Virginia provincial proclivities merge with national patterns, and he initially favored for president former Wilsonians Newton D. Baker and Owen D. Young. Fearing a higher tariff and lowered immigration barriers if Tammany prevailed, Glass seconded Swanson. Byrd, wary of national campaign effects upon his future, followed along. Another Wilsonian, Franklin D. Roosevelt, kept in touch with Swanson in the spring of 1928 and, along with New York senator Robert F. Wagner, diligently worked to commit southern senators such as Swanson to Al Smith. Smith had deadlocked the 1924 convention, preventing McAdoo's nomination, but in April 1928 Wagner confided to Roosevelt that Smith's campaign progressed nicely: "The Senators of the Southern States have mellowed considerably. . . . Most of them are actually friendly to our mutual friend." Swanson soft-pedaled Smith's candidacy, the most difficult ever presented him by a Democrat.[45]

Smith's candidacy created vast problems in Virginia, still rural, Protestant, and militantly prohibitionist. But Virginia's provincialism was matched by that of Tammany warrior Smith, whose world, one contemporary defined, began at Coney Island and ended at Buffalo. Speculation circulated that Smith was bound to northeastern business interests, favored lowered immigration bars, and endorsed high tariffs to placate Massachusetts and New Jersey. Although Glass thought Virginia to be "totally contrary" toward Smith, he was popular in wet centers such as Norfolk. Swanson soothed the peppery politician by urging him to write the Virginia Democratic platform so that it "be not injurious and accentuate the fact of his [Smith's approaching] nomination." At the Roanoke state Democratic convention, Swanson reviewed Glass's work and drew advice from a receptive Congressman Moore for prohibition, taxation, economy, and farm planks. The state's "Big Four," Swanson, Glass, Hooker, and newly elected national committeeman Byrd, poured "oil on troubled waters." Each with one-half vote, fourteen delegates of Virginia's forty-eight apparently preferred Smith, but Glass, upon addressing the convention, was interrupted by calls of "How do you stand on Al Smith?"[46]

At the humid 1928 Houston national Democratic convention, Swanson sought to pry loose eighty-eight Virginians—delegates and their alternates—for Smith. He cooperated with Smith's state leader, the fifty-four-year-old Norfolk lawyer and state senator James S. Barron, an Episcopalian and native of Richmond County who had practiced law briefly in New York. Symbolizing

Smith's popularity among Tidewater politicians, Barron claimed to be "for Virginia first and his own section second." Glass's preference for Cordell Hull of Tennessee surfaced when the Lynchburg senator voted to seat an anti-Smith delegation from Louisiana and, during a speech by Cannon, Glass and Senator Millard Tydings of Maryland exchanged blows before being separated. Following Smith's nominating speeches, Swanson apparently seized the Virginia state placard in the melee and joined the demonstration, angering Byrd. On the first and nominating ballot chairman Swanson reported Virginia's vote as six for Smith and eighteen for Hull. Had a second ballot occurred, four more Virginia votes would have been cast for Smith, the *Norfolk Virginian Pilot* reported.[47]

Reminiscent of Alton Parker's actions in 1904 on the gold standard, nominee Smith qualified his support of the party's prohibition plank. He selected another northeastern Roman Catholic wet as party chairman, vice-president of E.I. Dupont de Nemours, John J. Raskob. Upon this news, the carefully seamed Virginia Democratic coalition unraveled. Before the Houston convention, Bishop Cannon had catalogued for Swanson his two-year opposition to Smith and now called for Anti-Smith Democrats to meet in Asheville, North Carolina, to support Republican nominee Herbert Hoover and prohibition. The Anti-Smith convention listed four reasons to oppose Smith: his "repudiation" of the prohibition article, his wet proclivities, his selection of a "wet" Republican as chairman of the national Democratic Committee and his relationship to Tammany Hall. Smith's Roman Catholicism was officially ignored, but Cannon on other occasions had denounced what he estimated to be the narrowness and bigotry of the Irish New York Roman Catholic hierarchy. Worried Virginia state chairman Hooker complained in mid-July to vice-presidential nominee Joseph T. Robinson of Arkansas that Virginia Democrats were "sorely disappointed and many are in open revolt and actively and openly opposing Governor Smith's election." In August, Swanson and Byrd sent Glass to ask Smith to moderate his wet views, but he returned having taken "a futile trip beyond the fact that you, Byrd and I are in a position of having given Smith fair warning against any disaster that may ensue."[48]

Swanson dismissed Cannon's preachment that "dry southern Democrats" were being "asked to commit moral suicide for political office." Seeking a fourth term as senator, he refused in May 1928 to consider any gubernatorial candidate for the next year until after the election. In July, he met with other Virginia officeholders to endorse Smith. Cannon coordinated his activities with Republican leaders C. Bascomb Slemp and Joseph S. Frelinghuysen of New Jersey, and exorted Virginia anti-Smiths to register thousands of nonvoters. Norman Hamilton warned in October, "We are sorely in need of assistance, as we are up against a strong combination of 'old line' Republicans, Kluxism and Cannonism." Although Smith's religion was a major factor, his inept politics and controversy over enforcement of the Eighteenth Amendment, beyond all other issues, furnished Cannon glue for his anti-Smith Virginia coalition. Glass mounted a political jehad against Cannon; Byrd waxed censorious. At a rally in Richmond with the Democratic vice-presidential nominee Robinson, Swanson claimed he had been opposed to Smith initially because he knew "it would mean a fight." But upon his nomination, "I was for him." Byrd later claimed Swanson deserted the Smith campaign. Yet, in October, Swanson campaigned in the Tidewater, being keynote speaker at Hickory Ground at an "Old Time Rally" and also visited the Valley in behalf of the Democratic ticket. In later years, Swanson would be remembered by emerging Colgate Darden, future congressman and governor, as the center of "considerable wrangling about his stand in the Al Smith campaign." His senatorial colleague Hugo Black of Alabama recalled, however, nationally Swanson "took an exceptionally active part in the 1928 campaign." But, not only did President-elect Hoover count Virginia his by 164,000 to Smith's 140,000 votes, Republicans gained congressional seats in the Ninth, Seventh, and Second districts—defeating in the latter instance eight-year veteran Deal.[49]

Reelected without significant opposition, Swanson reprimanded Cannon by suggesting a sermon on "thou shalt not bear false witness against thy neighbor," given the ill-founded rumors circulated about the Democratic presidential nominee. While obtaining additional inaugural tickets for Cannon, Swanson also advised Glass to be "quiet and calm and appear undisturbed as though nothing had occurred." He, Glass, and Byrd agreed that "those who had their religious and prohibition prejudices inflamed to the point of leaving the Democratic party temporarily should be permitted to return without question." For Cannon, Virginia Anti-Saloon League superintendent David Hepburn, and minister of Norfolk's Grace Methodist Episcopal Church South J. Sydney Peters, nothing would be offered. Glass observed to Byrd that, in private, "Swanson cusses them more picturesquely and more emphatically than either you or I could hope to do." Had he known of Cannon's continuing electoral activities, he would have been more inspired.[50]

Cannon now threatened the Virginia political order. Some timid local Democrats suggested new state Democratic leadership with persons more bland and less objectionable to Cannon. The bishop proposed to Joseph D. Eggleston, Jr., a fellow anti-Smith and president of Hampden-Sydney College, that the anti-Smith organization be broadened to win the Virginia governorship in 1929 "outside the Democratic party with Republican assistance." In 1930, Cannon would then offer an independent candidate to succeed Glass. Selected anti-Smith organizers met in February 1929 in Lynchburg to formulate a course. By the month's end, Virginia Democrats in Washington overheard rumors that a $500,000 Republican campaign fund would be funneled into the autumn Virginia general election. As the only southern state, among those voting for Hoover, holding state elections in 1929, Virginia received full attention by the national Republican organization. In June, an anti-Smith convention at Roanoke nominated William Mosely Brown, a youngish professor of psychology at Washington and Lee University. Two weeks later, recalling William Mahone's tactics, two thousand Republicans in Richmond at their state convention seconded Brown's nomination. In the autumn elections, anti-Smith chieftains, notably Peters, cooperated with the Republican patronage dispenser C. Bascomb Slemp and Second District congressman Menaclus Lankford of Norfolk.[51]

Given regional objections to another western Virginia governor, Swanson considered possible Tidewater candidates who would detract from the Cannonites. Mapp held some potential for that mission, but he had persistently opposed Byrd and his policies; despite Mapp's dry Methodism, he had serious liabilities—one that suggested Cannon could influence him as in former days. Further, Swanson heard warnings in June 1928 that he might face Mapp, if elected governor, in the 1934 senatorial primary. With only the greatest difficulty would Glass come to Mapp. Two other eastern candidates—Lieutenant Governor Junius E. West of Suffolk and Rosewell Page, a former second state auditor, Richmond bar president, and Hanover delegate—stirred some interest. A fourth candidate, former attorney general Pollard, was presently a law professor and dean at the College of William and Mary. An active Baptist dry, he could lead his fellow religionists back into the Democratic fold. Pollard had campaigned for the Byrd constitutional reforms and would be, as Byrd later testified, "entirely loyal" to him. Given earlier campaigns, Pollard saw "no reason to expect any special consideration at the hands of Senator Swanson."[52]

Concluding a congressional session and having discussed options with Virginia congressional colleagues, Swanson wrote to Reed, among other persons, that he was "very desirous of seeing you with reference to the gubernatorial situation in Virginia." Increasingly aligned with Byrd, rapidly becoming his *éminence grise,* Reed agreed to either Richmond or Washington as a site for "five or six" to "start the ball rolling." For some time, Byrd had been inflating it for Pollard, and Swanson set Washington for the meeting that occurred in the early days of March 1929.[53]

Swanson accepted Pollard in preference to Mapp, who decided to run again. In the lowest primary vote of the decade, he lost to the former anti-machine gubernatorial candidate of 1917, by 107,000 to 29,000 votes. Swanson congratulated Pollard upon his primary victory and observed, "Your campaign left no bitterness." He advised him to deliver a broad keynote speech against Brown and then send copies to newspapers and to every Democratic voter: "Select the issues upon which your campaign will be conducted." Thus, Pollard would prevent Brown from gaining the initiative. Swanson encouraged Pollard to obtain contacts with the "entire labor factions among the State" and added that "we must handle this situation with skill in order to eliminate division." Swanson placed his office at Pollard's disposal and collected funds not only from his resources but from Glass's "intimate firends . . . on the grounds" that the latter's reelection in 1930 was in the balance. Swanson and Glass apportioned them directly "to each congressional district as may seem best" and avoided any being "wasted at central headquarters." Glass slashed at Cannon through his Lynchburg papers and revealed long-hoarded information that damaged the bishop's moral leadership. The organized Virginia prohibition forces wavered. Although Brown obtained the largest vote a non-Democratic gubernatorial candidate had accumulated for some time, his 99,000 ballots could not match Pollard's 169,000. After jubilation that regular Democrats had "manhandled . . . Hoovercrats," Swanson recommended that a rapid registration of voters, particularly in the white counties, be accomplished by May 1930 to discourage opposition to Glass's reelection. Byrd quickly agreed. Despite "hundreds of letters" and numerous delegations seeking his candidacy, under Swanson's influence, Trinkle refused to challenge Glass. In the autumn election of 1930, Glass avoided opponents and the Democrats regained two congressional districts lost in 1928.[54]

Although Cannon remained active in Virginia life, lawsuits, wrangling over prohibition, and revelations alleging personal and financial misbehavior reduced his influence. His sponsorship of education and other social reforms had aided Swanson in early political campaigns, presenting a leaven that reduced inclinations within the political establishment to favor property interests at the expense of social concerns. Most recently, paralleling pronouncements of the Federal Council of Churches, Cannon had led forty ministers to sign "an appeal to industrial leaders of the South," calling for employers to meet voluntarily with their employees to discuss questions "of wages, housing, shorter hours, especially of women and children, and a reasonable limit of child labor." A rebirth of labor activity that led Virginia trade-union membership to rise from twenty thousand to thirty-nine thousand occurred between 1926 and 1930. Ironically, despite attempts by authorities at Dan River Mills to develop "industrial democracy," widely publicized labor unrest in the Southside evidenced a growing class alienation and economic adversity.[55]

After an across-the-board 10-percent wage cut authorized by mill president H.R. Fitzgerald, and following effective local propaganda by Textile Workers Union vice-president Frank Gorman and Virginia Matilda Lindsay of the Woman's Trade Union League, elements of the city's business cadres and even the Ku Klux Klan responded positively to the local union's organizational campaigns. Fitzgerald refused to bargain, however, and the union struck on September 29, 1930. A mill shareholder, Judge J.T. Clement issued injunctions against picketing and Fitzgerald refused Pollard's mediation. When violence occurred, the governor ordered one thousand National Guardsmen into Danville. In December, American Federation of Labor president William Green and Swanson discussed the matter in the latter's office. Seeking a national reputation, Byrd had previously volunteered his aid and Swanson approved Green's suggestion that Byrd perform as arbitrator. Green visited Danville and issued a plea for arbitration while noting Byrd's willingness to participate. But Fitzgerald refused any compromise. Pollard's troops and growing local fears that textile violence from other strikes in the southern piedmont might spread to Danville, in addition to Fitzgerald's intransigence, broke the strike within a few weeks.[56]

Repeating a habit of decades, Swanson returned during Eastertide 1931 to his Pittsylvania County home. He gossiped with colleagues between reminiscences and hunting and fishing stories, and evaluated information and editorial opinion from over the state furnished by his secretary, Oden, and by Hamilton, Drewry, Price and other regional associates. One item of conjecture may have included Editor Jaffe's call for an "out and out liberal party." Lulie Swanson had earlier left for Paris to serve as a hostess at the United States pavilion at the Colonial Exposition. Swanson planned to join her and, as part of his duties on the Senate Foreign Relations Committee, to visit legations of the United States in Western Europe. Attending the War Policies Commission in Washington before leaving for Europe at the end of May, Swanson stayed at a hotel rather than reopen his closed home on R. Street. At the commission meeting he fainted in the Senate office building's caucus room from what his physician described publicly as "acute indigestion." He reassured the press that the senator needed a stricter diet and a few days' rest. Speculation bubbled in Virginia, and Swanson postponed his departure for Europe until July 5.[57]

As evidenced by the commotion over his illness, Swanson's central importance in Virginia politics complemented his influence at the national level. During the 1920s, he had achieved significant prestige in American foreign affairs and within the Democratic party. These developments formed a prologue to his final public accomplishments.

Claude A. Swanson as a freshman United States Senator, about 1914.

A young Swanson at the time of his election to the United State House of Representatives, about 1892.

Governor Swanson in mid-oratorical flight at the Jamestown Tercentennial celebration in 1907.

Senator Thomas Staples Martin, a frequent Swanson political ally and a major Democratic senatorial leader, about 1914.

Below left, Senator John W. Daniel, a Swanson benefactor and a moderate force in Virginia politics, in 1901. *Below right,* Rorer A. James, publisher of the *Danville Register*, a partisan Southside spokesman and Swanson confidant, about 1916.

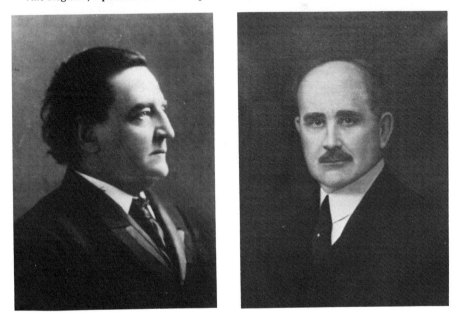

Right, Governor Westmoreland Davis, Swanson's 1922 opponent, about 1920. *Below left,* Representative Andrew J. Montague, a former governor and 1901 Swanson opponent, about 1915. *Below right,* Carter Glass in 1901, later a congressman, secretary of the treasury, and senator, and a Swanson adversary until the 1920s.

Above left, Representative Henry D. Flood, a Swanson political associate and Martin lieutenant, in 1901. Above right, Walter A. Watson in 1901, a Swanson ally and later a judge and congressman. Below left, Richard E. Byrd, Speaker of the Virginia House of Delegates and stormy petrel of Virginia politics, about 1910. Below right, Harry F. Byrd, Sr., later governor and U.S. senator, a factional antagonist of Swanson, about 1916.

Secretary of the Navy Swanson and Ambassador to Mexico Josephus Daniels with President Roosevelt during a review of the fleet in New York Harbor, May 31, 1934.

Franklin D. Roosevelt with his first cabinet, December 1933. *Clockwise from left,* Roosevelt, William Woodin, Homer Cummings, Swanson, Henry Wallace, Frances Perkins, Daniel Roper, Harold Ickes, James Farley, George Dern, and Cordell Hull.

Secretary Swanson greets officers of the fleet at Pearl Harbor on October 2, 1933.

Senator Swanson and journalist Ray Stannard Baker meet on a Washington street about 1919.

Swanson as Secretary of the Navy, February 1939.

10

Hares and Hounds
1921-1932

Within the Senate during the 1920s, Democrat Claude Swanson grew in influence and in authority. The Senate became his political home, as he settled in amid party hacks and hierarchs, committee chairmen and senior colleagues. Younger members discovered his engaging wit, useful advice, and astute bargaining; in 1932, a colleague acknowledged that, in senatorial matters, he was the "shrewdest politician and diplomat" in the Senate.[1]

Each constituent request received the attention of his seasoned office staff led by Archibald Oden. Whether seeking subsidies for highways or maintaining full repair schedules at Norfolk Navy Yard, Swanson flexed a skilled political craftsmanship. Occasionally forced to espouse issues contrary to his preferences, he confessed half humorously in the Senate cloakroom that "there comes a time in the life of man when he must rise above principle." For example, he admitted that "prohibitionist hounds" had chased the wet Virginia hares "into every briar patch." But a growing antiprohibitionist sentiment threatened to breed a new hare "with sharp teeth," willing to repeal dry laws. "While I am presently riding with the hounds, no hound will change into a hare any quicker than I will if I find the hares putting the hounds to rout." As one of his last acts as a senator, he voted for repeal of the Eighteenth Amendment. He also enjoyed repeating his description of a typical senator: For four years after election, he can be a statesman, but during the last two he is bound to be a politician. Six months preceding an election a senator might "do whatever he thought the majority of his constituents wanted even if he thought them wrong." He diagnosed such a senator as having a "six months pulse." But, as the helmsman tacks to the wind yet maintains his course, Swanson's accomplishments during the decade revealed his continuing commitment to earlier political standards.[2]

Numerically more substantial immediately after elections of three Republican presidents, a shadowed Republican senatorial majority ruled. Although the House generally deflated such tendencies, Senate Democrats and western Republicans agreed frequently to legislation reminiscent of the Wilson era or anticipating the New Deal of the 1930s. Democratic senators sporadically evidenced a superior discipline to the Republicans. In mid-decade, southerners on standing committees held twenty-one of thirty-four available ranking minority positions and 60 percent of Senate Democrats hailed from southern or border states. Minority leaders Oscar Underwood (from 1920 to 1923) and John T. Robinson (after 1923) represented former Confederate states. Swanson distrusted Underwood's leadership and his corporate leanings but found Robinson of Arkansas an abiding friend with an agreeable world view. By decade's end, Robinson, Swanson, and Mississippian Pat Harrison held "daily conferences . . . in [Swanson's] room at the Capitol" to review and to anticipate Senate developments. The Virginian also had a seat on the eleven-person Democratic Steering Committee that nominated party members for Senate committees.[3]

As chairman of the Democratic senatorial Election Committee, Swanson sought to secure state-level Democratic unity and searched for senatorial candidates with realistic election chances, both conditions being necessary for successful fund raising. In Maryland he pushed Albert C. Ritchie as a Democratic unifier, and in Kentucky Swanson used William G. McAdoo to soothe party differences and favored Alben W. Barkley for the Senate. Given harmony, Swanson argued Senate Democrats could take "the affirmative in politics," "impress the country by legislation enacted," give direction to foreign affairs, and move the United States away "from being isolated and remaining powerless and useless." Bernard Baruch frequently raised funds, and Swanson often telephoned the South Carolinian at his Wall Street offices. In Congress, a conscious cadre worked to continue the Democratic program of the Wilson years and to regain Democratic hegemony. Swanson, Robinson, Harrison and James W. Collie of Mississippi, Peter Gerry of Rhode Island, Cordell Hull of Tennessee, Finis J. Garrett and John Nance Garner of Texas, and William A. Oldfield of Arkansas were included in the group. Republican senators knew Swanson to be an influential force in the Senate and majority leader James W. Wadsworth remembered him as "a born politician" who judged "the political effect of any action which he or the Senate might take." He also found that Swanson's "views ran into larger fields than that on many occasions."[4]

Swanson's committee assignments revealed his standing among party and Senate colleagues. In 1921, eleven years' seniority alone did not explain his position as ranking minority member on the Foreign Relations Committee. By 1924, it contained seven Democrats: Swanson, three other southerners, and three westerners, two of whom were born in the South. On the Naval Affairs Committee, he cooperated more with senators from seaboard states than with fellow southerners. Of seven Democrats on the committee in 1924, six counted the ocean a neighbor along with seven of the eight Republicans. Voting upon complicated matters of foreign policy or naval legislation, Swanson often served as a "cue-giver" for his less-well-informed party colleagues. Membership on the Public Buildings and Grounds Committee and later membership on the Rules Committee placed him at two junctions of patronage and preferment. Proposals for federal buildings, land purchases, assignment of Senate office space, and oversight of the Library of Congress and the Smithsonian Institution were some functions of these committees.[5]

On Public Buildings and Grounds, he early endorsed a frequently proposed national archives facility. In 1912, a committee review elicited Swanson's positive response, and he cited slipshod storage of land receipts, pension papers, and Treasury documents. A year later, Congress funded planning activities and reorganized administration of public buildings by establishing the Public Buildings Commission, chaired by Treasury Secretary McAdoo. As a member, Swanson helped draft a recommendation for an archives building that was authorized in 1916. War priorities shelved the proposal, and unrealized plans left a snarled set of problems for peacetime. In March 1919, the second Public Buildings Commission secured control over allotment of public space, excepting the White House, Capitol, Smithsonian Institution, and Library of Congress. As one of eight members, Swanson advocated anew an archives facility "in which we could take care of our valuable records." To house partially an expanding federal government, the commission under chairman Reed Smoot proposed in 1926 a huge, one-hundred-million-dollar package for the archives, internal revenue, commerce, labor, supreme court, and other public buildings. In 1928, $8 million funded the depository plans, and, in September 1930, ground was broken for its construction. Completion and further expansion of the commission's earlier plans followed as the New Deal prescribed public works to cure the Great Depression.[6]

Farmer distress garnered Swanson's attention, sharply focused during the decade by two senatorial campaigns. Early in the decade, Virginia agrarians advanced reform proposals through the newly formed Farmers' National Council that determined to elect either farmers to Congress or to assist their "friends in Congress in their campaign for reelection." Lobbyists for the more sedate American Farm Bureau Federation organized an avowed interest group, the farm bloc, led by Iowa senator William S. Kenyon. Amid his 1922 reelection race, despite the bureau's low membership in Virginia, Swanson joined the farm bloc of representatives and senators. One historian of this farm crisis held that constituent demands forced the bipartisan coalition into being; western radicals George Norris and Robert La Follette "held little more in common with . . . Swanson . . . than sympathy for agriculture." In reality the agrarian bloc contained persons who frequently cooperated, who favored Wilson administration farm programs, and who held similar world views. In 1921, for example, on amendments to the 1918 Revenue Act to adjust federal taxes, Swanson and La Follette agreed on seventeen pivotal votes treating taxes upon estates, holding companies, corporations, and other forms of invested wealth. The Wisconsin leader and Swanson voted against the revised bill that still won Republican Warren G. Harding's signature.[7]

A roll-call analysis of the busy Sixty-seventh Congress of 1921 to 1923 demonstrated that Swanson voted more frequently for proposed agrarian legislation than any other member of the farm bloc or similarly inclined senator. As one who best represented "the characteristics all the bloc members share in common," Swanson, seven confessed farm-bloc Democrats, twelve party colleagues, and Republican La Follette were the most persistent in their advocacy of farm legislation. Republican voting patterns uncovered a highly fragmented response. Democratic cohesion made possible legislation acceptable to agrarians in the Sixty-seventh Congress: a three-year appropriation of $1 billion to store and to export farm goods through the War Finance Commission, federal grain exchange regulation, augmentation of the Federal Trade Commission by allowing the Department of Agriculture to oversee meat packing firms, an emergency tariff to protect some domestic agricultural goods, continued federal aid to highways, removal of agricultural cooperatives from federal antitrust laws, addition of a farmer to the Federal Reserve Board, and extended due dates for federal loans.[8]

Wartime habits and earlier reform movements encouraged Virginia agrarians to file their complaints in Washington. Swanson adapted for his use Farm Bureau and Farmers' National Council propaganda, affirmed agrarian aggressiveness touting active government, and drew upon the Department of Agriculture. In January 1922, concurrent with the National Agricultural Congress in Washington, Swanson condemned conditions that allowed farm profits to decline and those of manufacturing to grow. Bankers loaned money to plant and to raise crops but refused credit for storage and for other marketing devices. "It is in his wretched methods of selling and distribution where [a farmer's] greatest losses occur," Swanson observed. Federal farm credits, cooperatives, and financing would allow "industrious and frugal farmers [to] . . . buy farms, improve them and thus become freeholders." Parcel post, public roads, reduced transportation costs, and research stations would sustain farmers' success. "Every panic and every financial depression which has cursed this country invariably has been preceded by a great fall in agricultural products." His oratory hinted at simmering Virginia class feuds between the "country people" and the town, between merchant, factor, and farmer.[9]

Until farm profits could repay existing loans, production and marketing aids would not greatly benefit Virginia farmers, but even cooperatives and pooling projects sparked intense controversy among rural citizens. Tariff protection for agricultural commodities gained some southern support; the Southern Tariff Association, for example, echoed western demands for these government defenses. Swanson refused to take such a protectionist path. In tariff debates during the summer and autumn of 1922, he voted in 171 roll calls, only two of which were to increase tariff schedules: augment the duty upon peanuts and remove vegetable oils from the free list, both resulting from an intense protectionist drive by Virginia peanut growers. He voted against the 1922 Fordney-McCumber tariff, persuaded that its rates were "extortionate." In the autumn congressional elections, party publicists censured the high "Republican tariff" and contributed to Democratic gains of seventy-six seats in the House and eight in the Senate. The Fordney-McCumber agricultural duties furnished agrarians few significant economic gains. As Swanson had warned, one contemporary study contended that farmers obtained "$125,000,000 additional income per year . . . and . . . paid $426,000,000 more for the goods they bought."[10]

Evolving from World War I, the McNary-Haugen plan projected a government corporation that would buy specified commodities when a particular crop fell below a ratio price, or, as it came to be known, a parity price. Purchasing the domestic surplus, the corporation could sell in the world market where demand set the price. To avoid federal deficit spending, farmers would pay an equalization fee, and surplus revenues would be distributed annually through a script system. A flexible tariff schedule to be adjusted by the president would prevent foreign farm products from flooding the American domestic market. Blocked in 1921 by western farm leaders, Congress considered a new version in 1924 and passed similar bills in 1927 and 1928 that were vetoed by President Calvin Coolidge. Swanson disapproved of the early drafts, and, in 1927, he failed to vote when the bill cleared the Senate; he voted against it in 1928 and helped to sustain Coolidge's veto. He preferred removal of the equalization fee, which was, to his mind, an additional tax. Virginia interests—truck farmers and fruit growers aided by Governor Harry Byrd—sought to exempt their crops from equalization fees and marketing agreements. As important as any consideration, the McNary-Haugen proposals, as the *Norfolk Virginian Pilot* reminded, were "essentially a protectionist measure" and "a pet theory of the Northwest."[11]

Swanson approved an alternate scheme, the export debenture plan, that began appearing on legislative agendas in the mid-1920s. Agricultural exporters would be given a certificate, stating the difference between the world market price and the tariff on their exported crop. The paper, receivable at par by the Treasury, could be used by any importer to pay tariff charges on any products. The rebate formula would be determined by Congress and 50 percent of the tariff revenues would be assigned annually to refund debentures. The plan would include among other staples "tobacco, cotton, cotton waste, and manufactured products thereby" and generally pleased Virginia rural and urban entrepreneurs. The National Grange also preferred it to the more cumbersome McNary-Haugen schemes. In September 1928, the Virginia Grange reformed and elected as its state master John R. Horsley, an old friend of Swanson's and a former state legislator. He reinvigorated moribund lodges and pursued the Grange's legislative proposals to sensitize Swanson further. In a special 1929 session of Congress to resolve farm difficulties, Swanson joined Norris and other militant farm relief advocates to place the debenture plan in an agricultural marketing bill.[12]

In May 1929, Swanson sided with Norris again. After having endorsed Al Smith in 1928, Norris joined Democrats on the Committee on Agriculture and Forestry to probe President Herbert Hoover's agricultural proposals, but the House balked at inclusion of the debenture measure in an agricultural relief bill. Swanson and forty-five colleagues refused the conference committee's deletion, and he explained that the plan would "equalize conditions as between the farmer and the highly protected industries under the present and proposed tariff of the Republican party." In mid-June, the Senate bowed to the House and abandoned debentures in the Agricultural Marketing Act of 1929. Swanson accepted the act's creation of a farm board to loan money to cooperatives, to sponsor new marketing techniques, and to purchase crop surpluses. Again, in October, debenture forces amended a proposed tariff with the plan while Swanson worked behind the scenes. Being bound by a pair, he would have voted aye, but the House again refused to agree. A "record" had been made, and in 1935 legislation allocated 30 percent of custom revenues to aid agricultural exports and to reduce farm surpluses.[13]

Swanson had favored federal wartime investments in the Tennessee Valley to produce synthetic nitrates at Muscle Shoals, but he questioned peacetime plans first to manufacture inexpensive fertilizer at the Shoals and then to generate hydroelectric power by private companies. Corporate interests—Henry Ford, American Cyanamide, and power monopolies—failed to secure unified endorsements from farm groups. The Federal Farm Bureau favored Ford, then the American Cyanamid bid. As early as 1920, Swanson's approval of the Federal Power Commission indicated a bias toward government ownership and regulation. He continued to monitor the commission's activities, noting in 1930 that he feared Hoover had "strangled [it] by lack of funds through a conspiracy" of power companies. In 1921 he also voted to continue government expenditures at the Shoals. The Ford proposal gained approval in the House in 1924, but, despite widespread southern congressional endorsement, Senate opposition arose from suspicion of Ford's true intentions. Norris's counterproposal for government operation of the Shoals won the favor of the Farmers' National Council while other private power companies objected to Ford. Swanson joined Norris to postpone Senate action until December 1924 as the Virginia Democrat argued for more information on fertilizer costs. Before Senate debate could occur, Ford withdrew his offer.[14]

Swanson then opposed Underwood's motion to lease the Shoals to private concerns. During debate that defeated the Underwood plan, Swanson favored an unsuccessful amendment for government operation. He then agreed with Norris's provisions for safeguards to prevent the facility from falling into private, monopolistic hands. Upon introduction by the Nebraskan of his initial comprehensive plan for Valley development, in March 1928 Swanson questioned those senators still desiring an Underwood-style solution. They had not revealed how cheaply fertilizer might be produced nor had they a value upon the government's initial investment. "Is not the Government entitled to the same protection that a private individual would have?" Swanson voted for the Norris bill only to suffer Coolidge's veto. Although his Virginia colleague Carter Glass labeled it a dangerous precedent, Swanson assented to Boulder Dam's construction on the Colorado River, pleasing his western allies and stepping beyond simply converting wartime facilities. During 1929, engineering estimates of the Muscle Shoals region indicated greater amounts of water resources than earlier anticipated, and, in April 1930 Swanson again joined the majority, composed of western and southern senators, to pass the Norris plan. The House refused to follow. In February 1931, he acted in a similar fashion, but Hoover vetoed the project. Eventually, in May 1933, a Democratic president signed the legislation into law.[15]

Federal road fund legislation kept Swanson's loyalties throughout the decade. He agreed that the states should help repair federally financed roadways, but he suggested army machinery be used as well. Responding to agrarian calls for feeder roads, he objected to allocating federal funds exclusively for interstate projects. Representing heavily populated New York, Senator Royal S. Copeland in February 1925 questioned an appropriation formula that awarded states funds by taking more money from New York than the state received. Swanson admitted that he had contributed to formulation of the dispersal ratio of one-third population, one-third territory, and one-third post-road mileage. Copeland mused, "I knew some artist had a hand in it." Swanson professed consternation; the formula had never been criticized. Pennsylvania's David Reed fared no better. Not only dismissing states' rights as an argument in this instance, Swanson cleverly prevented last-minute legislative calendar alterations and other parliamentary devices meant to detour the legislation. Aware of Virginia's growing conservatism toward state-road funding at the decade's conclusion, he argued that localities should be allowed to match federal road funds if the state refused.[16]

Occasionally, as in 1929, Swanson could seize partisan staves. He not only punished Hoover farm policies, he tussled with Republicans against protective rates. Although his own party had in the previous year promised vaguely to maintain tariffs for legitimate businesses and a high-wage standard, in that sense favoring protectionism, it pledged to balance differences between domestic production costs and overseas cost and to reduce "those monopolistic and extortionate tariff rates bestowed in payment of political debts." Personally "bitterly opposed to the tariff bill," Swanson accused Finance chairman Reed Smoot of Utah, Reed of Pennsylvania, and Hiram Johnson of California of preparing a partisan bill and simply announcing to Democrats their proposals. Confusion ensued. Seven months after debate had begun, Swanson sketched "a disorganized [Republican] party going to the White House, a scattered mob, to appeal to its leader to reach a decision." Hoover, Swanson chided earlier, if he "abandons the leadership, if he has no convictions and no advice," invites demagogues to the fore. Swanson would rally Democrats and the so-called progressive Republicans, agrarian insurgents, to defeat the "exactions and iniquities and enormities contained in this bill."[17]

Through August and September 1929, Swanson helped the Democratic National Committee criticize more broadly the proposed tariff. Rather than benefit farmers, Hoover's tariff revisions "favored manufacturing interests at the expense of the consuming public." By midsummer 1929, fifty foreign countries protested the proposed increased tariff schedules. Sensitive to overseas markets, Swanson warned of retaliation; he saw in the growth of customs unions in Europe a danger to American goods, commenting to Secretary of State Henry L. Stimson that "we might be fighting for our lives." The Virginian emphasized that "prosperity of this country is in spots" and, to aid the consumer, reduction of duties on those products of corporations whose "profits are excessive" was needed. He chided the House, dominated by Hoover, for passing a high-tariff draft. Following Hoover's request to speed Senate deliberations in October 1929 Swanson noted that the legislation slowed because of inborn inequities and Hoover's refusal to explain his ideas on flexible rates adjusted by the executive. Fellow Democrats and Swanson continued to chip at internal cracks in Republican unity, observing the Republican "progressives" in conflict with "reactionaries." Amid the onset of the Great Depression in the spring of 1930, the Republicans pushed to pass the bill.[18]

Swanson and a majority of the Senate scrambled party allegiances further by attaching the export debenture plan to the Senate version of the tariff. He disdained a tariff on Philippine sugar or any duties on the archipelago's products. It would be "vicious and wrong and contrary" to tax the Philippines in such a manner. This bickering resulted in an amendment to grant independence to the island, but Swanson demurred. Although "sorry [that] we ever annexed them," he would not exploit ten million inhabitants by taxation or release them unprepared into a threatening oriental world. Recalling the 1900 Democratic platform and his belief that the "Constitution follows the flag," obligations had been incurred that required that "deliberations should be broad and states-manlike." By March 1931, however, he became convinced that Congress was determined upon independence and ceased opposition. In early 1930, moving from a committee of the whole, the Senate prepared to vote on the passage of the tariff. Perhaps suspecting that the expanding depression would fuel additional calls for protectionist amendments, Swanson objected to "the same discussion, the same contests, and same prolonged effort . . . for the various industries." Subsequently, he gained abandonment of the committee of the whole, replacing the parliamentary device with the motion to reconsider that speeded Senate action. On only eight motions did he favor either a higher tariff on an item or an existing high rate. Few Senators, Republican or Democrat, could match or better that record.[19]

On final consideration in the Senate of the Hawley-Smoot tariff, Swanson voted with twenty-nine Democrats, eleven Republicans, and one independent against its passage. Five bolting Democrats, four of them southerners, gave the bill its two-vote margin, and Hoover then signed it. As early as June 1929, Swanson had labeled the revenue proposal "a great calamity for the people." In August 1930, Swanson drew editorial praise from the *New York Times* when he asserted that the act produced foreign reprisals and disrupted international trade. His figures for June 1930 revealed American exports at a six-year low and, within the next year, a 35-percent additional decline occurred. On the Senate floor in March 1931, he accused the Republicans of using governmental powers "in the last seven years . . . to distribute wealth created by the people into the pockets of the few." Opposition to such favoritism, Swanson asked, "has been the issue of Democracy, has it not?" Visiting Europe in August 1931, he pointed to the American tariff as an essential cause of depressed world markets.[20]

Swanson furnished for the recently reorganized Democratic National Committee and the party's senatorial election committee criticisms of the tariff for the 1930 elections. Representing equally each state and inclined therefore toward rural and small-town attitudes, the National Committee fell into renewed conflict with its chairman John J. Raskob. He publicly favored no tariff revisions, and Smith, among others, agreed. Although Democratic House and Senate leaders avoided open disagreement with Raskob, Swanson and his low-tariff allies continued to berate the Hawley-Smoot tariff. This denouement contributed to Franklin D. Roosevelt's progress toward the 1932 Democratic presidential nomination, as the New York governor had not been among Raskob's tariff endorsers. Swanson now used the tariff not only against Republicans but also against potential Roosevelt opponents within the party.[21]

Swanson continued to accept some programs that established new relationships between federal and local governments. Following a report by the federal Children's Bureau, legislative consciences sponsored in 1918 funding to promote "the welfare and hygiene of maternity and infancy." In 1921, with Swanson's approval, the Sheppard-Turner Act appropriated $1.5 million in Virginia and in other states for an experimental system of child health and prenatal care offices, staffed by competent nurses. Virginia allocated more funds than formerly to obtain federal matching dollars. During the legislation's life, infant mortality in the state fell by 9 percent and maternal deaths by 11 percent. In June 1926, to renew funding, Swanson presented petitions from the Virginia Health Commission, women's groups, nursing associations, and individual rural physicians for continuation. Without federal assistance, they claimed, the nursing program would falter.[22]

Since 1922, the American Medical Association and regional physicians' groups had censured the bill and would persist in doing so. In 1926, Glass opposed its renewal, and the legislation lapsed in June 1929. Those laboring to revive and to redirect the program in 1931 emphasized rural health needs. The new proposal nearly succeeded in establishing federal subsidies for individual health units which were to be staffed by a physician, a sanitary expert, and a nurse. It failed passage, lacking a final Senate vote. In 1931, Swanson hid his preference by pairing with a Senate colleague, but his true attitude was revealed when he voted against a motion to recommit the bill and thereby kill it—a motion that failed. His pair, as did Glass, favored recommittal. Northern senator David Walsh denounced the legislation as a "wedge to state control or national control of the practice of medicine," and the U.S. Public Health Service lobbied against direction by the federal Children's Bureau. The decline of organized women's influence, a faltering economy, and inconsistent presidential leadership further contributed to defeat. The rural push behind the program furnished, however, continuing evidence of a vital coalition, committed to responding to constituent need—even if advancing beyond earlier reform limits.[23]

Contrary interests also tugged at Swanson to separate him from rural sectional alliances. In January 1925, he spoke for an amendment that obliged the Department of Agriculture to certify to the shipper the class, quality, and condition of livestock. Closer to the great eastern markets, Virginia cattlemen such as Henry Stuart would benefit from the legislation, but the senator met national opposition from the East and West. He also discovered western states' taxing unduly products of cottonseed oil and suggested that retaliation by eastern states could include prohibiting shipment of beef over two days old. Encouraged by Byrd, Swanson lobbied for Virginia fruit growers to avoid being included in stabilization corporation activities. Washington state interests joined. Apparently these two areas held marketing advantages and suspected that less competitive areas—such as Michigan—would form holding cooperatives to dump more apples on the world market. Sensitive to threats to overseas trade, Swanson correctly noted that dumping would encourage other nations to retaliate. In 1930, Great Britain banned American apples "under the pretense of protecting [Great Britain] . . . from a fruit fly"; Argentina followed suit. The earlier militant farm bloc obviously could suffer from conflicting sectional economic interests. More may have existed, but Swanson sought to soothe disruptive attitudes by "cooperation, by conciliation, by sensibly trying to settle the problem outside and not on the floor of the Senate."[24]

Swanson's success in local legislation manifested itself occasionally in Senate debate. He cleared paths to return surplus federal installations to Virginia control, petitioned for construction of the Arlington Memorial Bridge, and pushed dozens of private relief bills through sometimes menacing Senate agendas. If federal agencies ignored Virginia, Swanson claimed unfair treatment. When he resorted to this argument to obtain a veterans' hospital, Senate Finance chairman Smoot somewhat wearily replied, "Virginia will have a hospital." In continuing and expanding the federal naval presence at Norfolk, Swanson gained Norris's grudging admiration: the Virginian, through his "able way, although very technical way," had guaranteed that the yard would be given the opportunity to modernize elderly battleships and probably "everything else at Norfolk." Swanson modestly replied: "I hope so. I want the best possible work done."[25]

Federal reliance upon tobacco taxes meant that the senior senator from Virginia needed to survey revenue proposals to avoid more increases. During the decade, the weed provided over $3 billion to the federal treasury. World War I taxes proved most difficult to abolish. Swanson and his fellow tobacco congressmen divested these taxes in the Revenue Act of 1926, but consumer taxes remained. William A. Reed of Richmond's Larus and Brother tobacco corporation, concerned over the 5-percent decline in its company's tobacco plug and snuff sales, asked Swanson to initiate reduction of the eighteen cents per pound federal tax. Consulting with the ranking Democrat on the Senate Finance Committee Furnifold Simmons, Swanson tried but failed. Facing national economic dislocation and decreasing federal revenues after the 1929 stock-market crash, however, Swanson resisted successfully increasing levies upon tobacco products. In January 1932, with Reed, he visited the Democratically controlled House and secured assurances from Speaker Garner and chairman of the Ways and Means Committee James Collier of no additional tobacco taxes. Representatives Charles R. Crisp of Georgia and Robert L. Doughton of North Carolina also agreed to oppose an increase, and Swanson obtained promises from Democratic senators to resist any advance.[26]

Reed also funneled other tobacco industry concerns to Swanson. In communication with officials at Imperial Tobacco Company and Liggett-Myers, American and British-American tobacco corporations, he wrote Swanson to hasten passage of a treaty with revolutionary Turkey. Benefits would follow for those "who are dependent on Turkish Tobacco for . . . cigarette brands." Reed protested a Cuban duty on his Edgeworth brand and all other tobaccos at six dollars per pound. Following the death of tobacco millionaire and Republican James B. Duke, Reed visited Washington to lobby his Democratic friends "to extend such aid as was possible to the Duke Estate" to avoid heavy federal inheritance taxes. Glass and apparently Swanson gave Reed reason to believe he would receive their aid.[27]

Swanson, however, defended farmers by fending off menacing moves to restrict farmer marketing cooperatives. He spoke against proposals in Congress to force "co-ops" to submit expensive and time-consuming reports to federal agencies. Nor did he favor federal taxes placed upon them. In 1925, he contributed his parliamentary skills to aid Norris to require the Federal Trade Commission to investigate the Imperial and American tobacco companies. Both corporations held connections with Duke interests. Allegations circulated that the two corporate giants used their resources to hamper the Tri-State Tobacco Growers Cooperative Association by refusing significant purchases of tobacco;

others—such as R.J. Reynolds and Liggett-Myers—obtained large amounts of leaf from the farmers' pooling operation during the crop years from 1922 through 1924. Eventually, the Republican-dominated commission authored a report denying any significant role played by Imperial or American. Cooperative leaders and other growers labeled it whitewash to favor Republican Duke's interests. Later the Department of Agriculture reported that the two corporations were "largely instrumental in causing ultimate failure" of the cooperative.[28]

Small-town businessmen and warehousemen openly contested the entrepreneurs in the cooperative. In Virginia, in the heart of the flue-cured Old Belt region, cooperative membership stood highest numerically. To challenge the co-op, warehouse owners organized the Virginia-Carolina Warehouse Association, financed by local boards of trade and warehousemen. The *Southern Tobacco Journal* filled with anticooperative opinion. William Reed's brother, Leslie H. Reed of the Imperial Tobacco Company, advised the *Journal'* s editor on means to receive financial support from Imperial funds. But Swanson had joined the cooperative in 1922 during his senatorial reelection campaign, and these events placed him in difficult straits. His public record identified him on the side of the cooperative; privately, he probably dealt in disingenuous fashion with the Reeds and warehouse spokesmen, not unlike his treatment of the gold bugs in the strife-ridden 1890s.[29]

Swanson also worked for new projects—parks, memorials, and federal buildings—for Virginia localities. Usually he would enter in the Senate a proposal to be studied for its viability. The resolution would then be referred to the proper committee where clustered friendly senators. The particular committee request led to a study, appropriately funded. Upon completion of the investigation, the committtee would author a recommendation that carried considerable authority with other senators. By this time in the process, Swanson and other Virginians were no longer publicly observable. Coordination, however, through the House and with local boosters required precise timing. In June 1930, having secured Senate approval for $1 million to be expended through the Monument Parks bill for a Virginia project, Swanson encountered disorganization. Having had a "great deal of difficulty in getting the bill through the Senate," Swanson lost half of his appropriations owing to House conferees' mistakes. He complained, "It will be some time before we are able to get another $500,000 dollars." He correctly observed that "the vague promise to add the lost half at a future date would be difficult to realize."[30]

For fourteen years following World War I, Swanson introduced or husbanded legislation establishing a national military park at Yorktown, a park in the Shenandoah Valley and Great Smoky Mountains, a memorial at Appomattox surrender ground, recognition of Bull Run and the Civil War battlefields around Richmond, memorials at Williamsburg, a federal road to Mount Vernon, memorial bridges over Virginia water courses and the Potomac, and a susquicentennial celebration of Cornwallis's capitulation at Yorktown. These activities conjointly enriched Virginia landowners and the state's tourist industry.[31]

Keeping watch over Virginia interests included evaluating nominees to federal regulatory commissions. Coolidge's nomination of Thomas L. Woodlock to the Interstate Commerce Commission exhibited such an instance. A

New York resident and railroad director, Woodlock claimed Democratic allegiance, but investigation revealed he had voted Republican in the three previous presidential elections. Such evidence raised the hackles of Democrat Swanson, but it was not decisive in his estimate of Woodlock. Although the Farmers' National Council questioned Woodlock's close association with the railroads and banking interests, Swanson knew that profit from exporting Appalachian coal, iron ore, and limestone through Virginia ports partially depended upon low freight rates to keep a competitive edge over Baltimore and other outlets closer to the mineral fields. In addition, the Esch-Cummins Act of 1920 had placed interstate rail rates more closely under the federal wing, increasing the commission's local impact.[32]

Given a recess appointment by Coolidge, Woodlock faced again Senate approval in December 1925. Obliquely attacking Woodlock's fitness, Swanson dismissed a contention that commissioners should dole out "abstract justice" and demanded regional representation in the commission so that, "in a contest . . . between the various parts of the country," sections should be reassured that they were "before a court that will look after their interests and will know their situation." Coal transportation rates fixed by the commission became a major portion of the controversy over Woodlock's head. Swanson forced the regional argument to move the comission to favor Virginia in important cases. The harassed Woodlock voted in the majority in a favorable "decision . . . in connection with coal rates." Pennsylvania opposition was bought off by Coolidge who promised Senator David Reed to appoint a Keystone State resident to an early vacancy. So intense did debate become that the membership refused to place the roll-call vote on Woodlock in the *Congressional Record*. Swanson joined, as did other Senators from upper southern coal states, irrespective of party, to approve him by a vote of fifty-two to twenty-five. Regional opposition came from southeastern seaboard states south of Virginia and the northern tier of western states from Michigan to the Pacific.[33]

Akin to these events, following a successful nomination of a southerner, Coolidge failed to obtain another choice in January 1927, owing to the nominee's ties to railroads, regional coal interests, and his residency in Pennsylvania. Even more startling, the Senate, in March 1928, raised objections to reappointing commission chairman John T. Esch. Senators from the coal states of Kentucky, Tennessee, West Virginia, and Virginia offered searching questions over his ICC rate decisions, and the Virginia General Assembly sent Swanson a resolution decrying the commission's record of "excluding for Virginia products competitive markets outside" the state. Swanson accused Pennsylvania of having "prospered a great deal under the Commission's system of rates." That body, he observed, "arrogated to itself the position of being industrial master of America." Rather than sponsor competition, it had dampened it. The Senate then passed a resolution to investigate conditions in the West Virginia, Pennsylvania, and Ohio coalfields to determine if railroads and coal owners combined to keep miners' wages low. Owing to Esch's role in coal rate cases, lingering grievances over the Esch-Cummins legislation, regional disgruntlement, and farm bloc animosity, Esch was defeated by a vote of thirty-nine to twenty-nine. Only northeastern Democrats would accept Esch. On this occasion, Norris and

La Follette aligned with the Republican minority, but Swanson welcomed nine midwestern Republicans to the Democratic fold. Whether these contests represented continuing agrarian commitment to effective federal rate regulation, regional competition, partisan politics, growing significance of federal regulatory commissions, or labor-union activity, the reform rhetoric generated furnished metaphors for the New Deal to follow.[34]

Quarrels over commission appointments certainly revealed in the 1920s regional alignments, forming and dissolving, to propose alternatives and objections to Republican leadership goals. In January 1924, thirty-nine senators elected Democrat Ellison D. Smith of South Carolina chairman of the Senate Interstate Commerce Committee, in part because of his opposition to the Esch-Cummins Act. A coauthor, Albert Cummins of Iowa, lost his chairmanship as a result, a victim of revenge. Although absent, Swanson revealed by his pair that he would have voted for Smith. One year later, by a vote of forty-six to thirty-nine, senators authored a "stinging rebuke" by refusing to approve Charles B. Warren, Coolidge's nominee for attorney general, who was accused of being a close associate of the Sugar Trust. A long-time foe of the industry, Swanson and ten other southern Democrats joined the core of thirty who had voted against Warren, marking the first occasion in sixty years that the Senate had refused a cabinet nominee.[35]

Swanson was surprised at how far the profit-motive would drive some entrepreneurs. To protect public naval oil reserves, Swanson voted in 1920 to award control of the underground reservoirs to the secretary of the navy. Reserve proponents had been "satisfied that as the Secretary . . . had the administration of these naval reserves they would be used for the benefit of the Navy." Unfortunately for the lawmakers, envisioning another Daniels—not Harding's Secretary Edwin Denby—as the enforcer, thereafter followed the Teapot Dome scandal as Denby illegally granted entry to the reserves. Swanson could not fathom a secretary who had so ravaged the navy. In 1926, following a sharp price increase in crude oil, gasoline, and kerosene, he accused oil producers of market manipulation and asked for a Federal Trade Commission investigation. As in the tobacco cooperative investigation and other studies in the middle and late 1920s, Swanson and the Senate majority apparently were pressuring the commission to preserve competition. But Coolidge's businessmen commissioners continued muffling regulatory expression as they found no evidence of corporate manipulation of fuel price, despite an "increasing rate of profit in all branches." The commission offered information that local and regional jobbers and retailers had combined to peg prices. Swanson noted that "every time the . . . Commission has investigated the rapid increase . . . , [fuel] prices have gone back reasonably, while profits . . . have never seriously been impaired."[36]

Word that the Aluminum Company of America had ignored Federal Trade Commission rulings and that Coolidge's attorney general lagged in calling the corporation to task led the Senate to direct the Judiciary Committee to investigate the Justice Department's role. Dominated by Democrats and insurgent Republicans, the committee reported to the Senate that an examination of the aluminum company's activities should be undertaken. Swanson played Thomas Walsh's straight man in the discussion on the Senate floor, and the Virginian agreed that the corporation held "an absolute monopoly of virgin aluminum" and had cornered the scrap market "in defiance of the court decree and . . . the Sherman Anti-Trust law." The resolution to investigate failed by three votes.[37]

In 1924, Swanson spoke for a constitutional amendment to move the presidential inauguration from March to earlier in the year to avoid the traditional short session from the December after a presidential election to inauguration. In addition to removing "lame duck senators," the reform would prevent "most of the jokers contained in bills, which are afterwards disclosed, . . . on account of the haste incident to the short session." Five years later, he spoke for such an amendment to avoid "legislation by blackmail" in the short session. He opposed adding provisions for a single, six-year presidential term or national initiatives that would permit voters to amend the constitution. He had no objections to voters approving amendments passed by Congress provided the states continued to define the electorate. Within the Senate, he argued against overbearing House use of the latter's constitutional privilege of initiating revenue acts. While shortening some Senate procedures and successfully using cloture in the World Court debates, he complained, "The House decides without debate and we debate without deciding." Correspondingly, he frequently served as a resource on parliamentary procedure for the Senate.[38]

Swanson's constitutional scruples were frayed by political necessity. He unearthed states' rights bromides as necessary to his argument of the moment. In a short essay in March 1926, as "a recognized authority upon constitutional questions," Swanson placed sovereignty with the people and government suited to their purposes "in accordance with their desires." The unique written basis for government resided in the state and the federal constitutions that composed a system of central efficiency wedded to local liberty and states' rights. These circumstances permitted effective government of the larger territory of the United States. In the Senate, he defended southern franchise restrictions. In a boiling controversy over southern insistence that the prohibition amendment be enforced in the North, some publicists and senators called attention to the South's ignoring the Fourteenth and Fifteenth amendments. Swanson claimed the latter amendment did not provide universal manhood suffrage but only prevented "discriminating in suffrage on account of race, color or previous condition of servitude." The "ignorant, shiftless and corrupt voter" deserved disfranchisement. He refused to admit that blacks were mistreated; by meeting residence, property, and educational requirements, they could vote in Virginia. Contemporaneously, obviously sensitive to northern censure, Swanson promoted in Virginia a move to reduce voting restrictions and defended the state's allotment of representatives, citing discrimination in assigning congressional districts.[39]

At the conclusion of the 1920s, however, natural disasters led Swanson to approve legislation augmenting further federal authority and increasing state reliance upon Washington. After the 1927 Mississippi flood and criticism of the Senate's inactivity, Swanson performed as a ringleader to underwrite federal flood-control projects. Contention was avoided by the Democratic conference resolving differences with the Republican majority before floor debate began. Not since his entry into Congress in 1893, Swanson testifiied, had greater cooperation and conciliation occurred, and he summarized the Senate's decision as one of the "greatest advances which has been made for years looking to the development of our country." After further conference with the House, the bill passed with Coolidge's misgivings, awarding $325 million for flood control and channel stabilization. Significantly, earlier proposals for local matching contributions were omitted in the final version.[40]

In 1929, $6 million in federal loans went to farmers in Virginia and in other southeastern seaboard states suffering hurricane damage. The next summer, in the midst of a devastating twenty-two state drought, Swanson asked Harry Byrd, Virginia drought relief director, to send ideas on what "legislation, if any, can be enacted to benefit Virginia." Byrd estimated that $5 million would cover only one-half the damage in "the greatest economic disaster to the Valley since the Civil War." In Southside warehouses, piles of worthless tobacco accumulated. Byrd favored loans for large landowners and easing credit restriction by the Federal Reserve for banks. Smaller farmers should be given federal loans only on materials needed for crops, with the materials being sold by the government. Before the Senate Agriculture and Forestry Committee, Swanson went beyond Byrd's suggestions, however. He argued, "We did not act parsimoniously when we fed the distressed of Europe." Sixty million dollars must be loaned for relief, including medical and food supplies. He denied that the request was sectional: "It applies to a condition." The House objected to the amount and to loans being used for food. Hoover, Swanson reported, seemed to have intervened. Compromise led to a forty-five-million-dollar appropriation, devoid of food loans, although Swanson contended that the monies would be "a loan, not a dole, not a gift." Swanson and other senators pushed a second bill liberalizing procedures for loans that would include medicine and food. Swanson accused the president and his followers of willing to feed a mule working in the Valley of Virginia but not a working man. The bill approved in February contained an additional $20 million for food loans. Farmers, small-town merchants, and bankers gained while Hoover's public image suffered; Congress grew attuned to relief needs.[41]

In the Senate sessions of the 1920s, Swanson sustained regional agrarian alliances and economic groups to further reforms of earlier years. Refusing narrow ideological limits such as those of Glass, he upheld party platforms. His insightful parliamentary skills were recruited by various senators—from Norris to Simmons. Had Swanson been a senior member of important domestic committees such as Interstate Commerce, Agriculture and Forestry, or Finance his opinions may have been more easily observed, and he more outspoken. Given Democratic minority status, party necessities perhaps impelled him; his personal values certainly led him to favor rural projects, from improved roads to medical care. In the international field, however, in matters of the navy and foreign affairs, his role was far more public and more easily identified.

11

Prodigious Shadow
1921-1932

Between the presidencies of Woodrow Wilson and Franklin D. Roosevelt, Claude Swanson emerged as a principal in shaping Democratic foreign affairs and naval preparedness policies. Ranking Democrat on the Navy and Foreign Relations committees, he navigated a sea of paradoxes. The United States sought national security outside the League of Nations but participated in a series of disarmament conferences amid nervous competition among the major naval powers. The United States focused upon Asia, measuring especially Japan's emerging sea power, while, in the Atlantic, Great Britain and the United States entertained a wary suspiciousness that verged toward overt rivalry. Republican administrations flirted with the League by participating gingerly in various nonpolitical League activities, but entry into the World Court formed the central debate defining American relationships with the international body. In addition, vexatious problems of war debt repayment, immigration ratios, and tariff formulas existed. These patterns altered after 1929 amid alarms and excursions. The United States sank into economic depression, and Swanson witnessed the rise of armed aggression across the world. [1]

While continuing Wilson strategies that had opened much of the world to American economic penetration, Warren G. Harding and Secretary of State Charles Evans Hughes stalled on the League of Nations, utilizing only those Wilson foreign policies that were popular and useful for Republicans. Swanson worked futilely to rally the Democrats. In April 1921, Senate Wilson Democrats opposed a resolution, earlier vetoed by Wilson, that would permit a separate peace with Germany and Austria, abandon the Versailles settlement, and further dilute League support. Democratic amendments to declare simply the war at an end failed by a margin of two to one. In July, the Hughes peace resolution passed thirty-eight to nineteen. [2]

Covertly, Wilson attempted through Swanson and other senators to intrude in the Senate debate over the Hughes-sponsored German peace treaty. During a visit with Wilson at his home on S. Street, Swanson suggested a public statement signed by influential Democrats opposing passage of the Germany treaty. Instead, Wilson countered that he should organize a Democratic senatorial caucus that "can bind its members and then seek my counsel." Swanson desisted, hoping instead to postpone the vote to check the treaty, but powerful party dynamics prevented the treaty from becoming a binding party measure. Running for reelection and sensitive to pro-German voters in Nebraska, Gilbert Hitchcock took a "wobbly course" and dissuaded minority leader Oscar Underwood from his earlier opposition to the German treaty. More comfortable with Harding's New Era than Wilson's New Freedom, Underwood had apparently gained party leadership only by "promising to bow to Hitchcock in all matters" pertaining to the League, to the armistice, and to peace negotiations. Noting that William Jennings Bryan also found the Germany treaty acceptable, Swanson admitted to Wilson that, on two occasions, party caucuses had concluded "it would not be wise" to make the separate treaty a party issue. Despite Swanson's "doing all" that he could "to solidify democratic *[sic]* opposition," he observed only twenty dissenting senators on October 18, 1921. Austrian and Hungarian peace treaties passed by similar margins. Significantly, Hitchcock and Underwood voted with the majority of sixty. Some Democratic senators, Swanson included, believed Underwood had prevented a successful Democratic opposition.[3]

The new treaty failed to resolve residual problems of the war. American citizens and their government held claims against Germany for tens of millions of dollars, and Swanson interpreted the treaty as requiring the Germans either to pay the claims or to cede German property seized during wartime. Various properties, including 4,800 patents, merchant ships, and corporations, had been assigned to the Alien Property Custodian by the Wilson administration. Under Harding, the office fell to spoilsmen who looted it. Nonetheless, Swanson continued to reject restitution of remaining properties until Germany met its treaty obligations. From a political standpoint, he reminded voters of the Harding scandals, emphasized the ill-framed Republican peace treaty, and embarrassed Republican administrations for failing to defend American claimants. Following a ruinous German inflation, a rescheduling of German war payments was patched together which awarded some relief to American petitioners.[4]

To unsnarl the European reparations tangle, return of German properties was considered essential. Bernard Baruch advised it would "close the circle" by a "proper adjustment of the German reparations," and he suggested Swanson favor immediate restitution. The former Wilson advisor admitted that some means to repay Americans who lost property and lives should have been developed, but the country should not "be forced to international brigandage." Swanson refused to budge, holding Germany to requirements of the Republican-authored treaties. In commercializing the German debts, Congress expected the Treasury to underwrite monetary adjustments. Swanson questioned whether this wasn't just another way of having the American taxpayer pay German bills. By 1928, American and German claimants had become so vocal in their demands that Congress worked out a solution. Still, huge sums to compensate German ship owners bothered Swanson: "What makes these ships more valuable now than they were when ships were in great demand?"[5]

Allied war debts had become an even more unsettling domestic and international perplexity. During the postwar period, Swanson defended expenditures for food relief: "Wisdom, sense and judgment require us not to have

Europe in a state of starvation, because starvation produces . . . conditions that are opposed to order and the best interests of humanity." But the billions of dollars loaned during and after the war, the "war debts," he did not consider charity. The total amount—nearly $11 billion in intergovernmental debt and $3.5 billion in private loans—startled Swanson and his Virginia neighbors who had been recently forced to pay their state Civil War debt. They believed, as did other Americans, that the money had been borrowed in good faith. Partially raised through public bond sales, the loans would be assumed by the federal treasury if not repaid by Europeans. In contrast, Europeans viewed these debts as subject to negotiation. Wilson had rejected that opinion despite Great Britain's decision to write off its loans to continental allies. He conceded to a suspension of interest payments for the next two or three years, but the unresolved issue was forwarded to the offices of Republican presidents.[6]

Swanson was not insensitive to the burdens faced by nations in debt to the United States. He knew the United States to be the world's creditor, with "great sums due" it. Irretrievably involved in the world, the United States should act with confidence, not be "timid, vacillating and frightened by our own prodigious shadow." His immediate solution was more trade, and he condemned high protective tariffs that prevented it. Had lower schedules been in effect as he wished, foreign debtors more easily would have acquired dollars for repayments. The Republican Senate established, instead, the World War Foreign Debt Commission, which negotiated interest charges and repayment schedules. Protesting abnegation of the Senate's duty, Swanson cautioned that no repayment agreements be consummated without the Senate's full knowledge. Swanson voted with the majority in February 1923 to adjust great Britain's debt of $4.5 billion and to approve debt renegotiations with smaller European countries. He commended the League of Nations role in rebuilding Austria. In Belgium's case, there existed "no need to bargain or quibble over a settlement with so heroic a nation and . . . people," Swanson contended; Virginians admired the "courage, the splendid valor and sacrifice exhibited" by Belgium during the war. He felt otherwise, however, about Italy.[7]

The Italian settlement in 1926 spaced more than $2 billion in repayments over a period of sixty-two years at an average interest of .4 percent. The Democratic minority objected to this low negotiated rate when compared to Italy's ability to pay. Swanson ranked Italy as "one of the five great powers of the world" and contended that it could certainly afford to pay more. Mississippi's Pat Harrison joined the Democratic chorus, noting that Reed Smoot had only allowed thirty minutes for the Finance Committee to discuss the topic. Swanson expressed amazement, playing to insurgent Nebraska Republican Robert B. Howell's contention that, given the proposed schedule, Italy would never repay the principal. Americans were committed to interest rates of 4.5 percent on money loaned to Italy, receiving only a pittance of interest in return, complained the Virginian. In the key vote to recommit, twenty-four southern and western Democrats with nine Republican midwesterners, "progressives," voted nay, but forty-two Republicans and twelve Democrats carried the majority. The Democratic division prevented embarrassing Republicans in a congressional election year.[8]

Swanson did not form these viewpoints within a domestic vacuum. In August 1923 he, with Joseph T. Robinson and other congressional representatives, sailed to Copenhagen to participate in the Interparliamentary Union, made up of representatives of the parliamentary bodies of the world to consider resolutions of global importance. While witnessing the runaway German inflation, Swanson admitted that reparations and the debts hinged one upon another, but in negotiating with the United States, European nations should separate the two: "No questions of reparations were involved at the time of creation of this indebtedness, and hence should not be subsequently injected." Three years later, attending a similar meeting in Geneva, Swanson found the Europeans less cordial, although he considered liberal the debt settlements developed during the intervening months. He blamed some of the bitterness on unfortunate boasts by the Foreign Debt Commission that France would pay to the point of bankruptcy.[9]

The French debt, tied to that nation's quest for security, proved most vexatious. Initial debt adjustment agreements reached in 1926 were not approved by the Senate until December 1929. During this period, French and American groups complained of the huge outstanding principal of $4.2 billion. To reduce Franco-American tensions, support accumulated for Britain's earlier suggestion that inter-Allied debt be canceled. In December 1926, a group of Columbia University historians and political scientists called for yet another international conference to revise downward the debt structure to remove "the growing odium" surrounding European-American relations. Swanson responded with an "especially caustic attack." Partially, partisanship motivated him as Nicholas Murray Butler, Columbia president and active Republican, had endorsed his faculty's initiative, but Swanson considered the proposal open to misinterpretation, encouraging false French hopes, and thereby accentuating ill will. To cancel or to revise the existing repayment schedules—"the most liberal and generous ever made"—would be "untenable and intolerable." The *New York Times* editors found Swanson intemperate on this subject, but in December 1929 he moved to favor a considerable further downward revision of the French debts.[10]

A third renegotiation in 1929 of German reparation payments produced a false dawn, as the world approached the brink of economic disaster. In 1931, President Herbert Hoover announced a one-year moratorium on payments and inferred that negotiations would be undertaken to reduce further repayment schedules. Before the president published his decision, he notified congressmen. Baruch helped to reduce Senate opposition by meeting with Thomas Walsh, Carter Glass, Swanson, and "a lot of others." In December, Swanson was paired "aye" in accepting the moratorium. Swanson's response to war debts between 1919 and 1933 had been sectional but not inflexible. The issue encouraged division within the Democratic party. The urban northeast Democrats favored reduction; the southern Democrats did not. Not until the 1932 campaign did the Democratic platform refer specifically to war debts and then to oppose their cancellation. Swanson eventually accepted renegotiated, reduced, long-term payments. He viewed cancellation, however, as the loss of millions of dollars in tax funds that could have been used for highways, medical services, lower taxes, and the navy. In Swanson's mind, the very nations disputing debts were spending huge sums to build their fleets to armed perfection.[11]

Wilson had used America's navy as a stern force in the war and a political pawn in peace. He and his navy secretary Josephus Daniels decided upon a postwar naval expansion to enforce Wilson's vow to make the world safe for democracy. Both followed the service's General Board recommendations to construct a navy second to none. Wilson also espoused disarmament through the League of Nations and would offer his emerging fleet as a bargaining tool in postwar diplomatic encounters. Speaking for the navy in committee and floor debate, Swanson favored naval expansion; at the same time, he considered national disarmament to be a worthy goal for American foreign policy. But, in 1919, Republicans and disgruntled Democrats revised naval plans, abolishing much of the new construction and proving that Henry Cabot Lodge and his colleagues believed the world to be safe enough, protected by the British fleet.[12]

Thereafter, events went from bad to worse for the navy. External and internal squabbling over strategic and tactical application of the airplane and the submarine fomented career anxieties of officers, dividing the department. Dissident admirals—especially anglophile William W. Sims—publicly condemned the navy's direction, thereby provoking congressional investigations. Some reformers accused Daniels of surrendering to business interests while disabusing "everything British." Following Harding's election, William E. Borah encapsulated these attitudes in a resolution to seek British, American, and Japanese naval disarmament outside the League. Swanson consoled and counseled Daniels during the Senate hearings and defended the General Board's definition of what constituted a modern navy. When the House typically pared the navy budget to the marrow, the Senate Naval Affairs Committee added $100 million. Local Virginia interests pressured Swanson. One Newport News precinct worker pleaded, "With no merchant [ship] work [the] Navy killing puts our city in the village class." In March 1921, Swanson proposed that the fleet desperately required two aircraft carriers, each with an eighty-plane capacity, and he objected to further personnel cuts. At least 120,000 men, he advised the Senate, must man the ships "you have in Turkey, the ships you have in China, and the ships you have all over the world." In addition, he shielded navy yards from criticism; yet, he and other navy partisans failed, in vote after vote.[13]

Disarmament through the League now shifted to disarmament through bilateral treaty, catching the public fancy. Harding and Hughes proposed a disarmament conference that convened eventually in Washington in November. Economic recession, Wilson's disarmament proposals, agrarian unrest, and an approaching election convinced Swanson to accept disarmament to save "the financial solvency of the world . . . [now] in jeopardy." He questioned whether America's own decisions, "her determination to remain isolated . . . , assuming no responsibility to aid or keep stabilized a chaotic and disturbed world," had not been a principal factor in contemporary world unrest and rearmament. Had other nations looked to their own safety when the United States failed to join the League? Admitting Great Britain's dependence upon the sea, Swanson denied her the option of dominating it. The United States must resolve problems with

Japan in the northern Pacific as China held the key to the Far East; the Open Door should remain. In China, "no more spheres of influence and no more special concessions should be allowed."[14]

Structuring strategy to oppose the Washington disarmament conference, Swanson concentrated upon the willingness of Hughes and Harding to permit Japan a larger Pacific role. Major legislative counterattacks were fashioned against two of the treaties of the conference. The Yap treaty between the United States and Japan removed the United States' objection to Japan's suzerainty over the League-mandated island. A second agreement, the Four Power Pact, designed to end the Anglo-Japanese alliance, created a nonaggression agreement between the United States, Great Britain, Japan, and France which bound its signatories to respect insular dominions and possessions of each. Swanson opposed acceptance because it would reduce further in the public's mind any need for America to join the League. Also, the navy professionals, diminished in influence by Hughes's proposals and in near panic, had raised storm flags over growing Japanese naval strength. Wilsonian Democrats and, ironically, isolationists Robert La Follette and Borah resisted the Four Power Pact and attempted to form a sufficient minority to defeat it; but Senate minority leader Underwood had "helped negotiate the Treaty and [was] unqualified committed to its ratification." Some Democrats suggested Underwood's removal as Democratic leader, but Republicans carried enough votes to pass the treaty. The Yap concessions received similar treatment. So heavy were the majorities—sixty-seven to twenty-seven for the pact and sixty-seven to twenty-two for the Yap treaty—that no additional resistance developed against the remaining conference treaties submitted to the Senate by Harding.[15]

Swanson approved the Nine Power and Five Power naval pacts produced by the Washington conference. He could accept the former, which codified the Open Door for China, allowed for Chinese national territorial integrity, and required consultation among signatories should problems develop. But the second agreement would result in a drastic reduction of projected American naval strength. Swanson later expressed privately his dissatisfaction over the sapping of the budding battle fleet, then publicly decried the loss of "76 warships . . . that would have given [to] the United States power 'to sweep and control the seas.' " Post-Jutland battleships became the steel backbone of the fleet, however, while a shortage of cruisers continued. The United States and Japan agreed also to freeze the arming of their Pacific possessions, leaving Japan to fortify her home islands and the United States to secure Hawaii. Challenged by Westmoreland Davis in the August 1922 Democratic primary, Swanson did not openly attack arms limitations agreements. He knew that disarmament, as a term, meant naval disarmament to the president, to the Senate, and to the public, and made the best of adversity. Now for the next fifteen years, "limitations rather than competitive expansion would characterize the international naval system."[16]

To realize disarmament agreements, Secretary of State Hughes and his advisors decided to finish the nearly completed battleships *Colorado* and *Washington* at New York Shipbuilding Company and to scrap the other partially built ships and those on drawing boards. Cost projections indicated that finishing these 35,000-ton vessels would be least expensive. Between December 1921 and March 1922, fending off Lodge and Joseph S. Frelinghuysen of New Jersey, Swanson intervened and the *Washington* was replaced by the *West Virginia*, only 62 percent complete at Newport News Shipbuilding and Drydock Company. Daniels and Homer Ferguson played a prominent role in keeping the ship that would maintain employment of persons at Hampton Roads until December 1923. Other vessels in the area were sacrificed, however, including the 43,200-ton *North Carolina* at Norfolk Navy Yard. [17]

The Emergency Fleet Corporation decided that the world's largest ship, the German-built *Leviathan,* should be reconditioned for resale to a private firm to improve American transatlantic passenger services. The estimated overhaul reached $10 million, but the ship's length permitted only a few yards to berth it. Sponsoring Norfolk Navy Yard, Swanson discovered that only private yards would be allowed to bid on the project. When Newport News Shipbuilding, however, submitted the lowest estimate, Massachusetts senator Lodge maneuvered to permit Charlestown Navy Yard at Boston to obtain the ship. On the eve of contract-signing for the *Leviathan,* Swanson hectored Lodge's proposal to move the ship to "the nearest shipyard." "Nearest to what? Nearest to politics? Nearest to where the political power is?" Working through Emergency Fleet chairman Joseph W. Cavell, who from experience and in attitude was strongly biased toward private yards, Swanson kept the *Leviathan* at Newport News. Influential Saxon Holt of the city reported on Swanson's dividends: "The people . . . deeply appreciate your efforts in behalf of this city in aiding in securing the contracts for the completion of the *West Virginia* and the repairs to the *Leviathan.*"[18]

Swanson influenced the division of naval appropriations through his service on the subcommittee for the naval budget and admitted he generally spoke "for the Navy, whether more money is asked for it or not." In 1923, he defended adroitly $6 million for the adjustment of gun elevations to lengthen battleship battery range to twenty miles by pointing to Great Britain's earlier, similar modifications. During this period, "modernization" of battleships took place: switching from coal to fuel oil, improving armaments, and reworking fire controls. The Norfolk yard obtained in 1925 the *Texas* and the *New York* for refitting; each project required $3 million and employed one thousand workers for two years. After attending hearings on General William "Billy" Mitchell's attempt to establish a separate air force, Swanson and Rhode Island's Peter G. Gerry helped to preserve the navy's beleaguered air arm, although many senators favored reorganization of the air service. Swanson also continued to defend other navy yards on both oceans, when not in conflict with Virginia priorities, thereby earning gratitude from their senators.[19]

Details concerning naval operations and personnel policies passed from Swanson through the Naval Affairs Committee to the floor of the Senate. Long before they appeared in that marble chamber, requisite agreements had been bonded. Upon Swanson's entry into debate, he appeared to alert Democratic colleagues and similarly inclined Republicans to the issue at hand. In contending for at least a 100,000-man navy, he strove for a carefully adjusted salary system between regular and reserve officers and men. Salaries and ratings of yard employees and Navy Department personnel earned his attention. As the committee screened marine and navy promotions, he continued to prevent a top-heavy officer corps. He preferred "to see the officers of the Navy at sea" as "that is what a Navy is for." He also would retire aging officers so that "younger men have opportunities for promotion." Combating a bias against naval air officers within the department, he considered that, after ten years of air service, navy fliers should be allowed to transfer to other branches of the fleet to avoid dismissal for declining physical abilities. A member of the Naval Academy's Board of Visitors, the former teacher and education reformer endorsed demanding academic standards for midshipmen. Fearful that instruction levels would lower if naval officers replaced civilians, and perhaps defending a Virginia constituent, he believed "no civilian instructor who went to the Academy, under a contract, implied or otherwise, ought to be treated badly." He responded favorably to granting navy nurses retirement benefits and effectively argued for a congressional investigation of the submarine S-4 disaster to avoid "a coat of whitewash" that could impair naval efficiency.[20]

Swanson remained perturbed about the incomplete aspects of the Washington treaty. Neither submarines nor aircraft ratios had been defined, and craft under 10,000 tons' displacement threatened to proliferate. Both plane and sub threatened an American navy based upon surface-controlling battleships. In April 1924, as an amendment to the naval appropriations bill, the Senate petitioned Calvin Coolidge to call another disarmament conference, inviting the Washington Conference signatories to conclude additional agreements for surface and submersible ships under 10,000 tons. Swanson successfully proposed that a request be included to limit personnel who could "be maintained in the respective Navies." Agreeable to a second meeting, he chided Republicans and a "derelict" President Coolidge who refused a League invitation to participate in disarmament discussions. No effective disarmament could occur "until the United States is a party to it." Then, not only could taxes be reduced, but, inferentially, potential enemies such as Japan could be hedged about by international agreements.[21]

During an April 1924 discussion of immigration quotas, Swanson questioned an earlier "gentlemen's agreement" giving Japan authority to select Japanese immigrants to the United States. When Coolidge and Hughes proposed codifying it, Swanson refused, comparing it to a surrender of the right to admit one's choice of guests into one's home. Public opinion favoring Japanese exclusion broadened to include Asians in general. Since the 1920 Democratic platform had agreed to an existing near-exclusion of Asiatics, Swanson criticized the State Department for making "understandings of the . . . effect of treaties and committing us to foreign matters so as to avoid the [Senate] treaty making power." Two days later, the Japanese ambassador selected an inflammatory term—"grave consequences"—to illustrate Japan's response should fair treatment be denied. A journalistic storm erupted, and Swanson abandoned an immigration ratio allowing some Japanse immigration for one that virtually prohibited admittance. Citing the Four Power Pact and the dismantling of the American fleet, Swanson complained, "We made concession after concession to Japan, but we seem not to have been able to settle the differences." Other factors—an approaching presidential election, Democratic courting of the Far West, Senate Democrats' moves to split the Republican majority, nativism, and rampant nationalism—led also to passage of the bill. The 1924 Democratic platform condoned "exclusion of Asiatic immigration."[22]

Prospering in the China tobacco trade and selling "by the million pounds," Virginia tobacconists in 1918 grew suspicious of "Japan taking over the Chinese business." One trader noted, "If we were to set down on paper our opinion . . . of Japan's commercial morality, our letter would not get past the censorship." Japan extended loans to China which were underwritten by Chinese taxes on wine and tobacco, provoking tobacconists' concern. Second to Great Britain, China became a significant importer of Virginia bright tobacco during the period from 1923 through 1929. Much of the imported tobacco was in raw form as China accelerated her own manufacturing, but the market shrank upon emergence of internal political conflict. One Swanson correspondent in 1926 feared that the withdrawal of American naval forces would not only endanger American lives and property but also would harm the tobacco trade. Swanson forwarded to Secretary of State Frank B. Kellogg the tobacconists' request that "an adequate force of marines and minimum of four destroyers" be sent to Hankou to protect American interests and show the flag to the "Bolshevic Canton government." A former senator, Kellogg responded by dispatching the *Truxton* and the *Pope* with a warning concerning the low water level of the Yangtze River in winter.[23]

Japan seized Manchuria in late 1931, and Swanson concurred with the response of Kellogg's successor Henry L. Stimson. Cautioning him not to "take any steps leading to war," Swanson aided Stimson in assessing Senate and Foreign Relations Committee attitudes; the secretary of state found him "helpful as he usually is." As the crisis deepened, Swanson proposed that the United States "move the fleet to Hawaii, merely as a demonstration," but Stimson considered such an action too strong. By mid-August 1932, Stimson's non-recognition of the Japanese puppet state of Manchukuo relieved Swanson of his concern that Stimson might "take a step which would" force the United States "to back down or go to war." The nation was opposed to war and both men agreed that only a direct attack by Japan could provoke an American armed response.[24]

Toward Soviet Russia, Swanson gradually departed from the policy of nonrecognition established by Wilson and sustained by his three Republican successors. Despite almost unanimous initial opposition by business leaders and labor spokesmen to diplomatic relations with the Soviet Union, Swanson seriously considered agrarian suggestions for trade agreements to offset American farm distress in the early 1920s. Debating a resolution to investigate the Soviet government in December 1923, Swanson and George Norris questioned Secretary of State Hughes's harsh reception of Russian overtures to make amends for having unilaterally canceled debts owed to the United States. As a member of a subcommittee to evaluate recognition of Russia, Swanson directed most of his questions to discover the relationship between the Soviet government and the Communist party. Preferring to assess diplomatic recognition, he would not meddle in Russian internal affairs. In contrast, the *London Times* in

1926 called Swanson a "bitter opponent" of Russian recognition. He had monitored Russian expansive tendencies, cautioning, for example, that the Soviet government threatened to seize Bessarabia, which had been assigned to Romania by the 1919 peace settlements. In December 1932, following Franklin Roosevelt's election, Swanson asked for a review of the nonrecognition policy to consider trade and diplomatic ties. He predicted that a majority of Democrats and "progressive" western Republicans would agree. A year later, recognition was granted.[25]

The League Council in 1920 created the Permanent Court of International Justice, but not until February 1923 did Harding submit the court protocol for Senate approval. From the Foreign Relations Committee, initially, Lodge and Borah favored only a court apart from the League. To Swanson, such tactics resembled the 1919 bonding of irreconcilables and strong reservationists against the Wilson League. Harding and Hughes then agreed to plan for distinct separation of League and court as necessary for American approval, but Swanson and Key Pittman vigorously disagreed. A shuffling of the membership of the Foreign Relations Committee removed all but one Democratic court opponent, and strenuous efforts by Robinson prevented appointment of a notorious anti-League Democrat, James Reed of Missouri. Only five committee Republicans remained opposed and Chairman Lodge adopted delaying tactics. In early 1924, he appointed anti-League, pro-court senator George Wharton Pepper of Pennsylvania to chair a review subcommittee comprised of Swanson, Pittman, and anti-court senators Frank Brandegee of Connecticut and Henrik Shipstead of Minnesota. This committee rehashed arguments, but the witnesses testifying before it favored the World Court and American adherence to its protocol.[26]

Encouraged that "nearly all the Democrats" he knew indicated that they were "willing to join this court." Swanson pushed Lodge to introduce a Senate resolution approving the Harding-Hughes court plan. Wilson's death a few weeks earlier acted as an emotional catalyst in the plan's favor, but majority leader Lodge continued to obfuscate. In May 1925, by introducing a motion favoring the Harding-Hughes court, Swanson tested Harding's successor, Coolidge, and his earlier promise to brook no delay with the proposal. Amid the familiar histrionics of the anti-League faction, Swanson defended before the Senate in December 1925 reconsideration of the court question. By then the Foreign Relations Committee membership had altered extensively.[27]

Death and circumstance left but five of the 1919 committee members who had hamstrung American entrance into the League. Chairman Lodge's demise the previous month reduced Republican party discipline and removed a wily League and Harding-Hughes World Court foe. His successor, Borah, performed at best as a reform-bent Republican maverick, at worst as a destructive loner. Wisconsin's Irvine Lenroot, the fourth-ranking Republican on the committee, did give the court a positive reception; with only one session's committee exprience he, in effect, ceded initiative to the Democratic minority. Its leader, Robinson, and the other Democratic pro-court senators, Swanson, Pittman, and Thomas Walsh, surrounded new Democratic member Reed, who had finally obtained a seat owing to reasons of seniority and party harmony. Swanson led the court fight in the committee and in the Senate.[28]

With irreconcilables gravely reduced, controversy centered upon the court's advisory function to the League. Paramount in the effort to separate the League from the World Court, one of its judges, a University of Virginia graduate who had been trained in Republican state departments and who was adamantly opposed to American entrance into the League, John Bassett Moore, pontificated extensively: given its existing advisory relationship to the League, the court was hindered from practicing international law. If sufficient reservations could be attached, noted a correspondent, "to disgust the Democrats," acceptance of the Harding-Hughes court was in the balance. Aware of these tactics, Swanson defended the court resolution and projected images of the Wilsonian prophesy in a three-hour comprehensive Senate speech. Describing court functions and procedures in careful detail, he responded to arguments before the opposition could voice them. In the ensuing weeks, he prevented Reed's motion to recommit. When Borah described what he thought to be hobgoblins flying about court membership, Swanson replied that if they were "going to consult our fears about everything that might occur" they would accomplish nothing.[29]

During December and January, in a series of meetings endorsed by Coolidge and Secretary of State Kellogg, Swanson polished necessary compromises. Included were Lenroot, Pepper, Robinson, Moore, and Thomas Walsh. Four earlier Hughes reservations were slightly altered and an additional fifth reservation introduced by Swanson required American consent before the court could rule on any "item which the United States" had or claims to have had "an interest." Responding to fears that Japan might seek a court investigation of American immigration policies or that the repudiated Confederate debt of 1861-1865 might be contested by foreign creditors, the fifth reservation formed the net that caught Senate approval. Invoking cloture, the Senate accepted each amendment, including the "Swanson Reservation," passing the total compromise by a vote of seventy-six to seventeen. During concluding days of debate, Edith Bolling Wilson, accompanied by Lulie Swanson, sat in the Senate's presidential family seats. Upon approval of the court protocols as amended, the Wilsonians celebrated the Senate's acceptance of a modicum of the League covenant. In defeat, irreconcilable Hiram Johnson snarled that the minority Democrats had carried the day.[30]

A few weeks later over Washington and New York radio stations, Swanson interpreted Senate action, and speculated that in 1914 such a mediatory agency might have avoided war. In September 1926, attending an executive committee meeting of the Interparliamentary Union in Geneva, he listened as a League-convened conference of World Court signatories discussed American reservations. Earlier denying that he represented the American government, he nonetheless succinctly informed diplomats that, for the Senate to approve membership, the American reservations must be accepted. In part, he was protecting his flank. Borah, in Washington, had cast his suspicions upon the League meeting and dared the State Department to send representatives. Swanson earlier had approved American entry along the lines of the Harding-Hughes court and could have been conciliatory and publicly compromising. Now he was bound to the Senate's will, ruffling feelings among some of the European diplomats. American minister to Switzerland Hugh Gibson relayed gossip to

Kellogg that Swanson had been "overbearing" and that one delegate believed his statements prevented a more "friendly view" of reservations by the Europeans. Although the American fifth reservation proved to be a stumbling block, the conference produced a conciliatory statement. Neither Coolidge nor Kellogg pursued possible further understandings.[31]

In April 1928, Swanson complained of Coolidge's "lack of energy and enthusiasm" for court membership. He encouraged Kellogg in November "to try to get the governments to accept [the United States'] reservations." To review the court statutes, the League Council authorized a committee in December that included the elder internationalist Elihu Root who had visited Washington before his departure where he "had long talks with . . . Swanson, [Thomas] Walsh and Borah" as well as with Kellogg and other interested senators. In March 1929, Root obtained a compromise proposal, the Root formula, which provided that the United States could signify its opposition to any League advisory request to the court and, if overridden by League members, could withdraw without discredit. Newly elected President Hoover and Kellogg consulted with Swanson, Walsh, and Borah. The Democrats agreed to the formula. Hoover and Swanson also believed that the League Council should postpone consideration of the court revision until September to allow the Senate to digest an overcrowded agenda, to deflate potential criticism, and to permit consideration of the revision concurrently with the signatory powers. Swanson also volunteered to lead the Democrats in the fight for approval.[32]

In early September 1929, Swanson sponsored the Root plan with Secretary Stimson. Over the Columbia Broadcasting System's National Radio Forum, he assured listeners that the present proposal held "no danger" and, if it was not adopted, peace conferences and disarmament agreements were futile. Equality of treatment with League members could be expected. But the gloom of a spreading depression and a congressional election year led Hoover not to submit the protocols; he feared, according to Stimson, that Borah intended to embarrass him, that anti-League groups planned to use their power in the elections, and that Swanson was not fully trustworthy. Finally, in December 1930, partially owing to Swanson's agreement through Stimson, Hoover delivered his adherence request to the Senate. Inspired by an interview with Edward Bok of the American Peace Foundation, Swanson now argued for consideration in March 1931. He upbraided Douglas Freeman, *Richmond News Leader* editor, who questioned his commitment to the court. Swanson struggled to extract the court proposal from committee, but he and his colleagues failed by one vote. Not until March 1932 did the committee move for reconsideration, but Swanson was in Geneva as a delegate to a disarmament conference. Even then he advised Robinson in the new effort. But depression legislation continued to take first priority while Japanese aggression and disturbed European conditions detracted as well. One authority concluded that his absence "left the minority leadership with[Key] Pittman, a somewhat less enthusiastic champion of the World Court, which may have contributed to the lack of unity in the ranks of Court supporters." Soon Swanson left the Senate. The World Court proposal, a potential symbol of American commitment to the rule of law rather than of force, would be, like the League, consumed by worldwide aggression.[33]

The concept of the outlawry of war bloomed in the late 1920s. In early 1927, French foreign minister Aristide Briand proposed a bilateral pact with the United States which aimed to reduce Franco-American tensions and to shield France from Germany. Kellogg broadened the proffered treaty by inviting all nations to concur in a multilateral statement renouncing war as an instrument of national policy. Signed in August 1928, the Pact of Paris became still another symbol for peace forces in the United States. Swanson supported the treaty, an action interpreted by the *New York Times* as a signal that Democratic senators would vote for the bill. Coolidge submitted the treaty in December, and the Foreign Relations Committee held hearings. To deflate nationalist opposition, Swanson obtained Kellogg's agreement that there was "no obligation, moral or legal, for [the United States] to go to war." Wars of self-defense would not be confined to any specific territory and neither the Locarno Pact nor the League obligations of other signatories would be affected. Reported quickly to the Senate, the treaty received Swanson's aid; as a skilled parliamentarian, he helped Vice-President Charles Dawes unravel an agenda knot that placed the pact ahead of debates over a naval cruiser bill. [34]

In his supporting speech to the Senate, Swanson reviewed the pact's origins and chronological development and found no impairment to the "right of absolute and unlimited self defense." The League covenant remained whole. While Great Britain had reserved certain territories that would permit no interference, the Monroe Doctrine would remain healthy and unabraided. He also criticized the agreement by observing that the wars of the previous century would have fallen under the self-defense exception, each nation involved having claimed that excuse. The proposed pact, in Swanson's view, would not have prevented World War I or restrained any of the participating governments. It held "no tribunal, no instrumentalities for the settlement of international differences." This, to Swanson, was its "fatal defect." Only one senator voted nay on its last reading. In remembering those who had masterminded its passage, the Senate's presiding officer listed Swanson with Borah, Robinson, Charles Curtis, Thomas Walsh, and Arthur Vandenberg of Michigan. The passage of the Kellogg-Briand Pact resulted from considerable bipartisan effort, but it remained, in Swanson's words, only "a noble gesture." [35]

Swanson declined to follow Republican policy in the Near East. After 1919, a revolutionary Turkish government had emerged from the shambles of the Ottoman Empire, but Wilson heartened Armenians, a defiant, Christian minority within the new state, by endorsing their self-determination. Given previous depredations against them by Moslem Turks, Armenians received backing from American religious leaders, including Methodist bishop James Cannon, Jr., who condemned Turkish treatment of Christians. Within the United States, an Armenian nationalist group sponsored independence. In 1924, Hughes submitted to the Senate the Lausanne Treaty, establishing diplomatic and trade relations, while ignoring the Armenian question. By that time oil companies were accused of serving their own interests in sponsoring the treaty. The Democratic platform in 1924 condemned the Lausanne Treaty that bartered Armenian rights; Armenia had been betrayed and Wilson's promises broken. [36]

Secretary Hughes initially encouraged Swanson to accept the treaty, but the senator worried over the fate of missionary schools and of minorities within the new Turkish nation. He also refused to allow American capitulatory rights to be surrendered. Hughes recommended that Allen W. Dulles, State Department Near East expert, furnish additional information and explicate the department's views. In January 1925, after extensive discussion with Dulles, Swanson still harbored doubts, especially concerning the treaty's effects upon trade and the tariff. Another counselor, Henry Morgenthau, Sr., Wilson's Ambassador to Turkey, heatedly opposed settlement, citing for Swanson's benefit a long list of alleged abominations perpetrated by Turkish leaders. Although tobacco manufacturing interests in Virginia wanted adoption for those who were "dependent on Turkish tobacco for [their] cigarette brands," Swanson felt more keenly Cannon's antitreaty crusade. Utah Democrat William H. King performed as the primary opponent, but Robinson and Swanson hunted for votes against the treaty also. As an example of their tactics, Burton K. Wheeler later admitted complete ignorance of the matter and confessed that Swanson secured his negative vote "as a personal favor." On January 18, 1927, the treaty failed by six votes from receiving the necessary two-thirds' majority.[37]

Professional diplomats like Joseph C. Grew judged that domestic political considerations alone induced Swanson and his colleagues to defeat the treaty. Grew, as principal American negotiator shaping the Lausanne proposals, understandably was disappointed; his interpretation spread into studies of the period. He also harbored typical bureaucratic and State Department grievances against practicing politicians such as Swanson. When Coolidge appointed Grew American ambassador to Turkey, Armenian-American leader Vahan Cardashian and other anti-Turk elements immediately raised objections. Interviewed by the Senate Foreign Relations Committee, Grew feared partisan retribution from "a solid phalanx of democrats led by Senators Swanson and King," but he escaped rejection, despite reconsideration of his nomination by King. The Senate concurrently delved into functions of the Foreign Service Personnel Board and multiplied department career anxieties. Swanson received annual invitations to observe its deliberations upon promotions, demotions, or removals in the foreign service. In addition, the secretaries of state, the treasury, and commerce, Swanson, and three other congressmen composed the Foreign Service Buildings Commission that appropriated funds for furnishings for consular buildings, foreign service offices, and ambassadors' homes. Swanson's motivations were masked, but his former colleague on the Foreign Relations Committee, Hughes's successor, Kellogg, wrote a Virginia Republican in 1928 that Swanson, one of the "most valuable members" of the committee, had convinced Kellogg he never played "party politics with foreign affairs."[38]

Subsequently, elements of the rejected Turkish treaty passed the Senate piecemeal. In February 1930, the Senate consented to a reciprocal, nondiscriminatory trade agreement. Offering a long memorandum prepared by the determined Cardashian, Swanson recalled broken promises made to Armenia, but the State Department and new secretary Henry Stimson convinced Swanson to agree to the new proposal. He did so, rationalizing his vote by observing that no extraterritorial rights of the United States had been surrendered. In the case of

Turkey, in addition to his Methodist-influenced conscience, Swanson committed himself to maintaining Wilsonian policies, which in the mid-twenties merged into the Democratic platform. By 1930, national priorities had changed and the old Wilsonian projected world order, when applied to Turkey, no longer served.[39]

In Latin America, Swanson pursued a path of moderation which eschewed intervention in Mexican affairs. Although the American press reported bandit raids, revolutionary take-overs, assertive Latin American nationalism, and alleged Communist infiltrations, Swanson and Robinson proposed to resolve Latin American difficulties through discussion and arbitration. Democratic national platforms moved from a 1920 resistance to "imposing from outside a rule upon" Mexico's "temporarily distracted councils" and defense of the "right of the United States to demand full protection for its citizens" to a 1924 vague greeting of goodwill. In 1928, the platform specifically requested "non-interference in the elections or other internal affairs of any foreign nation. . . . Interference in the purely internal affairs of Latin America must cease." Swanson stressed in October 1925 at the Pan-American Union its cultural and commercial benefits and especially its intercessory role. He used the example of Argentina, Brazil, and Chile mediating United States–Mexican problems. In sponsoring passage of the Isle of Pines Treaty that would return it to Cuba, he cited Latin American ill will generated by continued occupation; he also sought to prevent Cuban abrogation of treaty rights at the United States naval base at Guantanamo. National pledges, its faith and honor, should be kept, as they were "more important than the enrichment of a few." In treating with Latin America, he did not favor sending military arms to recognized governments: "We should not support either side of a revolution." The United States must desist from making "general rules about recognition, that the thing must be governed by expediency."[40]

Oil aggravated American-Mexican relations. In 1917, a revolutionary Mexican government prepared to seize drilling sites under its constitutional prerogatives. From 1919 to 1920, Senator Albert B. Fall of New Mexico deliberately attempted to provoke American intervention in Mexico. During extended hearings Bishop Cannon conveniently testified that where the Methodist Church operated in Mexico no property had been molested; furthermore, he did not believe that intervention was a proper solution to the Mexican problem. Swanson also opposed Fall's intercessory recommendations in the Foreign Relations Committee, but, despite negotiations with Mexico, intermittant, anguished complaints from American oil corporations and investors continued throughout the decade. In 1925, Cannon complained of destruction of church property and harm to non-native clergymen. Yet, in 1926, Swanson still opposed intervention and cautioned that "heated expressions of opinion can do no good and might possibly interfere with negotiations." In 1928, he condemned Republican diplomats for insensitivity in their treatment of Latin America, and, in the midst of a presidential election, for a radio audience he identified Mexico and Nicaragua as objects of continuing "imperialistic departures" by the United States. Owing to debate over importation of agricultural labor in the midst of a sprawling depression, Swanson in April 1930 objected to singling out Mexico for stricter restrictions. It would be, he claimed, an "offense to the Mexican people" and preferred using, if necessary, a quota system that applied to all Latin American countries. The muddle over Latin American immigration consumed much of the session, but the House refused to make any adjustments.[41]

Swanson responded similarly to a prolonged crisis in Nicaragua. The United States had maintained an armed presence in the Central American country since 1912, but upon withdrawal in 1925, a revolution erupted. American forces returned; to stabilize the government, the Coolidge administration endorsed the Conservative party leader Adolfo Diaz. Despite claims that his faction had been armed by Mexicans and infiltrated by Communists, Juan B. Sacasa, the Liberal party head, was preferred by Swanson, by a majority of Senate Democrats, and by midwestern Republican "progressives." Swanson undoubtedly met Sacasa when he visited the United States and, in committee hearings, the senator called attention to the killing of civilians by U.S. air attacks and the repressive role of the Conservatives. In executive session, Swanson, the *New York Times* reported, led a "grilling" of Kellogg on continuing support of the Diaz government. He also questioned the political composition of the Nicaraguan National Guard and the intentions of rebel general Augusto Sandino. Swanson knew that naval appropriation bills were now in jeopardy as opponents of the administration's intervention policies fought to attach limiting amendments. He then defended the marines' presence in Nicaragua as a guarantee of free elections, but, in January 1931, he advised Stimson "to get entirely into Nicaragua, or to get out all together." He opposed "repeatedly sending marines to Nicaragua" and interfering with affairs in that land. Leave the country to Sacasa, he counseled, because continued endorsement of Diaz or those of his stripe harmed Nicaraguan and American relations in the region.[42]

Toward Panama, Swanson was far more possessive. He believed that the United States held "absolute sovereignty" over the zone and should not surrender it. Not only did Hampton Roads benefit from the Panama Canal, the navy considered it a vital link in national defense. For this generation of Americans, the Big Trench also symbolized the nation's initiative, progress, and technical accomplishment. Swanson vacationed in the zone in 1923 and stopped at Haiti and other Caribbean islands. When the canal and Panama's rights came before the League, Swanson responded that the United States would "not tolerate any interference in this matter . . . from any source whatever." Despite his public stance, Swanson accepted a mutual defense treaty that permitted Panamanians easier access to the zone.[43]

Swanson's leadership had moved from response to initiation in the fields of naval policy and foreign affairs. Recognized as "a leading representative of the Senate group adhering to the principles of Woodrow Wilson," the shrewd, smiling Virginian presented Democratic alternatives to Republican proposals. The noisy anvil of necessary campaign politics hid the more persistent theme of bipartisan cooperation, and Stimson knew, for example, that, during political campaigns, Swanson "had an adverse interest in the results of the election." Hoover and Stimson "could not count on him not to be swayed by that adverse interest." But the secretary of state would talk "over questions . . . with him freely and found him . . . very helpful." This cooperation emanated from Swanson's bipartisan consultations in the Senate. When he succeeded, as estimated by Vice-President Dawes, Swanson frequently did so owing to "unceasing work." Long-time Virginia political writer K. Foster Murray of the *Norfolk Virginian Pilot* called Swanson at the decade's end "probably the most influential Democratic Senator." But between 1929 and 1933, events occurred that led to his appointment as a cabinet secretary.[44]

12

The Wise Thing to Do
1929-1933

Events between 1929 and 1933 led Claude Swanson to accept appointment as secretary of the navy in Franklin D. Roosevelt's administration. In advocating the navy, in proposing acceptance of the 1930 London naval treaty, and in participating in the 1932 Geneva disarmament conference, he advanced to the forefront of senators in both parties in foreign relations and in naval affaris. His friendly relationship with Roosevelt and his political sagacity as well as national and Virginia political developments, encouraged Swanson's elevation to the Roosevelt cabinet.

Swanson frequently used informal meals and dinners as background to fathom senatorial attitudes; his home frequently provided a comfortable site for fruitful conversation. Amid Swanson's library of navy and Civil War books he intiated many guests into the Virginia mystique, making handy use of it to accompany his political personality. His table reflected bounty from the Commonwealth's fields and orchards. Henry L. Stimson recorded a Swanson dinner as "quite a pleasant company of a rather political character" replete with conversation "about old times," and "gossiping about the Senate, President Wilson and the League of Nations." At Senate luncheons, for business and entertainment, Swanson jocularly masked a searching intelligence while seeking votes as a means to an end. After the 1928 Republican presidential victory, he cautioned his boasting Republican dinner companions not to discuss "who killed Cock Robin." Conversations from these convivial meetings formed much of the gist of senatorial politics during these years.[1]

In the late 1920s, navy topics increasingly appeared in Swanson's conversation. Congress in 1929 debated authorization of fifteen 10,000-ton cruisers to be built over a three-year period. Displaying his parliamentary aplomb and acumen, he identified lackadaisical planning in cruiser construction as the source of America's most serious naval defect. Busily building the swift ships, Great Britain had resisted further treaty limitation at a recent disarmament conference and held a cruiser ratio of thirteen to five over the United States. To Swanson, the "best guarantee. . . of a continuation of peace" between Great Britain and the United States rested in cruiser equality. The nation must also match Japan, who had built beyond America's present cruiser strength. "Our rights in China. . . will be ultimately sacrificed" unless the navy was strengthened, for it is "folly. . . to leave our national safety and our vital interests only to peace preachments." Avoiding an extended filibuster and negotiating construction assignments between private and public yards, he maneuvered the cruiser bill through the Senate. An opponent congratulated Swanson and Naval Affairs chairman Frederick Hale of Maine "for the magnificent way they have steered through the legislation."[2]

A year before passage of the bill, Swanson confided to a Virginia associate his intention to have a cruiser built at Norfolk Navy Yard and to have a proposed aircraft carrier "assigned to Newport News." His evenhandedness was necessary with both Virginia yards because each sought "advantage over the other." He generally provided ship repair for navy yards and ship construction for private yards. The latter preferred new construction since costs could be more easily controlled. Early cruiser construction billets did not go to Norfolk, however. Other navy yards obtained three new cruiser projects. Newport News gained the carrier, beginning work in 1930 on the *Ranger.* Apparently, Swanson had compromised. The same week the cruiser bill passed, Norfolk yard won the *Pennsylvania* for modernization at an estimated cost of $8 million, to be followed by the *Arizona.* Ironically, employment pressures generated by machinist locals sometimes influenced naval policy as much as secretaries of state. Before the arrival of New Deal public works projects, Swanson often emphasized that these contracts provided employment for economically depressed shipbuilders. Internal trade-offs abounded, and Swanson frequently calmed Newport News Shipbuilding general manager Homer Ferguson's apprehensions.[3]

Should further moves to limit naval armament occur, the cruiser act allowed Herbert Hoover to postpone construction. In July 1929, he and novice prime minister Ramsey MacDonald of Great Britain jointly issued a statement halting cruiser construction. Swanson objected that until a treaty was signed, Hoover had exceeded the law and abused Congress. Only "when Great Britain" realized that America was "firmly determined to have a Navy substantially equal" would any agreement be made. In late September, after interviewing the navy's General Board, Hoover discussed naval affairs with Hale and Swanson to gain information for a MacDonald visit. Rumors also circulated that the two senators would serve on the American delegation to a prospective disarmament conference in London. By continuing precedents, established by Warren G. Harding and Calvin Coolidge, of including Democrats at armament limitations conferences, Hoover would avoid Wilson's 1919 failure to take any senators to the Versailles Treaty discussions.[4]

Evaluating MacDonald's speech to Congress in 1929, Swanson became convinced that the prime minister was promoting "amicable relations" and was amenable to naval parity between the two countries. In a Memorial Day address, to assure America's defensive posture, Hoover repeated Swanson's arguments that parity could be achieved through decrease of armaments rather than increase. As in 1922, Swanson expected no great building program to advance the nation to existing treaty schedules. He thought the coming conference should adopt rules for sea warfare similar to extant land warfare regulations so that sea battle would "be humanized and civilized." Undoubtedly, he meant to curb submarine and air attacks that would bedevil battleships and new, thin-skinned cruisers. But, instead of Swanson, Hoover sent to the conference Pennsylvania's David Reed and Joseph Robinson. In so choosing, Hoover stirred criticism owing to their low rank on the Foreign Relations and Naval Affairs committes, and some senators complained directly to Hoover of his failure to select Swanson.[5]

Coupled with the necessary two-thirds vote of the Senate for treaty approval and his friendly relationship with Robinson, his position as cue-giver among Senate Democrats and his seniority permitted Swanson a role in negotiations nevertheless. To resolve an early conference contretemps over cruiser ratios, Swanson expressed from Washington his opinion that, in effect, the Senate would accept a solution: "Great Britain and the United States may, if they so desire, exactly duplicate each other's cruiser fleet, ship for ship, ton for ton, and gun for gun." The American delegation expressed its appreciation for his counsel. On February 6, 1930, a public statement by the delegation chairman, Secretary of State Stimson, outlined American positions in agreement with those of Swanson and the Senate. Stimson surmised that the delegation would seek immediate parity in every class of navy ship with Great Britain, a reduction of battleships, equality of lowest possible tonnage in destroyers, aircraft car-riers, and submarines. Abolition or strict regulation of submarines received endorsement. Then Stimson wired his aide in Washington, inquiring "What does Swanson think?" Joseph P. Cotton replied that Swanson "was very much pleased" and indicated the senator would withhold public judgment until the conference completed its work.[6]

The London conference also considered an Atlantic consultative pact similar to the Pacific's Four Power Treaty of 1922. Swanson informed Stimson through Cotton that the Senate would not be favorably inclined and that he did not "relish political pacts." Instead, he preferred specific naval agreements on cruiser concessions. Political agreements encouraged long debates in the Sen-ate, which bred disharmony and disarray in naval matters. In an interview with a *London Times* correspondent, Swanson had earlier objected to any Mediterra-nean agreement similar to the 1922 Four Power Pact. Swanson claimed the United States had no insular possessions there, and the reporter surmised that Swanson intended to discourage an Atlantic agreement by introducing the Mediterranean as an issue. Cotton also reported to Stimson that Swanson "does not like Japan and consequently does not want to give them much." The Hoover administration bowed to "overwhelming Senate opposition" and withdrew proposals for such an understanding. Swanson would modify his position in 1932, indicative that he frequently represented drifting Senate opinion.[7]

In extensive hearings by Foreign Relations on the completed treaty, Swan-son raised questions to anticipate its foes while evidencing that he "was by no means dominated by the Admirals." Did the treaty protect the nation's commer-cial fleet? Did it assure naval equality between the United States and Great Britain? Did it provide replacement schedules for America's aging destroyer squadrons? What were the relative merits of six-inch guns over eight-inch guns on treaty cruisers? Could merchant ships be easily armed with six-inch guns? What convinced the navy that submarines were defensive weapons? Had the

navy been consulted concerning abolishment of undersea weapons? In responding to this and to other committee members' lines of questioning, the admirals
revealed a badly divided leadership that shied away from political pronouncements, preferring to hide their partisanship in disagreement over technical and
strategic issues. Although Senate Naval Affairs chairman Hale and the General
Board of the navy opposed the treaty, Swanson managed its passage.[8]

In July 1930, opening debate in a two-hour speech, Swanson reviewed
recent naval history. He cited the Wilsonian origins of the doctrine of equality
with Great Britain or any other nation's navy. After the Washington conference,
neither Harding nor Coolidge had permitted development of America's sea arm,
but the passage of the 1929 cruiser bill had prompted Great Britain to call the
London conference. Swanson claimed provisions of the treaty certified American home waters to be safe; he warned his listeners that "the military mind"
construed safety "as synonymous with 'superiority.' " He opposed such superiority over all fleets because it would create "fear, irritation, and suspicion."
Revealing a broad knowledge of naval technology, tactics, and strategy, he
endorsed the United States' decision to favor guns and armor over speed.
Despite heated controversy over the merits of six-inch or eight-inch guns, no
great difference existed for him. He applauded reduction of submarine tonnage
and restriction upon the undersea raiders in attacking merchant ships. Despite a
shortage, he knew that destroyers could be built quickly if needed. Given
American naval supremacy in the western hemisphere, a necessary $1 billion in
ship replacement costs could be spread over the next decade. The treaty passed,
with nine dissenters. In the words of one historian, it marked a victory of
"internationalists over isolationsts, . . . of international good will over . . .
isolation. . . . The civil authorities triumphed over the military."[9]

In the ensuing Congress, Swanson requested funds to nurture the fleet at
treaty levels. The London agreement permitted battleship modernization but no
new construction. Pleading that, if appropriations to refit the *New Mexico,
Idaho,* and *Mississippi* were withheld "in the present session, thousands of men
will be thrown out of employment in the Navy yards," he won the latter two
ships for Norfolk Navy Yard. Despite protest from proponents of the Brooklyn
yard, Secretary of the Navy Charles Adams kept the battlewagons on course to
Norfolk. Swanson overstated his true expectations in debate, being willing to
take less, which "was realistic with the construction thus permitted," and
received Stimson's congratulations in "having saved the money for the Navy."
Under seige by the depression, Hoover cut authorization for eleven new destroyers to five and trimmed by December 1931 $59 million from the navy budget.
Disgruntled, Hale and Swanson met with their House counterparts, Congressmen Fred Britten of Illinois and Carl Vinson of Georgia to support a House
resolution to investigate what Hoover's fiscal policies posed for the navy. In
1932, Vinson would sponsor an even larger construction bill.[10]

As a member of both the Senate Foreign Relations Subcommittee to study
silver exchange rates and the Public Buildings and Grounds Committee to
survey consulate and embassy requirements, Swanson and his wife toured
western Europe during the brooding summer of 1931. Interviewing financial
ministers in London, Berlin, Prague, Vienna, Paris, and Geneva, he discussed a

possible accord to reduce economic difficulties between France and Germany. In Paris, Swanson met with Premier Pierre Laval, and in Berlin he conferred with German president Paul von Hindenburg and Chancellor Heinrich Bruening. He investigated opportunities to reduce "cost of maintenance of marine services," and he received encouragement from Britain's Labor government. Swanson also suggested international agreements on silver rates. He pondered implications of German battleship construction and problems bred by America's earlier separate peace with the Wiemar Republic. During his Berlin visit, he attended a state dinner with Secretary Stimson, and, returning on board the *Leviathan,* he and Stimson held extensive conversations "over questions of the policy of the [State] Department." The secretary of state "found him, as always in the past, very helpful." Upon return, Swanson endorsed Hoover's one-year moratorium on war debt payments but opposed any further scaling downward of debts. He suggested a five-year cessation of naval construction, aware that replacement tables for overage ships would then favor the United States. He was drawn deeper into European politics, being selected as a delegate to the long-planned General Disarmament Conference at Geneva under League auspices. [11]

Hoover had encountered hitches in formulating a delegation. Swanson had volunteered, but Hoover found him to be "a little anxious to go." Stimson favored Swanson, who suggested to the president that Stimson head the delegation and David Reed of Pennsylvania be a member. Although both declined, Reed discussed with Stimson the delegation composition and agreed that Swanson "would make a good member. . . [and] very hard to match" with a Republican senator. On December 17, Swanson accepted the president's invitation as did Democrat Norman Davis. Pennsylvania senator George Wharton Pepper encountered business obligations. Republican Dwight Morrow agreed to chair the group but died three days later. American ambassador to Great Britain, former vice-president Charles G. Dawes, became the object of entreaties; he asked Stimson if he was "satisfactory to Senator Swanson." Reassured, Dawes became chairman, but upon returning to the United States, Dawes was appointed to direct the Reconstruction Finance Corporation. To Swanson's pleasure, Stimson now assumed leadership of the delegation with Undersecretary Hugh Gibson as acting chairman. President of Mount Holyoke College and peace activist Mary Emma Woolley and professional diplomat Hugh Wilson were appointed, but a Republican senator was not. Technical advisors and secretaries completed the cast. [12]

During briefing sessions, world politics, military strategy, tactics, and technical details were reviewed for the delegates. Swanson requested press reports from Great Britain, France, Germany, and Japan to delineate current opinions. His encompassing bonhomie and self-confidence stirred resentment in delegation advisor J. Pierrepont Moffat who described him "with an unlighted cigar, interrupting the conversation from time-to-time with jocular remarks." Hugh Wilson criticized what he understood to be Swanson's evaluation of various nations' positions as "good," "bad," or "unjust." Referring to French demands, Swanson asked "Do you believe that this is a righteous claim?" The elitest diplomat pondered upon Swanson and his fellow Americans using their consciences "without regard to. . . limitations of knowledge" to

"The American Delegation Crosses Lake Geneva," a European comment on the
Geneva Disarmament Conference of 1932, inspired by Emanuel Leutze's famous
"Washington Crossing the Delaware," with Swanson cast as Washington.

measure actions of nations. But Swanson, even Wilson admitted, "knew his
subject thoroughly."[13]

During these interviews, Swanson offered his view of world politics while
exchanging valuable insights. Although severely limited by existing agreements, the navy, President Hoover agreed, served as the United States' principal
arm, while the army occupied the "lowest terms, even for the maintenance of
internal order." Swanson accepted the concept that the American battle fleet
rested upon the battleship; he did not think it likely that the United States would
ome under aerial bombardment but the canal zone could be a target for
commercial planes converted to bombers. Swanson considered that restriction
of air power orginated with Great Britain, "who for the first time. . . had
become dangerously vulnerable as a result of military aviation." While he would
not initiate a motion to abolish submarines, he would join those nations
proposing such an idea. German and French differences "were based
upon. . . military power and that social and political problems would be greatly
modified by a change in the military situation." France appreciated a "stable and
efficiently armed" Germany as the single effective barrier against Russian
intrusion into western Europe, and French interests required that Chancellor
Bruening remain in power. Under no circumstances should the United States

agree to a security pact with France now. At Geneva, the Americans must approach "a final solution. . . by degrees." Swanson discussed also the sizes of the conference's five committees—political, military, naval, air, and economic—aware that the Senate kept committees small.[14]

Swanson joked with Stimson that he was the only member who enjoyed discussions on technical details. For example, replacement of airplanes, if limited by treaty, would be difficult as technology advanced beyond political control. New planes could rapidly replace older planes and horsepower limitations were "almost impossible," as lighter metals allowed swifter and more deadly designs within existing standards. Would aerial bombardment be considered the same as artillery bombardment? If proposed, he did not believe the United States would suffer from abolition of aircraft carriers. Benefits would accrue as only aircraft from carriers at that time could assault the mainland. Otherwise, he would maintain existing armament limitations. The existence of a new American naval construction bill, being readied in Vinson's House Naval Affairs Committee, "would prove extremely helpful" to bring other nations to favor limitations. He confided that the Senate supported a ban on chemical warfare and conjectured that any future conflict would originate between France and her allies and Germany, Italy, and "other dissatisfied countries." New weapons could upset the total balance, but the economic depression should encourage arms limitations. Joshing the secretary of state, contemplating means of agreement at Geneva, Swanson observed that "the only method whereby anything could be accomplished in the Senate was either by unanimous consent or by exhaustion." Stimson considered consent unlikely and exhaustion quite probable at Geneva.[15]

Swanson found Geneva to be a restful indian summer for his public career. Fellow delegate Woolley, Swanson's wife, his stepson Douglas Deane Hall, and his sister Margaret Swanson boarded the *President Harding* with the senator on January 20, 1932. At dockside, Swanson admitted he was "not too optimistic . . . but . . . hopeful. . . . If something does not come out of the conference, then the Lord help us." Several thousand peace advocates, attended by blaring band music, displayed posters and banners, cheered speaker Lillian D. Wald, and presented peace petitions, one with 400,000 signatures. After an eight-day voyage, the entourage was greeted at Cherbourg by the French mayor who sounded a theme common to the fifty-four delegations assembling in Geneva: "Good Luck. . . . Disarm everybody except" us. As depression-ignited political brawls erupted in the United States, the *Norfolk Virginian Pilot* estimated that Swanson's presence in Geneva provoked "green envy" among his stateside colleagues, who pictured him "ensconced in a hotel suite overlooking beautiful Lac Leman, three thousand miles from Washingon's unholy mess."[16]

To his sister Blanche, Swanson wrote, "Geneva at the moment seems to be the hub of the universe, with all the problems of the world reverberating at this center." Failure of the conference, he confided, "would be the signal for a race in armaments that will wreck the world financially and probably bring on another war." On February 3, he addressed the American people over transatlantic radio. "I suppose I was heard in Pittsylvania." Junius Fishburne in Roanoke cabled him that "it was the finest and clearest transatlantic broadcast he had ever heard."[17]

In a nearby building, the League Council debated in tardy fashion an undeclared war between China and Japan, and Swanson admitted privately that the League labored under a severe handicap "in dealing with so strong a nation as Japan," while the United States and the Soviet Union remained outside the body. After a month of meetings, Swanson concluded that guarantee of French security was the key to disarmament success: "Something must be done to save their face with their home people and to satisfy them politically." In early March, Swanson, revising an earlier opinion, argued for a United States Senate resolution "authorizing the President to call a consultation of the signatories whenever any emergency, a violation or threatened violence arose" and advised Robinson to "talk it over with [Thomas] Walsh, Borah, and Dave Reed." Robinson and William E. Borah opposed the move, and, by transatlantic telephone, Robinson told Swanson that it would serve only to irritate Congress. Stimson considered Robinson overly cautious and "influenced by the presidential year" elections. Robinson's failure to accept the bipartisan proposals, Stimson recorded, would "be a pretty sad disappointment"[18]

On March 19, Swanson described for an American radio audience unstable German political conditions, his opposition to budgetary limits on armaments, and conference disagreements. Stimson joined the delegation in April. Friction between French and American delegates grew, owing in part to Gibson's mistakes. German and French elections nearly suspended serious discussion, but Swanson felt relief upon reelection of Hindenburg in Germany; Andŕe Tardieu's eventual defeat by French voters proved disruptive to the conference. Discussions at month's end produced such differing conclusions by the participants that the conference passed beyond posssible success. Various persons—MacDonald, Tardieu, John Simon, Swanson, Davis, and Stimson—gathered for dinner at Stimson's rented villa and partook of a "good deal of chatting around in separate groups in the library." Woolley, Swanson, Simon, and MacDonald held meetings over consultative pacts, also. The key meeting occurred on April 22; thereafter, despite American efforts to reach definite conclusions, little was accomplished. Stimson returned to Washington in early May, and Swanson found small evidence for optimism. To resolve the deadlock, despite Stimson's objections, Hoover authored a ten-point proposal in June which would scrap tanks, prohibit chemical warfare, ban heavy mobile guns, forbid bombers, and outlaw bombardment of civilians. He would reduce by one-third land weapons and land armies and shrink by one-fourth battleship tonnage as well as that of aircraft carriers, cruisers, destroyers, and submarines. The president intended to "reduce offensive strength compared to defensive strength in all nations."[19]

Swanson placed Hoover's proposal before the Naval Committee, which immediately tangled over battleship classification. Swanson catalogued the present United States navy as defensive because the nation maintained no land army to transport to foreign shores and battleships were more effective and cheaper than expensive coastline defenses. Should battleships be abandoned, the American defense plans, bereft of cruisers, would need redrafting. After the Japanese responded that submarines were truly defensive, Swanson countered that new hearing devices extended the sleek subs' offensive capabilities, and only a few years before they had been labeled "assassins of the sea" for their attacks against merchant ships in World War I. He opposed French requests to enlarge naval ratios or to bar ship-launched scout planes. In June 1932, substituting for Gibson, he refused agreement on a joint British-French call for cancellation of war debts. If armament expenditures were also cut by the debtors, he would be more amenable. Hoover revived also the earlier Swanson consultative suggestion, and he asked Davis and Swanson to include the concept in the 1932 Democratic platform. Partially incorporated into both party platforms, the concept indicated some success at bipartisanship.[20]

In Geneva, Swanson employed a "fervid Southern eloquence" amid "great clouds of smoke from his cigar." Wilson recalled that he considered battleships "a symbol of the American home," and he "swore and bedamned that he would sink these submarines." Amazed European delegates required, as journalist John Whitaker humorously recalled, "translation of his remarks into English as well as French." His "spread-eagle oratory" outraged certain "feather duster diplomats. . . who tried to dismiss him as a troublesome fool." Whitaker suggested that "if they think [him]. . . a fool let them try to beat him in a political campaign for Senator from Virginia." Occasionally in the evening he visited the bar of the Hotel des Berges and matched wits with reporters, "the great press"—a phrase Swanson found amusing. As governor of Virginia, he had been "inspired to search the classics of Greece and Rome and to delve into the Holy Scriptures." In Luke 19:3, he found first mention of the fourth estate: Zacchaeus sought "to see Jesus 'and could not for the press.' " Questioned as to when he would vote wet, his eyes twinkled and he replied, "I'm going to vote wet three minutes before the state of Virginia, Sir."[21]

Demanding "equality of armaments" in principle, upon conclusion of the conference's initial stage, Germany withdrew in July 1932. The American delegation returned upon the *Leviathan,* and Lulie Swanson placed "her taboo" upon any further disarmament discussions for the remainder of the voyage. Swanson speculated whether any foundations for peace had been dug at Geneva. Tentative agreements over chemical and biological warfare had been framed, and aerial bombardment of civilians neared outlaw status. Yet, he sensed that the American delegation and its proposals resembled an American train running upon European tracks, using "a different signal system." He would have gone beyond Hoover's limits and complained that the president lacked "confidence in [the] delegation to give them a free hand." It also lacked coordination, as acting chairman Gibson's leadership had dissatisfied him. With the proper leader, they "should have gotten the Hoover plan for disarmament passed by a great majority in the General Committee and referred over to January [1933] for consideration," and "public opinion would have gathered behind it." Arriving in New York City on August 5, he appeared from his pictures heavier than usual, his hair wind-blown, his ruddy face a mask of crisscrossing wrinkles. He bragged to Carter Glass that his health was "better. . . than for many years in the past." Stimson pleased the Swansons by meeting them at the Washington train station upon their arrival. Shortly after his return, the senator was drawn into the roiling presidential contest between Hoover and Franklin D. Roosevelt.[22]

As a rule, Swanson sought the most available Democratic candidate to avoid disrupting the party. Influential in selecting Democratic senatorial candidates and in application of campaign funds, he complained to Bernard Baruch before the 1928 election, "It is this agitation of candidates that keeps the party in turmoil." But personal ties with Roosevelt since the Wilson era, fretful years of Democratic debacles, and Roosevelt's great political savvy inclined Swanson to support his candidacy. His closest senatorial associates—Cordell Hull, Robinson, and Thomas Walsh, for example—came to similar conclusions. Certainly early acceptance of Roosevelt would prevent the Democratic division and dislocation experienced in the two recent presidential campaigns. Following Hull's withdrawal, Roosevelt emerged as the candidate of the Senate Democratic leadership.[23]

In supporting Roosevelt, Swanson ran counter to Virginia developments. As early as January 1928, Harry Byrd had been mentioned as a potential presidential candidate, and, in February 1930, House of Delegates member William N. Tuck of South Boston had heard of Byrd's presidential availability from as far away as New York. A few weeks later, state game commissioner A. Willis Robertson predicted that Byrd's tour of Kentucky guaranteed that the latter would "figure prominently in the next National Convention." Swanson probed the former governor's intentions with several flanking movements, one of which suggested that he run against the incumbent Republican congressman in his district. Swanson saw no advantage in following Tammany Hall's Al Smith and John J. Raskob. Both men had ventured to near-Republican stands on tariff policy and appeared too eager to please eastern corporate interests. As important, Swanson wished to avoid another debate over prohibition and its enforcement. He could give lip service to dry Harry Byrd as a favorite-son candidate to maintain state party unity and to avoid national candidates campaigning for Virginia delegates to the national convention.[24]

In July 1930, a New York industrialist, Owen D. Young, floated a presidential boomlet that attracted Glass and Fourth District congressman Patrick H. Drewry. Byrd learned that the former refused to reply positively to Byrd's candidacy and the latter was "gravely critical and adversely inclined" toward it. William A. Reed complained to Stuart Bryan in October that *Richmond News Leader* articles represented "a movement to discredit Harry Byrd's Administration" to the harm of his presidential aspirations. In November, Governor Roosevelt won reelection in New York by a massive majority, and Swanson moved definitely to his column. To split southern Democrats from Roosevelt, Raskob then sponsored a motion to permit the Democratic National Committee to formulate endorsements for high tariffs and for repeal of prohibition. Should they pass, Roosevelt as a committee member could be caught between wets and drys. Smith and Raskob knew they had little to lose in southern precincts. Southern Roosevelt leaders, led by Hull, Robinson, and Swanson, orchestrated opposition to undo Raskob's ploy. Virginia's and other Democratic House delegations passed resolutions directing their state committee delegates to defeat the Raskob plan, and committeeman Byrd followed their lead. To thwart Smith, Roosevelt flexed his southern congressional muscle, and an angry Raskob broke with him. Such a rift pleased Swanson who could inform his Virginia associates that Roosevelt had antagonized Tammany.[25]

Hull used Swanson to muster senatorial forces against Raskob. In late March 1931, with Byrd, Hull, and Robinson to discuss strategy, Swanson apparently noted that the only successful Democratic presidential candidates since 1892 had been anti-Tammany in their political affiliations. Reviving a suggestion Roosevelt had discarded, Byrd would cut the prohibition knot by calling for a national referendum. Robinson agreed, Hull mildly objected, but Swanson "very vigorously opposed." Citing Byrd's apparent anti-Raskob stance, Swanson's office composed and Hull distributed a news release of the meeting. Reed cautioned Byrd that, from his actions, Swanson apparently wanted to get Byrd "out of the picture and in the meantime he is preparing his for the next [senatorial] election." Swanson now circulated stories of Byrd's suitability for the vice-presidential nomination, and Byrd heard that the senator's Washington friends were at work "overtime in their efforts to block any chance" for Byrd's presidential candidacy. Drewry volunteered "to take charge" of Byrd's campaign in the House of Representatives, but Reed warned Byrd "to beware of Greeks bringing gifts." Byrd admitted, "Pat, of course, is spokesman for Swanson." In July 1931, Reed and Byrd met Raskob in New York City, and the wily financier dangled the presidency before them, predicting that Smith would not run and that he, Raskob, "was going to oppose Franklin Roosevelt to the bitter end."[26]

Roosevelt in 1931 formally visited Virginia twice, in July to address the University of Virginia's Institute on Public Affairs and in October to participate in the 150th anniversary of Cornwallis's surrender at Yorktown. At Charlottesville, he condemned "too much local government" producing excessive costs for the taxpayer, and his extemporaneous remarks for greater economic planning led the two thousand listeners to applaud loudly. Byrd interpreted this reception as having placed him "to some extent in the position of running on the ticket with him as [his] Vice President." Roosevelt visited Lexington and Richmond, following a social agenda that allowed "friendly conversation" with the most active Virginia Democratic leaders.[27]

During his July junket, Roosevelt called upon Byrd at his forty-room Rosemont mansion. The two politicians did not mention the vice-presidency, and Byrd and Governor John Garland Pollard made no commitments "in any way to him." One week later, Pollard suggested Byrd announce as the southern candidate for president, but Byrd neither refused nor accepted, as he fruitlessly hunted for reasons to break openly with Swanson. As estimated by political journalist K. Foster Murray, Swanson purposely avoided disharmony by even risking "appearing to play second fiddle to Byrd" as head of the Virginia Democratic party.[28]

In September 1931, Swanson again attempted to draw Byrd and his "closest friends to Roosevelt." Swanson planned to sponsor Byrd as a favorite-son candidate and to convert the Virginia delegation to Roosevelt at the national convention. But Roosevelt opposition in Virginia was manifested not only in Byrd's political ambitions but in ideological factors as well. Reed observed that anyone with "even a few acres of land" should fear the New Yorker as president. "He would lead us into the dole and every other fool proposition of putting the government in business he could put over."[29]

The New York governor returned to Virginia in October 1931. As chairman of the Yorktown commission to celebrate Cornwallis's surrender, Swanson introduced him to the Tidewater's political gatekeepers. The sesquicentennial commemoration also welcomed Hoover, General John J. Pershing, and Marshal Henri Pétain of France. Following four days of intense activity, Swanson fell ill with what doctors described as indigestion, but he called it his "little spell exaggerated by the press." Swanson received a concerned note from Roosevelt: "You are like me. You throw everything you have with all your enthusiasm and vitality into what you are doing." The country "needs your service. . . and we cannot afford to have you laid up." Swanson accepted Roosevelt's invitation to visit in Albany in late December 1931.[30]

Swanson increased circulation of Byrd's availability for vice-president. To flush Byrd into the open, Lieutenant Governor James H. Price, long-term Swanson friend, wrote the Valley grower as to his intentions for that office. Swanson also successfully recruited Virginia's congressional Democratic delegation for Roosevelt. Former opponent, Eighth District congressman R. Walton Moore had become a Swanson advisor on foreign policy and a close friend. Even Congressman Harry Tucker, considering Byrd not to be presidential timber, favored Roosevelt. By the end of 1931, among the delegation only Congressman Clifton Woodrum of the Sixth, Thomas Burch of the Fifth, and "possibly Glass" were not "for Roosevelt and committed to him." Bryd continued to exchange communications with Roosevelt.[31]

In early December 1931, Swanson assembled "our friends together," including Pat Harrison, Hull, and westerner Thomas Walsh with Roosevelt's alter ego, Louis Howe. They evaluated a Howe-drafted resolution to cap potential factional eruptions in the national committee by denying any "possibility of its expressing its opinion, directly or indirectly, on any national question." A concerned Swanson worked slowly through various personalities involved in the leadership cadre of the committee. Two weeks later, committee vice-chairman Byrd received from Howe similar suggestions, a copy of which the diminutive Roosevelt agent sent to Swanson. Swanson, Hull, Byrd, and "others" met in Washington to stop Raskob again. The two senators proposed that statements and proposals concerning the committee be submitted in June to the national convention. By then, issues that Raskob could raise would be deprived of practical significance. Swanson undertook to encourage senators and congressmen "in Washington [to convince]. . . their respective national committeemen" to approve the suggestion. Byrd apparently informed Raskob of these events and, at the latter's request, he hurried to New York "to consult. . . about the recommendations."[32]

On January 4, 1932, Howe, Swanson, and Hull met with Byrd to count noses on the national committee. Nearly 90 of the 106 members would oppose Raskob's ploy. Outnumbered and probably well-informed by Byrd, Raskob suggested that the committee do exactly what Swanson and Hull had concocted in December. So dominating were the Roosevelt forces that they selected Chicago as the convention site among those suggested by the New Yorker. The next day in the Senate, Swanson coddled Byrd's close advisor Reed who revealed to Byrd that he "had quite a talk with Claude Augustus. . . [who] is doing all he can for you and me, and is leaving his affairs in our hands while he goes abroad. . . . He says he has fixed it so the [Virginia] legislature will endorse you." In the center of Swanson's political lair, Reed also, at Swanson's suggestion, met to discuss tobacco taxes with Speaker John Nance Garner and Congressman James Collier, both members of the House Ways and Means Committee.[33]

Swanson had convinced Reed, who had returned to Richmond, of his loyalty to Byrd. Given pervasive evidence of Roosevelt's command of party machinery, Swanson's effusiveness toward Reed was but another feint to guard the senator's outer marches in the Old Dominion. If Byrd would consider the vice-presidency, Roosevelt might well choose him, as the former's balance-the-budget, pay-as-you-go posture would stand Roosevelt well in the depression politics of 1932. Swanson would then have few difficulties in Virginia in the 1934 senatorial primary. In any event, his imminent departure for the Geneva Disarmament Conference would relieve him of having to reveal to Virginians his commitment to Roosevelt instead of favorite son Byrd. Swanson remembered his failure in 1912 to endorse initially Virginian Woodrow Wilson for the Democratic nomination. He would not now oppose openly another Virginian; he sailed to Europe convinced that Democratic politics were going according to a Roosevelt plan.[34]

At about the time Swanson landed at Cherbourg, Smith announced his willingness to accept the presidential nomination. Powerful press lord William Randolph Hearst endorsed Garner, owing to the Texan's anti-internationalist bias. Byrd told Howe, however, that all was well in the Democratic National Committee; he heard the most favorable reports about the "meeting in Washington" and urged Howe, "Give my best to Franklin." Although continuing his contact with Howe, Roosevelt, and James A. Farley, Byrd, on a short visit to New York city, found it inconvenient to meet with Farley, Roosevelt's field general.[35]

In mid-March 1932 from Geneva, Swanson wrote various Virginians inquiring about political affairs. He expected "several months" to go by before he could return home and "take part" in any campaigns. Although he undoubtedly received frequent resumes from Archibald Oden and other stateside associates, he feigned ignorance of events. For example, he knew that "Virginia was reapportioned congressionally with. . . few changes" when writing Moore about hearing from him "and the course of political events at home." Responding, Moore endorsed Roosevelt, hoping he soon would "develop sufficient strength to receive the nomination," but fearing the convention would "manage to commit suicide" owing to Smith's candidacy and the gathering of favorite sons. He believed Byrd an "avowed candidate. . . without the slightest prospect of being placed on the ticket." Moore had heard that his campaign managers in reality preferred Newton Baker, with Byrd in second place, all designed "to block Roosevelt." Swanson also complained to Reed that little of a political nature appeared in the international edition of the *New York Herald* and asked to be filled in.[36]

Reed's response to Swanson verified Moore's assumptions. Although Roosevelt appeared forging ahead, Reed retorted that he had "yet to see a businessman of any prominence in New York or elsewhere who do [sic] not think it would be a stupendous blunder to nominate him." Hoover, then, would win. Roosevelt's chief accomplishment in New York was to leave the state "a deficit of a hundred million dollars" that year. Roosevelt, Reed reasoned, must win on the first ballot or not at all. "Harry has a wonderful chance." Swanson probably forwarded this information to Roosevelt forces in Washington. In May, Robinson wrote Swanson: "Roosevelt seems assured of the Nomination, but the opposition . . . among the Conservative Democrats seems. . . to be increasing."[37]

Nearly all the would-be Roosevelt challengers attended the Democratic Jefferson Dinner in Washington on April 13. Among them, Byrd addressed the group and endorsed a national referendum on the prohibition amendment. Smith welcomed him as "a prodigal son," and journalistic opinion evaluated Byrd's prohibition proposal as a direct challenge to Bishop James Cannon, Jr. A photostatic copy of the speech, marked in blue pencil, went to Albany for Roosevelt to read. Byrd had raised the issue that had been muffled in March 1931 and January 1932 in the Democratic National Committee. If it became heatedly debated, prohibition could well split the Roosevelt forces. The following day, Howe learned, Byrd attended "a very secret conference, consisting of Smith, Raskob, [Jouett] Shouse, and several others. . . at which. . . some plans to get some life in the [stop Roosevelt] movement were discussed." To Howe, "Harry Byrd is joining the ranks of the enemy."[38]

In Virginia, with Swanson out of the country, Byrd was assured control of the state delegation and drew closer to Carter Glass. Reed had confirmed that Swanson would not return before the national convention. Byrd workers concentrated upon removing Roosevelt delegates to the state convention. At Richmond, on June 9, the Virginia convention's "Byrd bandwagon" made "it impossible to find out other candidates'" support. "A good many" of the Virginia delegates favored Baker, the old Wilsonian, and "Roosevelt men were being sidetracked." Preferring an orderly repeal of the Eighteenth Amendment, state Senator C. O'Connor Goolrick started a backfire by censuring Byrd's prohibition referendum as a radical departure from the Constitution. A convention compromise produced only a recommendation that the national party consider Byrd's solution to prohibition, but the unit rule placed Virginia's twenty-four votes under Byrd's banner. Pollard helped convince Glass to nominate Byrd. From Geneva, Swanson angled for Roosevelt, and his letters proved sufficient, with Drewry's efforts, to convince Reed that this "talking about the Vice Presidency . . . has done more harm than all the other agencies combined." So effective had the wile been that, of the Virginia Byrd delegates to the national convention, "very few, if any, took the view that Harry had a chance." At Chicago, however, had Garner not released his votes to Roosevelt on the fourth ballot, the sought-for deadlock might well have occurred. The New Yorker and the Texan became the Democratic nominees. Swanson telegraphed Roosevelt his congratulations, pledging "to aid in every possible way."[39]

Returning to Washington in August 1932, Swanson assembled his agenda, conferred with Oden, read correspondence, and finished details of his report on the Geneva conference to Secretary Stimson. Early the next week, he renewed Senate relationships and, with Key Pittman among others, assessed Roosevelt's prospects. Minority leader Robinson and other senior Democratic senators convinced Swanson to coordinate Democratic senatorial campaigns, thirty-three in number. Pittman advised Roosevelt that he might "find it enjoyable and probably profitable to talk to Claude at an early date." On August 11, Daniel C. Roper, Swanson, and Pittman lunched with Farley, the new Democratic national chairman. Then, the four Democrats ambled off to the Washington Press Club for a Farley interview. After a stay in Chatham, Swanson attended in Richmond the state Democratic committee meeting that rallied party leaders, who "vociferously applauded . . . [Swanson] as he said he had returned to engage in Democratic hostility against the enemy." Meeting Governor Pollard, he assured him that Byrd could find a place in a Roosevelt cabinet and asked Pollard of his future plans. Swanson attempted to dine privately with Byrd but the cagey former governor "asked Sam Ferguson to be present," which prevented Swanson's conferring with Byrd alone. On August 18, Swanson visited his beloved Hampton Roads where Norfolk celebrated its 250th anniversary and four former governors, Andrew Montague, Swanson, Westmoreland Davis, and E. Lee Trinkle, and incumbent Pollard received distinguished service medals. Nearby, within photographic range, stood Swanson colleagues Norman Hamilton, Price, Drewry, John R. Saunders, and assorted local leaders.[40]

By Labor Day, Swanson bolstered the Senate compaigns, aided by Virginian Edwin A. Halsey, secretary of the Senate minority. On Saturday, September 10, Swanson, Senator Robert F. Wagner of New York, and industrialist Young discussed with Roosevelt at Hyde Park unemployment and international problems. Preparing his first campaign move westward, Roosevelt mulled over senatorial prospects with Swanson. While Farley was absent with Roosevelt on the western swing, Swanson and Senator David Walsh remained in New York City to serve in advisory capacity at campaign headquarters in the Hotel Biltmore. Senators Pat Harrison and John S. Cohen of Georgia joined them. During the autumn electioneering Swanson compensated for Farley's lack of experience in national politics, as, close by Farley, he assisted the New Yorker. Farley recalled he never sought Swanson's advice "without getting a clever suggestion, . . . without offending anyone and without hurting the cause."[41]

To focus senatorial campaign issues, Swanson claimed the depression had been "largely produced by the provisions" of the Hawley-Smoot Tariff Act and that Hoover's counterarguments that blamed world war economic upheavals were mere alibis. Why had Hoover not mentioned these pending aftershocks when he served as secretary of commerce? Why had he not published his observations during the 1928 presidential election? Delighted, Swanson encountered great unity among Democrats. By the middle of September, he noticed local candidates grabbing at the coattails of Roosevelt, whose popularity was proving greater than theirs. A few weeks before the election, Swanson predicted a Democratic Senate with a working margin of six to ten seats. The Republican "campaign of fear" and claims of holding unto themselves "all the patriotism and ability in the country" earned the old Democrat's scorn. He also collected campaign funds; Baruch, for one, contributed an initial $20,000 in early September. Roosevelt carried the field in November. By a margin of fourteen seats, the Senate became Democratic for the first time since 1919. The

House held nearly a three-to-one Democratic ratio. These election results pleased Swanson as much as any during his long political career.[42]

To keep Byrd off balance, Swanson suggested to his Virginia friends that, for the 1933 Democratic primary, a ticket be floated composed of Drewry for governor and Goolrick for attorney general. He backed congressional candidates Byrd considered hostile. Byrd feared Swanson intended a portion of Baruch's contributions for the Virginia Second District contest between Colgate Darden and Menaclus Lankford to place Tidewater Democrats under obligation for the 1934 Senate election. Both Swanson and Byrd realized that the leadership role within the Virginia Democratic party would be resolved within the next eighteen months. Byrd observed: "The great crisis of our wing of the organization will come during the [1933] gubernatorial election. Every enemy we have will concentrate upon us, aided and abetted by Swanson." As no new Pollard appeared nor an internal crisis similar to the anti-Smith campaign to force agreement upon a gubernatorial candidate, federal patronage control was necessary to guarantee Byrd any chance of success.[43]

During mid-November 1932, Swanson conversed with President-elect Roosevelt in Washington. Deeply involved in planning Senate committee assignments, Swanson undoubtedly discussed the committees' composition. Swanson's own career may have received the New Yorker's attention, speculating upon Glass's invitation to become secretary of the treasury. Illness and ideological doubts hovered about Glass. He originally had favored Baker, a fiscal conservative, for president but reluctantly had made one radio speech for Roosevelt on November 1. Agreeable to seeing Byrd in the new cabinet, to Swanson he admitted worries that the exuberant Democratic victory would "lead to loose thinking and harmful action." Patronage conflicts emerged as Swanson approved of Hamilton for collector of customs at Norfolk while Byrd preferred the city's I. Walke Truxton. In early December, Swanson seemed certain that Glass was "responsive to [the] cabinet suggestion," or at least he telephoned Reed of his convictions. Not to be put off, Byrd alerted on December 10 such faithful retainers as Everett R. "Ebbie" Combs in the Ninth District to make no commitment to Swanson for the 1934 senatorial campaign. To control the Virginia Democratic party, Byrd could not permit Swanson to remain in the Senate and tried to convince Glass to refuse the cabinet appointment. Apparently successful, Byrd understood Swanson to be encountering increasing difficulties, to be considering resignation, and to be "fishing around for a cabinet appointment, preferably Secretary of the Navy." He believed that he gained Glass's agreement to stand against Swanson in patronage matters. But Glass vacillated over the cabinet offer.[44]

Virginia newspapers had conjectured upon Swanson's possible nomination to secretary of the navy. New Year's Day readers noted in the *Richmond Times-Dispatch* an estimate that he stood closer "personally to the President-elect than either Glass or Byrd." Other journalists reported Byrd as the object of an "organized effort to persuade" him to enter the 1934 Virginia senatorial race. Swanson visited Roosevelt on January 13 in New York City, ostensibly to discuss foreign affairs. At the same time, Roosevelt composed a list of potential cabinet members which included Glass as secretary of the treasury. Once more meeting the president-elect at the Mayflower Hotel in Washington, Glass discussed the Treasury appointment. Claiming ill health, Glass finally refused on February 3, and news reports made Swanson's move to the Navy Department highly probable. Swanson would turn seventy-two in 1934. His health could be seriously threatened by a vigorous reelection campaign. Two weeks later, after much thought, he accepted Roosevelt's offer. Immediately thereafter, Swanson invited Byrd to Washington. Swanson may have wished to protect his staff, or to have Byrd accept some of his patronage appointments, but the occasion, for Swanson at least, left lingering bitterness. Despite intense pressure, he did not resign early to give Byrd, expecting appointment by Pollard, a few days seniority over fifteen newly elected senators.[45]

Some Swanson confidants had entreated him to remain a senator, to oppose Byrd, and to fight "it out." Other persons dissatisfied with Byrd and his choice for governor, George Peery of the Ninth District, wanted Swanson's authority to boost other candidates. At the time, some uninformed observers decided Roosevelt wanted "his effective young ally" Byrd in the Senate. As late as January 30, 1933, Byrd had "heard nothing from Governor Roosevelt" and confessed that, as a new senator, he "could have of course little influence." A more realistic interpretation would be that Roosevelt preferred Glass out of the Senate and, knowing of Swanson's high standing in that body, to rely upon the older Virginian for senatorial support. Pollard would have appointed Byrd to the Senate in Glass's place, but it would not have resolved the younger man's Virginia political problems. Ironically, had Swanson, as a Roosevelt partisan, remained in the Senate, he might well have beaten an unappointed Byrd in 1934 in a free-swinging fight. But he took the bird in hand, moved to the executive wing of government, and left Byrd the Senate seat. An era in Virginia politics had ended. Swanson now directed his full attention to Roosevelt, his administration, and the emerging New Deal. The navy awaited.[46]

13

Second to None
1933-1939

A few weeks before his seventy-first birthday, Claude Swanson was sworn in as secretary of the navy. Younger journalists and recent arrivals in New Deal Washington frequently stereotyped him as a typical southern politician, replete with pince-nez secured by a long black ribbon, gray hair worn a bit long for the custom of the day, and a mustache from an earlier stylish mode. One State Department officer, reflecting his cultural bias, found Swanson's discursive manner objectionable; he "looked longer and seedier than ever. He sat back in his chair puffing away at his long, thin cigar and proceeded to utter pontifical statements" Appearances were deceiving. Swanson's network of political and personal relationships was matched in the cabinet only by that of Cordell Hull. Owing in no small part to this patient, aged, professional politician, the navy enjoyed exceptional treatment in an era of isolation and financial exigency. He coordinated navy publicity so effectively that, in 1938, Americans in public opinion polls believed, by a three-to-one-margin, that a larger American navy would prevent entry into war, while Swanson stood second only to Hull in having "done a good job" while in office.[1]

The New Deal cabinet that Swanson joined was noted for its variety. Washington insiders—Vice-President John Nance Garner, Swanson, Secretary of State Hull, and Commerce Secretary Daniel C. Roper—mixed with political novices on the national scene: Henry Wallace, Agriculture, Frances Perkins, Labor, William H. Woodin, Treasury, and Harold L. Ickes, Interior. The remainder, Postmaster James A. Farley, George H. Dern of War, and Attorney General Homer S. Cummings, were acquainted with national political currents. Perkins recalled Swanson, Roper, and Farley as the most partisan Democrats. Introduced to one another at church services before Roosevelt's inaguration, only Hull and Swanson knew to call for their departmental limousines. The remainder were left to flag down available transportation. Swanson's relationships with Hull and Dern, as well as the latter's successor Harry H. Wooding, were generally excellent. The secretaries of the navy and interior experienced difficult moments, made more so by Ickes's demeanor. Swanson and the rest of the cabinet found they had little in common with Woodin's replacement, Henry L. Morgenthau, Jr., The Virginian usually passed around cigars and circulated jokes at the beginning of cabinet meetings. He "would try to give him [Morgenthau] a cigar and he would look straight ahead and pay no attention to him." Swanson and Hull favored work relief quickly given, and, by accepting New Deal domestic legislation, they surprised some presumptive members. "Always very ceremonious of . . . appellations," Swanson and the other cabinet secretaries addressed on another as Mr. Secretary or Madam Secretary; only Roosevelt used first names in cabinet meetings. A generation later, Perkins recalled that Claude Swanson "had a great many things on the ball."[2]

For forty years, Swanson's department had been tugged between opponents and proponents of centralized decision-making. Except for brief periods before and during World War I, bureaus dominated the administrative system. Fresh to the navy, civilian secretaries frequently became "dependent upon them for information . . . to make . . . decisions." Appointed by the secretary since 1900, the General Board of the navy, composed of senior naval officers, advised on fleet plans, construction, and operations. In 1915, creation of the Office of Chief of Naval Operations had been a sop to consolidated authority advocates. Secretary Josephus Daniels, aided by Senators Benjamin Tillman and Swanson, had adroitly prevented the CNO from obtaining powers that might short-circuit the civilian secretary's political clout inside and outside the department. During the 1920s, tradition became a virtue. Admirals opposed unification and creation of a separate military air service, but squabbling over an air wing led to searing internal debates between air power and battleship supporters. Reorganization by Hoover, however, tended to strengthen the CNO at the expense of the General Board.[3]

Taken together, an opinionated, edgy, and suspicious crew made up the department in 1933. Although collectively a clannish group, each naval officer was accustomed, according to one authority, "to the idea that he was qualified to take the initiative and exert relatively unfettered authority over all activities within his charge." In diplomatic affairs, he habitually considered himself expert. Internal rivalry for preferment was intense, made more so by the "World War hump" of junior officers commissioned between 1918 and 1921 and a congressionally limited 100,000-man navy. Many faced early retirement or reserve status while a promotion freeze and a 15-percent salary reduction harmed the morale of the remainder. Represented by Harry E. Yarnell, Arthur J. Hepburn, Thomas C. Hart, and William D. Leahy, the 1897 Naval Academy class was emerging amid heavy competition to significant influence. Debates between "brown shoe" aviators versus "black shoe" surface officers continued. Reduction of civilian employees stirred political objections and labor complaints. The outgoing Hoover-appointed chief of Naval Operations, William V. Pratt, sniffed at Swanson's appointment as "a political choice [who was] . . . not much of an administrator." New chief of personnel Leahy discovered the navy in "a chaotic unsettled condition." Incoming budget officer James O. Richardson later praised Swanson for quickly creating "less friction in the Navy Department" than he had "ever known."[4]

Relieved at the exit of Hoover, Pratt, and Stimson, Leahy estimated Swanson to be "devoted to the Navy and a fully qualified expert in legislation." Within the department, young James Fife found Swanson "extremely well liked by everybody. . . . He let the Navy people run the Navy business" and used his political ability to resolve successfully "the problems of getting funds and the contacts with the Hill." Alert to morale-building details, Swanson knew many officers by name and permitted those under orders to carry alcoholic refreshments through dry states. After careful investigation of larger issues, he tended to select persons flexible in their thinking and to reinforce reformers in authority. As late as February 1939, he fought for advances in engineering opposed by "the conservative bloc in the navy." When governor of Virginia, he had preferred expert advisors. As secretary, he frequently agreed with technical chiefs and bureau heads at the expense of the General Board, investigative bodies, and the CNO.[5]

As a result, Swanson encountered a touchy chief William H. Standley, whose memoirs reflect a low opinion of the secretary. Although Swanson's physical resources diminished during his incumbency, Standley implied that the Virginian was severely enfeebled from its beginning. Early in his administration, Swanson favored Leahy as Standley's successor, leading the latter, in Leahy's opinion, "persistently and vigorously" to oppose his promotion. Because battleship service formed a requirement for line officers wishing to advance, Standley tried to block such an assignment for Leahy. He also fixed his wrath at strong-willed Ernest King when the Aeronautics bureau chief objected to poor staff work by Operations. King complained that Operations decided in contrary fashion upon discovery of Aeronautics' wishes. Standley "objected sharply" to Swanson's placing bureaus and offices "directly under and responsible to the Secretary of Navy." The secretary relied upon Leahy and King and kept them longer than normal at their bureau posts. As a result, budget officer Richardson noticed that Swanson built such an effective relationship with the navy's "higher echelon" that they frequently resolved controversies "rather than disturb the Secretary by referring disagreements to him."[6]

Swanson commanded an office staff with only two primary civilian aides. In addition, a former Marine Corps officer and distant relative of the President, Assistant Secretary of the Navy Henry Latrobe Roosevelt, and Swanson's reliable and effective former Senate secretary, Archibald Oden, contributed to Swanson's success in the early New Deal. Working with them, he avoided political traps. Richarson recalled Swanson reviewing a draft of a letter to Comptroller General John R. McCarl, composed by a naval officer and replete with intemperate phrases. Swanson asked, "You would like me to sign this letter?" Receiving an affirmative, the shrewd Virginian observed: "Long after I sign this letter, . . . [McCarl] will still have the power to make decisions adversely affecting the Navy, will he not? . . . Take this letter back and couch it in more temperate language." The secretary mused, "No sane man would slap a tiger in the face when his other hand is in the tiger's mouth." Richardson remembered also his "wisdom, kindness, sense of humor and of fair play, trust in and loyalty to his subordinates." Swanson later openly criticized McCarl for his refusal to grant travel funds to officers who had retired while on foreign assignment. Convincing the cabinet and Roosevelt, Swanson gave McCarl his first rebuff since appointment by Warren G. Harding in 1921; he also knew McCarl to be serving the final year of a fifteen-year term.[7]

Under the guise of economy, reorganization proposals reappeared. In 1933, Carl Vinson recommended greater centralization of authority under the Chief of Naval Operations. Both Swanson and the president recalled earlier bitter congressional debates during creation of the office. Preparing large appropriations requests, they preferred no additional congressional controversies over potential "militarism" residing in a navy "general staff" command concept. If given strengthened authority, professional officers might form political reefs for the White House and the secretary. Under the existing organization, Swanson could bridle such persons. Leaving Vinson's bill languishing in the House, he formed a smoke screen by appointing Assistant Secretary Roosevelt to chair an investigating board that included bureau chiefs Leahy and King. In January 1934, the Roosevelt board recommended few alterations. In reviewing them, Swanson objected even to an operations council that hinted at centralization. In the autumn of 1937, a general staff plan surfaced again and the president joked that word be passed "down the line through Operations and Navigation that anybody caught lobbying for a General Staff will be sent to Guam!" In March 1938 and in February 1939, Swanson helped negate similar Vinson reorganization plans as not "in the best interest of the Navy."[8]

Navy publicity concerned the secretary. He used press conferences and personal interviews while occasionally speaking on radio programs and at special events. But the old Virginian admitted that he "used to make a public speech on the slightest provocation—now never if [he could] avoid it." Swanson press conferences were noted for cordiality and mutual respect among the participants. Attended by Standley or Leahy, he held press conferences in his office in the war-built temporary navy buildings on Constitution Avenue. An admiral or captain dispensed cigarettes and press releases. The former would occupy the journalists, Swanson smiled, and then "they wouldn't ask so many questions;" the latter would ease their professional tasks. Believing that "a few fleas are good for the dog," he calmed subordinates indignant at disparaging remarks launched at the navy by a columnist or radio commentator. When a critic attacked and journalists demanded a response, Swanson refused to "use a sixteen-inch gun on a mosquito" or to "help . . . bring this man from the back page to the front page" of the newspaper. Swanson took special care with the foreign press and frequently granted personal interviews. In determining Swanson's success, his press aide emphasized his "kindly, tolerant and human" qualities that predominated.[9]

Roosevelt's fondness for the navy gave Secretary Swanson powerful political leverage but contributed also to his administrative chores. Lacking time to develop professional expertise, Roosevelt pursued his interest in the navy as an avocation. His experience as assistant secretary proved valuable but gave the president an overweening confidence in his naval opinions. He preferred to perform as his own navy secretary, and Swanson carefully adjusted to that inclination. Both men, however, were fast friends. The president insisted the secretary be "the direct agent and representative of the Commander-in-chief." Second, he expected Swanson to be the primary administrative officer enforcing the laws and expending naval appropriations. The New Yorker appreciated the Virginia's political sagacity, and Swanson freely discussed politics and other issues with the president more frequently than surviving manuscripts indicate. As important, Swanson could "pick up a telephone to get practically anything from his former associates in Congress." Within the riptide of depression-era politics, rebuilding the navy required carefully conceived moves based on painstaking assessments of congressional and public moods. Roosevelt and Swanson proved an effective combination.[10]

Swanson adapted easily to Roosevelt's political style. Presidential assistant and fellow Virginian Stephen Early cleared Swanson's speeches and those of other cabinet members early in the New Deal. On one occasion, Roosevelt suggested that a Swanson address "about the weakness of the Navy" should be "toned down." Also, when questioned by Japanese journalists in late 1933, Swanson checked with the White House before responding. In September 1933, before leaving for an inspection tour of the West Coast, Swanson took Standley and Henry Roosevelt with him to discuss with the president growing Cuban turmoil. Advised by Ambassador Sumner Welles, the president would avoid military intervention, but the White House conference decided upon a general naval alert. During a confidential press conference, Roosevelt gave details of Swanson's southern trip and ship movements in Cuban waters. The *Washington Evening Star* broke the story and other newspapers followed with headlines that Roosevelt had dispatched Swanson to Cuba. An angry Roosevelt summoned Early to issue a denial of intention to intervene and dictated a statement for Swanson to release from the *Indianapolis* departing Hampton Roads. Dutifully, the secretary complied. He refused to disembark from the cruiser during its two-hour stay in Havana harbor. The flag, however, had been shown to a Cuban junta, described by Welles as "radical" and "communistic."[11]

In the intensely nationalist New Deal, the president made the navy an extension of his political personality. When a majority of foreign news featured strutting dictators or bemedaled, grim-faced generals, the fleet furnished a handy, fresh symbol of American strength. Its photogenic quality, the dashing, glistening hulls, appealed to news editors. In May 1934, a great naval review in New York harbor not only stimulated business with a million-dollar payroll but furnished portraits of a windblown, square-jawed Roosevelt at the helm, surrounded by cabinet and naval officials. Using publicity techniques practiced during Daniels's term, Swanson's department sponsored Navy Day in October of each year, featuring speeches and "open ships" for civilian tourists. Some magazines, such as the *Scientific American,* unabashedly produced glossy treatments of the navy. Others, however, were more restrained.[12]

New York Times staffman and former naval officer Hanson W. Baldwin in 1935 complained that an inconsistent, ill-reasoned naval policy over the previous twenty years resulted from the navy's failure to educate the "public in the uses of a Navy or in the necessity" of defining such a policy. To Baldwin, the press had not been alert and the department had not provided "facilities for disseminating accurate information." More propaganda than education had resulted. The "open fleet" policy was labeled a "sideshow" simply to attract publicity. The *Nation, New Republic,* and *Christian Century* objected to naval expenditures and building programs. Critical congressional investigations such as those conducted by Gerald P. Nye and his committee tarred Roosevelt,

Swanson, and such varied groups as the American Legion, American Federation of Labor, Navy League, National Civic Federation, and Reserve Officers' Association with the same brush that darkened munition manufacturers and steel company executives. Even more widespread, budget cutters opposed to American involvement overseas frequently selected the navy as a target.[13]

The New Deal naval renaissance provoked great resentment from pacifists. In 1934, they focused upon the Vinson-Trammell legislation. The Mothers' Club of Bridgewater, Virginia, questioned Swanson: "Who is to fight the war the Vinson bill presupposes?" Women were not "raising our sons for any such purpose." National organizations—The Federal Council of Churches of Christ in America and the Women's League for Peace and Freedom—complained in similar tones. Naval Intelligence evaluated these groups and their statements. For example, Swanson forwarded to the president a report composed by Intelligence on the Midwest Institute of International Relations which drew upon files initiated during the Hoover administration. Revealing as much about the authors as their subjects, the resumé identified the institute as a continuing program of Northwestern University, sponsored by the American Friends Service Committee. Lecturers were identified as running "the gamut from extremely radical to mild 'Pink,' all of whom ably preached the doctrine of total disarmament." The officers calculated the institute to be "highly socialistic and at times communistic," bent upon undermining "National spirit by spreading communistic propaganda through school teachers, ministers, peace workers, and college students." They estimated the institute's resolution of protest to be "a clever and deliberate attempt to misunderstand [Roosevelt's] views."[14]

Roosevelt and Swanson followed a policy that the president labeled as "soft speaking." While regretting "to put censorship on Admirals," Roosevelt requested that no answer be given "professional pacifists" or "to 'hit' and assail them." Similar to Swanson's own approach, Roosevelt reminded Assistant Secretary Roosevelt to "spread the word about" in February 1934 to avoid such confrontations. He also cautioned the press to avoid speculation over naval developments because it "merely caused international reprisal statements." He asked Swanson in 1935 to instruct naval officers or government officials testifying before congressional committees to avoid answering questions that were "hypothetical." They should confine themselves to "discussion of the budget." In rebuilding the fleet, Roosevelt and Swanson incorporated confidentiality to defend national security, but they also used it to avoid domestic political ramifications.[15]

The Navy Department under Swanson excelled in transforming blueprints into gray-hulled reality. Although Hoover and the General Board had favored a long-range program to reach treaty strength, depression priorities disrupted these construction schedules. In the New Deal, Standley continued to argue for an orderly, gradual building program, but Swanson knew that long-term plans frequently found funds hard to come by. The secretary, in one of his initial pronouncements, recommended construction equal to the 1930 London Treaty agreements as "quickly as possible." He depended upon the naval committees for sustenance because their members represented the states of the yards and bases—the established interests. Other congressmen could be attracted by offers to develop their constituencies' resources through federal expenditures. House naval chairman Vinson of Georgia endorsed Swanson's call, and Florida senator Park Trammell of Naval Affairs joined the two southerners to resume an easy comradeship from previous years. After Trammell's death in 1936, David Walsh of Massachusetts replaced him, but similar sentiments continued. Gaining funding, Swanson practiced a political art that left nothing to chance and that emphasized an appropriation in hand ranked much higher than vague promises in the congressional bush.[16]

Navy budget requests normally were shaped two years before expenditure. The 1933 and 1934 budgets had evolved from the Hoover administration. The House Appropriation Committee formed a subcommittee that inspected every corner of the navy's proposals. An old acquaintance of Swanson's, Kansan William A. Ayres, chaired the subcommittee during Roosevelt's first administration to be succeeded by Kentuckian Glover H. Cary, then by North Carolinian William B. Umstead. The Senate subcommittee chairman, James F. Byrnes of South Carolina, and his colleagues, including three Naval Affairs members, reviewed the House-approved items, reintroduced some House-deferred projects, and responded to individual senators' concerns over naval base reductions. Effective working relationships with the Senate and House staffs were established. The secretary knew more than one bill had been influenced by chief clerks of these subcommittees. General navy legislation was centralized by Swanson in 1934 through the office of the Judge Advocate General, Admiral Claude C. Bloch, to avoid political difficulties with Congress, and a "legislative counsel" evolved. By 1939, under Swanson tutelage, the department became so adept at appropriation hearings that "suggested legislative procedures" formed an internal document for each request. These steps included the president expressing "his approval to Congress" and Swanson or the assistant secretary making "the first statement before the Committee with great earnestness." Each concerned bureau chief and appropriate staff person received memoranda on the legislation's progress. Included were fallback positions should considerable congressional opposition to a request develop. In 1933, however, the fleet could count afloat only 65 percent of treaty allotments. Unorthodox appropriation procedures were needed.[17]

During 1932, the Democratic House following Vinson's leadership had passed an authorization of $616 million for 120 ships to assure treaty strength during the next ten years. The Senate then refused to follow, and, in the autumn presidential campaign, naval strength became a minor issue, agitated principally by navy leadership. Hoover agreed that ship construction would be needed, especially if the Geneva Disarmament Conference failed, and released some relief funds for shipbuilding. Swanson undoubtedly discussed these issues in a meeting with President-elect Roosevelt in mid-November. A few days later, as reported by the *New York Times*, Roosevelt and Vinson agreed upon an efficient rather than a large navy. Vinson accepted a figure of $30 million per year for new ships, half of the 1932 House request. But Roosevelt was sensitive also to the Geneva conference's failing deliberations. Earlier, Swanson contended that the larger Vinson bill of 1932 could force agreement on arms limitation by Europeans when faced with an American fleet buildup, and probably so informed

Roosevelt. Thus, with the president's approval, he searched for other sources of naval funds, aided by Roosevelt's general memorandum to agencies to cease public work encumbrances until "a complete program for the construction of useful public works and unemployment relief" could be formulated.[18]

Swanson revived yard senator arguments but incorporated a new twist: naval appropriations meant domestic national employment. Vinson agreed. Economic theories floating into Washington concerning the salutary effects of work relief projects boosted Swanson's position. On March 20, 1933, less than two weeks in office, Swanson reminded the press that "naval construction should be considered with other public works included in any employment relief program Congress may vote." Presenting figures that for every $1,000 expended in ship construction, $850 went to labor, he postulated that, should Congress build the fleet to treaty strength by 1936, of the $1 billion needed, $850 million would be used for wages. Swanson relied upon Congress for relief appropriations to harvest immediately millions of dollars that the slower fleet rebuilding plans of Pratt and Standley would not have produced. By May 9, he encouraged the president that he could expect no congressional difficulty "with appropriating $46,000,000 for naval construction this year." On June 11, Swanson welcomed legislative agreement to appropriate an eventual $283 million in work relief funds for ships. Significantly, the navy had plans prepared, and, by December, 1933 vessels were on the ways in various stages of construction. Few New Deal relief projects were as quickly and competently begun. Roosevelt revealed Swanson's significant role in the affair by commenting, "Claude, we got away with murder that time."[19]

Seeking advantages for the navy, Swanson gave lip service to early budget cutting. He agreed with an unsuccessful Vinson suggestion to combine the Coast Guard and Naval academies. He flattered determined Bureau of the Budget officials and suggested coyly that the navy be awarded lump sum appropriations that would, in reality, give it greater and more flexible fiscal control. Rather than suffer a pay cut, civilian workers at Swanson's request accepted an additional half-day without pay. He reduced by one-sixth the time requirements of naval aviators to earn flight pay and abandoned Pratt's previous plans to lay up one-third of the fleet at a time. He cited that only $5 million could be saved by rotating battleships. Roosevelt assigned him 1,300 positions in reforestation and Muscle Shoals projects for naval officers removed from active service owing to budget reductions. In the summer of 1933, however, Swanson warned Roosevelt that the navy could not operate on proposed appropriations of $270 million for 1934. He requested more public works funds to purchase aircraft to equip new cruisers and carriers. In October, on a western inspection tour, he learned that the president had conceded his point and had instructed Assistant Secretary Roosevelt and Secretary Dern "to go together to Secretary Ickes with aviation requests" to obtain relief monies. The navy concluded 1933 with appropriations of $349 million.[20]

In his first annual report, Swanson affirmed that haphazard naval construction made drafting replacement schedules difficult. Regular and exceptional appropriations, including those of unbuilt ships from the Hoover years, were intended to answer the navy's most urgent needs: twenty destroyers, including four "heavy" 1,850 ton vessels, four light cruisers, four submarines, two aircraft carriers, and two gunboats. Battleship modernization also resumed. He admitted that two methods could achieve naval disarmament. The first, to decrease the fleet unilaterally, had already been tried without success. Other nations had refused to reduce their navies to the level of the United States. The other alternative, to construct a treaty fleet, would now be attempted. The awarding of contracts received careful attention. In July 1933, private ship-builders had been "practically without work." Congress had mandated equal treatment of public and private yards. Swanson coordinated complicated prob-lems of equitable distribution and had private bids scanned to avoid excess charges. Beneath the entire superstructure of naval rebuilding resided the political implications of construction assignments. Thus, Roosevelt approved each. Funds also were awarded to yards and bases for renovation and expansion. Pearl Harbor, Puget Sound, and Pensacola Air Station received the largest amounts. [21]

Scarcely had 1933 been toasted a success than Swanson and the department staff rushed to fashion legislative support for more appropriations. Taking a page from treaty tonnage limits, Swanson requested that, instead of authorizing an individual ship of so many tons, Congress approve aggregate tons in each class. A reworking of the 1932 Vinson House bill proposed to expand the fleet to treaty strength by 1939. Growing more dependent upon the department for leadership, Vinson and Trammell accepted it. Swanson and his aides advised congressmen by letter, by interview, and by telephone. During Senate hearings, he warned Trammell that a proposed amendment requiring half of an estimated one thousand planes should have their motors built in navy yards would result in delays from "three to four years" in the aircraft building program. The yards needed tools—they had "never manufactured aircraft engines." After extended discussions featuring Leahy, the navy share was reduced to at least 10 percent. Congress approved on March 27, 1934, the Vinson-Trammell Act that autho-rized 1,529,484 tons of ships. Swanson had achieved a primary goal of his secretaryship in fourteen months. Although appropriations came more slowly and emphasis upon replacements predominated, the navy had secured approval for a treaty fleet second to none. [22]

During debate on the bill, Swanson suffered his first serious illness as secretary. On December 14, 1933, he visited hospitalized colleagues Ickes and Dern only to return that evening as a patient, suffering from a respiratory infection with accompanying high blood pressure. He remained in the Naval Hospital as an ambulatory patient until the end of February 1934. Journalists reported he suffered from a "cold"; rumors of his early resignation circulated. Progress of the new naval legislation suffered. Yet, Swanson kept informed by telephone and through the assistance of naval aides. He undoubtedly signed letters composed by subordinates, but that was typical of him and other New Deal administrators. Trammell continued in contact, and Swanson responded in writing in January 1934 to House Appropriation Subcommittee inquiries. In mid-month, Roosevelt visited Swanson to assess the effects of his illness. He returned to cabinet meetings in March and was observed by Ickes as "looking very badly" and as having "difficulty in managing his cigarette." Swanson remained mentally alert. Physically, he had encountered a setback from which he would not recover.[23]

Criticism erupted over the navy's building program. Ickes, director of the Public Works Administration that furnished funds for many navy projects, had been "tremendously annoyed" in 1933 at the exceptional authorizations. Upon Roosevelt's instructions to release additional work relief funds for navy projects, Ickes became "even more disturbed . . . and again stormed the White House." Although overruled and ill-disposed to censure Roosevelt publicly, he made fund transfer difficult and detailed. Director of the National Recovery Administration Hugh Johnson's insistence that NRA codes governing work and manufacture be enforced led Roosevelt to request Swanson to certify that navy contractors and suppliers complied. Three days later, Swanson informed Roosevelt of the instant displeasure of Newport News Shipbuilding and Drydock Company. Hugh Johnson threatened to place the "whole naval construction program into the Navy Yards." Laughing, Roosevelt backed Johnson, and the private yards quickly capitulated. Swanson insisted that economy and expedition demanded forty hours as normal navy yard work week. This rankled John P. Frey of the American Federation of Labor's metal trades who reflected organized labor's desire for a thirty-hour week. In May 1934, Swanson irritated both capital and labor by warning that, if they could not settle a debilitating strike, he would transfer a nearly completed cruiser from New York Shipbuilding Corporation to a navy yard. The strike ended but grievances smouldered.[24]

After judicial destruction of the National Recovery Administration in 1935, the new National Labor Relations Board underwrote collective bargaining procedures for American labor. Struggling to build ships, the navy caught cross currents in contests between labor and private yard management. Some corporations, Newport News Shipbuilding for one, would avoid confrontation by continuing ill-concealed company unions. Others refused outright to bargain. In May 1935, a failure to arbitrate at Camden by officials of New York Shipbuilding launched a three-month strike; one owner, E.L. Cord, pledged to "close down the shipyard rather than do business with union labor." As press interest mounted, Roosevelt dumped the matter upon the department. Following confidential discussions with the White House, the department again issued an ultimatum to New York Shipbuilding to arbitrate or to "have contracts assumed by the government." A conference with Frances Perkins, labor and managment representatives, and Henry Roosevelt settled the strike. To complete on schedule seven delayed vessels, extra shifts were put to work. Perkins recalled a "very solemn" Swanson reporting these affairs to the cabinet. Committed to building long-postponed ships, the navy "always made a great stir. . . . In those days certain Navy people were likely to think any strike as comparable to treason."[25]

Naval priorities collided with other labor legislation. David Walsh and other congressmen sponsored a "little NRA" that would force holders of government contracts to employ persons at least at prevailing area minimum wages determined by Secretary Perkins, who held exemption authority. The department complained more about potential construction slowdowns than about having to enforce federal wage standards. Roosevelt initially dismissed such objections. He confided to his journalistic entourage that, as assistant secretary, he had learned "of the historic attitude of the Navy . . . toward that type of legislation." By the end of the decade, however, he also became more concerned over rapid construction. Upon passage of the Walsh bill, Swanson prepared to implement its provisions. In 1937, when steel corporations objected to a mandated forty-hour work week, he responded by suggesting that the government armor plate factory at Charleston, West Virginia, be reopened. Secretary of War Dern agreed. In 1938, the department, fearing "irrecoverable delays" in construction, opposed legislation to deny contracts to those firms refusing to follow edicts from the National Labor Board. Labor strife continued. In San Francisco, the navy depended upon civilian longshoremen to load its ships. Even after collective bargaining was forced upon the "Front," Swanson complained to the cabinet: "There's trouble on the West Coast. . . . We pay the going wage in the Port. We don't cheat them, but they won't work. . . . They're making demands we can't fulfill." Despite his earlier experience with yard labor, Swanson found the navy's primary charge of national defense ill-designed to adjust to the growing power of union labor.[26]

Private contractors by mid-1935 provided another reef to circumvent. Earlier in the year, the Nye Committee investigated the "Unholy Three," New York, Newport News, and Bethlehem shipbuilding corporations. They were accused of excess profits, intervention in foreign affairs, sponsorship of heavy armaments, and collusion among themselves and the Navy Department. Assistant Secretary Roosevelt and Admirals Samuel Robinson and Emory Land defended the navy before the committee. Land offered the shipbuilders small consolation: "They are my arch enemy, so far as doing business is concerned." Aeronautics head King disclosed that between 1927 and 1933 Pratt and Whitney had made a profit of 36 percent on engines while Wright Aeronautics had earned only 5 percent. Publicly, Swanson quickly denied department collusion. In 1933 and in 1934, internal investigations had produced only one accuser who furnished no convincing evidence. Swanson invited the press to help: "The Navy Department knows of no such individual, but should he exist I would like to have his name." Such accusations of excess profits aided the department in obtaining lower bids.[27]

Other corporate interests schemed to foster commitments for certain naval armaments. For instance, Swanson resisted blandishments of Ohio and California companies, their congressmen, and certain naval officers to continue to develop fragile, rigid airships. After crashes in 1933 of the *Akron* and two years later of the *Macon*, while admitting Congress could require it, he opposed replacements. On this occasion, both Standley and King agreed. The latter objected to the navy's being forced to develop dirigibles for eventual benefit of commercial projects. Germany's apparent success with the machines whetted arguments for American boosters. In March 1937, Swanson warned Vinson that hatching appropriation schemes for building more massive airships ran contrary to the president's plans. The spectacular conflagration of the *Hindenburg* reduced lobbying activities, but Roosevelt believed that Goodyear Rubber Company continued to press for federal funds "to salvage a fairly heavy speculative investment." Swanson refused a General Board favorable recommendation in 1937, preferring that "such development as is desirable be

undertaken by commercial industry or by the maritime commission."
Eventually, avoiding direct political confrontation, the president so altered
specifications of any proposed dirigible for navy use that no viable plans could
be realized; the navy shifted to blimps.[28]

Swanson and the department evaluated and amended various planning
documents. The secretary had a fix upon naval mobilization problems drawn
from his memory of wartime Washington. In 1930, appointed to the congressionally created War Policies Commission designed to "promote peace and to
equalize the burden and to minimize the profits of wars," Swanson, beginning in
March 1931, participated in discussions of mobilization plans. He recalled that
the navy "bought far beyond their need for consumption," but observed that
high, excess war profits taxes harmed productivity. Although he did not consider
price ceilings necessary in "every little hamlet in the United States," steel
pricing was another matter. Swanson questioned the efficacy of the navy
consulting board on weapon development and urged it to be reconstituted with
"leading technical men" in close cooperation with naval officials. He also
agreed with Homer Ferguson that the navy draft ship blueprints to anticipate
wartime construction, as plan composition frequently required half of the
completion time for a vessel.[29]

In reviewing a comprehensive army planning document prepared by Chief
of Staff Douglas MacArthur, the Virginian discovered that the General Board
had neither evaluated it nor moved toward "fixing up a plan of its own." Closer
cooperation followed during his secretaryship, especially in matters relating to
munitions. Bernard Baruch and others proposed additional plans to expunge
excess war profits, and the former War Industries Board director discussed his
proposals with Swanson and Roosevelt. Congressional movement toward neutrality legislation spurred Swanson's interest. In December 1934, to benefit
from the War Policies Commission reports and to reduce publicity given the Nye
Committee, Roosevelt convened a committee chaired by Baruch with cabinet
members Swanson, Hull, Morgenthau, Perkins, Wallace, and Dern. Included
were Johnson, transportation coordinator Joseph B. Eastman, Henry Roosevelt,
foreign trade advisor George Peele, and MacArthur. Roosevelt desired legislation "to take the profit out of war" as well as to order "things by law." The
Roosevelt's committee subordinated Baruch's goal to reduce profits and emphasized mobilization planning. The Nye Committee, however, attacked Baruch as
a wartime profiteer, and proposed administration legislation collapsed. House
Military Affairs chairman and former War Policies Commission member John J.
McSwain of South Carolina secured passage in the House of a bill to freeze
prices and wages in wartime, but it died in the Senate. The Navy Department
restructured its mobilization plans in 1936 and 1939. Swanson tightened
relations with research scientists, heretofore a moribund effort, to furnish
scientific advice. Authority disputes between bureaus and Operations officers
continued, however, and failure to tie planning closely to Swanson's office
occurred.[30]

Japan was the primary concern for Swanson and the navy in shipbuilding
and strategic planning. Caught in War Plan Orange and facing possible Philippine independence, the department had since 1922 shifted the fleet's main force

into the Pacific. By 1933, the Japanese navy, still within treaty limits, presented an order of battle larger and more modern than the American Pacific contingent. When questioned during his 1933 inspection of Pearl Harbor, Swanson emphasized an intention to build to treaty strength but dismissed the fleet's Pacific assignment as "merely an economy measure" because it was "cheaper to keep the vessels concentrated." He mentioned also that Pearl would become the most important American naval base. In the summer during the 1930s, fleet maneuvers continued generally north and west of the Hawaiian Islands. The Japanese protested, but Swanson condoned this fleet preparedness activity. Roosevelt certainly favored it, writing fleet commander James M. Reeves not to "forget that in planning for next summer [1935]," he should "train as many officers in Alaskan navigation as possible." By 1939, the war plan had been reworked, featuring a mid-Pacific defense line.[31]

Naval rebuilding programs also strengthened the position of the United States in arms limitation discussions. Swanson and Roosevelt continued in 1934 and 1935 a commitment to naval arms limitation through international agreement. Prompted by an approaching London conference scheduled at the conclusion of 1935, they suggested a tonnage reduction of 20 percent, thereby avoiding domestic accusations that they were abandoning existing treaties. Great Britain desired more favorable adjustments of existing treaties, while Japan spoke for naval equality with both countries. The department opposed any pro forma agreements, contending instead for a serious commitment to continue agreement of arms limitations. Swanson also disliked neutrality legislation by Congress. He mentioned the probable extension of American bases in the Pacific should Japan build beyond existing ratios. He also warned, should limitations be abandoned, "There is no telling where we would go in this [coming] conference." Earlier, in September 1934, Hull had informed him that Japan had secretly decided to terminate its Washington naval treaty agreements. Thus, comments by Swanson and Roosevelt toward continuing treaty commitments could be viewed only as suave political maneuvering. Swanson, however, convinced his cabinet colleague Perkins of his sincerity: "He was a great Pacifist, in the sense that he believed war could be prevented by the conscious action of intelligent men and nations."[32]

Following conversations with Swanson and department members, Roosevelt requested review of American Pacific bases and possible new categories of ships in December 1934. Five months later, Swanson recommended that plans be developed for a major outlying fleet base in the Philippines with subsidiary bases at Kiska, Samoa, and Guam. Certain mid-Pacific Islands—Wake, for instance—should be placed under naval authority. Pacific Coast and Pearl Harbor installations should receive major consideration. Implementation was tied to "requirements . . . which [would] develop out of the post [London] treaty situation." Roosevelt vetoed a Philippine base. Should the islands become independent, an American base would be "a military liability instead of an asset." In late July, Swanson and Roosevelt convened a joint press conference to discuss the Pacific situation. The secretary predicted that establishment of Pacific bases must be "inevitably considered" should the naval treaties expire: "If we lose the Philippines, the Navy might wish to go elsewhere in the Pacific."

Soon Swanson forwarded to the president photographs of Americans occupying the mid-Pacific islands. "Knowing of your interest in the Pacific Islands," Swanson observed, the men appeared "all healthy and . . . [were] able to catch some very fine fish." Swanson granted Pan American Airways permission to erect hangers and bases on Guam, Midway, and the Wake group. The department further sharpened its intelligence monitoring of Japan. Information from Ambassador Joseph C. Grew, sly interviews with Japanese officers, confidential Treasury reports, Asiatic squadron commanders' evaluations, and even cooperation with *New York Times* far eastern correspondent Hallett E. Abend provided Swanson and the department valuable intelligence estimates.[33]

In March 1935, Swanson saw "few prospects for future extension of naval armaments limitation." He listed new construction of capital ships by France, Germany, and Great Britain. Roosevelt responded by approving in July a project to replace the overage battleship *Arkansas* as well as by building twelve destroyers and six submarines in 1937. For the first time in thirteen years, the admirals could expect a new dreadnought. Ever cautious publicly, Roosevelt hinged the new ship upon expiration of existing treaties, all of which would cease December 31, 1936. He wanted nothing said of battleship planning "for a few months to come," but Swanson changed his mind. The following week, the secretary hinted to the press: "A battleship is under consideration but no decision has been reached whether we will ask for one or not." He also noted that no request for new cruisers or carriers had been submitted; all allowable by treaty had been authorized. In September 1935, preliminary battleship plans unrolled before Roosevelt's eager eyes. In March 1936, Japan withdrew from the second London conference, refusing any new agreements. As planned, Swanson and Roosevelt placed successfully the onus of withdrawal upon Japan, and Congress authorized two battleships in June. In the three years following 1933, despite Nye Committee activities, a general isolationist impulse, organized pacifist opposition, war scares in Europe, and deep depression, the Navy Department had obtained over $1.5 billion in ship authorizations. Swanson had eased many of these requests through dangerous congressional waters, and the lead time gained would be dramatically revealed in the naval battles of the early 1940s.[34]

To man these ships, Swanson petitioned for increased personnel allocations. Between 1933 and 1939, Congress and Roosevelt grudgingly increased authorized naval and Marine Corps personnel to 144,000. Actual numbers on duty usually fell five thousand below the maximum, forcing the navy in the early New Deal years to operate at 75 percent of normal ship complements. Swanson, however, observed that "the large number of applicants for enlistment . . . made it possible to select men of the highest type." Ship performances increased in efficiency as a result. Attempts to structure an equally efficient naval and marine reserve met delay owing to prickly problems between reservists and active regular officers. Retirement benefits and salary figured in the equation. The former assistant secretary of the navy pledged in December 1935 that "after twenty-two years of effort," he intended to "get results!" He requested Swanson and personnel officers to review unsatisfactory reserve proposals—sounding "as if they had been written in 1912"—in the White House for "a full hour."

Swanson took five admirals to convince Roosevelt of the cost of his proposals and to demonstrate the president's determination to the admirals. For the next two and one-half years, struggling through department politics, congressional hearings, and budget obstructions, a short, preliminary bill passed Congress in June 1938. Reserve categories were liberalized but Swanson never obtained a resolution to nagging manpower problems.[35]

In early February 1936, Swanson suffered a serious, life-threatening accident. Ill with a cold, he slipped in his bathroom, hit a chair, and fractured several ribs. Hospitalized, a week later he developed pleurisy in his left lung. Given his age, frail physique, and rising temperature, family members assembled, including his brother Henry C. Swanson, now Danville postmaster. But Swanson survived. Stepson Douglas Deane Hall reported him serene, relying upon his "sturdiness and strong constitution to pull him through." Obtaining daily reports, Roosevelt visited him and discovered that, although Swanson was "very weak, he had all the old light of battle in his eyes"; the president thought he would "get well by sheer will power." Although he suffered a relapse in late March which required Roosevelt to postpone a vacation trip, by April 10 doctors diagnosed the secretary as recovered sufficiently to enjoy a cruise on the *Sequoia*. On May 21, improved but requiring aid in walking and rising, he attended unexpectedly a cabinet meeting. To compound navy leadership problems, Assistant Secretary Henry Roosevelt died unexpectedly of a heart attack on February 22. Through the spring and summer, Admiral Adolphus Andrews and then William H. Standley, after the London Naval Conference, acted as secretary. As was his habit, Swanson vacationed at the Hoover fishing camp on the Rapidan in Virginia. In August, he called upon the president and in September officially resumed his duties. From this point, he was a semi-invalid.[36]

Roosevelt and Swanson over a period of months considered various persons to fill the assistant secretaryship. In August, rumors circulated that Charles Edison of New Jersey would be appointed. Swanson raised the issue again, in early September, as if to verify conjectures, and Roosevelt admitted he favored Edison. Although saddled with a hearing impairment, the businessman, reported Roosevelt, had "a sense of humor and, best of all, is wholeheartedly devoted to our cause." His father, inventor Thomas A. Edison, had chaired the navy's consulting board "through the war," and Edison himself had served in "the original NRA set up." This gave him experience that would benefit the navy, caught in difficulties over the new labor legislation. Roosevelt asked Swanson to interview him; the secretary "made inquiries" and gave his full endorsement. Not until the conclusion of Roosevelt's resounding 1936 reelection campaign did Edison receive his assignment. In January 1937, returning from the battleship division, Leahy assumed the Chief of Naval Operations billet. These two men carried much of the detailed administrative burden for Swanson for the remainder of his career.[37]

The secretary monitored, as did several other persons, Byrd's political movements and continuing flirtation with Wall Street. In August 1934, the president was notified through an informant at the Morgan Bank that Byrd had "organized a block of Democrats in the Senate" and "had already obtained 14 signatures and expected at least 22." Byrd intended to lead this faction, the report suggested, and "work with Republican members of the Senate" to oppose administration-sponsored measures. Roosevelt's overpowering congressional victory in November 1934 postponed that development and Swanson wrote, "I am overjoyed." In the spring and summer of 1935, Early and Oden observed carefully Byrd's activities as the press pictured him a vice-presidential possibility on an Al Smith presidential ticket. At the same time, with Swanson's encouragement, Roosevelt clubs were organized in many parts of the state, and to R. Walton Moore, despite Byrd's and Glass's anti-New Deal stance, "the sentiment in Virginia seems quite otherwise." Scanning photostats from Byrd's *Winchester Star,* Roosevelt tried unsuccessfully to interview the junior senator, who remained in Winchester to nurse his ill wife. Former Swanson associates Lieutenant Governor James H. Price and Norman Hamilton fashioned flank movements in Virginia. In 1936, the former announced his candidacy for governor in 1937, and Hamilton challenged anti-New Deal Representative Colgate Darden. Thereafter, Byrd denied any interest in the vice-presidency and Swanson considered the situation "very much clarified." He forwarded to Roosevelt addresses of six thousand Virginians who were "leading, active, and influential citizens." Hamilton won the Democratic primary in August 1936 on a Roosevelt platform that featured censure of Byrd and of Glass and endorsement of Price. One Virginia Roosevelt organizer bragged that the "contest put to the utmost the strength of the Byrd Organization," and it had failed. Despite Byrd's attempts to sponsor Thomas Burch for governor, Hamilton's victory contributed to Price's election the following year. [38]

The rebuilding program, however, occupied Swanson's attention. Admiral Land observed that national defense construction placed the navy between the "upper and nether mill stones." In World War I, one hundred companies sought naval contracts, but in 1935 only six, at most, could or would bid for the larger ships. Favoring repair work over new construction, government yards were at capacity. Homer Ferguson admitted that private yards submitted protective bids, gauging them to fit their available resources. Certain yards now emphasized specialized construction; Newport News won aircraft carriers over less technically proficient competitors. Private yard upkeep was included in their bids. Navy yard maintenance derived from normal naval operating expenses. Departmental dependence upon private designers resulted from government wage ceilings that prevented employment of superior craftsmen. In 1937, Roosevelt, probably at Swanson's request, ordered two new battleship contracts shifted to navy yards following high private bids. [39]

Throughout his secretaryship, Swanson encountered war scares. By telephone and by dispatch, he and his aides maintained a close and effective communication with Hull and Roosevelt on these occasions. In addition to Japanese restlessness, in 1934 the department leadership identified the European situation as a tinderbox. Leahy, for one, believed that war loomed more likely than in 1914, as only opponents' economic debilities prevented more active opposition to Adolf Hitler. Making a European war probable and frightening Congress into isolationist reaction, Hitler's co-fascist Benito Mussolini invaded Ethiopia in October 1935. Roosevelt labeled the event "alarming," and desired greater communication in the area. Hull and Swanson agreed. An American ship received orders to stand off French Somaliland "to maintain radio connection" with the American legation in Addis Ababa. The following year the Spanish Civil War featured German and Italian intervention. Roosevelt gave Swanson control of U.S. Coast Guard vessels operating in European waters and approved dispatch of ships to evacuate Americans. Both men viewed films of the bombing of the U.S.S. *Kane* by an "unidentified" airplane as the ship sailed thirty-eight miles from the Iberian peninsula. Immediately thereafter, press conjecture centered upon revival of the United States European Squadron, a possibility Roosevelt softpedaled. In December 1936, Japan and Germany signed the Anti-Comintern Pact, making them public allies, a suspicion that had been held by the Navy and State departments since 1934.[40]

The Sino-Japanese war expanded in the summer of 1937. The navy performed its traditional obligation of evacuating nationals, but Swanson kept purposely slim the Asiatic squadrons to avoid any serious losses from sudden attack. He directed that intelligence assessments be sent directly to the president. Despite agreement that China was "not a republic except in name and [was] not a democracy in any commonly accepted sense of the term," the navy leadership endorsed Chinese resistance. As Japan assaulted Shanghai, Roosevelt refused to invoke the Neutrality Act in the undeclared war, allowing China to purchase munitions and other war materials. In September, Swanson told the cabinet that the navy staff agreed that "if it was considered necessary to put Japan in its place, this was the right time to do it, with Japan so fully occupied in China." On October 5, Roosevelt called for a "quarantine" against international anarchy. In China waters, Admiral Yarnell reported from the *Augusta* on Japanese personnel, gunnery, ships, and planes. The first three impressed him; the last, he believed, were inferior. Should hostilities develop, he argued like Swanson for a war of "strangulation." The United States should pursue "an almost purely naval war," avoiding thereby a major land commitment. China should supply the manpower equipped by American material and led by American officers. Roosevelt found favor with "strangulation" as "it goes along with that word 'quarantine' " that he had "used in the Chicago speech last month." Despite an isolationist uproar, Roosevelt followed the navy's view. Then, the *Panay* incident occurred on the Yangtze.[41]

On Sunday, December 12, Japanese planes bombed, machine gunned, and sank the navy vessel carrying American embassy personnel and convoying three oil barges. Two sailors and a civilian were killed, eleven persons were wounded. Obviously a premeditated act, the attack caused the department to push for armed intervention with appropriate fallback positions. In the next four days, before the regular Friday cabinet meeting, the White House, army officials, and the department discussed various alternatives. As if the scene had been rehearsed, Swanson on cabinet day, "in his old feeble voice" called for war. Japan's present vulnerability—lengthened communication lines, dependence upon imports, and tangled commitments in the China war—would allow the United States to "lick Japan right now." Paralleling this hardline by the secretary, Leahy had forwarded to Roosevelt on the previous Wednesday a proposal for four battleships and four cruisers for fiscal 1939, an addition beyond the two battleships requested for 1938. Roosevelt also seriously considered a blockade with Great Britain of the Japanese home islands and thought of an embargo as well. He reminded Swanson before the cabinet, that he favored harnessing Japan, but "he didn't want to have to go to war to get it." But, by January 1938, Swanson and Roosevelt had unified the cabinet. Even pacifist Ickes, convinced that an inevitable war between fascist totalitarians and democrats loomed, agreed to a large navy bill for the spring of 1938. Supported by Swanson, naval officers, and the cabinet, Roosevelt began lobbying congress for naval increases.[42]

Careful administrative orchestration secured the largest peacetime navy supply bill to that date and the second Vinson bill. The first appropriated $500 million; the second authorized an addition of $1.5 billion in construction. Accomplished in the teeth of a rising war fright generated by pacifists, isolationists, and partisan Republicans, the legislation marked the second major phase of New Deal naval renaissance initiated by the appropriations of 1933 and 1934. It also produced the first full-dress congressional debate on foreign affairs during the New Deal era. Roosevelt warned in the first paragraphs of his state-of-the-nation address in early January 1938 of a "world of high tension and disorder." At the conclusion of the month, backed by his cabinet and encouraged by Swanson, he forwarded specific recommendations that would augment the army, increase by 20 percent the naval construction program, add two more battleships and cruisers to the 1938 schedule, and provide funds for experimental craft. Swanson concurrently launched a publicity campaign. He praised a long-range navy bomber flight to Hawaii which reflected the "soundness of the training methods and reliability of the materials employed by the Navy." The strengthened naval aviation cadet program had begun to bear fruit. He announced additions to the defense of Hawaii and Guam. Fleet maneuvers began, defending the West Coast against attack. Testifying before the House Naval Affairs Committee, Leahy warned of German, Japanese, and Italian coalignment following their recent anti-Communist pact. Hull also moved into the debate. Sponsored by the Departments of the Navy and War, special screenings of newsfilm of the recent *Panay* sinking flashed before the eyes of selected congressmen. Swanson furnished arguments for David Walsh to use in Senate Naval Affairs Committee hearings. He also opposed attempts to define a limited "American naval frontier" by isolationists.[43]

In August 1938, Swanson analyzed ship construction. The fleet's numbers had increased significantly from the 155 vessels he had counted in March 1933. With the presently authorized program, when complete, the navy would comprise 272 vessels, an aggregate of 1,517,480 tons. These engines of war would be led by eighteen new or refurbished battleships. Eight aircraft carriers, 18 heavy and 28 light cruisers would be flanked by 144 destroyers, 56 submarines, and auxiliaries. The last contained three highspeed tankers, prototypes of those that would supply the fleet around the world within a few years. Aircraft carrier and battleship designs led the world, and experimental landing craft and fast motor patrol vessels were under development. Improved aircraft prototypes were emerging and depression-inspired paycuts for the 116,000 officers and enlisted men were abandoned. In response to worsening European conditions, a "two ocean Navy" became a fact in September; the Atlantic squadron "temporarily" was reactivated, having been dormant since 1932, and in November received fleet status, led by four new battleships. In February 1939, Swanson boarded the *Houston* to review with Roosevelt the United States fleet's maneuvers in the Caribbean. There, both men decided upon the secretary's former naval aide, Harold C. Stark, as Leahy's successor in Naval Operations.[44]

These marked the last public activites in which Swanson participated. Fragile since 1936, his health became increasingly precarious. In January 1937, after standing for some time during a White House dinner, his legs weakened, his cane slipped, and he fainted. At the second Roosevelt inauguration, in part owing to a driving rainstorm, Swanson left early. Ickes pessimistically dismissed him as "neither physically nor mentally qualified" to serve; however, in October 1937, he admitted that Swanson seemed "to have Navy matters well in hand." Other persons close to Roosevelt considered that Swanson's illness projected a negative image of the cabinet. Being drawn closer to American naval planning after 1937, a British admiral noted in April 1938 that the secretary had "seen better days" and talked and walked "with difficulty." That autumn he suffered further deterioration. In April 1939, returning from the Caribbean, deeply tanned, he had considerable difficulty in making himself understood at cabinet meetings. A few days later, Daniels discussed Swanson's health with Roosevelt, who confirmed that Swanson "was too sick a man to do much." Roosevelt added, "I haven't the leart to let him go. He depends upon his salary for a living and I just couldn't ask him to quit." Others observers, such as the curmudgeonly Ickes, suspected that Lulie Swanson enjoyed too much being a cabinet wife to allow her husband to resign. Whatever the case, the Swansons were financially secure. Roosevelt could not bring himself to dismiss the friendly, now beloved, Virginian.[45]

Seeking relief from Washington heat, in June 1939, Swanson took up residence at the government's Rapidan camp near Criglersville, in Madison County. His family, brother, and sisters visited him. He fished in the cool waters of the grounds. On the morning of July 6, as the sun brightened green mountain glades, the seventy-seven-year-old Virginian suffered a severe stroke. Twenty-five hours later he died. Despite Lulie Swanson's objection to Byrd's presence on the funeral committee, he and the Virginia delegation participated in the stuffy state funeral in the Senate chamber. A huge crowd attended the brief Virginia graveside ceremonies at the family plot in Richmond's Hollywood cemetery. One observer estimated that among the thousands present was the largest gathering of public officials seen in Richmond in many years. They and their fellows bowed their heads as taps sounded, to be answered by an echoing bugle several hundred yards away. Rumbles from high, white thunderheads, stacked in order west of the Capitol, greeted departing mourners. The *Richmond News Leader* published an apt farewell: "Son of war and reconstruction, he lived to the eve of new destruction. Warring often, he did not fear the new contest. His end, we trust was of peace."[46]

14

Epilogue:
The Red Oak Breaks

The passing shadow of Claude Swanson's death stirred memories of his public career. A Richmond jeweler remembered him "from the time he was the Governor." Virginia had "lost one of her finest, truest and best beloved public servants." An agricultural expert recalled Swanson's passion for good roads and their relationship that began in "the early months of 1906 and the Jamestown Exposition of 1907," which had "ripened into a warm friendship, which, as the years went by, became more precious." An official of the Securities and Exchange Commission appreciated Swanson's contributions "to the life of our little private office group in 1924 at the famous [Democratic] Madison Square battle." An international lawyer identified Swanson as "one of those links to the past in our country which marked the beginning of the great battle for social justice and the rights of the ordinary man." Recounting pleasant social aspects of Swanson's Washington home, he remembered that "our home was [his] . . . stopping place when [in] . . . Philadelphia."[1]

An associate of over thirty years who served under Swanson as an innovative bureau chief of Supplies and Accounts, Rear Admiral Christian Peeples, remembered that the secretary compared himself to "the stout red oak, that though storms would come and go"; it would "bend but never break." Peeples regretted that it was "broken and with it goes a noble heart." The naval careerist considered Swanson, "regardless of his long illness, . . . a real asset to the Navy." The Virginian "not only knew and understood its heart and spirit, . . . he was always a tower of strength in Congress and with the public." An editorial in the *New York Times* praised Swanson: "For more than forty years he was a faithful and useful public man." A reporter disclosed that William D. Leahy "probably . . . closest to Mr. Swanson" was deeply affected by the passing of the "beloved Secretary." The *Richmond News Leader* revealed that admirals half seriously told of how at night they tucked their frail chief "into lamb's wool to be sure he would be alive in the morning." At a cabinet meeting, Franklin D. Roosevelt surprised Frances Perkins with the depth of his emotion by citing Swanson's passing as "a great loss." The president's office released a statement that hinted at Swanson's broader role in Democratic politics and New Deal administration by emphasizing his "wise counsel and philosophic understanding of human problems." Roosevelt declared in the statement, "I personally mourn the passing of a steadfast friend for more than a quarter of a century."[2]

Unrecorded sorrow was felt by "the thousands of his friends who had been proud to shake his hand and call him by his first name in Virginia towns and rural sections for almost half a century." As governor and congressman, Swanson had proven his value to these Virginians by giving them a sense of involvement in public affairs. His use of government agencies comforted and aided their aspirations. He publicized solutions that offered them escape from the sense of individual helplessness frequently bred by a spreading industrial economy. In his campaigns for increased credit, reduction of transportation costs, establishment of a rural post system, endorsement of public roads, and improvement of school systems, he sought for Virginia benefits enjoyed by urban northeasterners. He argued that constituents would have a voice by nominating agrarians to the evolving regulatory systems. Thus, South and West would be emancipated from domination by the Northeast. Swanson's role as a forger of coalitions and compromises most clearly revealed itself during the Wilson administration.[3]

His philosophy of government can be discerned more from his actions than from his words. In one of his earliest congressional addresses, he cited Edmund Burke, a popular choice of the day, to reinforce his argument that effective and orderly reform can be obtained through government. Legislation could not create wealth, but it was the most powerful "of all factors in controlling its distribution." Over the years, he inquired consistently as to how legislation affected this division. He knew that early industrial America had fostered a system that created millionaires with wealth beyond that of sovereign states. As a result, he attached to the tariff heavy significance as a battleground of class and regional conflict. Revisionary efforts here marked more than mere sham battles. Swanson also aided in the passage of legislation that stimulated the economy and redistributed federal tax revenue to benefit Virginia. In the summer of 1933, preparatory to the completion of his senior history thesis at Princeton University, William Sheldon interviewed the secretary. Swanson recalled for Sheldon the challenge of Populism in the 1890s. He emphasized his view that class politics, northeastern dominance of credit sources, and Democratic adjustment to the issues of the time were primary in the decade's political events. Such an interpretation, with minor adjustments, could be placed upon his later public career. Swanson bragged of his practical politics, but beneath compromises and pragmatic solutions stood a commitment to reform and a will-o'-the-wisp idealism.[4]

Swanson did not retreat before the evolving complexities of the modern world. He opposed William McKinley's brand of imperialism, but he would not have the United States withdraw from the international scene. Speaking in 1921, he described the civilization of the earth as "so interwoven in its interests, so interrelated that distressed conditions [anywhere] . . . are felt in the cotton fields of the South, the tobacco fields of Virginia and Kentucky, . . . the mines of the Rocky Mountains, and the factories of New England." Swanson helped move the nation forward into world affairs through collective security agreements and brute naval power. Frequently denied the former, he advocated the latter. Few senators have been as influential in navy matters. As a cabinet member, he proved again his administrative effectiveness.[5]

Although he claimed he did not "look for trouble," Swanson appreciated boldness, innovation, and action. To other colleagues he left the blowing of legislative trumpets; he orchestrated legislative accomplishment. Partly owing to his committee assignments, no major legislation carried his name, yet he influenced drafts to achieve significant congressional enactments. He dealt in the hardheaded world of the possible, of compromise, and of skillful parliamentary maneuvers. Not given to deep introspection, when circumstance permitted, he willingly advanced beyond the status quo. As an advisor to major Democratic figures of the early twentieth century—William Jennings Bryan, Wilson, and Roosevelt—he displayed an optimism and confidence drawn from his Methodist heritage, agrarian Virginia culture, and personal world view. As a Virginia politician, he could not ignore patterns of racial conflict, class exploitation, regional jealousies, or a shrinking electorate. He sought stability and, through stability, progress. Given such circumstances, it is difficult to imagine other tactics than those he used in Virginia that would have accomplished more. His record is not that of a party hack but that of a skillful legislative diplomat and an exceedingly wise executive encompassed in the personality of a professional politician. He did not nourish grudges; he sought friends and solutions.[6]

Once, during the New Deal days, a journalist asked Swanson about his political credo. "Liberal Democrat," he responded. Despite a request to expand his comment, he glanced at an oil portrait of Roosevelt over his desk, squinted a dark eye at his visitor and reiterated, "Liberal Democrat, that's all." Simplicity reigned; he favored ornate displays only in his oratory. Amid Virgina's spreading suburbs, his name is rarely memorialized—a junior high school here or a street there. After his death, the navy christened one of its new destroyers the U.S.S. *Swanson*. The vessel performed as a convoy escort in the undeclared Atlantic naval war between Germany and the United States. There, not unlike its namesake, the sleek gray warship executed the effective and difficult labor of seeing the mission through.[7]

Notes

Abbreviations

CAS	Claude A. Swanson
DNCC	Democratic National Committee Correspondence
JSH	*Journal of Southern History*
LC	Library of Congress, Washington, D.C.
NA	National Archives, Washington, D.C.
USNIP	*United States Naval Institute Proceedings*
VJE	*Virginia Journal of Education*
VMHB	*Virginia Magazine of History and Biography*

1. Rising Young Politician: 1862-1892

1. *Time*, July 17, 1939, 12.

2. William K. Boyd, editor, *William Byrd's Histories of the Dividing Line Betwixt Virginia and North Carolina* (Raleigh, 1929), 190-91; Maude Carter Clement, *History of Pittsylvania County, Virginia* (Lynchburg, 1929), 6-31; Walter L. Hopkins, "Rough and Tentative Notes on the Swanson Family of Virginia and Georgia," 1, Maud Carter Clement Papers (#9479), Manuscripts Department, University of Virginia Library; Mrs. O.A. Keach, "Revolutionary Abstracts from Northumberland County Records," *VMHB*, 34 (April 1926): 161.

3. Hopkins, "Notes on the Swanson Family," 2-5, 7; Marshall Wingfield, *Franklin County, Virginia: A History* (Berryville, Va., 1964), 209; C.B. Bryant, "Henry County: From Its Formation to the End of the Eighteenth Century, et. seq.," *VMHB*, 9 (July 1901): 139-40; (April 1902): 419; 10 (October 1902): 140; *Richmond Daily Whig and Advertiser,* April 3, May 5, 1835; Clement, *Pittsylvania*, 32ff. Clement confuses William Swanson II with his son William Graves Swanson; ibid., 256 n6.

4. Clement, *Pittsylvania*, 237-40; Carter Goodrich, "The Virginia System of Mixed Enterprise," *Political Science Quarterly*, 64 (September 1949): 355-87; Edward Pollock, *Illustrated Sketch Book of Danville, Virginia: Its Manufacture and Commerce* (Petersburg, Va., 1885), 20; A.J. Morrison, "Virginia Patents," *William and Mary Quarterly, 2d ser., 2* (January 1922): 153-54 n1.

5. *Richmond Daily Whig and Advertiser*, March 12, May 13, 31, 1836; Clement, *Pittsylvania*, 240-43; Pollock, *Danville*, 30; Charles W. Turner, "The Virginia Railroads, 1820-1860" Ph.D. diss., University of Minnesota, 1946), 55-59; Peter C. Stewart, "Railroads and Urban Rivalries in Antebellum Eastern Virginia," *VMHB*, 81 (January 1973): 3-22.

6. J.B. Swanson to M.C. Clement, March 26, 1928, Clement Papers; Swanson Ledgers, Swanson Family Papers (#38-83), Manuscripts Department, University of Virginia Library; Clement, *Pittsylvania*, 226.

7. Pollock, *Danville*, 3-36; Swanson Ledgers, Swanson Family Papers; *Richmond Times-Dispatch*, July 8, 1939; Nannie May Tilley, *The Bright-Tobacco Industry, 1860-1929* (Chapel Hill, 1948), 32-33, 200-203.

8. In late March 1865, Sutherlin convinced a Confederate demolition crew the futility of destroying the bridge over the Dan River. Jack P. Maddex, Jr., *The Virginia Conservatives, 1867-1879: A Study of Reconstruction Politics* (Chapel Hill, 1970), 68: Pollock, *Danville*, 52, 121; Swanson Ledgers, Swanson Family Papers; Tilley, *Bright-Tobacco*, 257; William L. Royall, *Some Reminiscences* (New York, 1909), 43-44.

9. Swanson's sisters and brothers were Blanche, Margaret, Julia, Sallie Hill, William Graves, John Pritchett, and Henry Clay Swanson, Whig antecedents being reflected in the name of his youngest brother.

10. *Richmond Times-Dispatch*, July 8, 1939; *New York Times*, July 8, 1939.

11. Parrish graduated in 1886 at Farmville, attended the University of Michigan, and received a Ph.B. at Cornell in 1896. She taught in Danville, Roanoke, State Normal School at Farmville Randolph-Macon Women's College, and State Normal School of Georgia; Parrish concluded her career as supervisor of rural schools of Georgia.

12. CAS to C.P. Swanson, August 10, 1873, in Swanson Scrapbook, unpublished material collected by Archie Beverly Swanson (#6572), Manuscripts Department, University of Virginia Library; Joseph D. Eggleston, Jr., "Claude Swanson: A Sketch," *VJE*, 1 (October 1907): 1; Thomas Whitehead, *Virginia: A Handbook* (Richmond, 1893), 48; *Danville Register*, September 22, 1914; Charles T. O'Ferrall, *Forty Years of Active Service* (New York, 1904), 327.

13. Venable delivered the French oration at the 1857 graduation in Chapel Hill. James T. Moore, *Two Paths to the New South: The Virginia Debt Controversy, 1870-1883* (Lexington, 1974), 9; Swanson Ledgers, Swanson Family Papers; Eggleston, "Claude Swanson," 1; A.J. Morrison, *The Beginnings of Public School Education in Virginia, 1776-1860* (Richmond, 1917), 17ff.; Cornelius Heatwole, *A History of Education in Virginia* (New York, 1916), 131; Maddex, *Va. Conservatives*, 214-17; Tilley, *Bright-Tobacco*, 363, 537-39.

14. Robert E. Withers, *Autobiography of an Octogenarian* (Roanoke, 1907), 218-221; Maddex, *Va. Conservatives*, 70-84, 276-96; Pollock, *Danville*, 123-24. Compare Moore, *Va. Debt Controversy*, 12-26.

15. B.W. Arnold, Jr., *History of the Tobacco Industry in Virginia from 1860-1894* (Baltimore, 1897), 46-47; Duncan L. Kinnear, *The First Hundred Years: A History of Virginia Polytechnic Institute and State University* (Blacksburg, Va., 1972), 53-56; Maddex, *Va. Conservatives*, 153-54, 169, 173, 180; Nelson M. Blake, *William Mahone of Virginia* (Richmond, 1935), 80-134. See Moore, *Va. Debt Controversy*, 14ff., for funding controversies.

16. Danville prices for 1870-1876 averaged 12.34, 11.64, 13.47, 20.45 and 13.32 cents per pound. Competition from the west in 1876 created serious national overproduction, from 381 to 581 million pounds. Blake, *Mahone*, 80-134; Maury Klein, *The Great Richmond Terminal* (Charlottesville, 1970), 31-32, 55-65; Maddex, *Va. Conservatives*, 278-79; Tilley, *Bright Tobacco*, 353-63; Arnold, *Tobacco Industry*, 50-52.

17. Leon G. Tyler, editor, *Virginia Biography*, 5 (Richmond, 1915), 5; *Richmond Times-Dispatch*, July 8, 1939; Eggleston, "Claude Swanson," 1.

18. Eggleston, "Claude Swanson," 1; Moore, *Va. Debt Controversy*, 59ff.; Maddex, *Va. Conservatives*, 218-32; Allan W. Moger, *Virginia, Bourbonism to Byrd, 1870-1925* (Charlottesville, 1968), 33-45.

19. *Richmond News Leader*, July 7, 1939; Kinear, *V. P. I.*, 33-56; John P. Cochran, "The Virginia Agricultural and Mechanical College: The Formative Half Century, 1872-1919, of Virginia Polytechnic Institute" (Ph.D. diss., University of Alabama, 1961), 67, 94-102; entry, October 1, 1879, March 19, April 2, May 8, June 5, 19, July 8, 17, 1880, Maury Society Records, Carol M. Newman Library, Virginia Polytechnic and State University.

20. Pollock, *Danville*, 121-23, 207; *New York Times*, November 26, 1883; Tilley, *Bright-Tobacco*, 255, 258; Kinear, *V. P. I.*, 56; interview, Douglas Deane Hall, September 8, 1960, Washington, D.C.; Eggleston, "Claude Swanson," 1; *Charlottesville Daily Progress*, August 2, 1910; *Richmond Times-Dispatch*, July 8, 1939; James Cannon, Jr., *Bishop Cannon's Own Story: Life As I Have Seen It*, Richard L. Watson, Jr., editor (Durham, 1955), 26-27.

21. W.T. Sutherlin contributed $1,000 to build cottages in 1883. Annie Deane Lyons's husband Peter had been the son of prominent Richmond lawyer James Lyons. Hall interview; *Randolph-Macon Monthly*, 4 (April 1882): 31; 5 (June 1883): 283, 286-87, 294; Cannon, Jr., *Own Story*, 24-28; Richard Irby, *History of Randolph-Macon College* (Richmond, 189?), 279 and passim; F. Joseph Mitchell, "The Virginia Methodist Conference and Social Issues in the Twentieth Century" (Ph.D. diss. Duke University, 1962), 4; Robert Dallek, *Democrat and Diplomat: The Life Of William E. Dodd* (New York, 1968), 27-28; James E. Scanlon, *Randolph-Macon College: A Southern History, 1825-1967* (Charlottesville, 1983), 143, 147, 160.

22. Moore, *Va. Debt Controversy*, 54-108; Charles C. Pearson, *The Readjuster Movement in Virginia* (New Haven, 1917), 26 and passim; Charles E. Wynes, *Race Relations in Virginia, 1870-1902* (Charlottesville, 1961), 20-24; C. Vann Woodward, *Origins of the New South* (Baton Rouge, 1951), 93-96; Carl N. Degler, "Black and White Together: Biracial Politics in the South," *Virginia Quarterly Review*, 47 (Summer 1971): 421-44; Maddex, *Va. Conservatives*, 293-94.

23. Moore, *Va. Debt Controversy*, 95-108; Moger, *Virginia*, 49-56; Klein, *Richmond Terminal*, 10-15, 55-65; *Lynchburg News*, July 26, 1883.

24. J.N. Wyllie to A.M. Scales, July 25, 1889, Alfred Moore Scales Papers, East Carolina Manuscript Collection, J.Y. Joyner Library, East Carolina University; CAS, *The Address of Hon. Claude A. Swanson, Delivered at Hanover Courthouse, September 18, 1905* (Norfolk, 1905), 3; *Ashland (?) Hanover News*, July 26, 1883; *Ashland Hanover and Caroline News*, February 7, 1885; Cannon, Jr., *Own Story*, 26-27; Pollock, *Danville*, 94; Walter T. Calhoun, "The Danville Riot and Its Repercusions on the Virginia Elections of 1883," *Studies in the History of the South, 1875-1922* in *East Carolina College Publications in History*, 2 (Greenville, 1966): 25-51; Moger, *Virginia*, 55-61; see reprint of "Coalition Rule in Danville" in *Appalachian Journal*, 1 (Spring 1973): 111-14, and Gordon B. McKinney, *Southern Mountain Republicans, 1865-1900: Politics and the Appalachian Community* (Chapel Hill, 1978), 66-68, 102-108.

25. CAS to J.N. Wyllie, October 7, 1885, Scales Papers; *Randolph-Macon Monthly*, 8 (October 1885): 28; University of Virginia, Matriculation Book: 1885-86, number 3, (#2464) Manuscripts Department, University of Virginia Library; University of Virginia, *A Sketch of the University of Virginia* (Richmond, 1885), 5, 7; William E. Larsen, *Montague of Virginia: The Making of a Southern Progressive* (Baton Rouge, 1965), 17-18; Phillip A. Bruce, *History of the University of Virginia, 1819-1919*, 4 (New York, 1921), 1-5, 82; *Virginia Magazine*, 25 (1885-86): 423, 504; U.S. Congress, *Congressional Record*, 67 Congress, 4 sess., 64 (February 17, 1923), 3822.

26. A.H. Byrd to F.R. Lassiter, November 28, 1886, George Cameron, Jr., to F.R. Lassiter, January 23, 1887, Frances Rives Lassiter Papers, Manuscript Department, William R. Perkins Library, Duke University; James T. Moore, "The University and the Readjusters," *VMHB*, 78 (January 1970): 89-91; Bruce, *University of Virginia*, vol. 5, 94-186. A more democratic university with law instruction equaling "any in the United States" is described in Henry W. Bragdon, *Woodrow Wilson: The Academic Years* (Cambridge, 1967), 65-89. Compare Evans C. Johnson, *Oscar W. Underwood: A Political Biography* (Baton Rouge, 1980), 14-17.

27. CAS to J.N. Wyllie, February 11, 1889, Scales Papers; CAS to John Inge, February 26, March 15, July 20, 1888, "Receipt, S.S. Hurt, Clerk of Court, Pittsylvania County," July 28, 1888, Claude A. Swanson Papers (#907), Manuscripts Department, University of Virginia Library; A.J. Montague to CAS, December 17, 1888, Andrew J. Montague Papers, Acc. 22001, Personal Papers Collection, Archives Branch, Virginia State Library; *Randolph-Macon Monthly*, 8 (December 1886): 92; *Virginia Magazine*, 26 (1886-1887), 122, 358. See Beverly Munford, *Random Recollections* (Richmond, 1905), 79-83, for a favorable assessment of Swanson as a lawyer.

28. CAS to J.N. Wyllie, February 11, 1889, Scales Papers; CAS to John Inge, July 20, 1888, Swanson Papers, UVA; W.L. Garrett to Harry Wooding, June 10, 1892, Harry Wooding Papers (#598), Manuscripts Department, University of Virginia; *Richmond State*, March 4, 1890; Munford, *Recollections*, 75-76; Moger, *Virginia*, 61-70.

29. Listed in the lobby of the Exchange Hotel with Swanson were William T. Sutherlin, William F. Rhea, James Hay, Edward Echols, and Edward W. Saunders. *Richmond State*, August

18-19, 1892; CAS to J.N. Wyllie, February 11, 1889, J.N. Wyllie to A.M. Scales, July 25, 1889, Scales Papers.

30. *Richmond Dispatch*, November 10, 1892; Moore, *Va. Debt Controversy*, 126-30; Blake, *Mahone*, 249; Whitehead, *Virginia*, 299.

31. Pollock, *Danville*, 118-19; O'Ferrall, *Forty Years*, 325.

32. In 1880, Franklin listed thirty-six, tax-paid distilleries. There were probably many more. "Schedule 3, Distilleries, 1880 Manufacturing, Franklin" in University of North Carolina at Chapel Hill, *Agricultural and Manufacturing Records of Fifteen Southern States* (Chapel Hill, 1963), 554; Whitehead, *Virginia*, 217ff.; Robert A. Hohner, "Prohibition and Virginia Politics, 1901-1916" (Ph.D. diss. Duke University, 1965), 2-3.

33. Edmund R. Cocke observed: "You can forecast for yourself the condition of Virginia women when the rural population have all become day laborers." E.R. Cocke to H.S. Tucker, July 12, 1892, Tucker Family Papers (#2605), Southern Historical Collection, University of North Carolina at Chapel Hill; William D. Sheldon, *Populism in the Old Dominion: Virginia Farm Politics, 1885-1900* (Princeton, 1935), 1-21, 95; Stanley B. Parsons, *The Populist Context: Rural versus Urban Powers in a Great Plains State* (Westport, 1973), 147; Norman Pollock, *The Populist Response to Industrial America* (New York, 1966), 13-24; Robert C. McMath, Jr., *Populist Vanguard: A History of the Southern Farmers Alliance* (Chapel Hill, 1975), 152-57; Arnold, *Tobacco Industry*, 41-55, 73-78; Tilley, *Bright-Tobacco*, 255ff.; Moore, *Va. Debt Controversy*, 126.

34. E.R. Cocke to H.S. Tucker, January 26, July 12, 1892, Tucker Family Papers; R.E. Byrd to J.A. Miller, February 8, 1892, Joseph A. Miller Papers, Manuscript Department, William R. Perkins Library, Duke University; Sheldon, *Populism*, 22-29; see Appendix A, ibid., for 1890 Alliance state platform. Maxwell Ferguson, *State Regulation of Railroads in the South* (New York, 1916), 61-64; Moger, *Virginia*, 93-107; Tilley, *Bright-Tobacco*, 268-69, 407-8; McMath, *Populist Vanguard*, 48-63.

35. E.G. Whittle to S.S. Hurt, October 1, 1892, Records and Minutes, Pittsylvania Alliance and Trade Union Records, 1890-92 (#38-92), Manuscripts Department, University of Virginia Library.

36. E.R. Cocke to H.S. Tucker, July 12, 1892, Tucker Family Papers; J.T. Ellyson to B.B. Gordon, October 12, 1891, Basil Brown Gordon Papers, Virginia Historical Society, Richmond; M.L. Shipman to William Mahone, February 2, 1892, William Mahone Papers, Manuscript Department, William R. Perkins Library, Duke University; V.D. Groner to Benjamin Harrison, August 17, 1892, Benjamin Harrison Papers, Manuscript Division, LC; Woodward, *New South*, 254-55.

37. *Warsaw Northern Neck News*, May 21, 1886; Mitchell, "Methodist Conference," 2-26; Cannon, Jr., *Own Story*, 70-78; Hohner, "Prohibition," 8-11; *New York Times*, September 21, 1892.

38. R.E. Byrd to F.R. Lassiter, April 25, 1892, F.R. Lassiter Papers; James Hay to H.D. Flood, April 18, 1892, Henry De La Warr Flood Papers, Manuscript Division, LC; John Goode to Grover Cleveland, April 19, 1893, Grover Cleveland Papers, Manuscript Division, LC; *Richmond State*, March 24, April 5, May 18-20, 1892; *New York Times*, May 19-20, 1892; compare *Richmond Dispatch*, April, May, 1892, and *Warsaw Northern Neck News*, April, May, 1892. Herbert J. Bass, *"I Am A Democrat": The Political Career of David Bennett Hill* (Syracuse, 1961), 190, 227.

39. "Wooding Autobiography," 52, J.W. Sheffield to Harry Wooding, March 18, 1892, W.L. Garrett to Harry Wooding, June 10, 1892, W.D. Tompkins to Harry Wooding, June 11, 1892, Wooding Papers; *Richmond State*, May 21, 1892, *Staunton Daily News*, August 26-27, 1892; *Richmond Dispatch*, August 26, 1892; *Cong. Rec.*, 53 Cong., 1 sess., 25 (August 25, 1893), 841-844.

40. E.R. Cocke to H.S. Tucker, July 12, 1892, B.T. Gordon to H.S. Tucker, July 4, 1892, Tucker Family Papers; B.B. Gordon to Grover Cleveland, September 9, 1892, Cleveland Papers; B.B. Gordon to W.F. Harrity, August 7, 1892, Gordon Papers; *New York Times*, June 29, 1892; Harry E. Poindexter, "From Copy Desk to Congress: The Precongressional Career of Carter Glass" (Ph.D. diss. University of Virginia, 1966), 154-70; Bass, *Hill*, 239.

41. "Minutes, Republican Pittsylvania Convention, Chatham, April 25, 1892," J.H.

Johnston to William Mahone, February 3, 4, 8, 1892, R.A. Wise to William Mahone, June 30, 1892, J.F. Cobb to William Mahone, July 29, 1892, W.H. Gravely to William Mahone, August 13, 1892, Mahone Papers; J.H. Johnston to Benjamin Harrison, May 13, 1892, J.S. Clarkson to Benjamin Harrison, July 24, 1889, Harrison Papers.

42. C.H. Pierson to Edmund Waddill, Jr., October 23, 1893, Mahone Papers; Sheldon, *Populism*, 45; Woodward, *New South*, 250-52; *Richmond Virginia Sun*, September 21, 1892; *New York Times*, September 17, 1892.

43. W.H. Gravely to William Mahone, September 2, 29, 1892, Mahone Papers; *Danville Register*, August 7, 1892; *Staunton Daily News*, August 26, September 3, 10, 1892; *Richmond Dispatch*, September 2, 22, October 23, 1892; *New York Times*, August 27, September 22-23, 25, 1892. Contrast Woodward, *New South*, 276.

44. J.S. Clarkson to William Mahone, September 6, 1892, Mahone Papers; *Richmond Dispatch*, August 26, September 13, 20, October 18, 23, 1892; *New York Times*, September 23-24, 1892; Sheldon, *Populism*, 87; Larsen, *Montague*, 33-34; Phillip A. Bruce, *History of Virginia*, 5 (Chicago, 1924), 503.

45. CAS to W.E. Tate, October 1, 1892, Claude A. Swanson Papers, Manuscript Department, William R. Perkins Library, Duke University; CAS to F.R. Lassiter, November 19, 1892, F.R. Lassiter Papers; *Danville Register*, October 27, 1892; *Richmond Dispatch*, October 23, 1892; *Richmond State*, May 20, 1892.

46. J.H. Johnston to William Mahone, August 26, 1892, W.H. Gravely to William Mahone, September 2, October 13, 1892, Mahone Papers; *Richmond Dispatch*, November 8, 10, 1892; *New York Times*, September 23, November 29, 1892; *Staunton Spectator*, August 31, 1892.

47. *New York Times*, November 14, 1892.

2. Faith with the People: 1893-1898

1. Camm Patteson to F.R. Lassiter, May 30, 1893, F.R. Lassiter Papers.

2. See John Hurt (#38-86) and William A. Garrett (#6356) Papers, Manuscript Department, University of Virginia Library; Albert D. Porter, *County Government in Virginia, A Legislative History, 1607-1904* (New York, 1947), 277-303.

3. J.F. Epes to F.R. Lassiter, January 31, February 15, 1893, F.R. Lassiter Papers; tally fragment, 1893, Tucker Family Papers; John Goode to Grover Cleveland, April 19, 1893, Cleveland Papers; J.B. Stephenson to CAS, June 5, 1901, in *Washington Post*, June 13, 1901; *Richmond Dispatch*, March 10, 30, April 15, 1893; Larsen, *Montague*, 28; J. Rogers Hollingsworth, *The Whirligig of Politics: The Democracy of Cleveland and Bryan* (Chicago, 1963), 1-6.

4. CAS to F.R. Lassiter, April 9, 1893, J.W. Daniel to F.R. Lassiter, May 10, 1893, F.R. Lassiter Papers; Allan Nevins, *Grover Cleveland: A Study in Courage* (New York, 1934), 516-20.

5. Hollingsworth, *Cleveland and Bryan*, 10-18; Nevins, *Cleveland*, 523-26; Moger, *Virginia*, 145-47.

6. Donald B. Johnson and Kirk H. Porter, editors, *National Party Platforms*, 1840-1972 (Urbana, Ill., 1973), 88; *Cong. Rec.*, 53 Cong., 1 sess., 25 (August 24, 1893), 841-45, (August 28, 1893) 1004-8; Moger, *Virginia*, 146-51.

7. Charles E. Wynes, "Charles T. O'Ferrall and the Virginia Gubernatorial Election of 1893," *VMHB*, 64 (October 1956), 437-41; *Richmond Dispatch*, April 15, May 25, June 6, July 18, 1893; *Warsaw Northern Neck News*, July 28, 1983; Klein, *Richmond Terminal*, 22ff.

8. Carter Glass to J.W. Daniel, August 18, 1893, John Warwick Daniel Papers, Manuscript Department, William R. Perkins Library, Duke University; *Richmond Dispatch*, August 18, 1893; Poindexter, "Glass," 173-74, Wynes, "O'Ferrall," 444-45.

9. W.H. Gravely to William Mahone, May 1, 1893, Mahone Papers; *Richmond Dispatch*, September 22, October 26, Novembr 3, 1893; Wynes, "O'Ferrall," 442-51; John H. Moore, "The Life of James Gaven Field, Virginia Populist" (M.A. thesis, University of Virginia, 1953), 228-32. Sheldon and Moger underestimate the white Populist vote and Kousser's figures are suspect. Sheldon, *Populism*, 95-105; Moger, *Virginia*, 109-111; J. Morgan Kousser, *The Shaping of*

Southern Politics: Suffrage Restriction and the Establishment of the One-Party South, 1880-1910 (New Haven, 1974), 174.

10. W.W. Scott to B.B. Gordon, January 29, 1889, Gordon Papers; W.A. Watson to F.R. Lassiter, May 25, June 4, 1892, T.S. Martin to F.R. Lassiter, November 13, 26, 1893, F.R. Lassiter Papers; R.E. Byrd to H.D. Flood, May 28, 1892, Flood Papers, LC; W.A. Anderson to J.S. Bryan, May 28, 1892, William A. Anderson Papers (#38-96), Manuscript Department, University of Virginia Library; Harry W. Readnor, "General Fitzhugh Lee: A Biographical Study" (Ph.D. diss., University of Virginia, 1971), passim; *Richmond State*, May 21, 1892.

11. *Richmond Times*, December 17-20, 1893; Larsen, *Montague*, 40-42; Kousser, *Shaping of Southern Politics*, 79-80; Woodward, *New South*, 371-72; Raymond H. Pulley, *Old Virginia Restored: An Interpretation of the Progressive Impulse, 1870-1930* (Charlottesville, 1968), 51; James A. Bear, Jr., "Thomas Staples Martin, A Study in Virginia Politics, 1883-1896" (M.A. thesis, University of Virginia, 1952), 160ff.; Klein, *Richmond Terminal*, 1ff.

12. Fitzhugh Lee to Grover Cleveland, April 7, December 25, 1893, Cleveland Papers; William G. Ray, "Thomas Staples Martin's Campaign for the United States Senate, 1892-1893" (M.A. thesis, University of Virginia, 1972), 62-64; Poindexter, "Glass," 189-92; Kaufman, "Flood," 26-30; *Richmond Dispatch*, April 26, 1893, February 8, 1894; see W.A. Jones to J.S.B. Thompson, November 25, 1894, William A. Jones Papers (#8649), Manuscripts Department, University of Virginia Library, and Flood Papers, LC, and F.R. Lassiter Papers, *circa* 1890-1902.

13. P.J. Otey to B.B. Gordon, August 23, 1893, Gordon Papers; Berryman Green to J.L. Hurt, March 2, 1893, Hurt Papers; *Richmond Dispatch*, December 2, 9, 12, 17, 22, 1893; Pollock, *Danville*, 44, 120.

14. CAS to S.G. Whittle, August 27, 1892, January 4, 1893, A.J. Montague to S.G. Whittle, February 1, 1896, Whittle Family Papers (#7973), Manuscripts Department, University of Virginia Library; *Richmond Dispatch*, January 17, 25, 1894; *Cong. Rec.*, 53 Cong., 2 sess. 26 (January 24, 1894), Appendix, 367.

15. *Cong. Rec.*, 53 Cong., 2 sess., 26 (March 1, 1894), Appendix, 643-44, (June 1, 1894), 5604-08, (June 1, 1894) 5606; Nevins, *Cleveland*, 597-603; Hollingsworth, *Cleveland and Bryan*, 25; Tilley, *Bright-Tobacco*, 376.

16. *Cong. Rec.*, 53 Cong., 2 sess., 26 (June 1, 1894), 5606; *Richmond Dispatch*, April 6, 17, May 3, 4, 16, 17, June 7, 1894; Hollingsworth, *Cleveland and Bryan*, 26-31; CAS to F.P. Cousins, January 20, 1894, Swanson Papers, Duke University; A.J. Montague to CAS, March 26, 1894, Montague Papers; Tilley, *Bright-Tobacco*, 215 and passim; Klein, *Richmond Terminal*, 235ff.; Moger, *Virginia*, 153.

17. Scott and Stringfellow to F.R. Lassiter, November 26, 1894, F.R. Lassiter Papers; C.T. Barksdale to William Mahone, May 22, 1894, T.G. Tatum to William Mahone, September 24, 1894, Mahone Papers; F.A. Magruder, *Recent Administration in Virginia* (Baltimore, 1912), 83-87; Moore, "Field," 243; Poindexter, "Glass," 195-97.

18. M.D. Martin to William Mahone, September 20, 1894, Mahone Papers; *Richmond Dispatch*, July 25, August 17, 24-25, 1894.

19. J.T. Ellyson to W.E. Bibb, October 10, 22, 1894, William E. Bibb Papers (#4171), Manuscripts Department, University of Virginia Library; *Richmond Dispatch*, August 10, 12, 24, September 18, 1894; *Richmond State*, August 24, 1894.

20. W.W. Cobbs to William Mahone, September 17, 1894, T.G. Tatum to William Mahone, September 24, 1894, M.D. Martin to William Mahone, September 20, 1894, Mahone Papers; *Lynchburg News*, August 25, 1894; *Richmond Dispatch*, September 4, 12, 24-25, October 24, 30, 1894.

21. Berryman Green to J.L. Hurt, October 17, 1894, Hurt Papers; U.S. House, *Contested Election Case of George V. Cornett vs. Claude A. Swanson from the Fifth District of Virginia* (Washington, 1895), 68, 70-74, 80.

22. A.J. Montague to W.T. Stiegleman, July 5, 1894, Montague Papers; *Cornett vs. Swanson*, 83-84.

23. J.H. Johnston to William Mahone, October 10, 22, 23, 1894, W.H. Pleasants to William

Mahone, October 22, 1894, C.T. Barksdale to William Mahone, November 22, 1894, Mahone Papers; *Cornett vs. Swanson*, 4ff.

24. *Cornett vs. Swanson*, 14ff.

25. Prohibitionist Sheldon received 249 votes. *Cornett vs. Swanson*, 5ff.; Berryman Green to Holmes Conrad, April 16, 1895, Cleveland Papers.

26. CAS to H.D. Flood, December 4, 1894, Flood Papers, LC; *Richmond Dispatch*, December 12, 1894; *New York Times*, December 12, 1894.

27. Thirty-three contested cases were eventually debated in the Fifty-fourth Congress (1895-1897). "Affadavit of J.J. MacDonald, December 17, 1894," Jones Papers; Chester H. Rowell, compiler, *Digest of Contested Election Cases, 1789-1901* (Washington, 1901), 502, 534, 537, 547. Contrast Larsen, *Montague*, 92-93.

28. T.S. Martin to F.R. Lassiter, March 18, 1896, F.R. Lassiter Papers; *Cong. Rec.*, 54 Cong., 1 sess., 28 (December 21, 1895), 284, (April 24, 1896), 4369; 2 sess., 29 (February 3, 1897), 1483-1501.

29. J.H. Hobson to William Mahone, January (?), June 3, 1895, W.W. Cobbs to William Mahone, July 25, 1895, E.P. Buford to William Mahone, July 25, 1895, J.H. Johnston to William Mahone, September 3, 1895, Mahone Papers; E.P. Buford to *Richmond Times*, August 3, 1895, Edward P. Buford Papers (#38-31), Manuscripts Department, University of Virginia Library; *Richmond State*, September 4, 1895; Sheldon, *Populism*, 111; Blake, *Mahone*, 252-53.

30. Fitzhugh Lee to Grover Cleveland, April 15, 1895, C.T. O'Ferrall to Grover Cleveland, April 16, 1895, Berryman Green to Holmes Conrad, April 16, 1895, Cleveland Papers; Fitzhugh Lee to J.L. Hurt, May 3, 1895, Hurt Papers; Fitzhugh Lee to H.S. Tucker, July 10, 1895, Tucker Family Papers; *Richmond State*, September 4, 1895.

31. W.W. Cobbs to William Mahone, August 23, 1895, Mahone Papers; H.D. Flood to CAS, January 17, 1896, Flood Papers, LC; Sheldon, *Populism*, 112; *Richmond Dispatch*, November 6-7, 10, 1895; *Richmond State*, November 7, 1895; Poindexter, "Glass," 221-22; Kaufman, "Flood," 38-40.

32. H.M. Price to H.S. Tucker, January 4, 1895, Tucker Family Papers; *Cong. Rec.*, 53 Cong., 3 sess., 27 (January 25, 1895), 1368-70, (February 2, 1895) 1701-2, (February 3, 1895) 1795-97; *Richmond Dispatch*, December 7, 1894, January 3, 8, 10, 1895; *Richmond State*, January 8, March 10, 1895; Nevins, *Cleveland*, 655.

33. T.S. Martin to J.L. Hurt, May 18, 1896, Swanson Papers, Duke University; Sheldon, *Populism*, 113.

34. *Richmond Times*, April 21, 1896.

35. CAS to W.B. Shepard, March 23, 1896, Swanson Papers, Duke University; *Richmond State*, August 9, 24, 1895; *Richmond Dispatch*, May 21, 1901; Poindexter, "Glass," 223-26; Doss, "Daniel," 185-87; Alfred W. Carter, "1896: Free Silver and the Virginia Democratic party" (M.A. thesis, East Carolina University, 1969), 24-28.

36. Carter, "1896," 34-35; Martin Scrapbook, 45, 72, Day-Martin papers (#38-159), Manuscripts Department, University of Virginia Library; *Cong. Rec.* 54 Cong., 1 sess., 28 (December 27, 1895), 353-55, (February 13, 1896) 1712, Appendix, 255.

37. Allen W. Moger, "The Rift in Virginia Democracy in 1896," *Journal Of Southern History*, 4 (February 1938): 315-17. Compare Moger, *Virginia*, 155-65. Sheldon, *Populism*, 138; Bear, "Martin," 203; Doss, "Daniel," 165-69; Larsen, *Montague*, 46; Pulley, *Old Virginia*, 56; Poindexter, "Glass," 225, 253; Carter, "1896," 106-14.

38. Carter Glass to J.W. Daniel, August 18, 1893, Daniel Papers, Duke University; Swanson sectional references, see *Cong. Rec.*, 53 Cong., 1 sess., 25 (August 24, 1893), 843-44; 2 sess., 26 (January 24, 1894), Appendix, 368-69, (March 1, 1894) 643-44.

39. *Richmond Dispatch*, June 4, 5, 1896; *Richmond Times*, June 3, 4, 1896; *New York Times*, June 4, 5, 1896; Carter, "1896," 61-67.

40. *Richmond Disipatch*, June 5, 1896; *Richmond Times*, June 5, 1896; *New York Times*, June 5, 1896; Carter, "1896," 68-69.

41. A.J. Wedderburn to F.R. Lassiter, September 2, 1896, F.R. Lassiter Papers; *Richmond*

Dispatch, June 5, September 2, 1896; *Richmond State*, August 4, September 3, 5-6, 1896; *New York Times*, November 7, 1896.

42. CAS to W.B. Shepard, March 23, 1896, Swanson Papers, Duke University; CAS to F.R. Lassiter, September 5, 1896, F.R. Lassiter Papers; Paolo E. Coletta, *William Jennings Bryan*, 1 (Lincoln, 1964), 115, 148; *Washington Post*, as quoted in the *Lynchburg News*, July 15, 1896; Poindexter, "Glass," 233-51; Carter, "1896," 72-87; Democratic National Committee, *Official Proceedings of the Democratic National Convention* (Logansport, Ind., 1896), 68a, 109-12, 313; Richard C. Bain, *Convention Decisions* (Washington, 1960), 155-57, Appendix C; U.S. House, *Contested Election of John R. Brown vs. Claude A. Swanson from the Fifth District of Virginia* (Washington, 1897), 743-44; *Richmond Dispatch*, July 7, 11, 1896; *Richmond Times*, July 18, 1896.

43. N.H. Hairston to W.H. Tyler, February 10, 1897, J. Hoge Tyler Papers, Special Collections, Virginia Polytechnic Institute and State University; *Brown vs. Swanson*, 245 ff.; Royall, *Some Reminiscences*, 202-3; *Richmond Dispatch*, October 4, 1896.

44. *Richmond Dispatch*, October 20, November 1, 1896; CAS to F.R. Lassiter, September 5, 1896, F.R. Lassiter Papers; *Brown vs. Swanson*, 265ff.

45. See J. Taylor Ellyson Papers (#4130), Manuscripts Department, University of Virginia Library, August, September 1897, for his influence over *Richmond Dispatch* editorials. *Richmond Times*, 1893-87; *Richmond State*, September, 1896; *Lynchburg News*, 1893-97; *Brown vs. Swanson*, 791; John S. Hopewell, "An Outsider Looking In: John Garland Pollard and Machine Politics" (Ph.D. diss., University of Virginia, 1976), 7.

46. Coletta, *Bryan*, 1: 189; *Richmond Dispatch*, October 13, November 1, 4, 1896; *Brown vs. Swanson*, 6, 243; *Warrock-Richardson Alamanac* (Richmond, 1893), 75, (Richmond, 1895) 86, (Richmond, 1896) 62.

47. CAS to E.W. Saunders, January 29, 1897, Claude A. Swanson Papers, Virginia Historical Society, Richmond; *Cong. Rec.*, 55 Cong., 2 sess., 31 (April 13, 1898), 3800-4, (April 23, 1898) 4212, 3 sess., 32 (February 23, 1899) 2236-37, (March 3, 1899) 2917; 56 Cong., 1 sess., 33 (March 16, 1900), 2988-96; *Brown vs. Swanson*, 3ff.

48. CAS to J.L. Tredway, February (?) 1897, R.A. James to J.H. Tyler, March 3, 1897, CAS to J.H. Tyler, March 17, 1897, T.S. Martin to J.L. Tredway, April 7, 1897, Tyler Papers.

49. N.H. Hairston to J.L. Tredway, April 4, 1897, Tyler Papers; T.S. Martin to F.R. Lassiter, March 18, April 9, 27, 1896, A.J. Montague to F.R. Lassiter, August 18, 1895, W.A. Watson to F.R. Lassiter, September 15, 1896, J.N. Button to F.R. Lassiter, September 18, 1897, F.R. Lassiter Papers; Larsen, *Montague*, 48-49, 53; William L. Chenery, *So It Seemed* (New York, 1952), 14.

50. H.C. Swanson to J.H. Tyler, June 8, June [25], 1897, R.A. James to J.H. Tyler, May 24, June 10, 1897, G.S. Shackelford to J.H. Tyler, May 25, 1897, N.H. Massie to J.H. Tyler, May 25, 1897, Tyler Papers; H.W. Fugate to F.R. Lassiter, July 31, 1897, F.R. Lassiter to R.E. Byrd, May 19, 29, 1897, F.R. Lassiter to T.W. Battle, May 8, 1897, A.C. Gordon to F.R. Lassiter, July 14, 1897, J.L. Moon to F.R. Lassiter, August 2, 1897, F.R. Lassiter to G.W. Morris, July 7, 1897, F.R. Lassiter Papers; G.B. Keezel to A.J. Montague, June 1, 1903, Montague Papers; *New York Times*, July 29, August 12-13, 1897; *Baltimore Sun*, August 3, 1896; *Richmond State*, March 17, June 27, August 13, 1897; *Roanoke Times*, July 27, August 13, 1897; *Richmond Dispatch*, August 12, 13, 1897.

51. *Roanoke Times*, August 5, 13, 20, 1897; *Warsaw Northern Neck News*, August 20, 1897; *Richmond Dispatch*, August 12, 13, 1897; *Richmond State*, August 13, 1897; Moger, *Virginia*, 168; Poindexter, "Glass," 268-76.

52. Contrast Larsen, *Montague*, 62, Moger, *Virginia*, 168, Virginius Dabney, *Virginia: The New Dominion* (New York, 1971), 430, and Poindexter, "Glass," 268-76. Swanson continued to vote for direct election at least through 1903. *Cong. Rec.*, 53 Cong., 2 sess., 26 (July 21, 1894), 7783; 55 Cong., 2 sess., 31 (May 11, 1898), 4825; 56 Cong., 1 sess., 33 (April 13, 1900), 4128; 57 Cong., 1 sess., 35 (February 13, 1902), 1722; *Richmond State*, February 6, May 27, 28, 1897; Francis B. Simpkins, *Pitchfork Ben Tillman: South Carolinian* (Baton Rouge, 1944), 285-309.

53. G.W.B. Hale to J.H. Tyler, March 8, 1897, Tyler Papers; Henry Maclin to F.R. Lassiter,

September 6, 1897, F.R. Lassiter to Henry Maclin, September 8, 1897, F.R. Lassiter Papers; Francis P. Miller, *Man from the Valley: Memoirs of a 20th Century Virginian* (Chapel Hill, 1969), 6-10; Cannon, Jr., *Own Story*, 78, 120ff.; McMath *Populist Vanguard*, 62; Arthur W. James, *Virginia's Social Awakening* (Richmond, 1939), 178-88; Ernest T. Thompson, *Presbyterians in the South, 1890-1972*, 3 (Richmond, 1973), 159-62ff.; John L. Eighmy, *Churches in Cultural Captivity: A History of the Social Attitudes of the Southern Baptists* (Knoxville, 1972), 41ff.; Mitchell, "Va. Methodist Conference," 4ff.; *Richmond Times*, April 1, 1896; *Richmond Dispatch*, July 28, August 12, 1897.

3. Platform Democrat: 1983-1903

1. Wayne E. Fuller, "The South and the Rural Free Delivery of Mail," *JSH*, 25 (November, 1959): 499-504; Herbert A. Gibbons, *John Wanamaker*, 1 (New York, 1926), 278-80; U.S. Senate, Post Office and Post Roads Committee, *Letter from Postmaster General in Response to Senate Resolution of Free Delivery of Mail in Rural Districts* (Washington, 1892), 1ff.

2. Fuller, "Rural Free Delivery," 506-9; *Cong. Rec.*, 53 Cong., 2 sess., 26 (March 24, 1894), 3242.

3. *Cong. Rec.*, 57 Cong., 1 sess., 35 (March 3, 1902), 2310-11, 2323-2331; U.S. House, Post Office and Post Roads Committee, *Rural Free Delivery Services* (Washington, 1902), 2-5; Fuller, "Rural Free Delivery," 508-10.

4. House Post Office and Post Roads Committee, *Rural Free Delivery Services*, 2; *Cong. Rec.*, 57 Cong., 1 sess., 35 (March 3, 1902), 2326, (March 8, 1902) 2540, (March 10, 1902) 2605; Fuller, "Rural Free Delivery," 510-21.

5. H.C. Coles to J.W. Collie, June 29, 1898, CAS to J.W. Collie, February 7, 1900, CAS to Mrs. M.E. Goolsby, March 10, 1900, April 17, 1900, Swanson Papers, Duke University; *Cong. Rec.*, 58 Cong., 2 sess., 38 (March 11, 1904), 3049, 3055, (April 12, 1904) 4716-21; *New York Times*, January 6, 7, March 2, 1904; *Norfolk Virginian Pilot*, March 11, 12, 1904; *Richmond News Leader*, July 24, 1903, January 5, March 11, 12, 1904; O'Ferrall, *Forty Years*, 327; U.S. House, *Report on Hay Resolution, Number 1395* (Washington, 1904), 20, 50-51, 190-91; see also Joseph L. Bristow, *Fraud and Politics at the Turn of the Century* (New York, 1952), 36ff.; A. Bower Sageser, *Joseph L. Bristow: Kansas Progressive* (Lawrence, 1968), 33-52.

6. *Cong. Rec.*, 53 Cong., 2 sess., 26 (April 10, 1894), 3646; 54 Cong., 1 sess., 28 (March 7, 1896), 2561; 2 sess., 29 (February 11, 1897), 1749-51, (February 12, 1897) 1754, 1771; 55 Cong., 2 sess., 31 (March 15, 1898), 2824; 55 Cong., 3 sess., 32 (January 19, 1899), 816, 822.

7. *Cong. Rec.*, 56 Cong., 1 sess., 33 (April 23, 1900), 4721, 4725; 56 Cong., 2 sess., 34 (February 6, 1901), 2020, Appendix, 268-71; Klein, *Richmond Terminal*, 26-29, 55-65, 286-94.

8. W.S. Showalter to James Hay, September 9, October 20, 28, 1902, James Hay Papers (#4221), Manuscripts Department, University of Virginia Library; *New York Times*, November 29, 30, 1903; *Cong. Rec.*, 56 Cong., 1 sess., 33 (April 26, 1900), 4721; 57 Cong., 1 sess., 35 (March 4, 1902), 2375-78; George C. Osborn, *John Sharp Williams: Planter-Statesman of the Deep South* (Baton Rouge, 1943), 104, 106-08, 120.

9. Champ Clark, *My Quarter Century in Politics*, 2 (New York, 1920), 264-65; Democratic National Committee, *Official Reports of the Proceedings of the Democratic National Convention* (Chicago, 1908), 161; Randall B. Ripley, *Majority Party Leadership in Congress* (Boston, 1969), 28; Kousser, *Shaping of Southern Politics*, 144; *Cong. Rec.*, 58 Cong., 1 sess., 37 (December 5, 1903), 532. See also Congressman Sereno Payne's remarks, ibid., 540; compare Osborn, *Williams*, 120 n60, 129, 138-39.

10. Woodrow Wilson, *Congressional Government* (New York, 1956), 65; Richard F. Fenno, Jr., *Congressmen in Committees* (Boston, 1973), 2-5; David W. Brady, *Congressional Voting in a Partisan Era: A Study of the McKinley Houses and a Comparison to the Modern House of Representatives* (Lawrence, 1973), 156-59.

11. James E. Watson, *As I Knew Them: The Memoir of James E. Watson* (New York, 1936),

295-96; Randall B. Ripley, *Party Leaders in the House of Representatives* (Washington, 1967), 36-37, lists Oscar Underwood the first House Democratic Whip in 1900. Watson is not cited as Republican Whip until 1905. Randall B. Ripley, "The Party Whip Organization in the United States House of Representatives," *American Political Science Review*, 58 (September, 1964): 564 n18, does not substantiate Watson's claim for Swanson. Yet, George B. Galloway, *History of the House of Representatives*, 2nd edition (New York, 1976), 142, and Neil MacNeil, *Forge of Democracy: The House of Representatives* (New York, 1963), 67, name Watson Republican Whip in 1899.

12. H.W. Wiley to C.W. Woodman, May 1, 1896, HR 54A-f 43.4, "Duty on Cuban Sugar and Tobacco," January 18, 1901, HR 56A-F 40.2, U.S. House, *Edited Version, Hearings Before Subcommittee of the Ways and Means Committee* (Washington, 1903), 12-13, HR-57A-f 38.1, Records of the House of Representatives, Ways and Means Committee, Record Group (hereafter abbreviated RG) 233, NA; *Cong. Rec.*, 55 Cong., 1 sess., "House Resolution, 1869," 30 (March 22, 1897), 151, (July 19, 1897) 2801-3.

13. CAS to J.L. Tredway, February (?), 1897, R.A. James to J.H. Tyler, March 3, 1897, CAS to J.H. Tyler, March 17, 1897, Tyler Papers; *Richmond State*, March 19, 1897; Washington, *Silver Knight and Watchman*, as quoted in *Lynchburg News*, April 24, 1897; Brady, *Congressional Voting*, 186; F.W. Taussig, *The Tariff History of the United States*, 8th edition (New York, 1967), 326-27; H. Wayne Morgan, *William McKinley and His America* (Syracuse, 1963), 276-77; William A. Robinson, *Thomas B. Reed: Parliamentarian* (New York, 1930), 351-52.

14. *Cong. Rec.*, 55 Cong., 1 sess., 30 (March 23, 1897), Appendix, 28-32, (March 26, 1897), 379, 381-82, (March 27, 1897), 400-1; *New York Times*, March 10, 1897; Taussig, *Tariff*, 326-27; Robinson, *Reed*, 352-54.

15. Brady, *Congressional Voting*, 53-54; Harold U. Faulkner, *The Decline of Lassiez Faire, 1897-1917* (New York, 1951), 59-61; Taussig, *Tariff*, 326-60; *Cong. Rec.*, 55 Cong., 1 sess., 30 (July 19, 1897), 2715-19, (July 21, 1897) 2802-3; *New York Times*, March 10, July 17, 18, 20, 1897; Tilley, *Bright-Tobacco*, 623.

16. *New York Journal*, March 29, 1898; Morgan, *McKinley*, 332-34, 369, 372; Lauros G. McConachie, *Congressional Committees* (New York, 1898), 42; David F. Healy, *The United States in Cuba, 1898-1902: Generals, Politicians, and the Search for Policy* (Madison, 1963), 17-27, 208; Elmer Ellis, *Henry Moore Teller: Defender of the West* (Caldwell, 1941), 310-12.

17. *Richmond Dispatch*, March 7, April 7, 10, 13, 15, 19, 1898; Dabney, *New Dominion*, 406; Harold U. Faulkner, *Politics, Reform and Expansion, 1890-1900* (New York, 1959), 266; Morgan, *McKinley*, 340-41, 347; *Cong. Rec.*, 55 Cong., 2 sess., 31 (June 6, 1898), 5567-68, (June 11, 1898) 5769; Readnour, "Lee," 220-50.

18. *Cong. Rec.*, 56 Cong., 1 sess., 33 (February 20, 1900), 2008-11, (February 22, 1900) 2079, (February 28, 1900) 2415.

19. *Cong. Rec.*, 56 Cong., 1 sess., 33 (March 19, 1900), 3046-48, (April 11, 1900) Appendix, 611; *Richmond Dispatch*, February 21, July 20, 1900; Morgan, *McKinley*, 464-65.

20. Democratic National Committee, *Official Proceedings of the Democratic National Convention* (Chicago, 1900), 113-21; *Richmond Dispatch*, July 20, 1900; Faulkner, *Politics*, 274.

21. *Cong. Rec.*, 57 Cong., 1 sess. 35 (December 17, 1901), 332-34, (December 18, 1901) 427, (March 4,1902) 2359.

22. *Cong. Rec.*, 57 Cong., 2 sess., 36 (December 18, 1902), 427-28, 431-32.

23. U.S. House, *Reciprocity with Cuba* (Washington, 1902), v, vi, 110, 123-24, 140, 146-47; *Cong. Rec.*, 57 Cong., 1 sess., 35 (April 18, 1902), 4418, 58 Cong., 1 sess., 37 (November 16, 1903), 265, 274-75, Appendix, 547-50, (November 19, 1903) 335-41, 389; Healy, *United States in Cuba*, 190, 194, 197-206.

24. CAS to F.R. Lassiter, August 9, 1900, F.R. Lassiter to CAS, August 14, 1900, F.R. Lassiter Papers; CAS to J.W. Collie, February 7, 1900, CAS to Mrs. M.E. Goolsby, March 10, April 7, 1900, CAS to B.S. White, March 27, April 17, 1900, Swanson Papers, Duke University.

25. A.J. Montague to CAS, October 8, 1898, CAS to A.J. Montague, October 10, 1898, Montague Papers; H.C. Coles to S.P. Epes, September 15, 1898, Sydney P. Epes Papers (#3654),

Manuscripts Department, University of Virginia Library; J. T. Ellyson to F.R. Lassiter, October 15, 1898, F.R. Lassiter Papers; Faulkner, *Politics*, 268-69.

26. Henry Maclin to F.R. Lassiter, September 6, 8, 1897, James Mann to F.R. Lassiter, October 22, 1897, T.S. Martin to F.R. Lassiter, October 23, 1897, F.R. Lassiter to W.A. Glasgow, October 4, 1898, W.P. Wall to F.R. Lassiter, November 5, 1898, F.R. Lassiter Papers; A.J. Montague to CAS, October 8, 1898, Montague Papers; T.S. Martin to Camm Patteson, February 15, 1898, T.S. Martin to H.D. Flood, May 11, 1898, Flood Papers, LC.

27. G.E. Smith to F.R. Lassiter, August 28, 1897, T.S. Martin to F.R. Lassiter, January 30, 1899, F.R. Lassiter Papers; W.A. Jones to A.J. Montague, January 21, 1899, Montague Papers; John Lamb to W.A. Jones, October 6, 1899, Jones Papers; Raymond H. Pulley, "The May Movement of 1899: Irresolute Progressivism in the Old Dominion," *VMHB*, 75 (April, 1967): 186-201.

28. W.A. Jones to A.J. Montague, January 21, 1899, Montague Papers; W.A. Anderson to A.A. Gray, March 29, 1898, R.W. Moore to W.A. Anderson, June 6, 1899, Anderson Papers; *Warsaw Northern Neck News*, March 17, July 21, 1899, *Roanoke Times*, March 29, 1899, *Richmond Dispatch*, June 11, 1899.

29. CAS to H.D. Flood, April 12, 1899, Flood Papers, LC.

30. W.B. Simmons to W.A. Anderson, April 28, 1899, Anderson Papers; F.R. Lassiter to W.L. Shands, April 17, 1899, G.J. Hundley to F.R. Lassiter, April 19, 1899, F.R. Lassiter Papers; *Richmond Dispatch*, April 16, 1899.

31. T.S. Martin to F.R. Lassiter, May 13, 1899, F.R. Lassiter Papers; W.A. Jones to W.A. Anderson, June 13, 1899, Anderson Papers; J.L. Tredway to J.A. Hurt, August 15, 1899, Hurt Papers; J.H. Tyler to W.A. Jones, April 11, 1905, Tyler Papers; *Richmond Dispatch*, March 14, 15, 17, May 11, 12, 1899, *Richmond Times*, May 11, 1899; *Norfolk Virginian Pilot*, May 11-12, 1899; *Roanoke Times*, May 11, 1899.

32. F.R. Lassiter to T.S. Martin, July 28, 1899, F.R. Lassiter Papers; J.L. Tredway to J.L. Hurt, August 15, 1899, Hurt Papers; *Norfolk Virginian Pilot*, July 30, August 9, December 8, 1899.

33. F.R. Lassiter to CAS, November 7, 1899, F.R. Lassiter Papers; *Norfolk Virginian Pilot*, September 3, October 6, 13, December 8, 1899; *Richmond Dispatch*, November 8, 1899.

34. James Hay to T.S. Martin, December 26, 1899, Flood Papers, LC; *Norfolk Virginian Pilot*, January 6, 1900; Robert S. Smith, *Mill on the Dan: A History of Dan River Mills, 1882-1950* (Durham, N.C., 1960), 51 n84.

35. F.R. Lassiter to CAS, March 5, 1900, F.R. Lassiter to T.S. Martin, March 5, 1900, CAS to F.R. Lassiter, March 7, 8, 1900, F.R. Lassiter Papers; *Richmond Dispatch*, March 3, 1900.

36. T.S. Martin to F.R. Lassiter, March 7, 9, 10, 1900, CAS to J.H. Tyler, March 8, 11, 1900, J.K. Jones to J.H. Tyler, March 9, 1900, CAS to F.R. Lassiter, March 8, 11, 1900, F.R. Lassiter Papers.

37. *Richmond Dispatch*, October 24, 1899; Moger, *Virginia*, 174; Larsen, *Montague*, 92.

38. A.J. Montague to T.W. Shelton, January 3, 1900, A.J. Montague to W.A. Anderson, January 18, 1900, Montague Papers; *Richmond Dispatch*, January 28, 1900.

39. T.S. Martin to F.R. Lassiter, March 29, 1900, F.R. Lassiter Papers; *Norfolk Virginian Pilot*, April 24, May 2, 3, 20, 1900; *Richmond Dispatch*, April 6, 21, 27, 1900; Poindexter, "Glass," 392; Kaufman, "Flood," 87-89.

40. *Norfolk Virginian Pilot*, March 25, 28, July 18, 1900; Martinsville, *Henry County Bulletin*, May 27, 1900; *Richmond Dispatch*, March 25, 28, 1900; Wynes, *Race Relations*, 57-58; Moger, *Virginia*, 186.

41. A.J. Montague to W.A. Jones, July 21, 1900, Jones Papers; F.R. Lassiter to T.S. Martin, September 20, 25, 1900, F.R. Lassiter Papers; CAS to H.D. Flood, July 30, August 9, 1900, Flood Papers, LC; CAS to F.R. Lassiter, August 26, 31, 1900, H.C. Coles to F.R. Lassiter, September 10, 1900, F.R. Lassiter Papers; CAS to D.P. Halsey, September 29, October 5, 1900, Don P. Halsey Papers (#375), Manuscripts Department, University of Virginia Library; Tilley, *Bright-Tobacco*, 424.

42. CAS to editor, *Norfolk Virginian Pilot*, November 14, 1899, in *ibid.*, November 19 and November 9, 14, 1899, June 12, 13, 14, 15, 16, 1900; *Richmond Times*, 1899-1901; Staunton *Augusta County Argus*, January 16, 1900; Moger, *Virginia*, 171; contrast for this period the *Roanoke Times, Washington Post,* and *Petersburg Index Appeal.*

4. Middle of the Road: 1901-1906

1. The remaining tobacco tax was still three cents higher than the prewar level. *Richmond Dispatch*, January 5, 9, 11, 24, February 9, March 2, 1901; *Norfolk Virginian Pilot*, February 5, 1901; *Roanoke Times*, June 1, 1901; CAS to D.P. Halsey, January 7, 1901, Halsey Papers; F.R. Lassiter to Pat Raferty, January 4, 190[1], F.R. Lassiter to E.G. Leigh, Jr., January 4, 1901, F.R. Lassiter Papers.

2. *Norfolk Virginian Pilot*, February 28, 1901; *Washington Post*, May 11, 20, June 6, 1901; *Roanoke Times*, June 1, 1901.

3. John W. Carter, *Hon. Stafford G. Whittle for Supreme Court Judge* (Martinsville, 1900), 2ff.; J.L. Tredway to J.H. Tyler, August 21, 1900, A.J. Montague to J.H. Tyler, August 25, 1900, A.A. Phlegar to J.H. Tyler, August 27, December 19, 1900, Tyler Papers; A.J. Montague to S.G. Whittle, August 24, 25, 28, September 6, 1900, CAS to S.G. Whittle, September 20, November 30, 1900, E.W. Saunders to S.G. Whittle, September 13, 1900, Whittle Family Papers; A.J. Montague to W.A. Jones, September 19, 1900, Jones Papers.

4. CAS to S.G. Whittle, January 4, 189[4], February 17, 27, September 20, November 28, 30, December 6, 10, 1900, E.W. Saunders to S.G. Whittle, September 18, 1900, Whittle Family Papers; T.S. Martin to W.H. Mann, January 19, 1901, William Hodges Mann Papers (#8330), Manuscripts Department, University of Virginia Library; F.R. Lassiter to J.H. Tyler, August 22, 1900, James Hay to J.H. Tyler, August 22, 1900, E.G. Leigh, Jr., to F.R. Lassiter, January 28, 1901, F.R. Lassiter Papers; CAS to F.O. Hoffman, February 4, 1901, John Warwick Daniel Papers (#158), Manuscripts Department, University of Virginia Library; A.J. Montague to W.A. Jones, February 3, 1905, Jones Papers; *Norfolk Virginian Pilot*, January 31, 1901; *Richmond Dispatch*, February 3, 16, 1901.

5. Magruder, *Recent Administration*, 87; *Richmond Dispatch*, April 26, 1901.

6. J.W. Daniel to D.P. Halsey, April 23, 1901, CAS to D.P. Halsey, April 27, 1901, Halsey Papers; CAS to H.D. Flood, April 15, 1901, Flood Papers, LC; *Richmond Dispatch*, April 27, 1901.

7. T.S. Martin to W.E. Bibb, December 24, 1900, Bibb Papers; *Richmond Dispatch*, August 15, 1900; Kaufman, "Flood," 69-71.

8. F.R. Lassiter to J.H. Tyler, July 21, 1898, J.W. Womack to F.R. Lassiter, July 25, 1898, F.R. Lassiter Papers; Kaufman, "Flood," 59 n10; T.S. Martin to H.D. Flood, April 20, 1901, J.L. Lee to H.D. Flood, April 27, 1901, D.H. Rucker to H.D. Flood, May 5, 1901, R.E. Byrd to H.D. Flood, May 29, 1901, Edward Echols to H.D. Flood, June 21, 1901, Flood Papers, LC; *Washington Post*, May 15, June 4, 1901.

9. F.A. Massie to F.R. Lassiter, April 2, 1901, F.R. Lassiter to F.A. Massie, April 14, 1901, F.R. Lassiter Papers; F.O. Hoffman to J.W. Daniel, May 27, 1901, June 4, 1901, Daniel Papers, UVA; J.H. Tyler to W.A. Jones, April 11, 1905, Jones Papers; *Richmond Dispatch*, March 13, 1901; *Norfolk Virginian Pilot*, May 26, 1901; *Washington Post*, May 12, 1901; Larsen, *Montague*, 103-04; contrast Moger, *Virginia*, 176.

10. CAS to S.G. Whittle, May 8, 1901, Whittle Family Papers; F.O. Hoffman to J.W. Daniel June 4, 1901, Daniel Papers, UVA; *Richmond Dispatch*, May 4, 10, 17, 1901; *Washington Post*, May 7, 17, 1901; *Norfolk Virginian Pilot*, May 16, 17, 1901.

11. *Richmond Dispatch*, May 21, 22, 23, 1901; *Washington Post*, May 21, June 13, 1901; *Norfolk Virginian Pilot*, May 21, 1901.

12. F.O. Hoffman to J.W. Daniel, May 27, 1901, Daniel Papers, UVA; *Norfolk Virginian Pilot*, May 21, 1901; *Richmond Dispatch*, May 29, 1901.

13. Smith, *Mill on the Dan*, 51-53; *Danville Labor Advocate* (n.d.), reprinted in *American Federationist*, 8 (May 1901): 167-69, (July, 1901) 244; *Washington Post*, May 28, 29, 1901; *Norfolk Virginian Pilot*, May 28, 29, 1901; contrast Poindexter, "Glass," 450-51; Melton A. McLaurin, *Paternalism and Protest: Southern Cotton Mill Workers and Organized Labor, 1875-1905* (Westport, Conn., 1972), 161-68.

14. *Washington Post*, May 30, 1901; *Norfolk Virginian Pilot*, June 20, 21, 27, 1901; *Richmond Times*, June 18, 1901; *Richmond Dispatch*, June 16, 1901; R.E. Byrd to H.D. Flood, May 29, 1901, Flood Papers, LC.

15. *Richmond Times*, August 11, 1901; *Richmond Dispatch*, August 13, 14, 1901.

16. *Norfolk Virginian Pilot*, August 14, 15, 1901; Larsen, *Montague*, 106-9.

17. *Richmond News*, November 8, 1901; *Richmond Dispatch*, December 7, 1901; Poindexter, "Glass," 459-61; Larsen, *Montague*, 111-12; see R.E. Byrd to H.D. Flood, October 5, 1901, Flood Papers, LC, for the "great distaste and disfavor" felt in the Valley toward the constitutional convention.

18. *Richmond Dispatch*, August 14, 1901; *Richmond Times*, August 14, 1901; *Norfolk Virginian Pilot*, August 14, 1901; *Washington Post*, April 27, 1901. Compare Pulley, *Old Virginia*, 78-81.

19. Rixey Smith and Norman Beasley, *Carter Glass: A Biography* (New York, 1939), 418; John Goode, *Recollections of a Lifetime* (New York, 1906) 28ff.; Wythe W. Holt, Jr., "The Virginia Constitutional Convention of 1901-1902: A Reform Movement Which Lacked Substance," *VMBH*, 76 (January 1968): 85; A.C. Braxton to R.T. Irvine, May 1, 1901, C.V. Meredith to A.C. Braxton, July 5, 1902, Allen Caperton Braxton Papers (#3329), Manuscripts Department, University of Virginia Library.

20. J.F. Rixey to W.A. Jones, October 27, November 22, 1899, Jones Papers; *Washington Post*, May 29, June 8, 23, 1901; *Norfolk Virginian Pilot*, June 7, 1901; entry, January 7, 1933, Henry F. Ashurst, *A Many Colored Toga: The Diary of Henry Fountain Ashurst*, George F. Sparks, editor, (Tuscon, 1962), 327.

21. Holt, "Constitutional Convention," 79, 83, 87-102; Porter, *County Government*, 342; Magruder, *Recent Administration*, 192-99; Victor D. Weathers, "The Political Career Of Allen Caperton Braxton" (M.A. thesis, University of Virginia, 1956), 58-81; Thomas E. Gay, Jr., "The Virginia State Corporation Commission" (M.A. thesis, University of Virginia, 1965), 37ff.; Jacob N. Brenamen, *A History of Virginia Conventions* (Richmond, 1902), 93.

22. Qualifiers include Wynes, *Race Relations*, 56-65; *Old Virginia*, 103-24; Poindexter, "Glass," 465ff.; Kaufman, "Flood," 93-112; Wythe W. Holt, Jr., "Virginia's Constitutional Convention of 1901-1902" (Ph.D. diss., University of Virginia, 1979), 99ff.; contrast Larsen, *Montague*, 107-8, and Moger, *Virginia*, 183-202.

23. CAS to H.D. Flood, July 25, August 13, September 4, 1902, Flood Papers, LC; CAS to S.G. Whittle, July 30, 1902, Whittle Family Papers; Eugene Withers to A.C. Braxton, July 24, October 4, 1902, A.C. Braxton to Eugene Withers, October 6, 1902, CAS to A.C. Braxton, July 8, 30, 1902, Braxton Papers; J.H. Lindsey, editor, *Report of the Proceedings and Debates of the Constitutional Convention, State of Virginia*, 2 (Richmond, 1906), 3058-61.

24. W.F. Rhea to H.D. Flood, October 1, 1902, T.S. Martin to H.D. Flood, November 3, 1902, Flood Papers, LC; CAS to E.S. Reid, March 6, 1902, Swanson Papers, Duke University; Kaufman, "Flood," 66.

25. W.W. Price to A.B. Williams, April 25, 1902, Braxton Papers; CAS to F.R. Lassiter, December 18, 1901, F.R. Lassiter to W.B. McIlwaine, February 11, 1902, R.C. Kilmartin to Jake Fleming, September 19, 1902, F.R. Lassiter Papers.

26. J.C. Wysor to A.C. Braxton, December 29, 1902, A.C. Braxton to J.C. Wysor, January 24, 1902, Braxton Papers; A.J. Montague to J.L. Tredway, February 17, March 13, 24, 1903, A.J. Montague to W.A. Jones, September 4, 1903, Montague Papers; W.C. [Walter Coles] to H.S. Tucker, April 25, 1902 (the latter was written on Ways and Means Committee stationery, Swanson's

committee assignment), Tucker Family Papers; *Richmond Times*, December 11, 1902, January 11, 1903; *Danville Register*, December 10, 1902; *Washington Post*, December 11, 1902.

27. W.A. Taylor to A.J. Montague, August 18, 1902, A.J. Montague to Joseph Whitehead, June 24, 1904, Montague Papers.

28. CAS to F.R. Lassiter, July 28, 1903, F.R. Lassiter Papers; M.C. Kern to E.S. Reid, September 7, 1901, Swanson Papers, Duke University; *Richmond News Leader*, February 18, 1903; *Norfolk Virginian Pilot*, October 28, 1903; Smith, *Mill on the Dan*, 110-11; U.S. Senate Judiciary Committee, *Hearings, Maintenance of Lobby to Influence Legislation* (Washington, 1913), 371-72.

29. A.J. Montague to T.F. Ryan, May 30, June 4, 1904, Montague Papers; CAS to H.D. Flood, May 10, 1904, Flood Papers, LC; CAS to D.B. Hill, August 28, 1900, David Bennett Hill Papers, Syracuse University; *Norfolk Virginian Pilot*, June 7, 8, 9, 10, 1904; Woodward, *New South*, 458-59; John R. Lambert, *Arthur Pue Gorman* (Baton Rouge, 1953), 312; Bass, *Hill*, 246; Thomas Fortune Ryan, "The Political Opportunity of the South," *North American Review*: 176 (February 1903), 161-72.

30. A.J. Montague to W.A. Jones, July 16, August 24, September 13, 1904, Jones Papers; A.J. Montague to W.A. Jones, May 25, 1904, Montague Papers; *Norfolk Virginian Pilot*, August 10, September 11, November 10, 1904; Weathers, "Braxton," 102-19; Richard B. Doss, "Democrats in the Doldrums: Virginia and the Democratic National Convention of 1904," *JSH* 20 (November 1954): 511-29.

31. H.S. Tucker to E.P. Wheeler, November 15, 1904, Tucker Family Papers; *Richmond News Leader*, April 23, November 28, 1904; *Staunton Dispatch and News*, August 8, 12, 1905.

32. *Richmond News Leader*, November 29, 1904; Andrew A. Buni, *The Negro in Virginia Politics, 1902-1965* (Charlottesville, 1967), 20-23; Kaufman, "Flood," 110-11.

33. J.R. Horsley to H.D. Flood, October 16, 1903, CAS to H.D. Flood, June 29, October 27, 1903, Flood Papers, LC; Marshall McCormick to H.S. Tucker, November 14, 1903, Tucker Family Papers; A.C. Braxton to J.C. Wysor, August 19, 1904, Braxton Papers; A.J. Montague to J.L. Tredway, March 13, July 1, 6, 1903, J.C. Gent to A.J. Montague, May 9, 1904, Montague Papers; S.H. Tyler to J.H. Tyler, July 3, 1903, Tyler Papers; *Richmond News Leader*, June 11, 1904; *Norfolk Virginian Pilot*, September 4, 1904.

34. CAS to H.D. Flood, June 29, 1904, Flood Papers, LC; W.A. Anderson to H.S. Tucker, December 4, 1903, H.S. Tucker to E.C. Venable, November 16, 1904, Tucker Family Papers; *Richmond News Leader*, March 14, 23, April 18, 1904.

35. J.T. Lawless to W.H. Mann, September 5, 1900, John Lamb to James Mann, September 18, 1900, H.D. Flood to W.H. Mann, August 29, 1900, January 7, 1901, T.S. Martin to W.H. Mann, January 19, 1901, Mann Papers; Henry C. Ferrell, Jr., "Prohibition, Reform and Politics in Virginia, 1895-1916," *Studies in the History of the South, 1875-1922* in *East Carolina College Publications in History*, 3 (Greenville, 1966), 185-87; Larsen, *Montague*, 222; *Richmond Times-Dispatch*, September 22, 1905.

36. W.H. Mann to James Cannon, Jr., April 4, 1908, James Cannon, Jr., Papers, Manuscript Department, Perkins Library, Duke University; Ferrell, "Prohibition, Reform, and Politics" 188-190; *Richmond News Leader*, March 23, April 13, 1904; *Norfolk Virginian Pilot*, April 17, 19, 1904; Cannon, Jr., *Own Story*, 120-25; Hohner, "Prohibition," 15-38.

37. Ferrell, "Prohibition, Reform, and Politics," 176-82.

38. Marjorie Faye Underhill, "The Virginia Phase of the Ogden Movement," (M.A. thesis, University of Virginia, 1952), 66-69; Heatwole, *Education in Virginia*, 277; Louis R. Harlan, *Separate and Unequal* (Chapel Hill, 1958), 135-56.

39. Charles W. Dabney, *Universal Education in the South*, 2 (Chapel Hill, 1936), 327; see Joseph D. Eggleston, Jr., and Robert W. Bruere, *The Work of the Rural School* (New York, 1918).

40. *Danville Register*, January 8, 1905; *Norfolk Virginian Pilot*, January 8, April 29, August 20, 1905.

41. J.S. Bryan to J.W. Daniel, January 13, 1905, Daniel Papers, UVA; *Richmond News Leader*, January 25, 1905; *Staunton Dispatch and News*, July 29, 1905; *Petersburg Index Appeal*, June 5, 1905.

42. S.C. Ferguson to H.D. Flood, January 30, 1905, Flood Papers, LC; *Richmond News Leader*, February 4, March 22, April 23, 1905; *Richmond Times-Dispatch*, July 7, 12, 1905; Larsen, *Montague*, 216-46.

43. R.C. Kilmartin to F.R. Lassiter, May 3, 1905, F.R. Lassiter Papers; J.D. Patton to J.W. Daniel, June 12, 16, 28, 1905, Daniel Papers, UVA; *Richmond News Leader*, January 27, 1905; *Richmond Times-Dispatch*, July 25, 1905.

44. *Roanoke Times*, August 3, 4, 1905; *Norfolk Virginian Pilot*, August 4, 15, 1905; *Staunton Dispatch and News*, August 8, 12, 13, 15, 1905; Crandal MacKay, *Claude Swanson and the Postal Scandal* (Alexandria, 1905), 8 pp.

45. J.N. Hutchieson to J.T. Ellyson, May 20, 1905, Ellyson Papers. See Jones, Tucker, and Tyler papers between January-September, 1905. Compare and contrast Larsen, *Montgue*, 233, 240-43; Moger *Virginia*, 210-12; Pulley, *Old Virginia Restored*, 127; Kaufman, "Flood," 130-34; Woodward, *New South*, 371-72; Harlan, *Separate and Unequal*, 156.

46. *Richmond Times-Dispatch*, August 23, 1905; *Staunton Dispatch and News*, August 25, 1905; W.H. Mann to H.D. Flood, March 9, 1905, H.D. Flood to W.H. Mann, March 13, 1905, Flood Papers, LC.

47. *Richmond Times-Dispatch*, August 10, September 19, October 17, 18, 1905; *Staunton Dispatch and News*, September 19, 1905; *Richmond News Leader*, November 4, 1905; Buni, *Negro in Va. Politics*, 51-53; Moger, *Virginia*, 66, 213, 219; CAS, *Address at Hanover Court House*, 3.

48. J.D. Patton to J.W. Daniel, September 14, 1905, Daniel Papers, UVA; J.T. Ellyson to W.A. Garrett, October 14, 1905, Garrett Papers; *Richmond News Leader,* October 4, 1905; *Danville Register*, January 15, 1905.

5. Concur and Cooperate: 1906-1910

1. A much reduced version of this chapter appears in Edward Younger and James Tice Moore, editors, *The Governors of Virginia, 1860-1978* (Charlottesville, 1982), 171-81. *Lynchburg News*, February 2, 1910; Harlan, *Separate and Unequal*, 156; Peter G. Filene, "An Obituary for the Progressive Movement," *American Quarterly*, 12 (Spring 1970): 20-34; John D. Buenker et al., *Progressivism* (Cambridge, 1977), passim; Dewey W. Grantham, *Southern Progressivism: The Reconciliation of Progress and Tradition* (Knoxville, 1983), passim.

2. Faulkner, *Decline of Laissez Faire*, 320-38;

3. For the era's booster spirit, see Carl Abbott, "Norfolk in the New Century: The Jamestown Exposition and Urban Boosterism," *VMHB*, 85 (January 1977), 86-96.

4. CAS to F.R. Lassiter, November 15, 1905, F.R. Lassiter Papers; B.P. Owen, Jr., to J.H. Tyler, August 8, 1905, Tyler Papers; *Richmond News Leader*, December 26, 1905.

5. *Richmond News Leader*, December 26, 1905, February 1, 2, 1906; *Norfolk Virginian Pilot*, February 1, 2, 3, 1905; Clipping, Swanson Scrapbook.

6. *Richmond Times-Dispatch*, February 2, 1906; *Norfolk Virginian Pilot*, January 31, February 12, 1906; *Richmond News Leader*, February 1, 1906; CAS, *Addresses, Messages and Proclamations* (Richmond, 1910), 3-30.

7. William A. Christian, *Richmond, Her Past and Present* (Richmond, 1912), 502 and passim; City of Richmond, *Richmond, Virginia, 1907* (Richmond, 1907), 16 pp.; Christopher Silver, *Twentieth-Century Richmond: Planning, Politics, And Race* (Knoxville, 1984), 12 and passim.

8. Ralph C. McDaniel, *The Virginia Constitutional Convention of 1901-1902* (Baltimore, 1928), 98-99; Larsen, *Montague*, 120; Magruder, *Recent Administration*, 196-97; Holt, "Constitutional Convention," 89-99.

9. Larsen, *Montague*, 149. Listening to Swanson's inaugural address were twenty-eight returning senators and thirty-three veteran delegates.

10. Bland Massie to H.D. Flood, April 11, 1902, Flood Papers, LC; CAS to C.T. Lassiter, August 28, October 4, November 17, 1905, Charles T. Lassiter Papers, Manuscript Department, William Perkins Library, Duke University; CAS to W.L. Garrett, October 4, November 17, 1905, E.S. Reid to W.L. Garrett, December 11, 1905, Garrett Papers.

11. Virginia General Assembly, *The Manual of the Senate and House of Delegates of Virginia, 1906* (Richmond, 1906), passim. This volume and the 1908 edition were used for assessment of internal legislative relationships. H.D. Flood to R.E. Byrd, January 15, 1906, H.D. Flood to A.C. Gordon, June 14, 1907, Flood Papers, LC; Hall interview; *Norfolk Virginian Pilot*, January 9, 11, 20, 1906.

12. R.A. James to W.A. Garrett, November 23, 1905, E.S. Reid to W.A. Garrett, December 11, 1905, W.A. Garrett Papers; H.D. Flood to R.E. Byrd, March 6, 1906, April 24, 27, May 29, 1907, R.E. Byrd to H.D. Flood, April 24, May 29, August 29, 1907, F.C. Moon to H.D. Flood, March 6, 1906, H.D. Flood to Walter Watson, May 29, 1907, Flood Papers, LC. See *Manual for Senate and House* for these sessions.

13. R.W. Withers to C.T. Lassiter, May 13, August 27, 1907, C.T. Lassiter to R.W. Withers, August 29, 1907, C.T. Lassiter Papers; R.E. Byrd to H.D. Flood, December 17, 1907, January 8, 14, 1908, T.S. Martin to R.E. Byrd, December 31, 1907, R.S. Turk to H.D. Flood, October 4, 1907, H.D. Flood to R.E. Byrd, January 8, 1908, Flood Papers, LC; *Norfolk Virginian Pilot*, May 5, 1907.

14. H.D. Flood to CAS, April 16, 1907, CAS to H.D. Flood, April 17, 1907, H.D. Flood to Edward Echols, September 2, 6, 1907, T.S. Martin to H.D. Flood, September 3, 1907, Edward Echols to H.D. Flood, September 5, 1907, Flood Papers, LC; C.T. Lassiter to F.W. Sims, December 7, 1907, C.T. Lassiter to N.B. Early, December 17, 1907, C.T. Lassiter Papers; *Norfolk Virginian Pilot*, August 30, 1907, January 8, 19, 1908; Poindexter, "Glass," 546; Moger, *Virginia*, 99, 102, 120, 232.

15. T.S. Martin to H.D. Flood, May 14, September 3, 1907, January 9, 1908, Edward Echols to H.D. Flood, September 5, 1907, W.H. Mann to H.D. Flood, January 3, 1908, Flood Papers, LC; G.B. Keezell to C.T. Lassiter, February 21, 1908, C.T. Lassiter Papers; *Washington Post*, June 8, 1901; Magruder, *Recent Administration*, 33, Raymond C. Dingledine, *Madison College: The First Fifty Years, 1908-1958* (Harrisonburg, 1959), 6-12. See *Manual of Senate and House* for these sessions.

16. C.T. Lassiter to John Whitehead, July 28, 1904, C.T. Lassiter to C.O. Hix, August 22, 1904, C.T. Lassiter to Northup and Wickham, September 3, 1904, C.T. Lassiter to Baker Asphalt Paving Company, October 1, 1904, C.T. Lassiter to CAS, January 9, 14, November 18, December 28, 1905, C.T. Lassiter to J.E. Willard, January 23, 1905, C.T. Lassiter to "Dear Sir," February 18, 1905, C.T. Lassiter to Henry Warden, February 21, 1905, C.T. Lassiter to Public School Teachers, Fourth Congressional District, March 6, 1905, CAS to C.T. Lassiter, November 17, December 8, 1905, C.T. Lassiter papers; Larsen, *Montague*, 176-79.

17. Memorandum to [P. T.] Otey, March 19, 1902, L.E. Johnson to Martin Dodge, June 27 (?), 1904, "National Aid to Road Building, 1892-1912" File 4, Bureau of Public Roads, RG 30, NA; CAS to C.T. Lassiter, December 6, 1905, C.T. Lassiter Papers; Virginia General Assembly, *Acts and Joint Resolutions Passed by the General Assembly of the State of Virginia during the Session of 1906* (Richmond, 1906), 50, 71-74; Virginia General Assembly, *Journal of the Senate of the Commonwealth of Virginia* (Richmond, 1906), (January 12, 1906) 34, (February 7, 1906) 171; *Cong. Rec.* 54 Cong., 1 sess., 28 (June 10, 1896), 6403-4, 56 Cong., 1 sess., 33 (December 8, 1899), 164.

18. R.W. Withers to C.T. Lassiter, August 22, 1907, CAS to C.T. Lassiter, December 26, 1908, January 21, 25, 1909, G.W. Rogers to C.T. Lassiter, January 18, 1909, C.T. Lassiter Papers; Frank M. Winston, "The Highway Policy of the State of Virginia" (M.A. thesis, University of

Virginia, 1943), 55-56; Virginia General Assembly, *Acts and Joint Resolutions, 1908*, 90-99; *Richmond News Leader*, June 15, 1906, February 10, 11, 1909; *Manufacturers Record*, 55 (February 4, 1909), 69.

19. Edward F. Overton, "A Study of the Life and Work of Joseph Dupey Eggleston, Junior," (Ph.D. diss., University of Virginia, 1943), 12-13. See J.D. Eggleston, Jr., to H.B. Frissell, March (?) 1902, in ibid., 554-88, for a catalog of Virginia school deficiences. Cannon, Jr., *Own Story*, 120; Moger, *Virginia*, 251-53; Thompson, *Presbyterians*, 3: 164-65, passim; *Richmond News Leader*, February 10, 1906; Virginia General Assembly, *Acts and Joint Resolutions, 1906*, 221, 350-52, 446-48; CAS, *Addresses*, 20; Carnegie Foundation for the Advancement of Teaching, *Sixth Annual Report of the President and Treasurer* (New York, 1911), 5, 65.

20. J.D. Eggleston, Jr., to H.D. Frissell, March (?) 1902, in Overton "Eggleston," 583-87; E.A. Alderman to Southern Education Board, November (?) 1906, Edward A. Alderman Papers (#1001), Manuscripts Department, University of Virginia Library; *Richmond News Leader*, January 24, 1906; Dabney, *Education in the South*, vol. 2, 326; Harlan, *Separate and Unequal*, 156-57.

21. Magruder, *Recent Administration*, 21; Eggleston, "Claude Swanson," 2.

22. H.D. Flood to J.N. Button, February 14, 1906, H.D. Flood to T.S. Martin, April 6, 1907, CAS to H.D. Flood, January 29, April 20, 1907, H.D. Flood to CAS, January 30, December 16, 1907, H.D. Flood to N.B. Tucker, January 30, 1907, Flood Papers, LC; *Richmond News Leader*, December 13, 14, 1906, February 5, 1907, April 17, 1908; Magruder, *Recent Administration*, 43.

23. J.D. Eggleston, Jr., to C.W. Dabney, October 17, 1933, in Dabney, *Education in the South*, 2:331; Eggleston, "Claude Swanson," 2.

24. *Norfolk Virginian Pilot*, June 19, 20, 23, 24, 25, 26, 27, 1909; Magruder, *Recent Administration*, 33-34.

25. E.A. Alderman to CAS, June, 28, 1909, Alderman Papers. Contrast Harlan, *Separate and Unequal*, 159-60.

26. H.D. Flood to G.H. Denny, January 4, October 7, 1907, CAS to H.D. Flood, August 31, 1907, Flood Papers, LC; Eggleston, "Swanson," 2; Dingledine, *Madison College*, 1-12; Moger, *Virginia*, 84, 252-53; Kinnean, *V. P. I.*, 174-76, 178, 197-98; *Virginia Journal of Education*, 1 (October, 1907): 17-20; J.D. Eggleston, Jr., "The Virginia Teacher's Pension Fund," *VJE*, 1 (April, 1908): 1-7; George B. Keezell, "History of the Establishment of the State Teachers College at Harrisonburg," *Virginia Teacher*, (May 1928): 133-40.

27. Magruder, *Recent Administration*, 59-60; Moore, *Virginia Debt Controversy*, 48, 88, 103-4; Woodward, *New South*, 406; Jack T. Kirby, *Darkness at Dawning: Race and Reform in the Progressive South* (Philadelphia, 1972), 104-7; compare and contrast Harlan, *Separate and Unequal*, 135-169.

28. CAS to J.E. White, February 20, 1907, in *Manufacturers Record*, 51 (February 28, 1907), 180; John E. White, "The Need of a Southern Program on the Negro Problem," *South Atlantic Quarterly*, 6 (April, 1907): 177-88.

29. *Richmond Times-Dispatch*, August 13, 1907; *Norfolk Virginian Pilot*, August 15, 1907; Brooks M. Barnes, "The Onancock Race Riot of 1907," *VMHB*, 92 (July 1984): 336-51.

30. A.C. Braxton to J.C. Wysor, December 27, 1902, June 15, 1905, Braxton Papers; Magruder, *Recent Administration*, 158-59, 176; Larsen, *Montague*, 130-33; McDaniel, *Constitutional Convention*, 84; *Norfolk Virginian Pilot*, September 15, 1905.

31. Virginia General Assembly, "Inquiry on Assessment of Railroads," Senate Document 4, *Journal of the Senate, 1906*, 3-8; Magruder, *Recent Administration*, 176-78; Ferguson, *State Regulation*, 69-71; *Norfolk Virginian Pilot*, October 25, 1907.

32. J.N. Button to H.D. Flood, August 8, 1906, Flood Papers, LC: *Richmond Times-Dispatch*, April 3, May 2, July 1, August 2, 1906; Magruder, *Recent Administration*, 159-60.

33. Camm Patteson to H.D. Flood, March 11, 1906, Flood Papers, LC; Virginia General Assembly, *Acts and Joint Resolutions, 1906*, 451-52; *Norfolk Virginian Pilot*, March 15, 1906; *Richmond Times-Dispatch*, July 3, 4, 19, 1906; Ferguson, *State Regulation*, 69-71, 76.

34. H.F. Byrd to H.D. Flood, October 20, 1908, Flood Papers, LC; *Danville Register*, November 7, 1905; Ferguson, *State Regulation*, 69-71, 76.

35. H.D. Flood to R.E. Byrd, March 16, 1906, Flood Papers, LC; B.T. Crump to H.S. Tucker, July 22, 1905, Tucker Family Papers; *Norfolk Virginian Pilot*, April 13, 1907; Larsen, *Montague*, 236-37.

36. R.C. Kilmartin to F.R. Lassiter, October 28, 1905, F.R. Lassiter Papers; H.D. Flood to A.C. Gordon, May 3, 1907, Flood Papers, LC; *Norfolk Virginian Pilot*, May 2, 3, 1907.

37. C.J. Faulkner to H.D. Flood, August 1, 1907, Flood Papers, LC; *Norfolk Virginian Pilot*, July 25, 28, 1907; *Richmond News Leader*, July 22, 1907; *Richmond Times-Dispatch*, July 27, 29, 1907; *Richmond Evening Journal*, July 22, 26, 1907.

38. Flood apologized lamely to Faulkner: "The feeling here in Virginia is pretty high and some action had to be taken." H.D. Flood to C.J. Faulkner, August 5, 1907, Flood Papers, LC; *Richmond News Leader*, August 3, 1907; *Norfolk Virginian Pilot*, August 4, 1907; *Richmond Times-Dispatch*, August 4, 1907; Ferguson, *State Regulation*, 77-80.

39. H.D. Flood to A.C. Gordon, May 3, 4, 1907, H.D. Flood to MacDonald Lee, March 4, 1908, H.D. Flood to W.N. Dawson, March 7, 1908, Flood Papers, LC; W.H. Mann to C.T. Lassiter, February 29, 1908, C.T. Lassiter Papers; J.M. McCormick to H.S. Tucker, February 28, March 5, 1908, Tucker Family Papers; W.A. Jones to H.C. Stuart, February 18, 1908, Jones Papers; Virginia General Assembly, *Journal of the House of Delegates of the State of Virginia, 1908* (Richmond, 1908), 647-665, (February 27, 1908) 696-97; *Norfolk Virginian Pilot*, January 22, 30, February 2, 4, 26, 28, 1908; *Richmond News Leader*, January 22, 23, February 26, 28, 1908; William H.T. Squires, *Through Centuries Three: A Short History of the People of Virginia* (Portsmouth, Va., 1929), 566; Jack T. Kirby, *Westmoreland Davis, Virginia Planter-Politician, 1859-1942* (Charlottesville, 1968), 54.

40. W.A. Jones to E.E. Montague, February 22, 1908, Jones Papers; H.D. Flood to R.E. Byrd, January 23, May 29, 1907, H.D. Flood to T.S. Martin, February 15, 1907, T.S. Martin to R.E. Byrd, December 31, 1907, Flood Papers, LC; *Richmond News Leader*, February 1, 2, 1907, March 5, 1908; *Norfolk Virginian Pilot*, July 1, 1906, July 7, 1907, February 4, March 27, 1908; McDaniel, *Constitutional Convention*, 85, 86; Virginia General Assembly, *House Journal, 1908*, 318-83, 716-21, (March 26, 1908) 1030-31; "Report of the Committee to Investigate Eastern State Hospital," House Document Number 3, ibid., 3-25.

41. C.T. Lassiter to F.R. Lassiter, April 7, 1908, C.T. Lassiter Papers; Virginia General Assembly, *Acts and Joint Resolutions, 1906*, 36-37, 248-250; Virginia General Assembly, *Acts and Joint Resolutions, 1908*, 266-74, 295; *Richmond News Leader*, March 27, 1906, March 14, 31, December 22, 1908; *Norfolk Virginian Pilot*, March 5, 1908; *Richmond Times-Dispatch*, July 8, 1939; James, *Social Awakening*, 2-6, 177-88.

42. CAS to H.D. Flood, January 29, September 7, 1907, H.D. Flood to J.R. Horsley, January 29, 1907, R.E. Byrd to H.D. Flood, February 9, 1908, Flood Papers, LC; clipping, Swanson Scrapbook; CAS to J.H. Tyler, November 5, 1906, December 26, 1907, Tyler Papers; C.T. Lassiter to F.R. Lassiter, January 18, 1908, C.T. Lassiter Papers; *Danville Register*, January 15, 1905; *Richmond News Leader*, February 28, 1907; *Norfolk Virginian Pilot*, March 20, April 1, 1908; *Charlottesville Daily Progress*, August 2, 1910.

43. CAS to Blanche Swanson, August 23, 1906, September 6, 1907, Swanson Scrapbook; CAS to H.D. Flood, September 14, 1906, December 13, 1909, H.D. Flood to Lewis Williams, October 3, 1906, H.D. Flood to T.S. Martin, April 16, 1907, J.R. Ellerson to CAS, December 11, 1909, H.D. Flood to H.F. Byrd, March 3, 1910, Flood Papers, LC; CAS to T.N. Page, March 15, 1907, T.N. Page to CAS, May 17, 1907, Thomas Nelson Page Papers, Manuscript Department, William R. Perkins Library, Duke University; L.W. Page to CAS, October 30, 1906, CAS to L.W. Page, October 6, 11, 21, 1906, File 1317, RG 30, NA; *Richmond Times-Dispatch*, July 5, 18, September 16, 20, October 11, December 15, 1906, April 21, 23, 26, May 5, June 13, 21, August 17, 1907; *Richmond News Leader*, June 26, 1906, February 10, 18, 22, March 5, April 15, 29,

September 30, November 10, 1909; CAS, "Virginia: An Address," VJE 1 (July 1908): 1-7, 17; Robert T. Taylor, "The Jamestown Tercentennial Exposition of 1907," *VMHB*, 65 (April 1957): 169-208; Magruder, *Recent Administration*, 171-73.

    44. CAS, *Addresses*, 115-31; *Richmond Times-Dispatch*, January 12, 1909.

    45. Eggleston soon encountered difficulty in the legislature without Swanson. Harlan, *Separate and Unequal*, 161; Eggleston clipping, February, 1910(?), Swanson Scrapbook; *Norfolk Virginian Pilot*, January 13, 14, 27, 1910; *Roanoke Times*, January 13, February 1, 1910; *Richmond News Leader*, January 12, 1910; *Richmond Times-Dispatch*, January 12, February 1, 1910; *Bristol Herald*, January 14, February 2, 1910; *Lynchburg News*, February 2, 1910; *Newport News Times Herald*, February 1, 1910.

6. The Latest Successful Comeback: 1906-1911

    1. R.A. James to W.A. Garrett, January 22, 1909, Garrett Papers; R.P. Caldwell to H.S. Tucker, February 27, 1909, Tucker Family Papers; *Richmond News Leader*, December 28, 1909.

    2. J.T. Ellyson to H.D. Flood, September 12, October 5, 1906, CAS to H.D. Flood, September 14, 1906, J.N. Button to H.D. Flood, April 2, 1907, Allen Potts to J.M. Herndon, December 15, 1908, Allen Potts to E.W. Saunders, December 15, 1908, Flood Papers, LC; R.A. James to W.A. Garrett, January 22, 1909, November 11, 1911, Garrett Papers; *Richmond News Leader*, May 8, 1906; *Richmond Times-Dispatch*, November 7, 13, 1906, November 6, 10, 1908, March 30, 1909.

    3. Entry, March 10, 1902, Walter A. Watson Diary, Virginia Historical Society, Richmond, Virginia. Parts of the diary have been published as Walter A. Watson, "Notes on Southside Virginia" in *Bulletin of the Virginia State Library*: 15 (September 1925). Alexander Hamilton to H.S. Tucker, March 27, 1903, J.O. Murray to H.S. Tucker, March 4, 1907, Tucker Family Papers; J.W. Daniel to H.D. Flood, September 22, 1906, H.D. Flood to T.S. Martin, April 16, 1907, Flood Papers, LC; *Norfolk Virginian Pilot*, March 21, 1908.

    4. CAS to J.W. Daniel, October 19, 1906, June 27, 1908, March 3, 1909, Daniel Papers, Duke University; R.A. James to W.A. Garrett, December 28, 1909, Garrett Papers.

    5. T.S. Martin to H.D. Flood, March 21, 1907, H.F. Byrd to H.D. Flood, October 20, 1908, Flood Papers, LC; H.S. Tucker to S.S.P. Patteson, April 13, 1905, A.C. Braxton to H.S. Tucker, April 25, 1906; G.S. Shackelford to H.S. Tucker, May 31, 1906, Tucker Family Papers.

    6. Carter Glass to W.A. Jones, June 26, 1908, Jones Papers; H.D. Flood to W.P. Barksdale, August 5, 1907, Flood Papers, LC; *Richmond News Leader*, January 29, 1903; *Norfolk Virginian Pilot*, March 18, 1908; Ferrell, "Prohibition and Politics," 192-93, 201 n34; Poindexter, "Glass," 440 n35.

    7. T.S. Martin to H.D. Flood, March 21, 1907, May 30, 1908, May 12, 21, 1909, H.D. Flood to T.S. Martin, February 15, 1907, H.D. Flood to W.H. Mann, January 16, 1908, Flood Papers, LC; J.F. Rixey to F.S. McCandlish, June 4, 1906, Jones Papers; R.C. Kilmartin to F.R. Lassiter, October 28, December 13, 1905, H.D. Flood to F.R. Lassiter, December 31, 1905, F.R. Lassiter Papers; C.T. Lassiter to F.R. Lassiter, January 18, 1908, R.C. Kilmartin to C.T. Lassiter, January 16, 1910, R.W. Withers to C.T. Lassiter, January 28, 1910, C.T. Lassiter Papers; CAS to J.T. Ellyson, September 8, 15, 1910, Ellyson Papers; *Richmond Times-Dispatch*, September 21, 1906, February 9, June 20, 1907; *Norfolk Virginian Pilot*, May 5, 1904, September 2, 1906, March 29, 1908.

    8. H.D. Flood to R.E. Byrd, November 8, 1907, CAS to T.S. Martin, September 8, 1910, Flood Papers, LC; W.A. Jones to C.C. Baker, May 17, 1906, Jones Papers; *Richmond Times-Dispatch*, November 13, 1906, April 27, 1908; T.K. Cartmell, *Shenandoah Valley Pioneers and Their Descendants: A History of Frederick County, Virginia, from Its Foundation in 1738 to 1908* (Berryville, Va., 1963), 124.

    9. H.D. Flood to T.F. Ryan, February 28, 1906, March 21, 1908, T.F. Ryan to H.D. Flood, October 30, November 19, 1906, January 2, 1908, H.D. Flood to Frederick Blynch, May 7, 1908,

H.D. Flood to Joseph Button, April 14, 1908, Flood Papers, LC; *Norfolk Virginian Pilot*, March 21, 25, 1908; *Richmond Times-Dispatch*, March 21, 1908; Coletta, *Bryan*, 1:396-97.

10. Carter Glass to W.J. Bryan, June 25, 1908, Carter Glass Papers (#2913), Manuscripts Department, University of Virginia Library; John Lamb to W.A. Jones, September 19, 1906, Jones Papers; J.H. Tyler to CAS, September 3, 1906, CAS to W.H. Tyler, September 5, 1906, December 27, 1906, A.F. Thomas to J.H. Tyler, September 8, 1906, Tyler Papers; *Richmond Times-Dispatch*, January 20, May 21, 1908; *Richmond News Leader*, February 18, 1908.

11. H.D. Flood to T.F. Ryan, March 21, June 5, 1908, J.N. Brenamen to H.D. Flood, March 29, 1908, T.S. Martin to H.D. Flood, May 4, 30, 1908, H.D. Flood to J.B. Trehy, May 20, 1908, H.D. Flood to G.H. Denny, May 27, 1908, Flood Papers, LC; W.A. Jones to W.H. Ryland, March 3, 1908, Jones Papers; CAS to W.H. Tyler, March 31, 1908, W.J. Bryan to J.H. Tyler, April 1, 1908, W.E. Harris to Mrs. W.H. Tyler, April 14, 1908, S.H. Tyler to J.H. Tyler, April 16, 1908, Tyler Papers; *Richmond News Leader*, May 16, 1908; *Richmond Times-Dispatch*, March 21, 26, 1908; *Norfolk Virginian Pilot*, March 21, 26, 1908.

12. Democratic National Committee, *Proceedings, 1904*, 81; G.H. Denny to H.D. Flood, May 30, 1908, E.W. Saunders to H.D. Flood, June 3, 1908, H.D. Flood to T.F. Ryan, June 5, 1908, T.S. Martin to H.D. Flood, June 5, 1908, H.D. Flood to T.S. Martin, June 5, 1908, Flood Papers, LC; *Richmond News Leader*, June 11, 12, 22, 1908; *Richmond Times-Dispatch*, June 9, 11, 1908.

13. Carter Glass to W.J. Bryan, June 5, 1908, Glass Papers; Carter Glass to W.A. Jones, June 26, 1908, Jones Papers; *Richmond News Leader*, July 8, 19, 1908; Democratic National Committee, *Official Reports of the Proceedings of the Democratic National Convention* (Chicago, 1908), 121, 195-200; Coletta, *Bryan*, 1:402-7; Richard C. Bain, *Convention Decisions and Voting Records* (Washington, 1960), 175-76, Appendix D.

14. E.A. Alderman to T.N. Page, November 9, 1908, Alderman Papers; T.S. Martin to H.D. Flood, June 20, 1908, H.D. Flood to T.F. Ryan, June 22, 1908, R.A. James to H.D. Flood, June 27, 1908, Flood Papers; LC; *Richmond News Leader*, July 22, October 6, 7, 1908; Larsen, *Montague*, 250-53.

15. Ferrell, "Prohibition, Reform and Politics," 175-224; compare and contrast Robert A. Hohner, "Prohibition and Virginia Politics: William Hodges Mann versus Henry St. George Tucker, 1909," *VMHB*, 74 (January 1966): 88-107, and Moger, *Virginia*, 215-19. W.A. Jones to H.S. Tucker, September 4, 1906, Tucker Family Papers; W.A. Jones to E.E. Montague, January 4, 1907, W.A. Jones to J.K. Ayers, January 16, 1907, W.A. Jones to R.L. Ailsworth, January 18, 1908, W.A. Jones to H.C. Stuart, February 18, 1908, H.C. Stuart to W.A. Jones, August 10, 1908, Jones Papers; W.H. Mann to James Cannon, Jr., October 24, December 5, 1908, Cannon Papers; *Richmond Times-Dispatch*, December 29, 1908, January 8, 21, February 1, 9, 1909; *Norfolk Virginian Pilot,* February 11, 1909.

16. T.S. Martin to H.D. Flood, May 14, 1907, July 23, September 10, 1908, W.H. Mann to H.D. Flood, September 16, 19, 1908, April 23, 1909, H.D. Flood to G.H. Denny, February 27, 1909, Flood Papers, LC; H.S. Tucker to G.B. Keezell, March 9, 1909, R.S. Ker to J.H. Rhudy, June 2, 1909, J.T. Clement to H.S. Tucker, August 19, 1909, H.S. Tucker to Alexander Hamilton, March 29, 1910, Tucker Family Papers; James Mann to F.R. Lassiter, April 8, 1909, F.R. Lassiter Papers.

17. W.H. Mann to James Cannon, Jr., October 24, 1908, Cannon Papers; H.D. Flood to G.H. Denny, June 28, 1909, H.D. Flood to T.S. Martin, August 3, 1909, H.D. Flood to A.S. Priddy, July 12, 1910, Flood papers, LC; *Richmond Times-Dispatch*, March 11, 12, 1909; *Norfolk Virginian Pilot*, July 25, August 25, 26, 1909; *Richmond News Leader*, March 16, 1911; Ferrell, "Prohibition, Reform and Politics," 210-21.

18. J.M. McCormick to H.S. Tucker, February 15, 1909, Eugene Withers to H.S. Tucker, August 20, 1909, Tucker Family Papers; T.S. Martin to H.D. Flood, March 21, 1907, CAS to H.D. Flood, October 7, 1909, H.D. Flood to G.H. Denny, November 8, 1909, Flood Papers, LC; *Richmond News Leader*, September 28, 29, 30, 1909; *Bristol Herald Courier*, October 30, 1909; *Newsport News Times Herald*, September 28, 1909.

19. Contrast Moger, *Virginia*, 218-22, Pulley, *Old Virginia*, 160-63, Hohner, "Prohibition," 106-7. J.M. McCormick to H.S. Tucker, February 15, 1909, H.S. Tucker to H.C. Stuart, September 8, 17, 1909, March 4, 1910, H.S. Tucker to A.C. Strode, September 11, 22, 1909, C.J. Faulkner to H.S. Tucker, December 3, 1909, H.S. Tucker to H.D. Flood, February 24, 1910, W.E. Harris to H.S. Tucker, August 12, 1911, Tucker Family Papers; C.C. Carlin to H.D. Flood, October 3, 1910, H.D. Flood to H.F. Byrd, March 3, 1910, Flood Papers, LC; *Roanoke Times*, March 1, 2, 4, 1910, *Richmond News Leader*, February 13, 1910, *Richmond Times-Dispatch*, January 31, March 4, 5, 1910.

20. H.D. Flood to CAS, January 22, 1910, W.E. Carson to H.F. Byrd, February 25, 1910, H.D. Flood to H.F. Byrd, March 3, 1910, CAS to H.D. Flood, March 14, 1910, Allen Potts to H.D. Flood, March 15, 1910, J.R. Ellerson to H.D. Flood, March 28, 1910, Flood Papers, LC; *Richmond News Leader*, January 7, 25, March 8, 9, 11, 16, 1910; *Newport News Times Herald*, March 17, 1910.

21. *Charlottesville Daily Progress*, August 2, 1910; *Roanoke Times*, March 17, 1910; *Richmond Times-Dispatch*, January 12, February 1, 1910; *Newport News Times Herald*, March 17, 1909; Cannon, Jr., *Own Story*, 139.

22. H.D. Flood to A.S. Priddy, July 12, 1910, Flood Papers, LC; press release, March 18, 1910, R.E. Byrd to H.D. Flood, March 18, 1910, H.D. Flood to W.H. Mann, March 20, 1910, Flood Papers, LC; CAS to James Hay, April 1, 1910, Hay Papers; *Richmond Times-Dispatch*, February 12, 15, 1910; *Newport News Times Herald*, March 18, 1910; contrast Kaufman, "Flood," 175-76.

23. Kaufman, "Flood," 174 n39; John Lee to H.D. Flood, March 15, 1910, H.F. Byrd to H.D. Flood, March 16, 1910, H.F. Byrd to R.E. Byrd, March 18, 1910, H.D. Flood to Carter Glass, July 11, 1910, H.D. Flood to A.S. Priddy, July 12, 1910, H.D. Flood to CAS, July 21, 26, 1910, Flood Paprs, LC; H.S. Tucker to Alexander Hamilton, March 29, 1910, Alexander Hamilton to H.S. Tucker, March 31, 1910, H.S. Tucker to H.D. Flood, April 9, 1910, Eppa Hunton, Jr., to H.S. Tucker, July 9, 1910, H.S. Tucker to W.A. Jones, July 16, 1910, R.L. Ailsworth to H.S. Tucker, August 17, 1910, Tucker Family Papers; CAS to Edward Daniel, August 5, 1910, Daniel Papers, Duke University; *Richmond News Leader*, June 30, July 12, August 1, 2, 1910.

24. CAS to James Hay, April 1, 1910, Hay Papers; Martin Stringfellow to H.S. Tucker, September 20, 1910, Tucker Family Papers; Richard L. Watson, Jr., *The Development of National Power, the United States, 1900-1919* (Boston, 1976), 136-61; George E. Mowry, *Theodore Roosevelt and the Progressive Movement* (Madison, 1947), 120-56; *Norfolk Virginian Pilot*, October 8, 1910.

25. CAS to J.T. Ellyson, September 15, 1910, Ellyson Papers; T.S. Martin to H.D. Flood, September 19, 1910, H.D. Flood to CAS, September 21, 1910, Flood Papers, LC; Martin Stringfellow to H.S. Tucker, September 20, 1910, J.A. Taliferro to H.S. Tucker, October 1, 1910, W.G. Harris to H.S. Tucker, October 20, 1910, W.A. Jones to H.S. Tucker, November 12, 19, December 19, 29, 1910, A.E. Strode to H.S. Tucker, November 29, 1910, Tucker Family Papers; Carter Glass to Rixey Smith, October 13, 1938, Glass Papers; *Norfolk Virginian Pilot*, October 8, 1910, May 3, 1911; *Lynchburg Daily Advance*, November 7, 10, 1910.

26. W.A. Jones to H.S. Tucker, January 8, 20, 30, 1911, Tucker Family Papers; J.G. Pollard to W.A. Jones, November 30, December 31, 1910, W.A. Jones to J.G. Pollard, December 1, January 19, 1911, John Garland Pollard Papers, Manuscripts Department, Earl Gregg Swem Library, College of William and Mary; *Richmond News Leader*, January 6, 24, 27, March 9, April 1, 1911.

27. H.D. Flood to R.E. Byrd, June 13, 1911, Flood Papers, LC; W.A. Jones to H.S. Tucker, March 6, 1911, Tucker Family Papers; Virginia Democratic League, *Handbook for Hon. William A. Jones and Hon. Carter Glass Addressed to the Democratic Voters in the Primary of September 7, 1911* (Richmond, 1911), 128 pp., Tyler Papers; *Richmond News Leader*, January 23, 27, March 8, May 3, 23, June 7, August 6, 1911; *Richmond Times-Dispatch*, August 20, 22, 1911.

28. CAS to F.R. Lassiter, November 29, 1892, F.R. Lassiter Papers; Carter Glass to W.S.

Copeland, January 19, 1911, T.S. Martin to W.S. Copeland, February 18, 1911, W. Scott Copeland Papers (#5497), Manuscripts Department, University of Virginia Library; R.S. Ker to Richard Gwyn, June 14, 1909, W.E. Harris to H.S. Tucker, January 24, 1910, January 10, 1911, W.A. Jones to H.S. Tucker, January 20, 1911, Tucker Family Papers; Raleigh Green to H.D. Flood, July 19, 1910, H.D. Flood to R.E. Byrd, November 29, 1910, W.S. Heath to H.D. Flood, June 19, 1911, R.A. James to H.D. Flood, December 27, 1913, Flood Papers, LC; C.B. Garnett to W.A. Jones, May 25, July 1, 14, 1911, W.A. Jones to C.B. Garnett, June 20, July 15, 1911, W.A. Jones to C.R. Hughes, June 26, 28, 1911, W.A. Jones to W.Y. Morgan, August 15, 1911, H.H. Baker to W.A. Jones, August 21, 1911, Jones Papers.

29. F.O. Hoffman to H.S. Tucker, June 20, 1908, W.L. Newman to H.S. Tucker, March 3, 1909, F.W. Morton to H.S. Tucker, June 14, 1909, W.A. Jones to H.S. Tucker, June 14, 1909, August 16, 1911, C.B. Garnett to "Dear Sir," August 25, 1911, J.C. Hemphill to H.S. Tucker, September 6, 1911, Tucker Family Papers; H.D. Flood to J.L. Hart, June 7, 1911, CAS to H.D. Flood, October 9, 1911, Flood Papers, LC; CAS to D.W. Owen, September 8, 1911, Charles A. Hundley Papers, Manuscript Department, William Perkins Library, Duke University; Moger, *Virginia*, 221-27; Pulley, *Old Virginia*, 165-67.

30. W.J. Bryan to J.H. Tyler, March 1, 1911, W.J. Bryan to W.A. Jones, August 7, 1911, Tyler Papers; Westmoreland Davis to W.A. Jones, July 7, 1911, C.W. Bryan to W.A. Jones, August 17, 1911, Jones Papers; R.H. Shultice to H.S. Tucker, October 8, 1910, Tucker Family Papers; *Richmond News Leader*, March 15, 1911.

31. CAS to D.W. Owen, September 4, 1911, Hundley Papers; CAS to W.A. Garrett, August 4, 1911, Garrett Papers; *Richmond Virginian*, August 29, 30, September 6, 7, 1911; *Richmond News Leader*, August 28, 1911; *Richmond Times-Dispatch*, September 1, 1911; Coletta, Bryan 1:388-89.

32. H.H. Byrd to H.D. Flood, September 14, 1911, Flood Papers, LC.

33. *Richmond News Leader*, September 8, 1911; *Richmond Times-Dispatch*, September 10, 1911.

7. Both Ears to the Ground: 1910-1917

1. *Cong. Rec.*, 61 Cong., 3 sess., 46 (December 6, 1910), 16, (December 16, 1910) 340, (January 13, 1911) 839, (January 27, 1911) 1537, (February 11, 1911) 2338, (February 28, 1911) 3639, (March 3, 1911) 4094; 62 Cong., 1 sess., 47 (April 20, 1911) 437, (June 12, 1911) 1924, 1966, (June 23, 1911) 2465-67, (July 7, 1911) 2714-18, (July 13, 1911) 2917, (August 4, 1911) 3592, 3593, (August 17, 1911) 4069; 62 Cong., 2 sess., 48 (May 5, 1912) 5930, 5955, 5959, (July 5, 1912) 8652, (August 2, 1912) 10049-53, (August 17, 1912) 11149, (August 19, 1912) 11271; 62 Cong., 3 sess., 49 (February 26, 1913), 4006.

2. U.S. House, *Joint Report of the Progress of Post-Road Improvement* (Washington, 1913), 2-4, 7-8, 16; U.S. House, *Federal Aid to Good Roads, Report of the Joint Committee on Federal Aid in the Construction of Post Roads* (Washington, 1915), 2ff.; W. Stull Holt, *The Bureau of Post Roads: Its History, Activities and Organization* (Baltimore, 1923), 13-18.

3. *Cong. Rec*, 53 Cong., 1 sess., 25 (October 18, 1893), 2628; 62 Cong., 2 sess., 48 (June 8, 1912), 7848-53.

4. H.D. Flood to T.S. Martin, February 15, 1907, James Hay to H.D. Flood, June 24, 1908, H.D. Flood to James Hay, October 11, 1910, H.D. Flood to Champ Clark, October 11, 1910, Flood Papers, LC; Champ Clark to W.A. Jones, June 20, 1908, Jones Papers; *Richmond News Leader*, January 21, 1904; *Norfolk Virginian Pilot*, June 20, 1906; George E. Mowry, "Election of 1912" in Arthur M. Schlesinger, Jr., editor, *History of American Presidential Elections, 1789-1968*, 3 (New York, 1971), 2148; Burton Ira Kaufman, "Virginia Politics and the Wilson Movement, 1910-1914," *VMHB*, 76 (January, 1969): 15-21; Bernard Baruch, *Baruch: Public Years* (New York, 1960), 7.

5. C.V. Gravatt to H.S. Tucker, September 20, 1911, W.A. Jones to H.S. Tucker, September 29, 1911, Woodrow Wilson to H.S. Tucker, November 29, 1911, B.R. Newton to H.S.

Tucker, December 12, 1911, Tucker Family Papers; Woodrow Wilson to Josephus Daniels, May 13, 1912, Josephus Daniels Papers, Manuscript Division, LC; Carter Glass to Stuart Gibboney, January 10, 1912, R.E. Byrd to Carter Glass, April 30, 1912, Glass Papers; R.E. Byrd to James Hay, March 24, 1911, Hay Papers; R.E. Byrd to J.H. Tyler, April 27, 1912, Tyler Papers; Lynn Helms to Woodrow Wilson, January 17, 1910, in Arthur S. Link, editor, *The Papers of Woodrow Wilson*, 20 (Princeton, 1975), 21; Arthur S. Link, *Wilson, The Road to the White House* (Princeton, 1947), 7, 23, 25; Larsen, *Montague*, 254-55.

6. E.A. Alderman to W.H. Page, July 12, 1912, Alderman Papers; G.H. Denny to H.D. Flood, January 17, 1912, H.D. Flood to H.H. Byrd, March 20, 1912, J.N. Button to H.D. Flood, March 21, 1912, H.D. Flood to Sands Gayle, April 11, 1912, W.E. Allen to H.D. Flood, April 24, 1912, Flood Papers, LC; Arthur S. Link, "The Underwood Presidential Movement of 1912," *JSH*, 11 (May, 1945): 230-45; Clark, *Quarter Century*, 2: 426; Link, *Road to the White House*, 339-40; Johnson, *Underwood*, 172-76; Dumas Malone, *Edwin A. Alderman* (New York, 1940), 270; Josephus Daniels, *The Wilson Era, Years of Peace, 1910-1917* (Chapel Hill, 1944), 520-21, 523-24.

7. T.S. Martin to H.D. Flood, April 3, 25, 1912, H.D. Flood to C.G. Craddock, May 14, 1912, C.G. Craddock to H.D. Flood, May 15, 28, 1912, Flood Papers, LC; T.S. Martin to James Hay, May 8, 14, 1912, Hay Papers; R.E. Byrd to H.S. Tucker, April (?), 1912 (?), Tucker Family Papers.

8. H.D. Flood to C.J. Campbell, May 16, 1912, Flood Papers, LC; T.S. Martin to James Hay, May 14, 1912, Hay Papers; H.S. Tucker to J.E. Willard, May 28, 1912, W.E. Harris to H.S. Tucker, June 4, 1912, Tucker Family Papers; *Norfolk Virginian Pilot*, May 22, 24, 1912; *Richmond News Leader*, June 28, July 6, 1912; *Norfolk Ledger Dispatch*, May 24, 1912; *Richmond Times-Dispatch*, June 28, July 6, 1912; *Roanoke Times*, May 24, 1912. Contrast Link, *Road to the White House*, 441-42.

9. H.D. Flood to H.F. Byrd, April 27, 1912, Flood Papers, LC; Pembroke Pettit to H.S. Tucker, November 3, 1913, Tucker Family Papers; E.A. Alderman to W.H. Page, July 8, 1912, Alderman Papers; *Richmond Times-Dispatch*, June 29, 1912; *Norfolk Virginian Pilot*, July 2, 1912; Bain, *Convention Decisions*, 94; Arnold Harry Skaar, "Woodrow Wilson and Virginia Politics, 1910-1912" (M.A. thesis, Virginia Polytecnic Institute and State University, 1968), 19-31.

10. H.D. Flood to G.H. Denny, July 8, 1912, Flood Papers, LC; *Norfolk Virginian Pilot*, July 2, 1912; Bain, *Convention Decisions*, 183-88; Link, *Road to the White House*, 447-56; Paola E. Coletta, *Bryan*, 2 (Lincoln, 1969), 63-74; Clark, *Quarter Century*, 2: 399-402; Mowry, "Election of 1912," 2149-50; Democratic National Committee, *Official Proceedings of the Democratic National Convention* (Chicago, 1912), 129ff.

11. *Roanoke Times*, July 2, 3, 1912; *Richmond Times-Dispatch*, July 5, 1912; Baruch, *Public Years*, 7; Mowry, "Election of 1912," 2151; Bain, *Convention Decisions*, 188-90; Johnson, *Underwood*, 188; Democratic National Committee, *Proceedings, 1912*, 325-26.

12. CAS to Woodrow Wilson, July 3, 9, 1912, Woodrow Wilson Papers, Manuscript Division, LC; *Richmond Times-Dispatch*, June 24, 1912; Mowry, "Election of 1912," 2160-61.

13. CAS to James Hay, July 27, 1912, Hay Papers; CAS to G.S. Shackelford, November 22, 1912, George S. Shackelford Papers (#3525), Manuscripts Department, University of Virginia Library; "An Address at a Birthday Banquet in Staunton, December 29, 1912," in *Wilson Papers*, 25: 632-40; Woodrow Wilson to H.S. Tucker, January 3, 1913, W.A. Jones to H.S. Tucker, January 7, 1913, Tucker Family Papers; H.S. Tucker to Woodrow Wilson, December 30, 1912, T.S. Martin to Woodrow Wilson, December 31, 1912, Wilson Papers; T.S. Martin to H.D. Flood, November 12, 1912, G.H. Denny to H.D. Flood, January 1, 191[3], R.E. Byrd to H.D. Flood, May 19, 1913, Flood Papers, LC; *Richmond News Leader*, December 30, 1912; *Baltimore Sun*, December 30, 1912; *Norfolk Ledger Dispatch*, December 31, 1912; Watson, *Development of National Power*, 164.

14. W.J. Bryan to H.S. Tucker, October 8, 1912, November 21, 1913, H.S. Smith to Woodrow Wilson, December 2, 1912, G.E. Chamberlain to H.S. Tucker, December 31, 1912, H.S. Tucker to Carter Glass, November 8, 1912, Andrew C. McLaughlin, "Review of John Randolph

Tucker, *Constitution of the United States: A Critical Discussion of Its Genesis, Development and Interpretation,*" *American Historical Review,* 5 (January, 1900): 367-71, in "December 1912" folder, Tucker Family Papers; Woodrow Wilson to Josephus Daniels, April 19, 1913, Daniels Papers; "Prenomination Friends," 1913, Woodrow Wilson to A.S. Burleson, June 25, 1913, R.H. Dabney to Woodrow Wilson, July 10, 1913, Albert S. Burleson Papers, Manuscript Division, Library of Congress; *Danville Register,* March 21, 1914.

15. W.G. McAdoo to CAS, July 30, 1913, CAS to W.G. McAdoo, September 13, 1913, 63A-F25, Senate Committee on Public Buildings and Grounds, RG 46, NA; CAS to W.J. Bryan, August 11, 1913, 110.13/27, Department of State, RG 59, NA; CAS to J.P. Tumulty, April 30, August 11, 25, October 28, 1913, June 17, 1914, CAS to Woodrow Wilson, November 15, December 22, 1913, January 21, 1914, Civil Service Commission to Woodrow Wilson, October 21, 1913, November 5, 1913, Woodrow Wilson to A.S. Burleson, June 4, 1914, Woodrow Wilson to J.P. Tumulty, January 28, 1915, Wilson Papers; Thomas R. Marshall, *Recollections of Thomas R. Marshall* (Indianapolis, 1925), 319; *Richmonds News Leader,* March 25, 1914.

16. Wythe W. Holt, Jr., "The Senator From Virginia and the Democratic Floor Leadership: Thomas S. Martin and Conservatism in the Progressive Era," *VMHB,* 83 (January 1975): 12-18. Holt incorrectly includes Swanson's assignment to Naval Affairs as part of Martin's compromise. Dewey W. Grantham, *Hoke Smith and the Politics of the New South* (Baton Rouge, 1958), 238-45; B.R. Tillman to W.M. Riggs, February 26, 1913, B.R. Tillman to J.W. Kern, March 8, 1913, B.R. Tillman, "Memorandum to the President to Go for What They Are Worth," March 8, 1913, B.R. Tillman to F.T. Simpson, March 14, 1913, B.R. Tillman to A.T. Smyth, March 24, 1913, B.R. Tillman to H.D. Tillman, May 28, 1913, Benjamin R. Tillman Papers, Robert Muldrow Cooper Library, Clemson University.

17. CAS, *Addresses,* 4; Hollingsworth, *Cleveland and Bryan,* 235-41; David Burner, "The Breakup of the Wilson Coalition of 1916," *Mid-America,* 45 (January 1963), 18; George B. Tindall, *The Emergence of the New South, 1913-1945* (Baton Rouge, 1967), 1-17.

18. Swanson owned at this time 950 shares in Dan River Mills stock, worth perhaps $15,000 and a 550-acre farm near Chatham. Senate, *Lobby to Influence Legislation,* 371-72; *Cong. Rec.,* 63 Cong., 1 sess., 50 (May 29, 1913), 1806, 1817, (September 8, 1913) 4482, (September 9, 1913) 4617, Index, 358-59; Smith, *Mill on the Dan,* 145; Taussig, *Tariff History,* 409-46; Frank Burdick, "Woodrow Wilson and the Underwood Tariff," *Mid-America,* 50 (October, 1968): 272-90; Arthur S. Link, *Wilson, The New Freedom* (Princeton, 1956), 177-97.

19. Carter Glass to Woodrow Wilson, December 29, 1912, Wilson Papers; *Cong. Rec.,* 63 Cong., 2 sess., 51 (December 8, 1913), 426-39; Link, *New Freedom,* 203-13, 230-37.

20. Carter Glass, *An Adventure in Constructive Finance* (New York, 1927), 55; *Cong. Rec.,* 63 Cong., 2 sess., 51 (December 8, 1913), 439, index, 496; *Norfolk Virginian Pilot,* November 9, 10, 11, 1913; *New York Times,* November 9, 13, 26, 28, December 1, 1913; Link, *New Freedom,* 235-38; Watson, *Development of National Power,* 177-81.

21. Robert K. Murray, "Public Opinion, Labor and the Clayton Act," *Historian,* 21 (May, 1959): 255-78, notes a large number of senators not voting as a sign of dissatisfaction with the Clayton Antitrust Act. Nineteen fourteen was an election year and even floor leader Francis G. Newlands was absent, running for reelection. *Cong. Rec.,* 63 Cong., 2 sess., 51, Index, 496; Link, *New Freedom,* 433-444; Watson, *Development of National Power,* 182; Moger, *Virginia,* 288-90.

22. *Cong., Rec,* 63 Cong., 1 sess., 50 (May 26, 1913), 1743-44, 1778; U.S. Senate, *Conditions in the Paint Creek District, Hearings* (Washington, 1913), 5-8, U.S. Senate, *Investigation of Paint Creek Coal Fields of West Virginia* (Washington, 1914), 1-8; *New York Times,* May 22, 28, June 10, 13, 1913; Harold E. West, "Civil War in the West Virginia Coal Fields," *Survey,* 30 (April, 1913), 37-50.

23. *Cong. Rec.,* 62 Cong., 3 sess. 49 (February 26, 1913), 4006-7; *Norfolk Virginian Pilot,* July 20, 1913; Moger, *Virginia,* 192-95.

24. T.S. Martin to C.T. Lassiter, February 8, 1913, C.T. Lassiter Papers; H.D. Flood to G.H. Denny, August 14, 1913, Flood Papers, LC; J.S. Williams to H.S. Tucker, November 11, 1912,

Tucker Family Papers; *Baltimore Sun*, August 26, 1912; *Norfolk Virginian Pilot*, July 15, 22, 1913; Charles Evans Poston, "Henry Carter Stuart in Virginia Politics, 1855-1933" (M.A. thesis, University of Virginia, 1970), 16-20; Ferrell, "Prohibition, Reform and Politics," 230-31.

25. R.R. Ailsworth to H.S. Tucker, August 17, 1914, Tucker Family Papers; R.E. Byrd to H.D. Flood, January 23 [1914], Flood Papers, LC; Ferrell, "Prohibition, Reform and Politics," 179-80, 231-36; Moger, *Virginia*, 307-13; Robert A. Hohner, "Prohibition Comes to Virginia: The Referendum of 1914," *VMHB*, 75 (October, 1967): 473-88; Kirby, *Davis*, 53-57; Robert A. Hohner, "Bishop Cannon's Apprenticeship in Temperance Politics, 1901-1918," *JSH*, 34 (February, 1968): 33-49; Jack T. Kirby, "Alcohol and Irony: The Campaign of Westmoreland Davis for Governor, 1909-1917," *VMHB*, 73 (July, 1965): 266; James H. Timberlake, *Prohibition and the Progressive Movement, 1900-1920* (Cambridge, 1963), 4-124; *Norfolk Virginian Pilot*, September 18, 1914.

26. H.F. Hutcheson to H.D. Flood, July 16, 1917, Chairman H.D. Flood, Personal Papers and Political File, Committee on Foreign Affairs, House of Representatives, RG233, NA; Eppa Hunton, Jr., to H.S. Tucker, July 20, 1914, R.W. Shultice to H.S. Tucker, August 3, 1914, H.S. Tucker to R.R. Ailsworth, August 11, 1914, Tucker Family Papers; R.A. James to W.A. Garrett, July 19, 1914, Garrett Papers; B.R. Tillman to H.C. Tillman, August 18, 1914, Tillman Papers; entry, September 23, 1914, Watson Diary; Robert A. Hohner, "The Prohibitionists: Who Were They?" *South Atlantic Quarterly*, 68 (Autumn 1969): 497-505; *Norfolk Virginian Pilot*, August 22, 1914.

27. *Cong. Rec.*, 63 Cong., 2 sess., 51 (September 4, 1914) 14974, 14978; *New York Times*, August 26, 1914; *Norfolk Virginian Pilot*, August 25, 26, 1914; Murray R. Benedict, *Farm Policies of the United States, 1790-1950* (New York, 1953), 158-59; Arthur S. Link, *Wilson, The Struggle For Neutrality, 1914-1915* (Princeton, 1960), 91-94, 100-1; Theodore Saloutos, *Farmer Movements in the South, 1865-1933* (Berkeley, 1960), 238-42; William G. McAdoo, *Crowded Years: Reminiscences of William G. McAdoo* (Boston, 1931), 298-300.

28. CAS to W.J. Bryan, March 23, 1915, H.R. Fitzgerald to CAS, March 12, 1915, W.J. Bryan to CAS, March 27, 1915, 165.102/419 RG 59, NA; Charles Catlett to H.D. Flood, December 21, 1914, Flood Papers, NA; *Cong. Rec.*, 63 Cong., 3 sess., 52 (February 11, 1915), Appendix, 377, 384, W.B. McEwen to W.G. McAdoo, December 1, 1914, in (March 2, 1915) Appendix, 642-43; Smith, *Mill on the Dan*, 146; McAdoo, *Crowded Years*, 301-10; Daniels, *Years of Peace*, 416-18.

29. H.C. Lodge to Theodore Roosevelt, February 4, 5, 8, 17, 19, 22, March 1, 1915, Theodore Roosevelt Papers, Manuscript Division, LC; *Cong. Rec.*, 64 Cong., 1 sess., 53 (August 18, 1916), 12825; Arthur S. Link, *Wilson, Confusions and Crises, 1915-1916* (Princeton, 1964), 340-41, *Struggle for Neutrality*, 740-41; McAdoo, *Crowded Years*, 306-7.

30. *Cong. Rec.*, 64 Cong., 1 sess., 53 (March 14, 1916), 4055-56, (March 15, 1916) 4114, (April 20, 1916) 6501, (April 21, 1916) 6581-83, (April 26, 1916) 6486, (May 1, 1916) 7122, (May 5, 1916) 7458, (May 8) 7567; Holt, *Bureau of Public Roads*, 16-20; "Press Conference, March 19, 1914," in *Wilson Papers*, 29: 355-56.

31. Archibald Oden to B.F. Oden, March 10, May 2, July 4, 1915, Flood Papers, LC; CAS to G.S. Shackelford, June 6, 1915, Shackelford Papers; CAS to D.W. Owen, August 20, 1915, Hundley Papers; J.G. Pollard to Carter Glass, December 20, 1914, January 8, 1915, Carter Glass to J.G. Pollard, January 6, 1916, J.G. Pollard to A.E. Strode, May 9, 1916, Pollard Papers; J.R. Crown to H.S. Tucker, December 23, 1915, Tucker Family Papers; *Lynchburg News*, October 18, 1914; *Richmond Times-Dispatch*, July 17, 1915; *Baltimore Sun*, December 16, 1916.

32. J.R. Crown to H.S. Tucker, January (?) 1916, Carter Glass to H.S. Tucker, January 6, 1916, C.B. Slemp to H.S. Tucker, January 26, 1916, Charles Curry to H.S. Tucker, February 9, 1916, Tucker Family Papers; *Baltimore Sun*, May 7, 1916.

33. Charles Catlett to H.D. Flood, December 1, 1914, Flood papers, NA; A.B. Williams to H.S. Tucker, October 15, 1915, Charles Curry to H.S. Tucker, June 30, 1916, W.A. Watson to H.S. Tucker, August 8, 1916, C.E. Hughes to H.S. Tucker, July 15, 1916, W.S. Marsh to H.S. Tucker, August 8, 1916, Tucker Family Papers; entry, April 20, September 24, 1914, Watson Diary; *Cong.*

Rec., 64 Cong., 1 sess. 53 (June 1, 1916), 9032; Larsen, *Montague*, 267-68; Link, *Confusions and Crises*, 325-27, 356-62.

34. CAS to Woodrow Wilson, October 7, 1915, Wilson Papers; CAS to H.D. Flood, July 20, 1915, H.D. Flood to J.W. Williams, October 8, 1915, H.D. Flood papers, NA; E.G. Leigh, Jr., to H.S. Tucker, October 22, 1915, Tucker Family Papers; Commodore B. Fisher, *The Farmer's Union* in *Publications of the University of Kentucky* 1, no. 2 (Lexington, 1920): 16.

35. James Cannon, Jr., to CAS, May 27, 1916, CAS to James Cannon, Jr., July 8, 1916, Cannon Papers; T.S. Martin to H.D. Flood, November 15, 1915, H.D. Flood to J.S. Peters, January 10, 1916, Flood Papers, NA; W.E. Harris to H.S. Tucker, January 16, 1916, Tucker Family Papers; *Norfolk Virginian Pilot*, January 11, 12, 22, 1916; Ferrell, "Prohibition, Reform and Politics" 239-42.

36. T.S. Martin to G.S. Shackelford, May 8, 18, 1916, CAS to G. S. Shackelford, May 9, 12, 1916, Shackelford Papers; H.F. Byrd to H.D. Flood, May 11, 17, 22, 1916, H.D. Flood to H.F. Byrd, May 15, 1916, W.F. Rhea to H.D. Flood, May 27, 1916, H.D. Flood Papers, NA; J.G. Pollard to Carter Glass, April 28, May 13, 19, 1916, Carter Glass to J.G. Pollard, May 1, 17, 1916, Pollard Papers; Carter Glass to H.S. Tucker, June 8, 1916, Tucker Family Papers; *Richmond Times-Dispatch*, June 1, 2, 3, 1916.

37. B.R. Tillman to Woodrow Wilson, January 5, 8, 1916, Tillman Papers; H.C. Lodge to Theodore Roosevelt, December 2, 1915, T. Roosevelt Papers; James Hay to H.D. Flood, November 9, 1914, J.N. Brenamen to H.D. Flood, June 11, 1916, H.D. Flood Papers, NA; *Norfolk Virginian Pilot*, January 10, 1916; *Cong. Rec.*, 63 Cong., 3 sess., 52 (March 3, 1915), 5237; Democratic National Committee, *Official Report of the Proceedings of the Democratic National Convention* (Chicago, 1916), 47, 75; Arthur S. Link, *Wilson: Campaigns for Progressivism and Peace, 1916-1917* (Princeton, 1965), 40-42; *Survey*, 36 (July 22, 1916): 424.

38. W.A. Watson to H.S. Tucker, July 19, 1916, Tucker Family Papers; *Cong. Rec.*, 64 Cong., 1 sess., 53 (July 21, 1916), 1372, (August 8, 1916) 12313; *New York Times*, July 22, 1916; Elizabeth H. Davidson, *Child Labor in the Southern Textile States* (Chapel Hill, 1939), 257-58; Stephen B. Wood, *Constitutional Politics in the Progressive Era: Labor and the Law* (Chicago, 1968), 67-68; Walter I. Trattner, *Crusade for the Children: A History of the National Child Labor Committee and Child Labor Reform in America* (Chicago, 1970), passim; Link, *Campaigns*, 56-60; Grantham, *Hoke Smith*, 300; *Survey*, 36 (July 22, 1916): 424.

39. W.A. Watson to H.S. Tucker, August 8, 1916, Tucker Family Papers; Smith, *Mill on the Dan*, 51 n84, 103-4, 171 n56; Davidson, *Child Labor*, 245-46; A.J. McKelway, "Protecting Negro Child Laborers in Virginia," *Survey*, 32 (August 15, 1914): 496; A.J. McKelway, *Child Labor in Virginia*, (New York, 1910), 1-12.

40. CAS to Woodrow Wilson, November 19, 1912, Wilson Papers; entry, March 17, April 13, 1913, in E. David Cronon, editor, *The Cabinet Diaries of Josephus Daniels, 1913-1920* (Lincoln, 1963), 10-11. 21; *Norfolk Virginian Pilot*, July 10, 11, 1913; Jerome M. Clubb and Howard W. Allen, "Party Loyalty in the Progressive Years: The Senate, 1909-1915," *Journal of Politics*, 29 (August 1967): 575; Henry C. Ferrell, Jr., "Regional Rivalries, Congress and MIC: The Norfolk and Charleston Navy Yards, 1912-1920," in Benjamin F. Cooling, editor, *War, Business and American Society: Historical Perspectives in the Military-Industrial Complex* (Port Washington, N.Y., 1977), 59-62; Coletta, *Bryan*, 2: 239-44; Brayton Harris, *The Age of the Battleship, 1890-1922* (New York, 1965), 151; George T. Davis, *A Navy Second to None: The Development of Modern American Naval Policy* (Westport, 1971), 196-97.

41. CAS to Josephus Daniels, June 3, 1913, Josephus Daniels to CAS, August 29, September 29, 1913, B.R. Tillman to Josephus Daniels, September 6, 9, 1913, H.A. Banks to CAS, September 17, 1913, Daniels Papers; B.R. Tillman to Josephus Daniels, March 5, 18, 1913, November 14, 1916, B.R. Tillman to J.W. Kern, October 2, 1914, B.R. Tillman to Woodrow Wilson, February 14, 1914, Tillman Papers; A.T. Mahan to Philip Andrews, September 24, 1910, in Robert Seager, II, and Doris D. Maguire, editors, *Letters and Papers of Alfred Thayer Mahan, 1902-1914,* 3 (Annapolis, 1975): 352-58; Ferrell, "Regional Rivalries," 62-64.

42. Entry, December 28, 1914, Bradley A. Fiske Diaries, Manuscript Division, LC; H.C. Lodge to Theodore Roosevelt, June 14, 1914, February 9, June 29, July 15, 1916, T. Roosevelt Papers; B.R. Tillman to Woodrow Wilson, September 14, 1914, B.R. Tillman to Josephus Daniels, January 27, 1914, Daniels Papers; U.S. House, *Preliminary Survey of Millcreek, Middlesex* (Washington, 1914) and *Norfolk Harbor and Vicinity* (Washington, 1914), passim; Karl Schriftgiesser, *The Gentleman from Massachusetts: Henry Cabot Lodge* (Boston, 1945), 102; John H. Garraty, *Henry Cabot Lodge* (New York, 1953), 315-16.

43. Entry, January 5, 1915, *Diaries of Daniels*, 87-88; B.R. Tillman to Victor Blue, January 26, 1915, Tillman Papers; Josephus Daniels to B.R. Tillman, February 2, 1915, Daniels Papers; Ferrell, "Regional Rivalries," 67; *Cong. Rec.*, 63 Cong., 3 sess., 52 (February 25, 1915), 4600-15, (February 26, 1915) 4700-2, (March 3, 1915) 5233-36.

44. Josephus Daniels to B.R. Tillman, September 18, 1915, January 11, 12, 1916; CAS to Josephus Daniels, October 30, 1915, Josephus Daniels to Woodrow Wilson, December (?) 1915, W.S. Benson to CAS, June 3, 1916, Daniels Papers; H.C. Lodge to Theodore Roosevelt, December 20, 1915, T. Roosevelt Papers; Harris, *Battleship*, 153; William R. Braisted, *The United States Navy in the Pacific, 1909-1922* (Austin, 1971), 171-79; Davis, *Second to None*, 226-31; Link, *Confusions and Crises*, 15, 35-36; Garraty, *Lodge*, 316-17.

45. B.R. Tillman to Boies Penrose, January 9, 1916, B.R. Tillman to CAS, January 23, 1916, B.R. Tillman to Josephus Daniels, February 3, April 23, June 22, 1916, B.R. Tillman to Samuel McGowan, February 15, 1916, B.R. Tillman to Woodrow Wilson, March 7, 1916, B.R. Tillman to W.A. Smith, June 21, 1916, Tillman Papers; B.R. Tillman to Josephus Daniels, January 11, 1916, Daniels Papers; U.S. Senate, Naval Affairs Committee, 64 Cong., 1 sess., *Report on the Naval Appropriations Bill* (Washington, 1916), 1-6; Robert G. Albion, *Makers of Naval Policy, 1798-1947*, Rowena Reed, editor (Annapolis, 1980), 125.

46. H.C. Lodge to Theodore Roosevelt, July 15, 1916, March 20, 1917, T. Roosevelt papers; H.C. Lodge to Theodore Roosevelt, July 10, 1916, in Henry Cabot Lodge, editor, *Selections From The Correspondence of Theodore Roosevelt and Henry Cabot Lodge, 1884-1918*, 2 (New York, 1925), 491-92. The latter letter does not appear in the Theodore Roosevelt papers nor does Lodge cite the above July 15, 1916, letter. Senate Naval Affairs Committee, *Report on Naval Appropriations, 1916*, 1-6.

47. *Cong. Rec.*, 64 Cong., 1 sess., 53 (July 13, 1916), 10924-27, 10928-47, (July 15, 1916) 11089-11114, (July 8, 1916) 11197-98, (July 21, 1916) 111384. See Braisted, *U.S. in the Pacific, 1909-1922*, 198-204, for an assessment of other contemporary pressures to expand the navy.

48. W.S. Benson, "Memorandum: Charleston Harbor Improvements," August 2, 1916, Woodrow Wilson to CAS, July 27, August 15, 1916, Josephus Daniels to Woodrow Wilson, August 15, 1916, Woodrow Wilson to Josephus Daniels, August 16, 21, 1916, Wilson Papers; *New York Times*, July 22, 24, 27, August 9, 17, 30, 1916; Watson, *Development of National Power*, 192-93; Daniels, *Years of Peace*, 35-63; Alex M. Arnett, *Claude Kitchen and the Wilson War Policies* (Boston, 1937), 99-108.

49. In four year periods, naval appropriations were: McKinley-Roosevelt (March 4, 1901-March 4, 1905) $107 million, Roosevelt (March 4, 1905-March 4, 1909), $83 million, Taft (March 4, 1909-March 4, 1913) $127 million, Wilson (March 4, 1913-August 22, 1916), $655 million. Josephus Daniels to Woodrow Wilson, August 21, 1916, Wilson Papers; Josephus Daniels to General Board, November 24, 1916, 4263-596, RG 80, NA; H.C. Lodge to Theodore Roosevelt, April 11, July 15, 1916, T. Roosevelt Papers; *Norfolk Virginian Pilot*, August 13, 16, 18, 1916; Link, *Confusions and Crises*, 38; George C. Herring, Jr., "James Hay and the Preparedness Controversy, 1915-1916," *JSH*, 30 (November 1964): 192-93, underestimates Virginia Guard pressure upon Hay.

50. W.G. McAdoo to CAS, January 4, June 16, 1916, W.G. McAdoo to Vance McCormick, June 22, 1916, William Gibbs McAdoo Papers, Manuscript Division, LC; CAS to R.C. Woolley, April 17, 1913, R.C. Woolley to CAS, May 1, 1913, February 9, 15, October 3, 1917, Robert C.

Woolley Papers, Manuscript Division, LC; John M. Blum, *Joe Tumulty and the Wilson Era* (Boston, 1951), passim; Daniel C. Roper, *Fifty Years of Public Life* (Durham, 1941), 293, 376.

51. B.R. Tillman to CAS, February 1, 6, 1917, B.R. Tillman to B.R. Tillman, Jr., February 9, 1917, B.R. Tillman to Josephus Daniels, February 23, 1917, Tillman Papers; *Norfolk Virginian Pilot*, November 11, 13, 17-19, 23, December 10, 15, 1916; entry, March 3, 30, April 1, 1917, *Diaries of Daniels*, 108, 125, 126; U.S. Senate, *Naval Appropriations Bill, Report 1101* (Washington, 1917), 1-2; *Cong. Rec.*, 64 Cong., 2 sess., 54 (February 27, 1917), 4378-83, (March 1, 1917) 4575-4612, (March 2, 1917) 4722-43; Ferrell, "Regional Rivalries," 68-69.

52. W.J. Bryan to CAS, February 9, 1914, 711.428/347B, August 1, 1914, 711.0012/531s, J.H.C. Barr to CAS, October 19, 1914, 812.63/26, October 20, 1917, 812.63/493, Robert Lansing to CAS, October 19, 1914, 812.63/26, CAS to Robert Lansing, October 22, 1917, 812.63/493, R.L. Dibrell to CAS, February 28, 1916, 641.116/52, RG 59, NA; *Cong. Rec.*, 63 Cong., 2 sess., 51 (April 21, 1914), 6971; 73 Cong., special sess., 77 (February 7, 1931), 4222; Patrick Devlin, *Too Proud to Fight: Woodrow Wilson's Neutrality* (New York, 1975), 439-41, 653, 656-67; Tilley, *Bright-Tobacco*, 278-80; Link, *Confusions and Crises* and *Campaigns*, passim.

53. The Zimmerman note had appeared so outlandish that Swanson verified it with the White House for an incredulous Lodge. H.C. Lodge to Theodore Roosevelt, March 2, 23, 1917, T. Roosevelt Papers; Robert Lansing, *War Memoirs of Robert Lansing, Secretary of State* (New York, 1935), 24, 238, 313; Link, *Campaigns*, 300-40; Devlin, *Too Proud to Fight*, 595ff.

54. *Cong. Rec.*, 65 Cong., 1 sess., 55 (April 4, 1917), 201-7.

8. Neither Hesitate nor Halt: 1917-1921

1. B.R. Tillman to B.R. Tillman, Jr., April 6, 1917, B.R. Tillman to J.S. Williams, April 20, 1917, B.R. Tillman to CAS, May 4, 23, August 1, 1917, CAS to B.R. Tillman, May 8, 9, 17, 29, 1917, Tillman Papers; "Head Usher's Diary, White House 1913-1921," Wilson Papers; *New York Times*, May 10, 1917; Seward W. Livermore, *Politics Is Adjourned: Woodrow Wilson and the War Congress, 1916-1918* (Middletown, 1966), 1-14.

2. Woodrow Wilson to CAS, April 26, 1917, Wilson Papers; Josephus Daniels to Woodrow Wilson, June 11, 1917, Daniels Papers; T.J. Wool to H.S. Tucker, June 29, July 14, 1917, Tucker Family Papers; entry, June 8, 9, 14, 1917, *Diaries of Daniels*, 162-64; *Cong. Rec.*, 65 Cong., 1 sess., 55 (June 7, 1917), 3290-92, (June 11, 1917) 3427-37, (June 12, 1917) 3535-38; *New York Times*, June 13, 1917; Ferrell, "Regional Rivalries," 67-70.

3. F.H. Hall, Memorandum, November 29, 1915; Woodrow Wilson to T.W. Gregory, February 19, 1917, T.W. Gregory to F.K. Lane, February 21, 1917, F.K. Lane to T.W. Gregory, February 24, 1917, T.W. Gregory to CAS, February 26, 1917, Woodrow Wilson to F.K. Lane, February 21, December 31, 1917, Wilson Papers; Josephus Daniels to CAS, September 29, 1917, Daniels Papers; entry, August 1, 1917, *Diaries of Daniels*, 185; *Cong. Rec.*, 65 Cong., 2 sess., 56 (December 17, 1917), 386-98; J. Leonard Bates, *The Origins of Teapot Dome: Progressives, Parties and Petroleum, 1909-1921* (Urbana, Ill., 1963), 115 and passim.

4. F.K. Lane to Woodrow Wilson, January 4, 1918, Wilson Papers; Josephus Daniels to Woodrow Wilson, January 3, 1918, Memorandum, January 9, 1918, Daniels Papers; entry, January 1, 9, 19, 1918, *Diaries of Daniels*, 261, 264, 269; *Cong. Rec.*, 65 Cong., 2 sess., 56 (January 15, 1918), 872-74, (January 16, 1918) 896, (January 17, 1918) 922-27, (January 18, 1918) 1006-8; Bates, *Origins of Teapot Dome*, 132 and passim.

5. W.G. McAdoo to CAS, February 28, 1918, McAdoo Papers; entry, January 9, 1918, *Diaries of Daniels*, 264-65; *New York Times*, January 9, 1918; *Cong. Rec*, 65 Cong., 2 sess., 56 (February 26, 1918) 2672-78.

6. *Cong. Rec*, 65 Cong., 2 sess., 56 (April 17, 1918) 5193-5211, (April 22, 1918) 5402, (April 24, 1918) 5547-48, (April 30, 1918) 5810-32, (May 1, 1918) 5838.

7. CAS to Josephus Daniels, March 8, 1913, 5834:27:4, April 16, 1913, 5834:27:2, June 6,

1917, 5267:666:1, W.C. Watts to Josephus Daniels, July 25, 1917, 5267-666:4, Jordan Brothers Lumber Company to T.S. Martin, August 18, 1917, 5267-704, B.M. Squires to W.B. Wilson, August 29, 1917, 5267-689, J.A. Franklin to F.D. Roosevelt, September 7(?), 1917, 5267-713, September 26, 1917, 5267-717, RG 80, NA; F.D. Roosevelt to Josephus Daniels, September 25, October 5, 1917, Navy Yard Employees to Woodrow Wilson, September 26, 1917, Woodrow Wilson to Josephus Daniels, March 7, 1918, Daniels Papers; entry, September 29, 1917, *Ashurst Diary*, 72; Bruce E. Field, "Norfolk in Wartime: The Effect of The First World War on the Expansion of a Southern City" (M.A. thesis, East Carolina University, 1978), passim; Ferrell, "Regional Rivalries," 70; Thomas J. Wertenbaker, *Norfolk: Historic Southern Port*, 2d edition, Marvin Schlegal, editor (Durham, 1962), 302-10.

      8. CAS to Mrs. R.E. Byrd, October 10, 1917(?), Harry Flood Byrd Papers (#9700), Manuscripts Department, University of Virginia Library; B.R. Tillman to Josephus Daniels, February 4, 1918, B.R. Tillman to CAS, March 9, April 29, 1918, Tillman Papers; Woodrow Wilson to CAS, December 11, 1917, Wilson Papers; J.P. Tumulty to D.C. Roper, November (?) 1917, Joseph P. Tumulty Papers, Manuscript Division, LC; Hall interview; *New York Times*, May 21, June 5, 1918; *Cong. Rec.*, 65 Cong., 2 sess., 56 (May 11, 1918), 6362, (July 6, 1918) 8738; Simpkins, *Tillman*, 538-45.

      9. W.K. Allen to H.S. Tucker, February 28, 1918, A.J. Montague to H.S. Tucker, January 16, 1919, Tucker Family Papers; W.E. Dodd to Claude Kitchin, January 27, 1918, W.E. Dodd to [D.R.] Anderson, October 13, 1918, Dodd Papers; entry, December 20, 1918, Watson Diary.

      10. W.A. Watson to H.S. Tucker, June 6, 1918, Tucker Family Papers; Josephus Daniels to F.D. Roosevelt, March 8, 1937, Daniels Papers.

      11. G.S. Shackelford to CAS, March 5, 1918, CAS to G.S. Shackelford, March 6, 1918, Shackelford Papers; entry, March 2, 1918, *Diaries of Daniels*, 286; *Cong. Rec.*, 65 Cong., 2 sess., 56 (March 21, 1918), 3831; David Burner, *The Politics of Provincialism: The Democratic Party in Transition, 1918-1932* (New York, 1968), 40; Livermore, *Politics Is Adjourned*, 245.

      12. Entry, January 3, February 21, 24, 1919, *Diaries of Daniels*, 364, 375; entry, October 11, 1918, *Ashurst Diaries*, 82-83; *New York Times*, November 12, 1918; *Cong. Rec.*, 65 Cong., 2 sess., 56 (October 1, 1918), 10986; 65 Cong., 3 sess., 57 (January 7, 1919), 1101-14, (February 26, 1919) 4889.

      13. J.P. Tumulty to Woodrow Wilson, February 1, 1919, Wilson Papers; *Cong. Rec.*, 65 Cong., 3 sess., 57 (January 22, 1919), 1857, (January 31, 1919) 2426-27, (February 1, 1919) 2496-98, (February 5, 1919) 2752, (February 8, 1919) 2969; Blum, *Tumulty*, 186-88; Alice Roosevelt Longworth, *Crowded Hours* (New York, 1935), 277 and passim.

      14. The *Cong. Rec.* reports only Swanson objecting to the Lodge motion, but the *Norfolk Virginian Pilot* reporter, probably J. Foster Murray, recorded that Martin and Swanson "joined in simultaneous objection . . . and the resolution went over under the rules." *Norfolk Virginia Pilot*, March 4, 1919; *Cong. Rec.*, 65 Cong., 3 sess., 57 (February 28, 1919), 4518 and passim, (March 4, 1919) 4967-74; T.S. Martin to Woodrow Wilson, July 27, 1919, Wilson Papers; Ralph A. Stone, *The Irreconcilables: The Fight Against the League of Nations* (Lexington, 1970), 52-76; Watson, *Memoirs*, 190-93.

      15. Stone, *Irreconcilables*, 72-74; Garraty, *Lodge*, 353-56; Arthur C. Walworth, *Woodrow Wilson*, 3d edition, 2 (New York, 1978), 272; Denna F. Fleming, *The United States and the League of Nations* (New York, 1932), 153-55; Henry C. Lodge, *The Senate and the League of Nations* (New York, 1925), 118-21; Herbert F. Margulies, *Senator Lenroot of Wisconsin: A Political Biography, 1900-1929* (Columbia, 1977), 266; W. Stull Holt, *Treaties Defeated by the Senate: A Study of the Struggle between the President and Senate over the Conduct of Foreign Relations* (Baltimore, 1933), 266-67.

      16. Key Pittman to Woodrow Wilson, November 11, 1918, Wilson Papers; Holt, *Treaties Defeated*, 249ff.; Blum, *Tumulty*, 182-84; Stone, *Irreconcilables*, 95-99.

      17. F.L. Polk to Robert Lansing, May 31, 1919, Woodrow Wilson to Robert Lansing, June 3, 1919, Wilson Papers; Woodrow Wilson to J.P. Tumulty, May 6, June 2, 13, 1919, J.P. Tumulty to

Woodrow Wilson, June 17, 1919, Tumulty Papers; Garraty, *Lodge*, 363-65; Stone, *Irreconcilables*, 96-115; Henry F. Pringle, *The Life and Times of William Howard Taft*, 2 (New York, 1939), 936-45.

18. F.L. Polk to Robert Lansing, May 31, 1919, Wilson Papers; CAS to A.S. Burleson, June 2, 1919, J.P. Tumulty to A.S. Burleson, June 25, 1919, Burleson Papers; *Cong. Rec.*, 66 Cong., 1 sess., 58 (July 10, 1919), 2336-39; entry, July 29, 1919, *Diaries of Daniels*, 429.

19. Entry, July 17, 1919, *Ashurst Diary*, 100; entry July 16, 1919, *Diaries of Daniels*, 426; *Cong. Rec.*, 66 Cong., 1 sess., 58 (July 14, 1919), 2532-42; *Danville Register*, July 12, 1919; *New York Times*, July 9, 12, 1919; *Norfolk Virginian Pilot*, July 12, 15, 1919; Blum, *Tumulty*, 201.

20. CAS to W.H. Taft, July 7, 1919, October 1, 1919, William Howard Taft Papers, Manuscript Division, Library of Congress; *Cong. Rec.*, 66 Cong., 1 sess., 58 (July 14, 1919), 2535-36; *Danville Register*, July 15, 1919; *New York Times*, July 15, 24, 1919; *Norfolk Virginian Pilot*, July 17, 24, 1919; U.S. Senate, Foreign Relations Committee, *Treaty of Peace with Germany: Hearings* (Washington, 1919), 499-552; Fleming, *League of Nations*, 297-336; John C. Vinson, *Referendum for Isolation: Defeat of Article Ten of the League of Nations Covenant* (Athens, 1961), 88-89, misinterprets Swanson's intention and other pro-League senators in downgrading Article Ten's significance.

21. *Norfolk Virginia Pilot*, August 16, 1919; *New York Times*, August 26, 1919; Margaret L. Coit, *Mr. Baruch* (Boston, 1957), 292; Baruch, *Public Years*, 135-37; Blum, *Tumulty*, 202-6; Senate, *Treaty of Peace with Germany: Hearings*, 5 and passim.

22. *Danville Register*, September 4, 1919; Josephus Daniels, *The Wilson Era, Years of War and After* (Chapel Hill, 1946), 480-81; George Wharton Pepper, *Philadelphia Lawyer* (Philadelphia, 1944), 129.

23. H.C. Lodge to H.S. Tucker, December 17, 1919, Tucker Family Papers; CAS to W.H. Taft, October 1, 1919, Taft Papers; Archibald Oden to L.C. Garnett, December 20, 1919, Pollard Papers; *Cong. Rec.*, 66 Cong., 1 sess., 58 (September 16, 1919), 5515, (September 26, 1919) 5976, (October 2, 1919) 6275, (November 6, 1919) 8014-20; Stone, *Irreconcilables*, 145; Margulies, *Lenroot*, 278-94, Garraty, *Lodge*, 375-76, 376 n8.

24. S.B. Woodfin to Peter Ainslie, August 18, 1917, Cannon Papers; H.F. Hutcheson to H.D. Flood, July 16, 1917, R.E. Byrd to H.D. Flood, July 13, 20, 1917, G.O. Greene to H.D. Flood, August 1, 1917, Flood Papers, NA; *Washington Star*, August 9, 1917; *Norfolk Virginian Pilot*, July 31, August 2, 8, 1917; *Richmond Virginian*, July 25, August 9, 1917; Cannon, Jr., *Own Story*, 164-66; Ferrell, "Prohibition, Reform and Politics," 237-42. Compare and contrast Kirby, *Davis*, 164-66.

25. C.T. Lassiter to H.A. White, May 14, 1917, C.T. Lassiter to R.C. Kilmartin, July 25, 1917, C.T. Lassiter Papers; J.N. Brenamen to H.D. Flood, June 19, 1917, J.T. Fitzpatrick to H.D. Flood, June 25, 1917, R.E. Byrd to H.D. Flood, July 17, 1916 [*sic*], July 20, 30, 1917, H.F. Byrd to H.D. Flood, July 30, 1917, Flood Papers, NA; J.G. Pollard to Carter Glass, December 20, 1914, Pollard Papers; J.G. Pollard to J.H. Tyler, September 11, 1917, Tyler Papers; J.G. Pollard to H.S. Tucker, August 15, 1917, Tucker Family Papers; *Norfolk Virginian Pilot*, July 13, 1917.

26. *Washington Star*, August 9, 1917; *Cong. Rec.*, 65 Cong., 1 sess., 55 (July 2, 1917), 4588-89, (July 6, 1917) 4752, 4759, (July 21, 1917) 5397, (August 1, 1917) 5666, (August 8, 1917) 5927.

27. J.M. Hart to Carter Glass, August 20, 1919, Glass Papers; A.J. Montague to H.S. Tucker, April 27, 1918, Tucker Family Papers; *Cong. Rec.*, 65 Cong., 2 sess., 56 (April 17, 1918), 5216; *Norfolk Virginian Pilot*, April 19, 1918.

28. T.S. Martin to Woodrow Wilson, July 27, 1919, Wilson Papers; G.M. Blake to H.S. Tucker, October 24, 1919, Tucker Family Papers; CAS to Lucy Day Martin, March 31, 1920, Day-Martin Papers; entry, December 20, 1918, Watson Diary; *Cong. Rec.*, 66 Cong., 1 sess., 58 (November 12, 1919), 8373, (November 13, 1919) 8417; 66 Cong., 2 sess., 59 (April 10, 1920), 5483-86, 5490; *Norfolk Virginian Pilot*, November 13, 1919; *Richmond Times-Dispatch*, November 13, 14, 15, 1919; *Danville Register*, October 24, November 13, 1919; *Petersburg Evening Progress*, October 25, November 13, 1919; *Roanoke Times*, November 13, 15, 1919.

29. R.E. Byrd to T.S. Martin, January 31, 1919, J.N. B[utton] to H.D. Flood, February 29, 1919, Flood Papers, LC; R.W. Shultice to H.S. Tucker, November 18, 1919, Tucker Family Papers; Moger, *Virginia*, 324-25; Johnson, *Underwood*, 295-96.

30. H.W. Robertson to H.F. Byrd, July 14, 1920, Byrd Papers; R.C. Slaughter to Martin Stringfellow, April 7, 1920, Tucker Family Papers; S.W. Watkins to H.D. Flood, March 15, 1920, Flood Papers, LC; Democratic National Committee, *Proceedings of the Democratic National Convention* (Indianapolis, 1920), 68-69; *Cong. Rec.*, 66 Cong., 2 sess., 59 (December 17, 1919), 759, (January 27, 1920) 2106, (April 22, 1920) 6063-65; *Norfolk Virginian Pilot*, April 23, July 14, 1920.

31. Memorandum, August 21, 1919, Woodrow Wilson to B.F. Buchanan, August 22, 1919, Wilson Papers; J.P. Tumulty to Woodrow Wilson, March 2, 1919, Tumulty Papers; *Norfolk Virginian Pilot*, May 5, 1918; *Danville Register*, July 17, 26, 1919; *Cong., Rec.*, 65 Cong., 2 sess., 56 (May 6, 1918), 6097, (October 1, 1918) 10986, 10988; 66 Cong., 1 sess., 58 (June 4, 1919), 635; Burl Noggle, *Into the Twenties: The United States from the Armistice to Normalcy* (Urbana, Ill., 1974), 84 and passim.

32. J.P. Holland to H.S. Tucker, December 3, 1919, H.S. Tucker to T.H. Downing, February 27, 1920, Tucker Family Papers: *Washington Star*, December 21, 1919; *Danville Register*, September 21, 28, 1919; Tilley, *Bright-Tobacco*, 450 and passim; Noggle, *Into the Twenties*, 49 and passim; James H. Shideler, *Farm Crisis, 1919-1923* (Berkeley, 1957), 46 and passim.

9. The Principle of Local Self-Government: 1920-1930

1. CAS to S.H. Swanson, August 10, 1922, Swanson Papers, University of Virginia Library; Hall Interview; *Norfolk Virginian Pilot*, October 28, 1923.

2. Carter Glass to H.D. Flood, October 2, 1920, Flood Papers, LC; J.C. Pollard to A.V. Shea, June 15, 1920, Pollard Papers; W.G. McAdoo to Carter Glass, July 21, 1920, Glass Papers; Democratic Committee, *Proceedings, 1920*, 68-69, 153-57; *Norfolk Virginian Pilot*, July 2, 1920; John D. Lyle, "The United States Senate Career of Carter Glass, 1920-1933" (Ph.D. diss., University of South Carolina, 1974), 39-41.

3. Carter Glass to H.S. Tucker, January 1, 7, 1921, Tucker Family Papers; J.N. Button to CAS, February 29, 1919, Flood Papers, LC; memoranda, April 15, November 23, December 7, 1922, Carter Glass to CAS, October 26, 1922, June 8, 1928, CAS to Carter Glass, October 24, 27, 1922, October 6, 1924, October 25, 1925, Glass Papers; *Norfolk Virginian Pilot*, November 16, 1919; *Baltimore Sun*, September 27, 1922.

4. C.C. Burns to E.R. Combs, September 30, 1920, Everett R. Combs Papers (#9712), Manuscripts Department, University of Virginia Library; W.A. Pratt to H.D. Flood, September 13, 1920, Flood Papers, LC; U.S. House of Representatives, *Contested Election Case of John Paul v. Thomas W. Harrison from the Seventh Congressional District of Virginia* (Washington, 1921), 3-33, 71-73, and passim.

5. R.A. James to Carter Glass, October 16, 1920, Glass Papers; D.L. Groner to W.E. Borah, November 12, 1920, William E. Borah Papers, Manuscript Division, LC; House, *Paul v. Harrison*, 197; Buni, *Negro in Va. Politics*, 77-81.

6. W.S. Battle, Jr., to CAS, November 29, 1920, CAS to W.S. Battle, Jr., December 1, 1920, CAS to R.H.T. Adams, December 2, 1920, J.P. Fishburn to CAS, December 7, 1920, Swanson Papers, University of Virginia Library; CAS to D.W. Owen, December 15, 1920, Hundley Papers; A.J. Stoffer to H.S. Tucker, December 16, 1920, Tucker Family Papers.

7. C.W. Mapp to R.E. Woolwine, July 12, 1920, Tucker Family Papers; S.L. Ferguson to H.F. Byrd, August 20, 1920, Byrd Papers; CAS to E.H. Hutchins December 6, 1920, Swanson Papers, University of Virginia Library; H.D. Flood to A.F. Thomas, December 16, 1920, Alsen Franklin Thomas Papers (#6096), Manuscripts Department, University of Virginia Library; Marvin E. Winters, "Benjamin Franklin Buchanan, 1859-1932," (M.A. thesis, University of Virginia, 1969), 46; Ronald E. Shibley, "G. Walter Mapp: Politics and Prohibition in Virginia, 1873-1941" (M.A. thesis, University of Virginia, 1966), 55-57.

8. J.R. Tucker to H.S. Tucker, November 15, 1920, D.H. Leake to H.S. Tucker, November 15, 1920, L.S. Epes to H.S. Tucker, November 9, 1921, Tucker Family Papers; *Danville Register*, July 30, 1921.

9. *Roanoke Times*, December 30, 1920; *Norfolk Virginian Pilot*, December 31, 1920; Willis, "Trinkle," 19, 49, 52, 62-65.

10. H.C. Lodge to H.S. Tucker, May 29, 1919, W.H. Short to H.S. Tucker, July 24, 1919, E.L. Trinkle to R.F. Leady, December 22, 1920, D.H. Leake to H.S. Tucker, December 24, 1920, Tucker Family Papers. Tucker later wrote Davis that Glass told him Swanson would have preferred Tucker. H.S. Tucker to Westmoreland Davis, February 17, 1922, Westmoreland Davis Papers (#6560), Manuscripts Department, University of Virginia Library.

11. CAS to R.A. James, March 18, 1921, CAS to J.A. Stone, May 31, 1921, CAS to R.H. Mann, February 26, 1921, "Campaign Notes," June-July 1921, CAS to H.G. Barbee, July 2, 1921, CAS to J.P. Swanson, July 19, 1921, CAS to C.R. Mitchell, July 19, 1921, C.V. Noland to CAS, September 3, 1921, Swanson Papers, University of Virginia Library; W.S. Copeland to CAS, October 21, 1921, Copeland Papers.

12. L.S. Epes to E.W. Hutchens, April 9, 1921, Tucker Family Papers.

13. "Speech of Honorable Henry St. George Tucker, Candidate for Governor, Richmond, Virginia, April 30, 1921," 20 pp., G.E. Smith to H.S. Tucker, May 5, 1921, Tucker Family Papers.

14. C.E. Geoghegan to H.S. Tucker, April 27, 1921, G.W. Mapp to P.L. Penn, June 10, 1921, J.M. Hart to H.S. Tucker, June 27, 1921, Tucker Family Papers; *Roanoke Times*, January 1, 1921; Willis, "Trinkle," 40; Shibley, "Mapp," 47-51. Compare and contrast Kirby, *Davis*, 131-33, 161.

15. R.E. Byrd to H.D. Flood, June 16, 1919, Flood Papers, LC; J.T. Clement to D.H. Leake, May 13, 1921, Tucker Family Papers; H.F. Byrd to H.D. Flood, January 19, 1921, S.L. Ferguson to H.F. Byrd, January 22, 1921, Byrd Papers; Andrew L. Shifflett, "Good Roads in Virginia, 1916-1923" (M.A. thesis, East Carolina University, 1971), 29-38, 70 and passim; *Danville Register*, July 11, August 20, 1919.

16. R.W. Woolley to H.S. Tucker, July 31, 1921; J.S. Bryan to H.S. Tucker, August 3(?), 1921, T.C. Johnson to H.S. Tucker, August 3, 1921, F.B. Hutton to H.S. Tucker, August 3, 1921, J.L. Tucker to D.H. Leake, August 3, 1921, T.J. Coles to D.H. Leake, August 4, 1921, J.E.B. Holladay to H.S. Tucker, August 4, 1921, B.R. Tucker to H.S. Tucker, August 4, 1921, A.B. Green to H.S. Tucker, August 4, 1921, Barton Myers to H.S. Tucker, August 6, 1921, D.H. Leake to H.S. Tucker, August 20, 1921, Tucker Family Papers; H.C. Stuart to W.S. Copeland, February 1, 1921, Copeland Papers; H.D. Flood to A.H. Crismont, July 6, 1921, Flood Papers, LC; N.H. Hamilton to CAS, March 17, 1921, CAS to H.F. Byrd, August 9, 1921, Swanson Papers, University of Virginia Library; *Danville Register*, July 22, 30, 1921, *Richmond Times-Dispatch*, August 3, 1921.

17. H.D. Flood to W.H. Landes, August 11, 1921, H.D. Flood to Turner McDowell, August 11, 1921, Flood Papers, LC; *Norfolk Virginian Pilot*, July 15, September 9, 1921, November 1, 4, 1921; *Richmond Times-Dispatch*, September 28, 1921; Willis, "Trinkle," 86-89; Buni, *Negro in Va. Politics*, 81-84.

18. R.M. Lynn to Carter Glass, August 29, 1921, Carter Glass to H.D. Flood, September 13, 1921, Glass Papers; H.M. Smith, Jr., to H.S. Tucker, August 20, 1921, Tucker Family Papers; W.S. Battle, Jr., to CAS, August 10, 1921, CAS to W.S. Battle, Jr., August 12, 1921, Swanson Papers, University of Virginia Library; Julian Gunn to H.F. Byrd, August 10, 1921, CAS to H.F. Byrd, August 15, 1921, Byrd Papers; Henry C. Ferrell, Jr., "The Role of Democratic Party Factionalism in the Rise of Harry Flood Byrd, 1917-1923," *Essays in Southern Biography* in *East Carolina College Publications in History*, 2 (Greenville, 1965), 146-66; Robert T. Hawkes, "The Career of Harry Flood Byrd, Sr., to 1933" (Ph.D. diss., University of Virginia, 1975), 43-44; Kaufman, "Flood" 254.

19. CAS to J.P. Swanson, October 15, 1921, CAS to J.N. Brenamen, January 6, 1922, CAS to W.C.N. Merchant, January 23, 1922, Kyle Morison to CAS, January 4, 1922, Swanson Papers, University of Virginia Library; H.F. Byrd to CAS, December 14, 1921, J.N. Brenamen to H.F.

Byrd, January 2, 1922, Byrd Papers; *Richmond News Leader*, December 8, 12, 1921; *Norfolk Virginian Pilot*, January 14, 31, 1922; *Danville Bee*, January 2, 1922; Kaufman, "Flood," 2 and passim.

20. *Danville Register,* May 21, 1921; *Norfolk Virginian Pilot*, February 23, 1922; *Waynesville Valley Virginian*, March 3, 1922; *Richmond Times-Dispatch*, March 8, 1922; Shifflett, "Good Roads," 116-20, 130-39.

21. CAS to W.A. Richeson, February 1, 1922, H.F. Byrd to CAS, May 1, 1922, CAS to H.F. Byrd, May 6, 1922, CAS to A.H. Sands, July 10, 1922, Swanson Papers, University of Virginia Library; CAS to H.F. Byrd, March 28, April 3, 1922, H.F. Byrd to CAS, March 27, 1922, Byrd Papers; *Waynesboro Valley Virginian*, March 3, 1922; *Richmond News Leader*, March 8, 1922; Shifflett, "Good Roads," 139-45.

22. *Norfolk Virginian Pilot*, March 3, 11, 12, 1922; L.S. Epes to E.W. Hudgins, April 9, 1921, Tucker Family Papers; Shibley, "Mapp," 61.

23. CAS to Joseph Whitehead, March 11, 1922, L.C. Major to CAS, March 10, 1922, G.L.H. Jordan to CAS, March 17, 1922, J.F. Cherry to CAS, April 7, 1922, CAS to J.W. Boltwood, April 14, 1922, P.H. Drewry to CAS, April 18, 1922, W.S. Forbes to CAS, May 7, 1922, W.D. Cardwell to CAS, May 18, 1922, Saxon Holt to CAS, June 16, 1922, N.H. Hamilton to CAS, July 5, 1922, CAS to N.H. Hamilton, July 6, 1922, H.L. Hooker to P.H. Drewry, July 12, 1922, L.S. Davis to CAS, July 15, 1922, Swanson Papers, University of Virginia Library; *Norfolk Virginian Pilot*, July 26, 1922.

24. Woodrow Wilson to H.M. Smith, Jr., July 22, 1922, CAS to Woodrow Wilson, August 4, 1922, Wilson Papers; H.L. Hooker to C.J. Duke, June 27, 1922, C.T. Lassiter to CAS, May 11, 1922, CAS to H.M. Smith, Jr., August 9, 1922, Swanson Papers, University of Virginia Library; CAS to E.R. Combs, July 12, 1922, Combs Papers; H.C. Bouldin to Josephine Sizer, July 20, 1922, S.H. To W.W. Moody, July 19, 27, 1922, George Bryan to Westmoreland Davis, July 27, 1922, C.W. Crush to Westmoreland Davis, July 30, 1922, Davis Papers; *Richmond Times Dispatch*, July 26, August 2, 1922; *Richmond News Leader*, January 31, July 1, 21, 1922; *Loudoun Times*, January 12, June 15, 1922; Kirby, *Davis*, 142-58.

25. CAS to Saxon Holt, June 19, 1922, CAS to J.T. Lawless, July 24, 1922, CAS to S.H. Swanson, August 19, 1922, T.J. Barham to CAS, August 18, 1922, Swanson Papers, University of Virginia Library; CAS to Carter Glass, October 27, 1922, Glass Papers.

26. CAS to H.F. Byrd, August 11, 1921, H.F. Byrd to CAS, January 4, June 15, 1922, CAS to G.R.B. Mitchie, July 21, 1922, CAS to R.E. Byrd, July 28, 1922, Swanson Papers, University of Virginia Library; CAS to W.A. Garrett, January 16, 1923, Garrett Papers; *Winchester Evening Star*, July 6, 15, 27, 1922; *Baltimore Sun*, July 15, 1922; *Norfolk Virginian Pilot*, July 21, 1922. Compare and contrast Hawkes, "Byrd," 52, Kirby, *Davis*, 159-62, Pulley, *Old Virginia*, 175-76, and Moger, *Virginia*, 333; Jospeh Fry and Brent Tarter, "The Redemption of the Fighting Ninth: The 1922 Congressional Election in the Ninth District of Virginia and the Origins of the Byrd Organization," *South Atlantic Quarterly*, 77 (Summer 1978); 352-70.

27. H.F. Byrd to W.A. Garrett, January 23, August 3, 1923, Garrett Papers; E.R. Combs to C.F. Beverly, September 5, 1923, E.R. Combs to H.L. Trolinger, September 26, 1923, Combs Papers; L.S. Epes to H.F. Byrd, December 7, 1922, Byrd Papers; Shiflett, "Good Roads," 132, 138, 207-9; Tilley, *Bright-Tobacco*, 392, 450-67; U.S. Senate, *The American Tobacco and the Imperial Tobacco Company* (Washington, 1926), 19 and passim.

28. E.R. Combs to G.C. Peery, November 20, 1923, E.R. Combs to A.K. Morison, November 20, 1923, Combs Papers; H.F. Byrd to R.E. Byrd, November 23, 1923, T.W. Ozlin to H.F. Byrd, December 19, 1923, Byrd Papers; *Richmond News Leader*, December 8, 1923; *Norfolk Virginian Pilot*, January 9, February 22, 1924.

29. Carter Glass to R.L. Ailsworth, January 30, 1924, Glass Papers; Lee N. Allen, "The McAdoo Campaign for the Presidential Nomination in 1924," *JSH*, 29 (May 1963): 211-28; Tindall, *Emergence of New South*, 242-43.

30. H.S. Tucker to J.W. Davis, September 2, 1922, April 4, June 6, August 16, 1923, June

14, 1924, Tucker Family Papers; Carter Glass to R.L. Ailsworth, June 14, 1924, Carter Glass to W.M. McAdoo, April 5, May 16, 1924, Glass Papers; H.F. Byrd to T.S. Martin, December 13, 1918, Byrd Papers; Lyle, "Glass," 85-93; *Norfolk Virginian Pilot*, June 8, 10, 11, 12, 1924; *Portsmouth Star*, June 11, 12, 17, 19, 25, 1924; Robert K. Murray, *The 103rd Ballot* (New York, 1976), 72-73, 75-78, 86-88.

31. W.E. Dodd to J.A. Woodburn, October 19, 1924, Dodd Papers; Carter Glass to CAS, July 4, 1924, Carter Glass to N.R. Hamilton, December 15, 1926, Glass Papers; *Richmond Times-Dispatch*, June 24, July 5, 7, 9, 1924; *Norfolk Virginian Pilot*, July 4, 7, 8, 12, 15, 1924; Democratic National Committee, *Official Proceedings of the Democratic National Convention* (Indianapolis, 1924), 75, 204-6, 208-309, 338 and passim.; Burner, *Politics of Provincialism*, 107-9, 114-27; Murray, *103rd Ballot*, 178, 181-82; William H. Harbaugh, *Lawyer's Lawyer: The Life of John W. Davis* (New York, 1973), 215-16.

32. H.F. Byrd to CAS, August 19, 1924, L.S. Epes to CAS, August 20, 1924, CAS to H.F. Byrd, August 21, 1924, Byrd Papers; *Norfolk Virginian Pilot*, July 15, 1924; Harbaugh. *Davis*, 216; Murray, *103rd Ballot*, 204 and passim.

33. H.F. Byrd to CAS, September 19, 29, 1924, CAS to H.F. Byrd, September 27, 1924, Byrd Papers; W.E. Dodd to CAS, November 2, 1924, "Memorandum for Senator Swanson," September (?) 1924, Dodd Papers; CAS to Carter Glass, October 6, 13, 1924, Glass Papers; Burner, *Politics of Provincialism*, 159.

34. *American Federationist*, 33 (April 1926): 500; 34 (July 1927): 881; (December 1927): 1522; 35 (February 1928): 159; (July 1928): 886.

35. R.W. Moore to R.L.C. Barrett, October 27, 1926, R. Walton Moore Papers, Franklin D. Roosevelt Library, Hyde Park, N.Y.; *Waynesboro Valley Virginian*, August 8, 1919, February 6, July 30, August 6, 1920, March 3, April 28, June 23, 1922; *Cong. Rec.*, 69 Cong., 1 sess., 67 (January 16, 1926), 2173, (February 27, 1926) 4684, (June 18, 1926) 11503.

36. R.W. Moore to H.S. Tucker, November 17, 1924, R.W. Moore to Carter Glass, June 5, 1925, Moore Papers; H.F. Byrd to CAS, April 13, 1925, CAS to H.F. Byrd, November 16, 1925, Byrd Papers; G.W. Mapp to Carter Glass, November 25, 1924, January 9, 1925, Carter Glass to G.W. Mapp, January 7, 1925, Carter Glass to R.M. Lynn, May 30, 1925, Glass Papers; J.G. Pollard to R.W. Moore, December 31, 1923, January 8, 1925, R.W. Moore to J.G. Pollard, January 2, December 20, 1924, January 6, 1925, Pollard Papers; Shibley, "Mapp," 68-83; Hopewell, "Pollard," 113-14; *Norfolk Virginian Pilot*, July 6, 1925.

37. CAS to Carter Glass, July 15, 1925, Glass Papers; H.F. Byrd to W.S. Copeland, August 22, 1925, Copeland Papers; James Cannon, Jr., to G.W. Mapp, December 1, 1924, June 8, 1928, Cannon Papers; H.F. Byrd to E.R. Combs, December 9, 1924, Combs Papers; H.F. Byrd to A.C. Thomas, November 25, 1924, Thomas Papers; R.W. Moore to C.O. Goolrick, March 17, 1925, Moore Papers; Shibley, "Mapp," 34 and passim; Hawkes, "Byrd," 67-77, 199.

38. CAS to H.F. Byrd, November 6, 16, 1925, H.F. Byrd to CAS, November 10, 28, 1925, Byrd Papers.

39. E.R. Combs to H.F. Byrd, December 25, 1925, Combs Papers; Willis, "Trinkle," 140-42, 153-54; Bruce, *Virginia*, 4: 511-13; Robert T. Hawkes, Jr., "The Emergence of a Leader; Harry Flood Byrd, Governor of Virginia, 1926-1930," *VMHB*, 82 (July, 1974): 259-81. See also Tipton R. Snavely et al., *State Grants-in-Aid in Virginia* (New York, 1933), passim. Compare and contrast Hawkes, "Emergence of a Leader," 265-81. Contrast George B. Tindall, "Business Progressivism: Southern Politics in the Twenties," *South Atlantic Quarterly*, 62 (Winter 1963): 93-94, 101-2.

40. Buni, *Negro in Va. Politics*, 73; *Norfolk Virginian Pilot*, May 17, 1928; *Richmond News Leader*, March 16, 1929; Joseph A. Fry, "Senior Advistor to the Democratic 'Organization': William Thomas Reed and Virginia Politics, 1925-1935," *VMHB*, 77 (October 1977): 452-60; Charles E. Wynes, "The Evolution of Jim Crow Laws in Twentieth Century Virginia," *Pylon*, 28 (Winter 1967): 420-21.

41. *Portsmouth Star*, May 21, 1924; *Norfolk Virginian Pilot*, August 5, 10, 1925; Nancy B.

Cuthbert, "Norfolk and the K.K.K., in the Nineteen Twenties" (M.A. thesis, Old Dominion College, 1965), 61 and passim; David B. Chalmers, *Hooded Americanism: The First Century of the Ku Klux Klan, 1865-1965* (New York, 1965), 130-33; Buni, *Negro in Va. Politics*, 102-3.

42. Alleghany Klan, No. 49, to H.F. Byrd, June 5, 1928, Letters received, Governors Office, Harry Flood Byrd Executive Papers, Archives Branch, Virginia State Library, Richmond; H.F. Byrd to W.T. Reed, September 22, 1931, W.T. Reed to H.F. Byrd, September 23, 1931, Byrd Papers; W.T. Reed to H.F. Byrd, September 24, 1931, Reed Family Papers, Virginia Historical Society, Richmond; *Norfolk Virginian Pilot*, October 11, 1928; Chalmers, *Hooded Americanism*, 232-33.

43. For additional criticisms see Joseph H. Saunders for the Virginia Educational Association, Superintendent Harris Hart and Douglas S. Freeman in "Public Hearing before Commission Appointed to Suggest Amendments to the Constitution, October 12, 1928," 1-13, 14-33, and "December 7, 8, 9, 1926," 179-313, J.T. Deal to H.F. Byrd, March 8, 1927; H.F. Byrd to Carter Glass, March 9, 1927, J.G. Pollard to H.F. Byrd, March 27, 1928, T.L. Farrar to H.F. Byrd, June 1, 1928, R.L. Ailsworth to H.F. Byrd, June 12, 1928, J.A. Lesner to H.F. Byrd, June 16, 1928, Letters received, Governor's Office, Byrd Executive Papers; H.F. Byrd to W.T. Reed, August 6, 1926, Reed Family Papers; *Norfolk Virginian Pilot*, May 1, 27, June 17, 1928; Shibley, "Mapp," 87.

44. R.W. Moore to H.F. Byrd, March 8, 1927, Moore Papers.

45. For divisive national themes, see Burner, *Politics of Provincialism*, 74-102. Carter Glass to CAS, June 8, 1928, Glass Papers; CAS to F.D. Roosevelt, March 28, April 6, 1928, R.F Wagner to F.D. Roosevelt, April 20, 1928, General Correspondence, F.D. Roosevelt Papers; Carter Glass to H.F. Byrd, May 31, 1928, Letters received, Governor's Office, Byrd Executive Papers.

46. CAS to Carter Glass, June 7, June 16, 1928, Carter Glass to CAS, June 8, 1928, Glass Papers; *Norfolk Virginian Pilot*, May 5, June 21, 22, 1928.

47. Carter Glass to CAS, June 8, 1928, Glass Papers; Democratic National Committee, *Proceedings of the Democratic National Convention, 1928* (Indianapolis, 1928), 67-68, 211-14; Hall Interview; *Norfolk Virginian Pilot*, June 26, 27, 28, 29, July 2, 1928; Burner, *Politics of Provincialism*, 190-201; Bruce, *Virginia*, 4: 517.

48. J.M. Hooker to J.T. Robinson, July 19, 1928, Carter Glass to CAS, August 16, 1928, Glass Papers; Burner, *Politics of Provincialism*, 201; Cannon, Jr., *Own Story*, 391 and passim.

49. In the three presidential elections in Virginia in the 1920s, the vote was: Democratic, 142,000, 140,000, and 140,000; Republican, 87,000, 73,000, and 165,000. CAS to W.S. Copeland, May 22, 1928, Copeland Papers; N.H. Hamilton to Carter Glass, October 15, 1928, Glass Papers; Colgate Darden to author, August 14, 1961, Hugo Black to author, August 21, 1961, author's possession; *Norfolk Virginian Pilot*, July 20, August 24, 26, September 11, October 4, 11, 1928; Cannon, Jr., *Own Story*, 273, 439, and passim; Michael S. Patterson, Jr., "Fall of a Bishop: James Cannon, Jr., versus Carter Glass, 1909-1934," *JSH*, 39 (November 1973): 493-518.

50. CAS to James Cannon, Jr., November 23, 1928, February 12, 18, 1929, Cannon Papers; CAS to Carter Glass, November 14, 1928, Carter Glass to H.F. Byrd, November 22, 1928, Glass Papers.

51. James Cannon, Jr., to J.D. Eggleston, November 12, 1928, Cannon Papers; C.B. Slemp to J.S. Peters, October 4, 1929, J.S. Peters to C.B. Slemp, November 22, 1929, C. Bascomb Slemp Papers (#9507), Manuscripts Department, University of Virginia Library; Carter Glass to CAS, November 12, 1928, Glass Papers; *Richmond News Leader*, February 6, 26, 1929; *Norfolk Virginian Pilot*, June 19, 27, November 22, 1929.

52. A.W. Robertson to CAS, June 5, 1928, Byrd Papers; H.F. Byrd to W.T. Reed, July 9, 1931, Reed Family Papers; J.G. Pollard to CAS, November 23, 1928, "Memorandum of Interview with Governor Byrd, November 14, 1828," Pollard Papers; H.F. Byrd to Carter Glass, November 26, 1928, Carter Glass to H.F. Byrd, June 3, 1929, Glass Papers; Shibley, "Mapp," 92; Hopewell, "Pollard," 148-55.

53. Swanson may have made an argument for Mapp to compromise with the Cannon drys, but certainly he referred to the regional issues as in R.C.L. Moncure to CAS, January 22, 1929, Reed Family Papers: "There is a great feeling toward the Southwest Virginia and Valley to the positions

they hold in the state." CAS to W.T. Reed, February 4, 13, 1929, W.T. Reed to CAS, February 16, 1929, Reed Family Papers; Hopewell, "Pollard," 154-55.

54. CAS to H.F. Byrd, April 4, 1930, H.F. Byrd to CAS, April 23, 1930, Byrd Papers; R.C. Garland to Harry Wooding, December 17, 1929, Wooding Papers; H.F. Byrd to CAS, May 9, 1929, Carter Glass to H.F. Byrd, June 3, October 3, 1929, H.F. Byrd to Carter Glass, October 25, 1929, April 23, 1930, Glass Papers; CAS to J.G. Pollard, August 7, 1929, *Williamsburg Speech of John Garland Pollard* (Richmond [?], 1929), 16 pp., Pollard Papers; *Richmond News Leader*, March 4, April 2, 10, 20, 29, 1929, Hopewell, "Pollard," 361; Shibley, "Mapp," 91-93.

55. Patterson, "Cannon versus Glass," 506-12; Julian R. Meade, *I Live in Virginia* (New York, 1935), 250 and *passim*; Cannon, Jr., *Own Story*, 368; George T. Starnes and John Hamm, *Some Phases of Labor Relations in Virginia* (New York, 1934), 125; Smith, *Mill on the Dan*, 245-94; Irving Bernstein, *A History of the American Worker, 1920-1933: The Lean Years* (New York, 1960), 3-13; Worth M. Tippy, "Why the Church Sympathizes with Labor," *American Federationist*, 33 (October 1926): 1308-10.

56. A.T. Stroud to H.F. Byrd, December 8, 1930, A.T. Stroud to J.A.C. Chandler, December 8, 1930, Byrd Papers; Bernstein, *Lean Years*, 37-40; Meade, *I Live in Virginia*, 6 and passim; Smith, *Mill on the Dan*, 293-327; Hopewell, "Pollard," 248-61; Tom Tippett, *When Southern Labor Stirs* (New York, 1931), 210-69.

57. H.F. Byrd to W.T. Reed, May 26, 1931; W.T. Reed to H.F. Byrd, May 28, 1931, Reed Family Papers; Norfolk *Virginian Pilot*, March 14, May 16, 1931; *New York Times*, May 16, July 5, 1931; Hall interview; Smith, *Mill on the Dan*, 412.

10. Hares and Hounds: 1921-1932

1. Key Pittman to F.D. Roosevelt, August 10, 1932, Key Pittman Papers, Manuscript Division, LC; H.L. Black to author, August 21, 1961, author's possession; Watson, *Memoirs*, 295-96.

2. CAS to P.S. Wilson, April 5, 1923, P.S. Wilson to CAS, April 6, 1923, File 481, Virginia, RG 30, NA; H.L. Black to author, August 21, 1961, author's possession; *Greensboro Daily News*, February 25, 1961; *Cong. Rec.*, 72 Cong., 2 sess., 76 (February 16, 1933), 4225, 4231; Pepper, *Lawyer*, 146; James F. Byrnes, *All in One Lifetime* (New York, 1958), 6.

3. CAS to J.T. Robinson, October 5, 1926, March 5, 1932, Joseph T. Robinson Papers, University of Arkansas Library; Carter Glass to R.L. Ailsworth, January 30, 1924, Glass Papers; compare and contrast Burner, *Politics of Provincialism*, 158-78.

4. B.M. Baruch to CAS, October 22, 1925, October 21, 1926, CAS to B.M. Baruch, October 23, 1925, J.T. Robinson to B.M. Baruch, March 27, September 24, 1925, B.M. Baruch to J.T. Robinson, November 6, 1926, Bernard M. Baruch Papers, Seely J. Mudd Manuscript Library, Princeton Univerity; James W. Wadsworth, Jr., *Reminiscences*, Oral History Research Office, Columbia University (New York, 1975), 112-13.

5. The concept of "cue-giver" is developed in Donald R. Mathews and James A. Stimson, *Yeas and Nays, Normal Decision Making in the House of Representatives* (New York, 1975), 78-111, as applied to the House a generation later. The same occurrence, if less consistent, may be observed in the Senate and by Swanson in the 1920s. Barbara Hinckley, *The Seniority System in Congress* (Bloomington, 1971), 108-113, limits the effect of seniority, emphasizing initial assignments and reassignments as primary. Yet, in allocation of office space, the Senate Rules Committee followed strictly seniority rankings. George H. Haynes, *The Senate of the United States: Its History and Practice*, 2 (Boston, 1938), 924; Eleanor E. Dennison, *The Senate Foreign Relations Committee* (Stanford, 1942), 144-45; George W. Pepper, *In the Senate* (Philadelphia, 1930), 38-39.

6. U.S. Senate, Public Buildings and Grounds Committee, *Government Archives: Hearings, March 1, 1912* (Washington, 1912), passim; U.S. House of Representatives, *Report of Public Buildings Commission* (Washington, 1914), 26 and passim; Cong. Rec., 65 Cong., 3 sess., 57 (March 4, 1919), 5018; 66 Cong., 1 sess., 58 (July 8, 1919), 2272-76; 67 Cong., 4 sess., 64

(February 10, 1923), 3413; 69 Cong., 1 sess., 67 (April 16, 1926), 7571-82, (April 28, 1926) 8360-73, (May 4, 1926) 8668-70; U.S. Senate, *Annual Report of the Public Buildings Commission* (Washington, 1927), passim.

7. George P. Hamilton, "Farmers National Council," *Nation*, March 15, 1919, 400; *Cong. Rec.*, 67 Cong., 1 sess., 56 (October 29, 1921), 7008-10, (November 7, 1921) 7524; Tilley, *Bright-Tobacco*, 449 and passim; Shideler, *Farm Crisis*, 156; Arthur Capper, *The Agricultural Bloc* (New York, 1922), 3-12.

8. Charles M. Dollar, "Southern Senators and the Senate Farm Bloc: An Illustration of Roll Call Analysis," 22 pp., paper delivered at the Thirty-first Annual Meeting of the Southern Historical Association, Richmond, Virginia, 1965; Lindsay Rogers, "The Second, Third, and Fourth Sessions of the Sixty-seventh Congress," *American Political Science Review*, 18 (February, 1924): 91-95; Shideler, *Farm Crisis*, 155-88.

9. *Southern Planter*, 82 (October 15, 1921): 10, (November 15, 1921): 10; 83 (January 1, 1922): 8; *Cong. Rec.*, 67 Cong., 2 sess., 62 (January 25, 1922), 1691-94; *New York Times*, January 24, 26, 1922; Orville M. Kile, *The Farm Bureau through Three Decades* (Baltimore, 1948), 47 and passim.

10. Compare and contrast Charles M. Dollar, "The South and the Fordney McCumber Tariff of 1922: A Study in Regional Politics," *JSH*, 39 (February 1973): 45-66; *Cong. Rec.*, 67 Cong., 2 sess., 62 (September 19, 1922), 12907; 71 Cong., 2 sess., 72 (February 7, 1930), 3223; Benedict, *Farm Policies*, 186-87; Taussig, *Tariff*, 454-61; Shideler, *Farm Crisis*, 187; *New York Times*, October 2, 1922; *Southern Planter*, 84 (June 15, 1923): 8, (December 1, 1923): 12-13.

11. *Cong. Rec.*, 68 Cong., 1 sess., 65 (March 10, 1924), 3898, 3961, 3965, (March 13, 1924) 4084; 69 Cong., 1 sess., 67 (June 24, 1926), 11868-72; 2 sess., 68 (February 11, 1927), 3518; 70 Cong., 1 sess., 69 (April 12, 1928), 6283, (May 25, 1928) 9880; *Norfolk Virginian Pilot*, May 24, 25, 1928; Donald L. Winters, *Henry Cantwell Wallace as Secretary of Agriculture, 1921-1924* (Urbana, Ill., 1970), 247-88; Benedict, *Farm Policies*, 207-38; Gilbert C. Fite, *George N. Peek and the Fight for Farm Parity* (Norman, Okla., 1954), 38 and passim.

12. Charles M. Gardner, *The Grange: Friend of the Farmer* (Washington, 1949), 124; John F. Davis, "The Export Debenture Plan for Aid to Agriculture," *Quarterly Journal of Economics*, 43 (February 1929): 250-77; John D. Hicks, *Republican Ascendancy, 1921-1933* (New York, 1960), 217-18; Richard Lowitt, *George W. Norris: The Persistence of a Progressive, 1913-1933* (Urbana, 1971), 299 and passim.

13. *Richmond News Leader*, May 10, 1929; *Cong. Rec.*, 71 Cong., 1 sess., 71 (May 8, 1929) 997-98, (May 14, 1929) 1269, (June 11, 1929) 2661, (June 14, 1929) 2886, (October 19, 1929) 4694; Lowitt, *Norris*, 416 and passim; Benedict, *Farm Policies*, 239-40; Gardner, *The Grange*, 174.

14. *Cong. Rec.*, 66 Cong., 2 sess., 59 (May 28, 1920), 7779; 3 sess., 60 (February 5, 1921), 2653; 68 Cong., 1 sess., 65 (June 3, 1924), 10282; 71 Cong., 2 sess., 72 (February 26, 1930), 4264; Preston J. Hubbard, *Origins of TVA: The Muscle Shoals Controversy, 1920-1932* (Nashville, 1961), 6 and passim.

15. *Cong. Rec.*, 68 Cong., 2 sess., 66 (December 16, 1924), 656, (December 19, 1924) 824, (January 8, 1925) 1454, (January 13, 1925) 1738, (January 14, 1925) 1808; 70 Cong., 1 sess., 69 (March 12, 1928), 4548, (March 13, 1928) 4635, (May 25, 1928) 9842; 2 sess., 70 (December 14, 1928), 603; 71 Cong., 2 sess., 72 (April 4, 1930), 6511; 71 Cong., 3 sess., 74 (February 23, 1931), 5716; Hubbard, *TVA*, 20 and passim; Lowitt, *Norris*, 244 and passim.

16. *Cong. Rec.*, 66 Cong., 3 sess., 60 (February 11, 1921), 2999, (February 17, 1921) 3606-11; 67 Cong., 1 sess., 61 (August 11, 1921), 4857-58, (August 16, 1921) 5062, (August 17, 1921) 5113-14; 68 Cong., 2 sess., 66 (January 30, 1925), 2708, (February 3, 1925) 2937, (February 6, 1925) 3124-28; 69 Cong., 1 sess., 64 (June 5, 1926), 10767, (June 11, 1926) 11149-50; 69 Cong., 2 sess., 68 (January 4, 1927), 1059.

17. CAS to W.T. Reed, June 4, 1929, Reed Family Papers; *Cong. Rec.*, 71 Cong., 1 sess., 71 (September 13, 1929), 3594, (October 31, 1929) 5003-4; Lawrence H. Fuchs, "Election of 1928," in Schlesinger, *Presidential Elections*, 3: 2613-14.

18. Entry, March 30, 1931, Henry L. Stimson, Diaries, 15: 198, Manuscript Archives, Yale University; *Cong. Rec.*, 71 Cong., 1 sess., 71 (September 10, 1929), 3494; *New York Times*, August 7, November 1, 1929; Taussig, *Tariff*, 496-98.

19. E.E. Schattschneider, *Politics, Pressures and the Tariff* (New York, 1935), 13 and passim; *Cong. Rec.*, 71 Cong., 1 sess., 71 (October 9, 1929), 4387, 4389; 2 sess., 72 (February 18, 1930), 3844, (March 4, 1930) 4698, (March 5, 1930) 4793-4800, 4826, (March 24, 1930) 6015, (May 15, 1930) 8975, (May 16, 1930) 9056; *New York Times*, April 3, 1930.

20. *Cong. Rec.*, 71 Cong., 1 sess., 71 (June 17, 1929), 2951; 2 sess., 72 (June 14, 1930), 10789-90; 3 sess., 74 (March 3, 1931), 6979-90; *New York Times*, August 4-5, 1930; August 9, 1931; *Norfolk Virginian Pilot*, June 14, 1930; David Burner, *Herbert Hoover: A Public Life* (New York, 1979), 297.

21. *New York Times*, June 14, August 4, November 2, 1930; Frank B. Freidel, *Franklin D. Roosevelt: The Triumph* (Boston, 1956), 177-78.

22. *Cong. Rec.*, 67 Cong., 1 sess., 61 (July 21, 1921), 4216, (November 21, 1921) 8053; E.G. Williams to CAS, May 6, 1926, B.B. Bagby to CAS, May 18, 1926, Mrs. R.S. Hopkins et al. to CAS, June 11, 1926 in 69 Cong., 1 sess., 67 (June 15, 1926), 11270-75; Grace Abbott, "The Federal Government in Relation to Maternity and Infancy," *Annals of the American Academy of Political Science*, 151 (September, 1930): 92-101.

23. *Cong. Rec.*, 69 Cong., 1 sess., 67 (June 15, 1926), 11270-71; 71 Cong., 3 sess., 74 (December 16, 1930) 811, (December 18, 1930) 1037-38, 1041, (December 17, 1930) 949, (January 10, 1931) 1913; Burner, *Hoover*, 222.

24. CAS to H.L. Stimson, July 9, 1930, H.L. Stimson to CAS, July 22, 1930, 842.61211/13, 21A., RG 59, NA; *Cong. Rec.*, 68 Cong., 2 sess., 66 (January 7, 1925), 1381-83; 69 Cong., 1 sess., 67 (June 9, 1926), 10991; 70 Cong., 1 sess., 69 (March 28, 1928), 5493; 71 Cong., 1 sess., 71 (May 10, 1929), 1104-5; Dollar, "Farm Bloc."

25. For an example of federal expenditures in the Norfolk area, the Second District, see the Seventy-first Congress's activity. *Cong. Rec.*, 71 Cong., 2 sess., 72 (June 28, 1930), 11992-93. Ibid., 66 Cong., 3 sess., 60 (February 11, 1921), 2999; 67 Cong., 4 sess., 64 (February 7, 1923), 3205, (February 12, 1923) 3483-84, 3486; 68 Cong., 2 sess., 66 (February 20, 1925) 4252, (March 3, 1925) 5274; 70 Cong., 1 sess., 69 (February 27, 1928), 3595; 72 Cong., 1 sess., 74 (January 6, 1931), 1465, (February 21, 1931) 5615.

26. W.T. Reed to CAS, December 13, 1927, April 23, 1929, December 22, 31, 1931, CAS to W.T. Reed, April 27, 1927, January 13, 1932, W.T. Reed to H.F. Byrd, January 5, 1932, Reed Family Papers; U.S. Treasury Department, Secretary, *Annual Report on the State of Finances for the Fiscal Year Ended June 30, 1940* (Washington, 1941), 480-82.

27. W.T. Reed to CAS, June 21, 1926, January 25, 1929, T.G. Burch to W.T. Reed, May 24, 1930, Reed Family Papers.

28. *Cong. Rec.*, 68 Cong., 1 sess., 65 (April 29, 1924), 7443-47; 2 sess., 66 (February 9, 1925), 3281, 3303; U.S. Senate, *The American Tobacco Company and the Imperial Tobacco Company* (Washington, 1926), 4-18, 32-35, 52; John T. Scanlon and J. M. Tinley, *Business Analysis of the Tobacco Growers Cooperative Association* (Washington 1929), 100-2; Tilley, *Bright-Tobacco*, 449-86.

29. Scanlon and Tinley, *Tobacco Growers Cooperative*, 15, 65, 112-45; Senate, *ATC and Imperial*, "Exhibit B," 104-9; G.E. Webb to L.H. Reed, February 23, 1923, L.H. Reed to G.E. Webb, March 12, 1923, in ibid., 68-69.

30. CAS to W.T. Reed, July 1, 1930, Reed Family Papers. See U.S. Senate, *Investigation of Battlefields in and around Fredericksburg and Spotsylvania Courthouse* (Washington, 1924), 3 pp., and *Creating Colonial Monuments in Virginia* (Washington, 1931), 2 pp.

31. U.S. Senate, *Shenandoah and Great Smokey Mountains National Parks* (Washington, 1926), 8 pp.; *Cong. Rec.*, 68 Cong., 2 sess., 66 (February 12, 1925), 3539, 69 Cong., 1 sess., 67 (May 13, 1926), 9362.

32. CAS to W.T. Reed, March 19, 1927, Reed Family Papers; *Cong. Rec.*, 69 Cong., 1 sess.,

67 (December 21, 1925), 1255-56; *New York Times*, January 25, February 7, 1925; Clarence A. Miller, *The Lives of the Interstate Commerce Commissioners and the Commission Secretaries* (Washington, 1946), 117-21; E. Pendleton Herring, "Special Interests and the Interstate Commerce Commission, II," *American Political Science Review*, 27 (December, 1933): 906-8; Harvey C. Mansfield, *The Lake Cargo Coal Rate Controversy* (New York, 1932), 88 and passim.

33. State delegations from Kentucky, Tennessee, West Virginia and Virginia—three Republicans and five Democrats—voted aye. CAS to W.T. Reed, March 19, 1926, Reed Family Papers; Miller, *Commissioners' Lives*, 120; *Cong. Rec.*, 69 Cong., 1 sess., 67 (December 21, 1925), 1257-57; U.S. Senate, *Journal of the Executive Proceedings*, 69 Cong., 2 sess., 64, pt. 1 (March 26, 1926), 802; *New York Times*, March 24, 25, 29, 1926; Harvey, *Coal Rate Controversy*, 141-71.

34. U.S. Senate, *Journal of the Executive Proceedings*, 70 Cong., 1 sess., 66, pt. 1 (March 16, 1928), 586-87; *Cong. Rec.*, 70 Cong., 1 sess., 69 (February 13, 1928), 2888, (February 16, 1928) 3096-97, (February 17, 1928) 3150-51; 71 Cong., 1 sess., 71 (June 12, 1929), 2740; 2 sess., 72 (May 7, 1930), 8487; Miller *Commissioners' Lives*, 105-6, 125; *New York Times*, February 22, 27, March 13, 17, 1928; Harvey, *Coal Rate Controversy*, 171-94.

35. *Cong. Rec.*, 68 Cong., 1 sess., 65 (January 9, 1924), 747; 69 Cong., special sess., 67 (March 10, 1925), 101, (March 16, 1925) 275; *New York Times*, January 10, 11, 1924, February 7, March 17, 1925; Shideler, *Farm Crisis*, 293; Lindsay Rogers, "First and Second Sessions of the Sixty-eighth Congress," *American Polticial Science Review*, 19 (November, 1925): 762.

36. Senate requested FTC studies including bakeries, cooperatives, and power companies. The latter investigation grew to be a basis for the Public Utility Holding Company Act of 1935. Susan Wagner, *The Federal Trade Commission* (New York, 1971), 27; *Cong. Rec.*, 68 Cong., 1 sess., 65 (January 29, 1924), 1597-98, (February 8, 1924) 10577; U.S. Senate, *Prices, Profits and Competition*, 19, 20 (Washington, 1928), 248-56.

37. U.S. Senate, Judiciary Committee, *The Department of Justice and the Aluminum Company of America* (Washington, 1926), 12; *Cong. Rec.*, 69 Cong., 1 sess., 67 (February 18, 1926), 4207-9, 4215-19 (February 26, 1926), 4622.

38. *Cong. Rec.*, 67 Cong., 1 sess., 61 (November 16, 1921), 7802; 68 Cong., 1 sess., 65 (March 18, 1924), 4418, 4420, (March 26, 1924) 5007-8; 70 Cong., 1 sess., 69 (May 21, 1928), 9330; 71 Cong., 1 sess., 71 (June 5, 1929), 2390-91; 71 Cong., 2 sess., 72 (May 19, 1930), 9117.

39. R.W. Moore to H.F. Byrd, March 8, 1927, Moore Papers; *Cong. Rec.*, 70 Cong., 1 sess., 69 (January 23, 1928), 1848-75, 71 Cong., 1 sess., 71 (May 15, 1929), 1323-28, (May 24, 1929) 1847-51, 1858-61, (May 28, 1929) 2076; *New York Times*, March 28, 1926.

40. Arthur W. MacMahon, "First Session of the Seventieth Congress," *American Political Science Review*, 22 (August, 1928): 663-64.

41. A first lien on crops secured the federal loan. H.F. Byrd to J.G. Pollard, August 11, 1930, Byrd Papers; W.T. Reed to H.F. Byrd, December 19, 1930, Reed Family Papers; U.S. Senate, Agriculture and Forestry Committee, *Hearings on Relief for Drought Stricken Areas* (Washington, 1930), 18-21; *Cong. Rec.*, 71 Cong., 3 sess., 74 (December 9, 1930), 395-96, (February 3, 1931) 3839-48; *Richmond Times-Dispatch*, February 3, 1931; Arthur W. MacMahon, "Third Session of the Seventy-first Congress," *American Political Science Review*, 25 (November, 1931): 939-42; compare and contrast Burner, *Hoover*, 263-64.

11. Prodigious Shadow: 1921-1932

1. Stephen Roskill, *Naval Policy Between the Wars, 1919-1929*, 1 (London, 1968), 19-20; L. Ethan Ellis, *Republican Foreign Policy, 1921-1933* (New Brunswick, 1968), passim; Robert H. Ferrell, *American Diplomacy: A History*, 3d edition (New York, 1975), 507-40.

2. *Cong. Rec.*, 67 Cong., 1 sess., 61 (April 30, 1921), 862-65, (July 1, 1921) 3299; Noggle, *Into the Twenties*, 151; Robert K. Murray, *The Harding Era: Warren G. Harding and His Administration* (Minneapolis, 1969), 139-40.

3. CAS to B.M. Baruch, September 30, 1921, Baruch Papers; Woodrow Wilson to CAS, July 13, October 10, December 13, 1921, CAS to Woodrow Wilson, October 12, 1921, J.R. Bolling

to CAS, October 13, 1921, Bainbridge Colby memorandum, October 14, 1921, Wilson Papers; *Cong. Rec.*, 67 Cong., 1 sess., 61 (July 1, 1921), 3283, (October 12, 1921) 6249, 6257, (October 18, 1921) 6438-39; Peter H. Buckingham, *International Normalcy: The Open Door Peace with the Former Central Powers, 1921-29* (Wilmington, 1983), 42-47.

4. *New Republic*, 32 (September 6, 1922), 33-34; *Nation*, 67 (August 1923): 103-4; *New York Times*, February 8, 1925; Murray, *Harding Era*, 479-81.

5. B.M. Baruch to CAS, December 16, 1925, May 27, June 3, 1926, CAS to B.M. Baruch, April 23, June 2, 1926, Baruch Papers; *Cong. Rec.*, 69 Cong., 1 sess., 67 (March 2, 1926), 4838, (April 2, 1926) 6764-66, (May 17, 1926) 9514-24; 70 Cong., 1 sess., 69 (February 16, 1928), 3098-99.

6. *Cong. Rec.*, 65 Cong., 3 sess., 57 (January 22, 1919), 1857-58; Ellis, *Republican Foreign Policy*, 22-24, 191-205; Carl P. Parrini, *Heir to Empire: United States Economic Diplomacy, 1916-1923* (Pittsburgh, 1969), 47-71, 254-59; Harold G. Moulton and Leo Pasvolsky, *War Debts and World Prosperity* (Washington, 1932), 25-70.

7. *Cong. Rec.*, 67 Cong., 4 sess., 64 (February 3, 1923), 2939, (February 16, 1923) 3786; 68 Cong., 2 sess., 66 (December 11, 1924) 447-48; 69 Cong., 1 sess., 67 (December 7, 1925), 974-75, (April 24, 1926) 8167, (April 27, 1926) 8278, 8282, (April 28, 1926) 8347; Ferrell, *American Diplomacy*, 511.

8. J.T. Robinson to B.M. Baruch, February 17, 1926, Baruch Papers; *Cong. Rec.*, 69 Cong., 1 sess., 67 (April 1, 1926), 6688-90, (April 19, 1926) 7744-46, (April 21, 1926) 7901; Moulton and Pasvolsky, *War Debts*, 86-87.

9. Leland Harrison to H.S. Gibson, July 31, 1926, 500 D/336, RG 59, NA; Union Interparlementaire, *Compte Rendu de la XXI Conference* (Geneva, 1923), 343-44, 374-82; *Norfolk Virginian Pilot*, October 2, 1926; *New York Times*, October 2, 1926, August 9, 1931.

10. *New York Times*, December 21, 22, 1926; *Cong. Rec.*, 71 Cong., 2 sess., 72 (December 16, 1929), 721; Moulton and Pasvolsky, *War Debts*, 87, 295-98; Melvyn P. Leffler, *The Elusive Quest: America's Pursuit of European Stability and French Security, 1919-1933* (Chapel Hill, 1979), passim.

11. Entry, June 19, 1931, Stimson Diaries, 16: 193; *Cong. Rec.*, 72 Cong., 1 sess., 75 (December 22, 1931), 1126; Burner, *Hoover*, 300-4; Ferrell, *American Diplomacy*, 511-12; George L. Grassmuck, *Sectional Biases in Congress on Foreign Policy* (Baltimore, 1951), 93-99.

12. Entry, November 20, 1918, February 21, 24, 1919, *Diaries of Daniels*, 350, 375; Josephus Daniels to Woodrow Wilson, January 25, 1919, Daniels Papers; Thomas H. Buckley, *The United States and the Washington Conference, 1921-1922* (Knoxville, 1970), 6-10; Harold and Margaret Sprout, *Toward a New Order of Sea Power: American Naval Policy and the World Scene, 1918-1922* (Princeton, 1946), 110-12; Roger Dingman, *Power in the Pacific: The Origins of Naval Arms Limitation, 1914-1922* (Chicago, 1976), 43-48.

13. W.E. Dodd to Josephus Daniels, November 22, 1918, W.E. Dodd to [E.H. (?)] Goodwin, December 29, 1918, Dodd Papers; E.B. Cameron to CAS, January 20, 1921, Swanson Papers, University of Virginia Library; entry, March 27, 1920, *Diaries of Daniels*, 510-11; U.S. Senate, *Suspension of the United States Naval Construction Program* (Washington, 1921), 28 pp.; *Cong. Rec.*, 66 Cong., 3 sess., 60 (December 14, 1920), 310, (March 1, 1921) 4131, (March 3, 1921) 4388-90; 67 Cong., 1 sess., 61 (May 12, 1921), 1360-61, (May 20, 1921) 1580-86, (May 24, 1921) 1684-85; Paolo E. Coletta, *Admiral Bradley E. Fiske and the American Navy* (Lawrence, 1979), 199-216; Braisted, *U.S. in the Pacific, 1909-1929*, 491-504; Dingman, *Naval Arms Limitation*, 100-4; Roskill, *Naval Policy, 1919-1929*, 52-53; Ernest Andrade, Jr., "United States Naval Policy in the Disarmament Era, 1921-1937" (Ph.D. diss., Michigan State University, 1966), 36-39.

14. Theodore Harris to CAS, November 21, 1921, Swanson Papers, University of Virginia Library; *Cong. Rec.*, 67 Cong., 1 sess., 61 (October 31, 1921), 7007-10; *New York Times*, July 12, November 1, 1921; C. Leonard Hoag, *Preface to Preparedness: The Washington Disarmament Conference and Public Opinion* (Washington, 1941), 89-123; Murray, *Harding Era*, 144-49; Buckley, *Washington Conference*, 18.

15. J.T. Robinson to B.M. Baruch, February 22, March 10, 21, 1922, Baruch Papers; *Cong.*

Rec., 67 Cong., 2 sess., 62 (February 28, 1922), 3193, (March 23, 1922) 4312, (March 24, 1922) 4486, 4489, 4497; Braisted, *U.S. in the Pacific, 1909-1922*, 624-25, 646-47; Buckley, *Washington Conference*, 142, 156, 182-83; Ellis, *Republican Foreign Policy*, 100-3; Merlo J. Pusey, *Charles Evans Hughes*, 2 (New York, 1963), 461-63; Joan Hoff Wilson, *American Business and Foreign Policy, 1920-1933* (Lexington, 1971), 46-47; Buckingham, *International Normalcy*, 53-71.

16. *Cong. Rec.*, 67 Cong., 2 sess., 62 (March 27, 1922), 4621, (March 30, 1922) 4784; 70 Cong., 2 sess., 70 (January 16, 1929), 1759-60; Sprout, *New Order*, 161-79; Ferrell, *American Diplomacy*, 519-21; Andrade, "Disarmament Era," 39-79; Dingman, *Naval Arms Limitation*, 215-19.

17. U.S. Navy, Bureau of Construction and Repair, "Vessels under Construction, United States Navy," October 10, 1921; memorandum, "Navy Department Plan," "Conference Memorandum," "Memorandum of A Conversation Held in Mr. Hughes's Room," December 13, 1921, Charles Evans Hughes Papers, Manuscript Division, LC; *Cong. Rec.*, 67 Cong., 2 sess., 62 (March 28, 1922), 4674; *New York Times*, February 14, 1935.

18. P.S. Jones to CAS, October 21, 1921, Saxon Holt to CAS, May 15, 1922, Swanson Papers, University of Virginia Library; *Cong. Rec.*, 67 Cong., 2 sess., 62 (February 11, 1922), 2428; *New York Times*, October 26, December 31, 1921, February 15, 1922; *Norfolk Virginian Pilot*, February 14, 15, 1922.

19. J.T. Robinson to B.M. Baruch, February 17, 1926, Baruch Papers; *Cong. Rec.*, 68 Cong., 1 sess., 65 (March 21, 1924), 4637, (April 12, 1924) 6210-14, (April 26, 1924) 7221-22, (April 28, 1924) 1731-32; 70 Cong., 2 sess., 70 (February 2, 1929), 2696; *Norfolk Virginian Pilot*, March 7, 1925, February 10, 1929; Roskill, *Naval Policy, 1919-1929*, 457, 562; Andrade, "Disarmament Era," 88-112.

20. *Cong. Rec.*, 66 Cong., 3 sess., 60 (February 12, 1921), 3059-60, (March 3, 1921) 4388-92; 67 Cong., 1 sess., 61 (May 20, 1921), 1726; 2 sess., 62 (June 16, 1922), 8819-25, 8856-58, 8860-67; 70 Cong., 1 sess., 69 (January 20, 1928), 1769-74, (January 27, 1928) 2125, (March 26, 1928) 5346-48, (April 30, 1928) 7424-25, (May 16, 1928) 8866-68; 71 Cong., 1 sess., 71 (June 4, 1929), 2317.

21. *Cong. Rec.*, 68 Cong., 1 sess., 65 (April 29, 1924), 7457-58.

22. Northern and Southern Democrats could agree upon Asian exclusion but not upon European. *Cong. Rec.*, 68 Cong., 1 sess., 65 (April 8, 1924), 5828-29, (April 14, 1924) 6302-13, (April 17, 1924) 6548-49; Rodman W. Paul, *The Abrogation of the Gentleman's Agreement* (Cambridge, 1936), 34-97; Pusey, *Hughes*, Vol. 2, 513-16; Johnson and Porter, *National Party Platforms*, 1: 235-36, 249; Russell H. Fifield, *Woodrow Wilson and the Far East* (Hamden, 1965), 10, 36-37, 48.

23. John Richards and Company to J.E. Hughes, August 2, 1928, J.E. Hughes to CAS, September 2, 1918, Robert Lansing to CAS, September 16, 1918, 693.119/203; CAS to F.B. Kellogg, November 29, 1926, F.B. Kellogg to CAS, December 3, 1926, 893.00/7883, RG 59, NA; Tilley, *Bright-Tobacco*, 335-36.

24. Entry, December 9, 1931, January 14, 1932, August 10, 1932, Stimson Diaries, 19: 141; 20: 50; 23: 135.

25. Entry, April 13, 1931, Stimson, Diaries, vol. 15, 240; U.S. Senate, Foreign Relations Committee, *Hearings, Recognition of the Present Government of Russia, Part 1* (Washington, 1924), 16-17, 21-30, 48-49, 97, 119; *New York Times*, December 4, 1932; *London Times*, October 11, 1926; Edward M. Bennett, *Recognition of Russia: An American Foreign Policy Dilemma* (Waltham, 1970), passim, Hoff Wilson, *Business and Foreign Policy*, xv; Selig Adler, *The Uncertain Giant, 1921-1941: American Foreign Policy between Wars* (New York, 1965), 52-55.

26. J.T. Robinson to B.M. Baruch, May 9, 1925, Baruch Papers; U.S. Senate, Foreign Relations Committee, *Hearings, Permanent Court of International Justice* (Washington, 1924), 26-138 and passim, *New York Times*, July 1, December 7, 1923; Murray, *Harding Era*, 368-72; Pusey, *Hughes*, vol. 2, 594-601; Dennison, *Senate Foreign Relations Committee*, 103-115; Ellis, *Republican Foreign Policy*, 69-71; Denna Fleming, *The United States and the World Court, 1920-66* (New York, 1968), 40-46.

W.J. Carr to CAS, March 20, 1928, 120.11/5c, May 9, 1929, 120.31/56a, RG 59, NA; F.B. Kellogg to C.B. Slemp, May 15, 1928, in Ellis, *Kellog*, 14-22, 243-44; Trask, *Turkish Nationalism*, 56-60; Walo H. Heinrichs, Jr., *American Ambassador: Joseph C. Grew and the Development of the United States Diplomatic Tradition* (Boston, 1966), 132-33. Contrast Daniel, "Armenian Question," 272-74; U.S. House of Representatives, *Report of the Progress of Purchase of Sites and Construction of Buildings* (Washington, 1929), passim, Buckingham, *International Normalcy*, 100.

39. Heinrichs, *American Ambassador*, 148; Trask, *Turkish Nationalism*, 113-14; *Cong. Rec.*, 71 Cong., 2 sess., 72 (February 17, 1930), 3779-80; Buckingham, *International Normalcy*, 104-6.

40. Entry, October 29, 1930, March 3, 1931, Stimson, Diaries, 10: 103; 15 135; *Cong., Rec.*, 68 Cong., 2 sess., 66 (January 15, 1925), 1865-69; 69 Cong., 1 sess., 67 (December 18, 1925), 1056-58; Johnson and Porter, *National Party Platforms*, 1: 222, 252, 274; Ellis, *Republican Foreign Policy*, passim; Noggle, *Into the Twenties*, 139-41.

41. James Cannon, Jr., to CAS, May 9, 1925, J.C. Grew to CAS, May 11, 1925, 812.404/261, RG 59, NA; U.S. Senate, Foreign Relations Committee, *Preliminary Report and Hearings, Citizens of the United States in Mexico*, 1 (Washington, 1920), 141-58; Cannon, Jr., *Own Story*, 214-17; *Cong. Rec.*, 71 Cong., 2 sess., 72 (April 2, 1930), 6349-53, (April 21, 1930) 7324, 7329, 7332, (May 13, 1930) 8843; *New York Times*, November 25, 1926, October 9, 1928; Clifford W. Trow, "Woodrow Wilson and the Mexican Intervention Movement of 1919," *Journal of American History*, 58 (June, 1971): 46-72.

42. *Cong. Rec.*, 70 Cong., 1 sess., 69 (April 16, 1928), 6521-25; (April 19, 1928) 6747-53, (April 25, 1928) 7192-93; U.S. Senate, Foreign Relations Committee, *Hearings, Use of the United States Navy in Nicaragua* (Washington, 1928), 19 and passim; *New York Times*, January 7, 10, March 10, 1927, April 18, 1931; William Kamman, *A Search for Stability: United States Diplomacy Toward Nicaragua, 1925-1933* (Notre Dame, 1968), passim; Adler, *Uncertain Giant*, 88-92; Ellis, *Kellogg*, passim, and *Republican Foreign Policy*, 46-72.

43. J.T. Robinson to B.M. Baruch, December 22, 1923, Baruch Papers; CAS to W. A. Garrett, January 16, 1923, Garrett Papers; *New York Times*, December 24, 1926, September 13, 1927.

44. Entry, November 7, 1930, September 9, 1931, Stimson, Diaries, 10: 130; 18: 1-2; entry, September 3, 1928, in Dawes, *Notes*, 111; *New York Times*, November 27, 1928; *Norfolk Virginian Pilot*, January 1, 1928.

12. The Wise Thing to Do: 1929-1933

1. Hall interview; CAS to W.T. Reed, April 13, 1929, Reed Family Papers; C.E. Hughes to CAS, January 22, 1925, 711.672/341A, RG 59, NA; H.F. Byrd to W.T. Reed, March 26, 27, 1931, Byrd Papers; entry, January 12, 1932, Stimson, Diaries, 19: 42; entry, December, 2, 1928, January 9, 1929, Dawes, *Notes*, 172, 225 and passim.

2. U.S. Senate, Naval Affairs Committee, *To Authorize Construction of Certain Naval Vessels* (Washington, 1928), passim; *Cong. Rec.*, 70 Cong., 2 sess., 70 (January 16, 1929), 1758-62, (January 24, 1929) 2192, (January 26, 1929) 2294, (January 28, 1929) 2529, (January 31, 1929) 2530, (February 21, 1929) 3954, (February 22, 1924) 4036-41, (February 27, 1929) 4538.

3. H.W. Farlow to CAS, July 25, 1922, Swanson Papers, University of Virginia Library; CAS to W.T. Reed, March 31, 1928, Reed Family Papers; *Norfolk Virginian Pilot*, February 10, 1929; *Cong. Rec.*, 71 Cong., 2 sess., 72 (May 28, 1930), 9709.

4. *New York Times*, August 4, September 29, 1929; Raymond G. O'Connor, *Perilous Equilibrium: The United States and the London Naval Conference of 1930* (Lawrence, 1962), 20 and passim; Ellis, *Republican Foreign Policy*, 155-90.

5. O'Connor, *London Naval Conference*, 58, notes Swanson's criticism of Hoover's cruiser suspension may have harmed his chances of attendance at London. In 1927, however, Coolidge

27. J.C. Grew to CAS, December 2, 1925, CAS to J.C. Grew, December 8, 1925, 767.9 15/12, 15/13, RG 59, NA; *Cong. Rec.*, 68 Cong., 1 sess., 65 (May 6, 1924), 7904; Sen Hearings, *Permanent Court*, 71; Dennison, *Senate Foreign Relations Committee*, 114-21; Flemi *World Court*, 47-51.

28. J.T. Robinson to B.M. Baruch, May 9, 1925, Baruch Papers; Dennison, *Senate Fore Relations Committee*, 118, 188-90; Margulies, *Lenroot*, 380-82.

29. *Cong. Rec.*, 69 Cong., 1 sess., 67 (December 17, 1925), 974-88, (December 18, 19 1075-89, (January 6, 1926) 1565-68, (January 18, 1926) 2295, 2589-93; Margulies, *Lenrc* 381-85; Dennison, *Senate Foreign Relations Committee*, 121-22; L. Ethan Ellis, *Frank B. Kell* and American Foreign Relations, 1925-1929 (New Brunswick, 1961), 226-27; Fleming, *Wc Court*, 52-67; London *Times*, December 18, 1925.

30. *Cong. Rec.*, 69 Cong., 1 sess., 67 (January 23, 1926), 2656-66, (January 26, 19 2739-62, (January 27, 1926) 2824-25; Margulies, *Lenroot*, 385-90; Dennison, *Senate Fore Relations Committee*, 121-22; Ellis, *Kellogg*, 226-27; Fleming, *World Court*, 52-67; Pep| *Senate*, 106-20.

31. *Cong. Rec.*, 69 Cong., 1 sess., 67 (February 18, 1926), 4203-5; S.P. Tuck to F Kellogg, September 14, 1926, in U.S. Department of State, *Foreign Relations of the United Sta 1926*, 1 (Washington, 1941), 17-25; *New York Times*, February 17, August 4, 24, 1926; El *Kellogg*, 228-29, 384-85; Fleming, *World Court*, 52-67. Both Ellis and Fleming are highly crit of the Senate.

32. F.B. Kellogg to Elihu Root, March 8, 1929, H.L. Stimson to Elihu Root, May 25, 19 in U.S. Department of State, *Foreign Relations of the United States, 1929*, 1 (Washington, 19 7-8, 12-13; *Cong. Rec.*, 70 Cong., 1 sess., 69 (April 9, 1928), 6076-78; *New York Times*, April 1928; Ellis, *Kellogg*, 229-30; Dennison, *Senate Foreign Relations Committee*, 124-25; Philip Jessup, *Elihu Root, 1905-1937*, 2 (New York, 1928), 434-42.

33. J.T. Robinson to CAS, February 3, 1932, CAS to J.T. Robinson, March 5, 19 Robinson Papers; W.T. Reed to CAS, December 13, 1930, CAS to D.S. Freeman, December 1930, Reed Family Papers; entry, November 12, December 3, 5, 6, 12, 1930, March 14, 30, A 13, 1931, Stimson, Diaries, 10: 148, 192-93, 199, 201, 218; 15: 156-57, 166, 198, 240; *Richm News Leader*, December 12, 1930; *New York Times*, September 6, October 4, 1929, December 1930; Dennison, *Senate Foreign Relations Committee*, 126-33.

34. Entry, December 20, 1928, Charles G. Dawes, *Notes As Vice President, 1928* (Boston, 1935), 191-92; U.S. Senate, *Hearings, General Pact for the Reunciation of War* (Wa ington, 1928), 4, 7, 13; *Cong. Rec.*, 70 Cong., 2 sess., 70 (January 4, 1929), 1121, 1138-39; Ad *Uncertain Giant*, 88-92; Ellis, *Kellogg*, 193-212; Robert H. Ferrell, *Peace in Their Time:* Origins of the Kellogg-Briand Pact (New Haven, 1952), passim.

35. Entry, January 15, 1929, Dawes, *Notes*, 235-37; *Norfolk Virginian Pilot*, January 6 1929; *Cong. Rec.*, 70 Cong., 2 sess., 70 (January 5, 1929), 1179-89.

36. James Cannon, Jr., to CAS, February 23, 1925, Cannon Papers; Schlesinger, *Presiden Elections*, 3: 2401, 2501; Robert L. Daniel, "The Armenian Question and American-Turk Relations, 1914-1927," *Mississippi Valley Historical Review*, 46 (September, 1959): 252-69; Ro R. Trask, *The United States Response to Turkish Nationalism and Reform 1914-1939* (Minneapo 1971), passim; Buckingham, *International Normalcy*, 102.

37. Swanson had defended Wheeler in an attack by the Justice Department during the Tea Dome affair. *Cong. Rec.*, 68 Cong., 1 sess., 65 (May 23, 1924), 9253-60; C.E. Hughes to C/ January 26, 1924, Hughes Papers; C.E. Hughes to CAS, May 6, 1924, 711.672/285b, January 1925, 711.672/341A, A.W. Dulles to CAS, December 2, 1924, 711.67/51A, RG 59, NA; He Morgenthau, Sr., to CAS and W.E. Borah, May 18, 1926, Borah Papers; W.T. Reed to CAS, J 21, 1926, Reed Family Papers; CAS to James Cannon, Jr., February 26, 1925, June 2, 19: Cannon Papers; Daniel, "Armenian Question," 270-75; Joseph C. Grew, *Turbulent Era: A Dip matic Record of Forty Years, 1904-1945*, 1 (Boston, 1952), 674-79; Trask, *Turkish Nationalism*, Buckingham, *International Normalcy*, 103-4.

38. "Proceedings, Foreign Service Building Commission, July 15, 1926," Borah Pape

desired to send Swanson, Andrew Mellon, and Kellogg to another conference, but Kellogg demurred, fearing it would be "overloading the delegation" and appear that the United States was "overanxious to have an agreement." F.B. Kellogg to Calvin Coolidge, May 27, 1927, in *Foreign Relations, 1927*, 1: 40-41; *New York Times*, October 21, 22, November 13, 1929.

    6. H.L. Stimson to J.P. Cotton, February 7, 1930, J.P. Cotton to H.L. Stimson, February 7, 1930, in *Foreign Relations, 1930*, 1: 21, Charles G. Dawes, *Journal As Ambassador to Great Britain* (New York, 1939), 145.

    7. J.P. Cotton to H.L. Stimson, March 6, 27, 1930, in *Foreign Relations, 1930*, 1: 48-49, 88-89; London *Times*, February 18, 1930; O'Connor, *London Naval Conference*, 92, 98.

    8. U.S. Senate, Foreign Relations Committee, *Hearings on Limitations of Naval Disarmament* (Washington, 1930), 2 and passim; *Cong. Rec.*, 71 Cong., special sess., 73 (July 10, 1930), 85-89; O'Connor, *London Naval Conference*, 116; Gerald E. Wheeler, *Admiral William Veazie Pratt, U.S. Navy: A Sailor's Life* (Washington, 1974), 294-308; Andrade, "Disarmament Era," 209-35, 294.

    9. The London *Times* correspondent estimated that Swanson supported the treaty owing to constituent endorsements. London *Times*, March 4, July 9, 1930; *Cong. Rec.*, 71 Cong., special sess., 73 (July 8, 1930), 12-23, (July 19, 1930) 336; O'Connor, *London Naval Conference*, 121.

    10. Entry, March 3, 1931, Stimson Diaries, 15: 135; *Cong. Rec.*, 71 Cong., 3 sess., 74 (December 15, 1930), 686, (January 6, 1931) 1457-58, (January 16, 1931) 2343, 2357-59, (February 20, 1931) 5512, (February 21, 1931) 5614, (February 27, 1931) 6240; *New York Times*, March 6, 31, July 2, September 30, December 2, 1931; *Norfolk Virginian Pilot*, March 5, 13, 1931.

    11. Entry, July 25, 1931, August 28, 1931, dictated on September 9, 1931, Stimson, Diaries, 17: 140; 18: 1-2; H.C. Hengstler to U.S. Lines, June 13, 1931, 124.01/588A, F.M. Sackett, Jr., to H.L. Stimson, July 21, 1931, 462.00296/4639, J.T. Marriner to H.L. Stimson, August 26, 1931, 751.62/153, W.E. Edge to H.L. Stimson, August 29, 1931, 751.62/154, RG 59, NA; *New York Times*, July 5, 23, August 1, September 4, October 4, 12, 1931.

    12. Entry, November 4, 1931, December 4, 13, January 5, 18, 1932, Stimson, Diaries, 19: 58, 128, 140-41, 157-58; 20: 9, 66; Dawes, *Journal*, 432; Hugh R. Wilson, *Diplomat between Wars* (New York, 1941), 262-64; Robert H. Ferrell, *American Diplomacy in the Great Depression: Hoover-Stimson Foreign Policy, 1929-1933* (New Haven, 1957), 205-6.

    13. CAS to J.T. Marriner, December 17, 1931, J.T. Marriner to CAS, December 18, 1931, 500 A154A4/582 1/2, RG 59, NA; entry January 5, 1921 in J. Pierrepont Moffat, *The Moffat Papers*, Nancy Harrison Hooker, editor (Cambridge, 1956), 53; Wilson, *Diplomat*, 268-70.

    14. "Memorandum of Meeting of American Delegates to the Disarmament Conference, January 5, 1932," passim.; "Memorandum of Conversation at Luncheon at the White House, January 5, 1912," passim; "Memorandum of American Delegation to the Disarmament Conference, January 7, 1932," passim; United States Delegation to the First Phase of the General Disarmament Conference, RG 43, NA.

    15. "Memorandum of Meeting of American Delegation to the Disarmament Conference, January 6, 1932," passim; "Memorandum on Conference in the Secretary's Office, January 7, 1932," RG 43, NA.

    16. H.L. Stimson to American Embassy, Paris, January 8, 1932, RG 43, NA; *New York Times*, January 21, 24, 1932, *Norfolk Virginian Pilot*, June 12, 1932; Hall Interview; Jeanette Marks, *Life and Letters of Mary Emma Woolley* (Washington, 1955), 131-32.

    17. CAS to Blanche Swanson, February 12 (?), 1932, Swanson Scrapbook.

    18. Entry, March 12, 15, 1932, Stimson, Diaries, 21: 59-60, 68; CAS to J.T. Robinson, March 6, 1932, CAS to Cordell Hull, April 27, 1933, Cordell Hull Papers, Manuscript Division, LC; CAS to R.W. Moore, March 14, Moore Papers; CAS to Carter Glass, March 12, 1932, Glass Papers; *New York Times*, February 4, 1932; Edward W. Bennett, *German Rearmament and the West, 1932-1933* (Princeton, 1979), 78 and passim.

    19. CAS to R.W. Moore, March 14, 1932, Moore Papers; CAS to Rixey Smith, May 6, 1932, Glass Papers; H.R. Gibson to William Castle, April 19, 21, 25, 1932, "Memorandum of Con-

versation Among Members," April 28, 1932, H.L. Stimson to H.R. Gibson, June 21, 1932, in *Foreign Relations, 1932,* 1: 104-9, 211-24; entry, April 20, 21, 25, 1932, Stimson, Diaries, 21: 130, 136, 154; *New York Times*, March 20, May 4, 1932; "Remarks of Senator Swanson Over National Broadcasting System to America, March 19, 1932," 10 pp., Swanson Scrapbook; Bennett, *German Disarmament*, 143-61.

20. Entry, June 22, 23, 1932, Stimson, Diaries, 22: 137, 142; "Memorandum of Transatlantic Telephone Conversation," June 22, 1932, in *Foreign Relations, 1932*, vol. 1, 215-18; *New York Times*, June 20, 1932; London *Times*, April 30, May 6, 1932; Johnson and Porter, *National Party Platforms*, 332, 344. Contrast Hoff Wilson, *Business and Foreign Policy*, 63.

21. Wilson, *Diplomat*, 268; John T. Whitaker, *And Fear Came* (New York, 1936), 130-32.

22. CAS to Carter Glass, August 10, 1932, Glass Papers; entry, August 5, 10, 1932, Stimson, Diaries, 23: 126, 135; *Norfolk Virginian Pilot*, August 6, 9, 1932; *New York Times*, August 6, 1932; Marks, *Woolley*, 146-47, 152; Stephen Roskill, *Naval Policy Between the Wars, 1930-1939* (Annapolis, 1976), 134 and passim; Hugh R. Wilson, *Disarmament and the Cold War in the Thirties* (New York, 1963), 11-29.

23. CAS to B.M. Baruch, November 18, 1926, Baruch Papers.

24. W.N. Tuck to H.F. Byrd, February 8, 1930, A.W. Robertson to H.F. Byrd, March 3, 1930, H.F. Byrd to N.B. Early, April 7, 1930, Byrd Papers; H.F. Byrd to A.D. Dabney, March 7, 1930, Junius W. Fishburne Papers (#6355), Manuscripts Department, University of Virginia Library; Brent Tartar, "A Flier on the National Scene: Harry F. Byrd's Favorite Son Presidential Candidacy of 1932," *VMHB*, 82 (July, 1974): 282-305; *Richmond News Leader*, May 1, 28, 1929; Burner, *Politics of Provincialism*, 197, 222; Freidel, *Triumph*, 177, and *FDR and the South* (Baton Rouge, 1965), 3-4, 38, 50-51; Cordell Hull, *Memoirs of Cordell Hull*, 1 (New York, 1948), 140-42; Tindall, *Emergence of New South*, 251-52.

25. A.T. Stroud to H.F. Byrd, July 10, 15, 1930, H.F. Byrd to A.T. Stroud, July 11, 1930, Byrd Papers; W.T. Reed to J.S. Bryan, October 22, 1930, W.T. Reed to H.F. Byrd, January 9, 1931, Reed Family Papers; *Norfolk Virginian Pilot*, March 1, 4, 5, 8, May 17, 1931; Freidel, *Triumph*, 178-81; Hull, *Memoirs*, 1: 140-41. Roosevelt responded favorably to the anit-Tammany sentiment. Burner, *Politics of Provincialism*, 248-49.

26. H.F. Byrd to W.T. Reed, March 27, July 9, 23, 1931, W.T. Reed to H.F. Byrd, July 24, 1931, Reed Family Papers; H.F. Byd to W.T. Reed, March 26, 31, 1931, W.T. Reed to H.F. Byrd, March 28, April 2, 1931, J.J. Raskob to H.F. Byrd, April 9, 21, 1931, H.F. Byrd to J.J. Raskob, April 8, 18, July 31, 1931, Byrd Papers; Cordell Hull to H.F. Byrd, July 16, 1931, H.F. Byrd to Garland Pollard, July 16, 28, 1931, Pollard Papers; *Norfolk Virginian Pilot*, March 26, 1931.

27. H.F. Byrd to W.T. Reed, July 9, 1931, Reed Family Papers; *New York Times*, July 7, 8, 1931; *Charlottesville Daily Progress*, July 6, 7, 1931; *Richmond Times-Dispatch*, July 7, 8, 1931.

28. H.F. Byrd to W.T. Reed, July 9, September 22, 1931, W.T. Reed to H.F. Byrd, September 23, 1931, Byrd Papers; J.G. Pollard to H.F. Byrd, July 15, 1931, H.F. Byrd to J.G. Pollard, July 16, October 13, 14, November 3, December 29, 1931, Pollard Papers; *Norfolk Virginian Pilot*, August 6, 1932.

29. W.T. Reed to H.F. Byrd, September 16, 1931, Reed Family Papers.

30. CAS to F.D. Roosevelt, November 25, 1931, Democratic National Committee Correspondence, and F.D. Roosevelt to CAS, November 16, 1931, F.D. Roosevelt Papers; *Norfolk Virginian Pilot*, October 15-16, 18, 20, 1931.

31. W.T. Reed to H.F. Byrd, November 28, 1931, Byrd Papers; H.F. Byrd to W.T. Reed, December 29, 1931, Reed Family Papers; "Report, Judge Bernard Ryan," July 29, 1931, DNCC, F.D. Roosevelt Papers; R.W. Moore to Mrs. C.A. Swanson, May 27, 1927, Moore Papers; Freidel, *Triumph*, 238-39.

32. L.M. Howe to CAS, December 3, 1931, L.M. Howe to H.F. Byrd, December 18, 1931, DNCC, F.D. Roosevelt Papers; H.F. Byrd to W.T. Reed, December 29, 1931, Reed Family Papers; F.D. Roosevelt to H.F. Byrd December 3, 1931, H.F. Byrd to F.D. Roosevelt, December 28, 1931,

Byrd Papers. For the latter letter, Byrd wrote two drafts, the first emphasized anti-Raskob aspects of the Hull-Swanson proposal, the second was more noncommittal.

33. F.D. Roosevelt to H.F. Byrd, December 3, 1931, Byrd Papers; H.F. Byrd to L.M. Howe, January 1, 1932, DNCC, F.D. Roosevelt Papers; W.T. Reed to H.F. Byrd, January 5, 1932, Reed Family Papers; compare and contrast Freidel, *Triumph*, 239-40. Freidel stresses James A. Farley's role in the above, not recognizing that of Howe.

34. H.F. Byrd to W.T. Reed, August 18, 1932, Reed Family Papers, reveals that Swanson, leaving for Europe, told Pollard he had arranged to have Byrd nominated for vice-president.

35. H.F. Byrd to L.M. Howe, January 18, March 17, 19, 29, April 6, 1932, J.A. Farley to H.F. Byrd, February 8, 10, 12, 1932, H.F. Byrd to F.D. Roosevelt, April 6, 1932, L.M. Howe to H.F. Byrd, April 28, 1932, DNCC, F.D. Roosevelt Papers; Freidel, *Triumph*, 275-80.

36. CAS to Carter Glass, March 12, 1932, Glass Papers; CAS to R.W. Moore, March 14, 1932, R.W. Moore to CAS, March 23, 1932, Moore Papers; CAS to W.T. Reed, March 14, 1932, Reed Family Papers.

37. Swanson also sent a letter to Byrd. W.T. Reed to CAS, March 23, 1932, W.T. Reed to H.F. Byrd, March 30, 1932, Reed Family Papers; J.T. Robinson to CAS, May 26, 1932, Robinson Papers.

38. Photocopy, Harry Byrd Speech, Jefferson Dinner, Washington, April 13, 1932, Richard Crane to L.M. Howe, April 23, 1932, L.M. Howe to Richard Crane, April 25, 1932, DNCC, F.D. Roosevelt Papers, *Richmond Times Dispatch*, April 14, 1932; *New York Times*, April 14-15, 1932; Harbaugh, *Davis*, 338-40.

39. W.T. Reed to A[rchibald] Oden, May 14, 1932, W.T. Reed to H.F. Byrd, May 23, 1932, Reed Family Papers; J.G. Pollard to H.F. Byrd, May 31, 1932, J.G. Pollard to Carter Glass, June 15, 1932, Pollard Papers; Richard Crane to F.D. Roosevelt, May 17, June 8, 1932, Louis Chawenet to F.D. Roosevelt, June 11, 1932, CAS to F.D. Roosevelt, July 4, 1932, DNCC, F.D. Roosevelt Papers; H.F. Byrd to Carter Glass, February 29, March 18, May 20, 24, June 16, 18, 20, 1932, Byrd Papers; *Norfolk Virginian Pilot*, June 5, 6, 10, 1932; Freidel, *Triumph*, 291-311; James M. Burns, *Roosevelt: The Lion and the Fox* (New York, 1956), 134-38.

40. Roosevelt replied to Pittman that he was "very anxious to see [Swanson]." Key Pittman to F.D. Roosevelt, August 10, 1932, F.D. Roosevelt to Key Pittman, August 13, 1932, Pittman Papers; H.F. Byrd to W.T. Reed, August 18, 1932, Reed Family Papers; CAS to Carter Glass, August 10, 1932, Glass Papers; entry, August 10, 1932, Stimson, Diaries, 23: 135-36; *Norfolk Virginian Pilot*, August 6, 9, 16, 17, 20, 1932; *New York Times*, August 11, 1932.

41. CAS to F.D. Roosevelt, September 6, 1932, CAS to J.A. Farley, September 3, 1932, DNCC, F.D. Roosevelt Papers; *New York Times*, September 11, 13, 1932; James A. Farley, *Behind the Ballots: The Personal History of a Politician* (New York, 1938), 161; Martha H. Swain, *Pat Harrison: The New Deal Years* (Jackson, 1978), 30-31.

42. H.F. Byrd to W.T. Reed, September 15, 1932, Reed Family Papers; *New York Times*, August 15, September 10, October 1, 18, 24, November 3, 1932.

43. H.F. Byrd to W.T. Reed, July 29, September 15, 16, 1932, W.T. Reed to H.F. Byrd, September 17, 1932, W.T. Reed to CAS, November 23, 1932, Reed Family Papers.

44. Carter Glass to CAS, November 15, 1932, Carter Glass to H.F. Byrd, January 30, February 4, 1932, Carter Glass to F.D. Roosevelt, February 7, 1933, Glass Papers; W.T. Reed to H.F. Byrd, December 6, 1932, H.F. Byrd to W.T. Reed, December 12, 1932, Reed Family Papers; H.F. Byrd to E.R. Combs, December 10, 1932, H.F. Byrd to W.M. Tuck, November 22, 1932, H.F. Byrd to Carter Glass, January 29-30, February 7, 1933, Byrd Papers; CAS to L.M. Howe, November 16, 1932, F.D. Roosevelt to CAS, November 17, 1932, DNCC, F.D. Roosevelt Papers; Lyle, "Glass," 273.

45. Key Pittman to F.D. Roosevelt, February 11, 1933, Pittman Papers; H.F. Byrd to W.T. Reed, February 22, 1933, W.T. Reed to H.F. Byd, February 28, 1933, W.T. Reed to Archibald Oden, March 1, 1933, Reed Family Papers; Carter Glass to M.H. McIntyre, January 18, 1933,

Carter Glass to F.D. Roosevelt, February 7, 1933, Carter Glass to H.F. Byrd, February 13, 1933, Glass Papers; *Richmond News Leader,* December 31, 1932, January 9, 11, 26, 1933; *Richmond Times-Dispatch*, January 1, 11, February 22, 26, March 2, 1933; *Norfolk Virginian Pilot*, February 21, 22, 28, 1933, *New York Times*, January 14, 1933; Frank B. Friedel, *Franklin D. Roosevelt: Launching the New Deal* (Boston, 1973), 145-50.

46. H.F. Byrd to W.T. Reed, February 27, 1933, Reed Family Papers; H.F. Byrd to Carter Glass, January 30, February 11, 1933, Carter Glass to H.F. Byrd, February 4, 13, 1933, Glass Papers. Contrast Freidel, *Launching the New Deal*, 148 and Burns, *Roosevelt*, 148.

13. Second to None: 1933-1939

1. Entry, March 16, 1933, *Moffat Papers*, 90-91; George F. Gallup, *The Gallup Poll, Public Opinion, 1935-1971*, 1 (New York, 1972), 93, 109; Frances Perkins, *Reminiscences*, Oral History Research Office, Columbia University (New York, 1976), book 4; 90, 176; *Newsweek*, July 17, 1939, 16; Time, July 17, 1939, 12.

2. Perkins, *Reminiscences*, book 4: 18, 21, 84, 89, 176, 185, 469, 545, book 7, 604; Roger W. Babson, *Washington and the Revolutionists* (New York, 1934), passim; John F. Carter, *The New Dealers* (New York, 1934), passim; Freidel, *Launching the New Deal*, 139-60; Keith D. McFarland, *Harry H. Wooding: A Political Biography of FDR's Controversial Secretary of War* (Lawrence, 1975), 153; Roper, *Public Life*, 285-95, 376.

3. In 1933, the eight bureaus were Aeronautics, Engineering, Medicine and Surgery, Navigation (Personnel), Supplies and Accounts, Yards and Docks, Construction and Repair, and Ordnance. Additional departments included the Marines, Naval Observatory, Judge Advocate General, Hydrographic Office, and Chief of Naval Operations. U.S. Senate, *Functions of the Department of Navy* (Washington, 1933), 2 and passim; Robert H. Connery, *The Navy and Industrial Mobilization in World War II* (Princeton, 1951), 12-22; Vincent Davis, *The Admirals Lobby* (Chapel Hill, 1967), 20-22, 38-40; Ferrell, "Regional Rivalries," 65-66; Roskill, *Naval Policy, 1919-1929*, vol. 1, 56-58; Albion, *Makers of Naval Policy*, 12 and passim.

4. Entry, June 15, 1933, Diaries, 1:1-II, 2-II, William D. Leahy Papers, Manuscript Division, LC; Harold C. Train, *Reminiscences*, Oral History Research Office, Columbia University (New York, 1966), 115; Thomas C. Hart, *Reminiscences*, Oral History Research Office, Columbia University (New York, 1966), 86-90; James O. Richardson, *On the Treadmill to Pearl Harbor: The Memoirs of Admiral James O. Richardson* (Washington, 1973), 462; Albion, *Makers of Naval Policy*, 93; Davis, *Admirals Lobby*, 39-42; Wheeler, *Pratt*, 365.

5. J.W. Reaves to W.D. Leahy, February 18, 1935, CAS to F.D. Roosevelt, February 15, 1939, F.D. Roosevelt Papers; entry, December 20, 1932, July 1, 1933, Leahy, Diaries, 2:36, 3-II; James Fife, *Reminiscences*, Oral History Project Office, Columbia University (New York, 1959), 73-73a; Harold G. Bowen, *Ships, Machinery and Mossbacks: The Autobiography of a Naval Engineer* (Princeton, 1954), 78-79; *Time*, July 10, 1933, 9-10.

6. Entry, January 10, 1935, February 12, 1935, Leahy Diaries, 2:20-II, 21-II; William H. Standley and Arthur A. Ageton, *Admiral Ambassador to Russia* (Chicago, 1955), 29, 43; Ernest J. King and Walter M. Whitehill, *Fleet Admiral King: A Naval Record* (New York, 1952), 240, 262-65; Richardson, *Memoirs*, 462; Alan G. Kirk, *Reminiscences*, Oral History Project Office, Columbia University (New York, 1972), 105, 110-111.

7. Richardson, *Memoirs*, 462-63; *Newsweek*, March 16, 1935, 11; entry, August 9, 1933, De Capo Press, *Complete Presidential Press Conferences of Franklin D. Roosevelt*, 2 (New York, 1972), 151-52.

8. F.D. Roosevelt to H.L. Roosevelt, March 2, 1934, F.D. Roosevelt to CAS, November 5, 1937, F.D. Roosevelt Papers; Press releases, May 1-7, 1933, pt. one, RG 80, NA; CAS to H.L. Roosevelt, May 8, 1933, CAS to F.D. Roosevelt, March 6, 1934, CAS to C.M. Vinson, March 15, 1938, February 9, 1939, in Elting E. Morrison, *Naval Administration: Selected Documents on Navy*

Department Organization, 1915-1940 (Washington [?], 1945), V-11, V-55, VI-2; entry, June 15, 1933, Leahy Diaries, 1-II.

9. *United States Naval Institute Proceedings*, 59 (May 1933): 750, 61 (January 1935): 146-47; *Newsweek*, June 2, 1934, 16; *Washington Evening Star*, May 24, 1933, March 28, 1936; *New York Times*, May 31, 1933, May 24, August 2, 1934, March 14, September 19-20, December 13, 1935, September 10, 1936, October 30, 1938.

10. F.D. Roosevelt to H.L. Roosevelt, March 2, 1934, F.D. Roosevelt to CAS, April 25, 1933, November 12, 1934, May 3, July 2, August 21, 1935, January 20, March 9, 1938, CAS to F.D. Roosevelt, June 11, November 27, 1934, April 1, June 29, September 20, 1935, January 7, 1936, January 24, 1938, F.D. Roosevelt Papers; entry, July 1, 1933, Leahy Diaries, 2:3; Train, *Reminiscences*, 207-8; Hart, *Reminiscences*, 82, 87-88; Albion, *Making Naval Policy*, 159; King, *Fleet Admiral*, 240-41, 266; Standley, *Admiral*, 28, 41; Roskill, *Naval Policy, 1930-39*, 2:179.

11. Contrast entry, September 6, 1933, Diaries, 262, Harold L. Ickes Papers, Manuscript Division, LC. Although a considerable portion of the Ickes diaries have been published, this study cites the unpublished, complete diaries. See Harold L. Ickes, *The Secret Diaries of Harold L. Ickes*, 1 (New York, 1953), 2, 3 (New York, 1954). CAS to S.T. Early, April 20, 1933, S.T. Early to CAS, April 22, 1933, H.L. Roosevelt to F.D. Roosevelt, October 20, 1933, F.D. Roosevelt Papers; *New York Times*, September 7, 8, 9, 1933; entry, September 6, 1933, *Roosevelt Press Conferences, 2*: 233-34, 237-38; Robert Dallek, *Franklin D. Roosevelt and American Foreign Policy, 1932-45* (New York, 1979), 60-64.

12. *New York Times*, June 1, 2, 3, 1934, August 1, 1935; *Scientific American*, 153 (November 1935), 231ff.; *Time*, June 11, 1934, 17-18; *Newsweek*, June 2, 1934, 16, June 9, 1934, 7, 19; *Roosevelt Press Conferences*, passim.

13. Alan R. McCracken, "Strictly Private Thoughts on Naval Publicity," *USNIP*, 61 (March, 1935): 381-83; Hanson W. Baldwin, "Wanted: A Naval Policy," *Current History*, 43 (November 1935): 125-30; M.A. Hallgren, "Drifting into Militarism," *Nation*, October 4, 1933, 372-74, "The Naval Crisis," *Nation*, November 21, 1934, 579, "Our Navy Madness," *Nation*, January 23, 1935, 88-89; "The Week," *New Republic*, February 7, 1934, 348; "Big Navy Roosevelt," *New Republic*, March 7, 1934, 89-90; "Hold Up Naval Contracts," *Christian Century*, 52 (February 1935): 230-32; Holden A. Evans, "Our Muscle-Bound Navy," *Colliers*, June 11, 1938, 9-10, 44-47; Robert A. Divine, *The Illusion of Neutrality* (Chicago, 1962), 57 and passim.

14. On a protesting letter from Walter W. Van Kirk of the Federal Council, Naval Intelligence officer Ellis Zacharias scrawled "Hooey!!" W.W. Van Kirk to CAS, October 7, 1933, A1-3/QN(331007), Mrs. F.D. Dove to CAS, February 25(?), 1934, and others in A1-3/QN(340226R), RG 80, NA; CAS to F.D. Roosevelt, July 3, 1934, F.D. Roosevelt Papers.

15. F.D. Roosevelt to H.L. Roosevelt, February 2, 1934, F.D. Roosevelt Papers.

16. C.M. Vinson to CAS, July 9, 1937 (A1-3/A189340213-8), May 24, 1939 (A1-3/A18340213-13), D.L. Walsh to CAS, March 23, 1938 (A1-3/A18340213-9) RG 80, NA; CAS to W.T. Reed, July 1, 1930, Reed Family Papers; *New York Times*, March 8, 1933; Wheeler, *Pratt*, 327-28; Robert G. Albion, "The Naval Affairs Committees, 1816-1947," *USNIP*, 78 (September 1952): 1231-35; Fife, *Reminiscences*, 73-73a; Stephen E. Pelz, *Race to Pearl Harbor: The Failure of the Second London Naval Conference and the Onset of World War II* (Cambridge, 1974), 70-72.

17. "Suggested Legislative Procedure," February 6, 1939, AL3/A18(380318-2), RG 80, NA; U.S. House of Representatives, *Navy Department Appropriations Bill for 1935: Hearings* (Washington, 1935), 3 and passim; Albion, *Makers of Naval Policy*, 176-77; Emory S. Land, *Winning the War with Ships: Land, Sea and Air-Mostly Land* (New York, 1958), 145-46.

18. CAS to L.M. Howe, November 16, 1932, F.D. Roosevelt to CAS, November 17, 1932, March 21, 1933, F.D. Roosevelt Papers; *New York Times*, February 19, September 30, October 27, November 30, 1932; entry, May 12, 1933, *Roosevelt Press Conferences*, 1:254-55; Dallek, *Roosevelt and Foreign Policy*, 35 and passim. Compare and contrast Freidel, *Launching the New Deal*, 432, and Pelz, *Race to Pearl Harbor*, 79-81.

19. M.H. McIntyre to H.L. Ickes, May 2, 1933, CAS to S.T. Early, May 9, 1933, F.D. Roosevelt Papers; *New York Times*, March 21, 1933; Pelz, *Race to Pearl Harbor*, 79; Land, *Winning the War*, 146.

20. CAS to F.D. Roosevelt, April 19, May 5, June 3, August 23, 1933, CAS to L.W. Douglas, May 3, 1933, F.D. Roosevelt to CAS, August 19, 1933, memorandum, F.D. Roosevelt to CAS, May (?), 1933, F.D. Roosevelt to H.L. Roosevelt, October 19, 1933, F.D. Roosevelt Papers; H.L. Ickes to H.L. Roosevelt, October 30, 1933, A1-3/VZ(33081), RG 80, NA, is a request for a breakdown of funds as to where they were expended and how long they would be needed. H.L. Roosevelt to H.L. Ickes, October 30, 1933, ibid.; *New York Times*, March 31, April 17, May 5, 1933; *Washington Evening Star*, May 24, 1933; Roskill, *Naval Policy*, 2: 491.

21. CAS, *Annual Report of the Secretary of Navy for the Fiscal Year, 1933* (Washington, 1933), 2-3, 8, 21; press release, pt. 1, August 29, 1933 (1), CAS to C.M. Vinson, April 18, 1934, A1-3/A18(340243:2), RG 80, NA; "Naval Construction Program, 1934," CAS to F.D. Roosevelt, July (?), 1933, H.L. Roosevelt to F.D. Roosevelt, July 26, 1933, August 22, 1934, F.D. Roosevelt Papers; Land, *Winning the War*, 146; Lynwood E. Oyos, "The Navy and the United States Far Eastern Policy, 1930-39" (Ph.D. diss., University of Nebraska, 1958), 112.

22. CAS to O.G. Murfree via W.H. Standley, November 29, 1933, Park Trammell to CAS, January 23, 1934, A1-3/A18(330510), memorandum, CAS to Park Trammell, January 23, 1934, A1-3/A18(330510), CAS to Park Trammell, February 24, 1934, A1-3/A18(340224), Materials on House of Representatives Hearings, January 22-24, 1934, in A1-3/A18(340101 to 340131), RG 80, NA; *New York Times*, January 10, June 21, 1934; Donald W. Mitchell, *History of the Modern American Navy* (New York, 1946), 348-53. Compare and contrast Standley, *Admiral*, 32-34.

23. *New York Times* and Ickes disagree over dates of Swanson's hospitalization. *New York Times*, December 15, 25, 1933, January 21, 1934; entry, December 16, 1933, March 2, 1934, Ickes Diaries, 392, 454; Park Trammel to CAS, January 23, 1934, A1-3/A18(330510), press releases, pt. 1, February 1934 (1), February 23, 1934, RG 80, NA; U.S. House of Representatives, *To Establish Composition of the United States Navy: Hearings, January 22-24, 1934* (Washington, 1934), 648 and passim.

24. F.D. Roosevelt to CAS, August 19, 1933, CAS to F.D. Roosevelt, August 23, 1933, F.D. Roosevelt Papers; H.L. Ickes to H.L. Roosevelt, October 30, 1933, A1-3/VZ(33081), RG 80, NA; Emory S. Land, *Reminiscences*, Oral History Research Office, Columbia University (New York, 1963), 130-31; *New York Times*, May 9, July 29, 1934; Hugh S. Johnson, *The Blue Eagle from Egg to Earth* (New York, 1935), 244; Irving Bernstein, *Turbulent Years: A History of the American Worker, 1933-1941* (Boston, 1970), 172 and passim.

25. Perkins, *Reminiscences*, 6: 273-74; entry, August 2, 1934, *Roosevelt Press Conferences*, 6: 75-78; *New York Times*, August 3, 8, 10, 16, 30, 1935.

26. Bernstein, *Turbulent Years*, 255-58; A.T. Church to Charles Edison, February 9, 16, 1939, A1-3/FS(380318-1), RG 80, NA; F.D. Roosevelt to CAS, December 28, 1938, F.D. Roosevelt Papers; Perkins, *Reminiscences*, 6: 273-74; entry, June 23, 1936, February 9, 19, 1937, *Roosevelt Press Conferences*, 7: 296; 9:155, 175; *New York Times*, April 22, 1938.

27. Land headed construction and Robinson, engineering. U.S. Senate, Special Committee on Investigating Munitions Industry, Naval Shipbuilding, *Preliminary Report* (Washington, 1935), 1-7, 106-8, 137, 318-22; *Washington Evening Star*, February 5, 1934; *New York Times*, January 31, February 14, 1935; Land, *Winning the War*, 146; Wayne S. Cole, *Gerald P. Nye and American Foreign Relations* (Minneapolis, 1962), 80-86; see CAS to F.D. Roosevelt, December 18, 1935, F.D. Roosevelt Papers, for problems in airplane procurement.

28. E.J. King to CAS, May 14, 1936, A1-3/ZR(350303-2), CAS to C.M. Vinson, March 5, 1937, A1-3/ZR(370113), Charles Edison to F.D. Roosevelt, September 8, 1938, and F.D. Roosevelt to Charles Edison, September 10, 1938, A1-3/ZR(390908), W.D. Leahy to F.D. Roosevelt, September 16, 1938, 1-3/ZR(380916), R.T. Secrest to F.D. Roosevelt, October 14, 1938, A1-3/ZR(381017), RG 80, NA; *New York Times*, February 14, 21, 1935; Richard K. Smith, *The Airships Akron and Macon: Flying Aircraft Carriers of the United States Navy* (Annapolis, 1965), passim.

29. *Cong. Rec.*, 71 Cong., 2 sess., 72 (July 2, 1930), 12266; U.S. House of Representatives, *War Policies Commission Hearings* (Washington, 1931), 15: 57-62, 288-92, 318-19, 488.

30. J.T. Robinson to B.M. Baruch, April 11, 1931, B.M. Baruch to CAS, December 12, 1934, Baruch Papers; Cordell Hull to F.D. Roosevelt, April 11, 1935, in Edgar B. Nixon, editor, *Franklin D. Roosevelt and Foreign Affairs*, 2 (Cambridge, 1969): 470-75, 475 n5; F.D. Roosevelt to CAS, December 26, 1935, CAS to F.R. Lillie, June 9, 1936, A1-3/ZR(350303), CAS to W.F. Durand, March 13, 1937, CAS to F.R. Lillie, April 26, 1937, F.R. Lillie to CAS, April 29, 1937, A1-3/ZR(350303-2), RG 80, NA; House of Representatives, *War Policies Hearings*, 401-68, 475, 480; Connery, *Navy and Mobilization*, 40-53; Baruch, *Public Years*, 266-69; Divine, *Illusion of Neutrality*, 72-72.

31. F.D. Roosevelt to J.M. Reeves, August 30, 1934, F.D. Roosevelt Papers; F.D. Roosevelt to CAS, May 3, 1935, in Nixon, *Roosevelt and Foreign Affairs*, 2: 495-96; *Washington Evening Star*, September 20, 1934; *New York Times*, February 7, April 4, May 3, 16, 1935; Pelz, *Race to Pearl Harbor*, 125-27; Roskill, *Naval Policy, 1930-39*, 2: 234; Louis Morton, "War Plan Orange: Evolution of a Strategy," *World Politics*, 11 (January, 1959): 224-25, 227, 240-41.

32. Cordell Hull to F.D. Roosevelt, September 18, 1934, in Nixon, *Roosevelt and Foreign Affairs*, 2: 216-17; CAS to F.D. Roosevelt, June 29, 1935, F.D. Roosevelt Papers; Perkins, *Reminiscences*, 4: 89; *Literary Digest*, January 6, 1934, 11; *New York Times*, May 24-25, June 7, August 2, 5, 1934; Pelz, *Race to Pearl Harbor*, 127-29; Dallek, *Roosevelt and Foreign Policy*, 86-91; Divine, *Illusion of Neutrality*, 73.

33. F.D. Roosvelt to CAS, December 17, 31, 1934, May 3, July 30, 1935, in Nixon, *Roosevelt and Foreign Affairs*, 2: 322-23, 330, 495-96, 573; CAS to F.D. Roosevelt, May 1, 1935, F.D. Roosevelt Papers; *New York Times*, March 14-15, August 1, 1935.

34. F.D. Roosevelt to CAS, July 2, 1934, in Nixon, *Roosevelt and Foreign Affairs*, 2: 546; CAS to F.D. Roosevelt, June 29, 1935, R.F. [Rudolph Forster] to H.M. McIntyre, September 16, 1935, F.D. Roosevelt Papers; *New York Times*, March 11, July 11, 1935, August 9, 1936; Roskill, *Naval Policy*, 2: 491; contrast Pelz, *Race to Pearl Harbor*, 202.

35. F.D. Roosevelt to Wilson Brown, December 4, 1935, CAS to F.D. Roosevelt, October 7, December 3, 1935, January 7, December 11, 1936, August 6, 1937, January 20, 1938, R.F. [Rudolph Forster] to M.H. McIntyre, December 10, 1935, D.W. Bell to F.D. Roosevelt, April 18, 1938, Adolphus Andrews to F.D. Roosevelt, May 25, 1938, F.D. Roosevelt to D.I. Walsh, June 4, 1938, F.D. Roosevelt Papers; *New York Times*, December 13, 1935; Roskill, *Naval Policy*, 2: 491; CAS, *Annual Report, 1934*, 13.

36. F.D. Roosevelt to Josephus Daniels, February 27, 1936, S.T. Early to F.D. Roosevelt, March 29, April 6, 10, 1936, F.D. Roosevelt Papers; entry, February 9, March 21, 1936, Ickes Diaries, 1388, 1444; *New York Times*, February 7, 14, 15, 16, 23, May 22, August 11, September 10, 1936.

37. CAS to F.D. Roosevelt, September 8, 15, 29, 1936, F.D. Roosevelt to CAS, September 12, 1936, F.D. Roosevelt Papers; entry, August 21, November 17, 1936, *Presidential Press Conferences*, 8: 88, 169; *New York Times*, November 18, 1936.

38. S.T. Early to F.D. Roosevelt, August 16, 1934, August 8, 1936, CAS to F.D. Roosevelt, October 1, November 7, 1934, September 4, 1935, June 29, 1936; Archibald Oden to S.T. Early, August 15, 1935, F.D. Roosevelt to H.F. Byrd, August 31, 1935, H.F. Byrd to F.D. Roosevelt, September 17, 18, 1935, photostats of *Winchester Star*, August 24, 30, September 5, 1935, F.D. Roosevelt Papers; R.W. Moore to W.E. Dodd, July 26, 1935, Moore Papers; Carter Glass to H.F. Byrd, July 2, 1934, Glass Papers; *Norfolk Virginian Pilot*, August 2, 5, 1936. Compare and contrast Darden, *Conversations*, 57-61.

39. Special Committee, *Preliminary Report*, 36-37, 54, 113, 144, 175-76, 273-74; *New York Times*, January 31, 1935; Donald L. Mitchell, "What Our Warships Cost," *Nation*, September 1939, 320-23. Swanson contributed to Congressman John J. McSwain's committee investigating the Emergency Fleet Corporation. *New York Times*, February 7, 1935.

40. CAS to F.D. Roosevelt, June 26, 1935, F.D. Roosevelt to CAS, June 28, August 21, 22,

1935; F.D. Roosevelt to Henry Morgenthau, Jr., August 5, 1936, memorandum to F.D. Roosevelt, September [?], 1936, F.D. Roosevelt Papers; entry, July 26, 1934, Leahy Diaries, 14-II; entry, August 11, 1936, *Roosevelt Press Conferences*, 8: 68; Hull, *Memoirs*, 1: 488, Divine, *Illusions of Neutrality*, 81-121.

41. Charles Edison to W.D. Leahy, July 29, 1937, CAS to F.D. Roosevelt, June 26, 1935, November 29, 1937, December 8, 1937, F.D. Roosevelt to CAS, June 28, 1935, W.D. Leahy to F.D. Roosevelt, November 30, 1937, H.E. Yarnell to W.D. Leahy, October 15, 1937, F.D. Roosevelt Papers; entry, September 19, 1937, Ickes Diaries, 2324, 2337; Divine, *Illusion of Neutrality*, 200-16; compare and contrast Dorothy Borg, "Notes on Roosevelt's 'Quarantine Speech,' " *Political Science Quarterly*, 72 (September 1957): 405-33.

42. Reflecting departmental attitudes, James R.O. Richardson believed the administration's response to American war fright to be conciliatory, "if not meek and supine." Richardson, *On the Treadmill*, 17: entry, December 18, 1937, Ickes Diaries, 2897-2801; W.D. Leahy to F.D. Roosevelt, December 15, 1937, A1-3/FS(371215), RG 80, NA; M.H. McIntyre to F.D. Roosevelt, January 15, 1938, F.D. Roosevelt to M.H. McIntyre, January 25, 1938, F.D. Roosevelt Papers; Dallek, *Roosevelt and Foreign Policy*, 153-55.

43. D.I. Walsh to CAS, March 23, 1938, CAS to D.I. Walsh, March 24, 1938, CAS to H.T. Bone, April 20, May 2, 1938, A1-3/A18(340213-9), RG 80, NA; *Cong., Rec.*, 75 Cong., 3 sess., 83 (January 3, 1938), 8, (January 28, 1938) 1187-88; *New York Times*, January 20, February 1-2, 6, April 1, 6, 22, 1938; Norman Alley, *I Witness* (New York, 1941), 284-86; Roskill, *Naval Policy, 1930-39*, 2: 469-70; *Literary Digest*, February 12, 1938, 4.

44. Swanson, with department concurrence, recommended Captain Edgar L. Woods as surgeon general but F.D. Roosevelt preferred Ross T. McIntire. CAS to F.D. Roosevelt, September 26, November 26, 1938, F.D. Roosevelt Papers; entry, March 5, 1939, Ickes Diaries, 3274; *New York Times*, August 30, 1938; *Norfolk Virginian Pilot*, September 3, 5, 1938; King, *Fleet Admiral*, 288-93; Allison Saville, "Claude Augustus Swanson," in *American Secretaries of the Navy, 1813-1972*, Paola E. Coletta, editor (Annapolis, 1980), 665.

45. Despite Ickes's dislike of Lulie Swanson, he expressed considerable sympathy for Swanson. Entry, July 7, 1936, January 10, 24, October 20, 1937, September 18, 1938, March 5, 18, April 1, June 11, July 8, 1939, Ickes Diaries, 1602-4, 1890-91, 1929-34, 1939, 2378, 2839, 3337, 3576-77. Admiral [S.J.] Myrick to A.E.M. Chatfield, April 14, 1938, quoted in Roskill, *Naval Policy*, 2: 362; "Notes on Franklin Roosevelt Conversation," April 14, 1939, Daniels Papers; Hall interview.

46. Entry, July 8, 1939, July 15, 1939, Ickes Diaries, 3571, 3576; H.S. Truman to Mrs. H.S. Truman, July 11, 1939, in Harry S. Truman, *Dear Bess: The Letters of Harry Truman to Bess Truman, 1910-1959*, Robert H. Ferrell, editor (New York, 1983), 414.

14. Epilogue: The Red Oak Breaks

1. J.F. Kohler to F.D. Roosevelt, July 8, 1939, R.H. Sexton to Mrs. C.A. Swanson, July 12, 1939, M.F. Doyle to F.D. Roosevelt, July 7, 1939, F.D. Roosevelt Papers.

2. C.J. Peeples to F.D. Roosevelt, July 8, 1939, F.D. Roosevelt Papers; Perkins, *Reminiscences*, 7: 639; *Richmond News Leader*, July 8, 1939; *Richmond Times-Dispatch*, July 8, 1939; *New York Times*, July 8, 1939.

3. *Norfolk Virginian Pilot*, July 8, 1939.

4. *Cong. Rec.*, 53 Cong., 2 sess., 26 (January 24, 1894), Appendix 368-70, (June 1, 1894), 5604-7; Sheldon, *Populism*, passim.

5. *Cong., Rec.*, 67 Cong., 1 sess., 61 (October 29, 1921), 7008.

6. *Norfolk Virginian Pilot*, July 8, 1939.

7. Hall Interview; *New York Times Magazine*, July 9, 1933, 3; Patrick Abbazia, *Mr. Roosevelt's Navy: The Private War of the U.S. Atlantic Fleet, 1939-1942* (Annapolis, 1979), passim.

Bibliographic Essay

While a history graduate student at the University of Virginia, I was presented the opportunity to study the public career of Claude A. Swanson, and discovered that only a few items from his correspondence were accessible. No significant additions have been made since that time. A biographer faces, then, a barrier that prevents easy entry into the intentions and views of the Virginian. This study has profited from the necessity of using parallel manuscript collections of friends and foes and other contemporary sources. A broader sweep than is normally true of political biographies results, and a forgotten Virginia emerges. Should a cache of Swanson material become available, only more details of his life would be revealed and the structure of this work would not be seriously altered. The notes provide the sources upon which this study rests; what follows is a commentary upon the most important.

Manuscripts

The University of Virginia's collection of Claude A. Swanson material represents the largest single body of the political records of the secretary. They include a family scrapbook, earlier Swanson family records, and the 1922 senatorial election records, circa 1920 to 1923, that furnishes the most complete record of his political campaigns. Smaller collections at Duke University and the Virginia Historical Society offer additional insights. The records of his governorship at the Virginia State Library are little more than pardons and similar official papers. Swanson's tendency to communicate in person or by telephone, especially after his rise to prominence, would probably have had a corresponding reduction in the utility of his career papers, even if they were available. Two possible fates have been offered: either he destroyed them upon the acceptance of the cabinet portfolio, or, more likely, they suffered irreparable damage from a leak in a Washington warehouse roof. Published Swanson gubernatorial material includes Claude A. Swanson, *Addresses, Messages and Proclamations* (Richmond, 1910).

Of the nearly ninety collections of diaries, record groups, and manuscripts consulted for this study, the following have proven to be the most useful and provide valuable cross certifications for themselves and other contemporary sources: Bernard M. Baruch, Princeton University; Harry Flood Byrd, University of Virginia and Virginia State Library; James Cannon, Jr., Duke University; Grover Cleveland, Library of Congress, Westmoreland Davis, University of Virginia; Josephus Daniels, Library of Congress; Democratic National Committee, Hyde Park; John Warwick Daniel, University of Virginia; William E. Dodd, Library of Congress; Henry De La Warr Flood, Library of Congress and National Archives; Carter Glass, University of Virginia; James Hay, University of Virginia; Harold L. Ickes, Library of Congress; William A. Jones, University of Virginia; Charles T. Lassiter, Duke University; Francis Rives Lassiter, Duke University; William Mahone, Duke University; Andrew J. Montague, Virginia State

Library; Key Pittman, Library of Congress; John Garland Pollard, College of William and Mary; Records of the Department of the Navy, National Archives; Records of the Department of State, National Archives; Reed Family, Virginia Historical Society; Joseph T. Robinson, University of Arkansas; Franklin D. Roosevelt, Hyde Park; Henry L. Stimson, Yale University; Benjamin R. Tillman, Clemson University; Tucker Family, University of North Carolina at Chapel Hill; J. Hoge Tyler, Virginia Polytechnic Institute and State University; Whittle Family, University of Virginia; and Woodrow Wilson, Library of Congress.

Appreciation is extended to Mr. Charles H. Ryland and Mrs. William A. Jones, III, for permission to quote from the William A. Jones Papers; to Mr. Junius R. Fishburne, Jr., from the Junius W. Fishburne Papers (University of Virginia); to Senator Harry Flood Byrd, Jr., from the Harry Flood Byrd Papers, to Mr. George G. Shackelford from the George S. Shackelford Papers (University of Virginia); and to Mrs. Elizabeth Copeland Norfleet from the W. Scott Copeland Papers (University of Virginia).

Contemporary Sources

Many previous studies of the period have depended upon Richmond newspapers to carry not only the narrative but the interpretative burden as well. The *Richmond Dispatch*, a Democratic mouthpiece, leaned toward an urban bias. The *Richmond Times* represented the psychology of the creditor class and was violently anti-Populist. Upon their combining, the new journal, the *Richmond Times-Dispatch*, supported the state's "progressives," as did the *Richmond News Leader*. The *Norfolk Virginian Pilot*, frequently unused in past evaluations, offers an important palliative for narrow interpretations of the Swanson era. Also significant and used selectively are the *Danville Register, Petersburg Index Appeal, Richmond State, Roanoke Times, Staunton Dispatch and News, Warsaw Northern Neck News*, and similar local newspapers. The *Washington Post* and *New York Times* covered Virginia political affairs well and frequently in detail before World War I. The latter paper furnished a primary pathway in elucidating Swanson's later career.

Public documents abound as valuable contributions to an understanding of the political environment in which Swanson existed. The *Congressional Record* and the many congressional hearings, reports, and other federal compilations, as the various U.S. Department of State, *Foreign Relations of the United States*, mark a second primary area not fully incorporated into previous estimates of Swanson. The contested election cases give the careful reader not only political information but social and economic insights also. The Virginia General Assembly's *Acts and Joint Resolutions, Journal of the House of Delegates of the State of Virginia*, and *Journal of the Senate of the Commonwealth of Virginia*, and publications of other state agencies, like J.H. Lindsay, editor, *Report of the Constitutional Convention, State of Virginia* (Richmond, 1906), provide revealing details of the era. Census and other statistical data are drawn from the various *Report of the Secretary of the Commonwealth*, Wilson Gee and John J. Carson, *A Statistical Study of Virginia* (Charlottesville, 1927), Ben J. Wattenburg, editor, *Statistical History of the United States* (New York, 1976), the various *Official Congressional Directory*, Alexander Heard and Donald S. Strong, *Southern Primaries and Elections, 1920–1950* (University, 1950), the various *Manual of the Senate and House of Delegates of Virginia*, and the *Warrock-Richardson Almanac*.

Contemporaries' commentaries and world views are exemplified by: Jacob N. Brenamen, *A History of Virginia Conventions* (Richmond, 1902); James Cannon, Jr., *Bishop Cannon's Own Story: Life as I Have Seen It*, Richard L. Watson, Jr., editor (Durham, 1955): Josephus Daniels, *The Cabinet Diaries of Josephus Daniels, 1913–1920*, E. David Cronon, editor (Lincoln, 1963); Charles G. Dawes, *Notes as Vice*

President, 1928–29 (Boston, 1935); *Complete Presidential Press Conferences of Franklin D. Roosevelt* (New York, 1972); Maxwell Ferguson, *State Regulation of Rail Roads in the South* (New York, 1916); John Goode, *Recollections of a Lifetime* (New York, 1906); Henry Cabot Lodge, editor, *Selections from the Correspondence of Theodore Roosevelt and Henry Cabot Lodge, 1884–1918* (New York, 1925); F.A. Magruder, *Recent Administration in Virginia* (Baltimore, 1912); Beverly Munford, *Random Recollections* (Richmond, 1905); William C. Pendleton, *Political History of Appalachian Virginia* (Dayton, 1927); James O. Richardson, *On the Treadmill to Pearl Harbor: The Memoirs of Admiral James O. Richardson* (Washington, 1973); Thomas Whitehead, *Virginia: Handbook* (Richmond, 1893); and Robert E. Withers, *Autobiography of an Octogenarian* (Roanoke, 1907).

Formal oral interviews include Douglas Deane Hall, Swanson's stepson, and selected memoirs of the Oral History Research Office, Columbia University. Primary is that of Frances Perkins, and appreciation is given to the Trustees of Columbia University for permission to use the above and other reminiscences in the collections cited in the notes. Hundreds of other interviews of an informal or anonymous nature have occurred over the years that have provided additional understanding of Swanson's career.

General Studies

The notes substantiate the great debt this biography owes to professional historians who have given insight and direction to the study of the United States during the late nineteenth and early twentieth centuries. The works of William R. Braisted, David Bruner, L. Ethan Ellis, Robert H. Ferrell, Peter G. Filene, Dewey Grantham, Maury Klein, Arthur S. Link, George E. Mowry, Burl Noggle, Stanley Parsons, Stephen E. Pelz, Randall B. Ripley, Stephen Roskill, Theodore Salutos, Nannie May Tilley, George B. Tindall, Richard L. Watson, Jr., C. Vann Woodward, and others have contributed factual and interpretive frameworks from which this work has greatly benefited. Although he misapprehends the Virginia reformers, Link's emphasis upon the continuity of reform in the century and Filene's notice that no one single species of Progressive existed, coupled with a criticism of the term's general vagueness, mark contrasting yet central themes of this narrative.

Among Virginia studies, the present generation received much of its current view of the state's politics and culture during the last years of Harry Flood Byrd's political organization. The attraction to move its existence into the era of the 1920s and turn-of-the-century politics was irresistible. There, the "progressives" and other reformers were considered underdogs to the dominant Martin machine as they were in the Virginia of Harry Byrd in the late 1940s and 1950s. Among the first to take such a point of view was Herman L. Horn, "The Growth and Development of the Democratic Party in Virginia Since 1890" (Ph.D. diss., Duke University, 1949). James A. Bear, Jr., "Thomas Staples Martin, A Study in Virginia Politics, 1883–1896" (M.A. thesis, University of Virginia, 1952), furthered the Martin machine image. In the early 1960s, using an interpretation drawn from the major Richmond dailies and the governor's papers, William E. Larsen, in his well-written *Montague of Virginia: The Making of a Southern Progressive* (Baton Rouge, 1965), produced the primary source for the "progressive" view. Later in the decade, incorporating his earlier studies on post-Reconstruction Virginia, Allen W. Moger accepted and based *Virginia, Bourbonism to Byrd, 1870–1925* (Charlottesville, 1968) upon Larsen, newspapers, and doctoral dissertations for the most part generated in the seminars of Edward E. Younger at the University of Virginia.

Other Younger students identified most of the reform activities as conservative reactions to radical agrarians. Raymond Pulley in *Old Virginia Restored: An Interpretation of the Progressive of the Progressive Impulse, 1870–1925* (Charlottesville, 1968), questions the reformers, as does Jack Kirby in *Westmoreland Davis, Virginia Planter-Politician* (Charlottesville, 1968); both include additional manuscript sources only then recently available. Two dissertations, Harry E. Poindexter, "From Copy Desk to Congress: The Pre-congressional Career of Carter Glass" (Ph.D. diss., University of Virginia, 1966), and Burton Ira Kaufman, "Henry De La Warr Flood: A Case Study of Organizational Politics in an Era of Reform" (Ph.D. diss., Rice University, 1966) added further important qualifications drawn from other Virginia newspapers and from the Flood Papers at the Library of Congress. No appreciable reinterpretation of the Martin machine occurred, however. Articles and or dissertations by Joseph A. Fry, Thomas E. Gay, Alvin H. Hall, Robert T. Hawkes, Robert A. Hohner, Wythe W. Holt, Jr., John S. Hopewell, Harry W. Readnour, Brent Tartar, L. Stanley Willis, as well as Edward Younger and James Tice Moore, *The Governors of Virginia, 1860–1978* (Charlottesville, 1982), provided further definition of the era. The present study has been enriched by these scholars. The advantages provided by recently opened or discovered manuscripts as well as a search of older collections allow it to advance beyond the parameters established by the above sources.

Index

Accomack County, Va., 132
Adams, Charles, 186
Addis Ababa, Ethiopia, 216
Agricultural Marketing Act of 1929, 155
Alabama, 101, 113, 139, 146
Alaska, 212
Albany, N.Y., 194, 196
Albemarle County, Va., 132
Alderman, Edwin A., 76, 77, 91, 102, 140
Alexandria, Va., 56, 60, 67, 108, 140
Allen, William, 33
Alliance Democrat, 16
Aluminum Co. of America, 163
American Bar Association, 87
American Cyanamide Corp., 155-56
American Farm Bureau Federation, 153, 154, 156
American Federation of Labor, 53, 149, 205, 209
American Friends Service Committee, 205
American Legion, 205
American Medical Assoc., 159
American Peace Foundation, 177
American Telephone and Telegraph Co., 61
American Tobacco Co., 12, 13, 24, 51, 96, 160
Amherst, Va., 111
Anderson, Henry W., 135
Anderson, William A., 47, 50; Attorney General, 59; on Board of Education, 77; co-authors Anderson-McCormick Act, 46; class attitudes, 60; condemns black franchise, 51; and constitutional convention, 59; declines senatorial campaign, 47; favors local option, 108; gubernatorial candidacy, 64; sues railroads, 80-81; and May Movement, 46; reelected, 69
Anderson-McCormick Act, 16, 24, 46
Andrews, Adolphus, 214
Anti-Comintern Pact, 216
Anti-Saloon League, 65, 86, 88, 91, 111, 127, 134, 142, 147
Anti-Smith Democrats, 146-48

Appomattox County, Va., 9, 161
Appomattox River, 1
Argentina, 159, 180
Arkansas, 146, 153
Arlington (Va.) Memorial Bridge, 159
Armenia, 178-80
Arrington, Ben, 33
Asheville, N.C., 146
Ashland, Va., 7, 9
Ashland Hotel and Mineral Well Co., 7
Atlanta, Ga., 39, 79
Atlantic and Danville Railroad, 98
Atlantic City, N.J., 96
Atlantic Coast Line Railroad, 39, 80
Atlantic Ocean, 10, 221
Augusta County, Va., 51, 80, 141
Austria, 166-67, 168
Ayers, Rufus A., 32, 64-65
Ayers, William A., 206

Bacon, Augustus O., 117
Baker, Newton, 124, 145, 195-96, 198
Baldwin, Hanson W., 204
Baltimore, Md., 102-3, 163
Baltimore Sun, 110
Bankhead, John, 113
Barbour, John S., 8, 13, 14, 22, 23, 24
Barbour, John S. (nephew), 58-59
Barham, R.P., 67
Barkley, Alben W., 153
Barksdale, C.T., 15, 33
Barksdale, William R., 134
Barron, James S., 145-46
Baruch, Bernard, 103, 153, 167, 169, 192, 197-98, 211
Baskin, J.L., 144
Bassett, John D., 144
Bedford County, Va., 1, 46, 59
Beirne, Richard F., 8, 10, 23, 71
Belgium, 168
Belmont, August, 103
Bennett, William W., 7
Berlin, Germany, 186, 187

minister, 64; on Mexico, 180; prohibitionist activities, 64, 91-92, 108; publishes *Richmond Virginian*, 97; reasons for opposing Smith, 146; and Turkey, 178-79
Cannon, Joseph, 40
Cardashian, Vahan, 179
Cardwell, William D., 73, 132-33, 136, 137
Caribbean, 218
Carlin, Charles, 88, 91, 93, 108, 128, 138, 140
Carnegie Foundation for the Advancement of Teaching, 76
Caroline County, Va., 96, 137
Carroll County, Va., 10, 12, 29, 61
Cary, Grover H., 206
Cascade, Va., 26
Cavell, Joseph W., 172
Chandler, J.A.C., 79
Charleston, S.C., 113, 115
Charleston, W. Va., 107, 210
Charleston Navy Yard (Boston), 172
Charlotte County, Va., 132
Charlottesville, Va., 9, 14, 87, 102, 128, 193
Charlottesville Daily Progress, 84
Chatham, Va., 9, 14, 16, 33, 57, 61-63, 71, 84, 110, 125, 135, 144, 196
Cherbourg, France, 189, 195
Chesapeake and Ohio Railroad, 48, 72, 73
Chesapeake Bay, 79, 113
Chicago, Ill., 31, 106, 194, 196, 214, 218
Chile, 180
China, 125-26, 170-71, 174, 183, 190, 216
Chincoteague, Va., 81
Christian Century, 205
Christiansburg, Va., 54
Churchman, John, 73, 80
Churchman Act, 80, 81, 82
Civil Service Review Committee, 38
Civil War, 3, 12, 17, 21, 34, 39, 50, 71, 87, 142, 161, 165, 168, 183
Clark, Champ, 40, 101-3, 117
Clayton Antitrust Act, 106
Clement, J.T., 135, 149
Cleveland, Grover, 10, 22, 31, 46, 57, 60, 63, 104, 106, 133; agrarian opposition to, 15-17, 24; carries Va., 8; contests Hill, 14; orders repeal of Sherman act, 20; patronage use by, 19, 21; vetoes Bland bill, 24
Cobbs, William W., 28
Cocke, Edmund R., 13, 15, 21-22, 28
Cohen, John S., 197
Coleman, George P., 135
Coles, Henry C., 38
Coles, Walter, Jr., 33, 62
College of William and Mary, 76
Collie, James W., 153
Collier, James, 160, 195

Colorado River, 156
Columbia Broadcasting System, 177
Columbia University, 169
Combs, Everett R. "Ebbie," 139, 198
Commoner, 98
Congressional Record, 43, 162
Connecticut, 175
Conservative Party of Virginia, 4, 8
Cook, Julia, 2
Coolidge, Calvin, 141, 165, 173, 178, 181, 186; appointees of, 161-63, 184; and Kellogg-Briand Pact, 178; vetoes McNary-Haugen bill, 155; vetoes Norris plan, 156; and World Court, 175-77
Copeland, Royal S., 156
Copeland, W. Scott, 17, 97, 134, 137
Copenhagen, Denmark, 169
Cord, E.L., 209
Cornett, George W., 25, 27
Cosby, John, 7
Cotton, Joseph P., 185
Covington, Va., 144
Cox, Edwin P., 73
Cox, James, 131
Criglersville, Va., 218
Crisp, Charles, 19
Crisp, Charles R., 159
Cromer, George W., 38, 40
Crown, John R., 110
Crump, Beverly, T., 80, 81
Crumpacker, Edgar D., 34
Cuba, 31, 42-43, 44-45, 47, 180, 204
Culpeper County, Va., 46
Cumberland County, Va., 12
Cummings, Homer, 124, 200
Cummins, Albert, 163
Curtis, Charles, 178

Daniel, Edward, 95
Daniel, John Warwick, 34, 46; and CAS, 25, 36, 57, 67, 87, 95; at constitutional convention, 86; death, 95; debates W.A. Jones, 35; defends lower rail rates, 81; described, 86-87; and Farmers' Alliance, 13; favorite son candidacy, 89; favors constitutional revision, 50; illness, 93-94; influence, 31-32; organizes honest election conference, 28; prefers Tyler, 21; reelected, 46
Daniels, Josephus, 121, 123, 125, 204, 218; CAS requests larger appropriations from, 113-15; dominates general board, 113; and naval oil reserves, 120; reorganizes navy, 114, 201; role in Navy Act of 1920, 120; supports Va. projects, 116, 119, 172; support for Wilson, 101, 122, 170
Dan River, 1, 2, 30
Dan River Mills, 63, 109, 112, 149. *See also* Riverside Cotton Mills